Ukraine

Restoring Growth with Equity:
A Participatory Country Economic Memorandum

World Bank Country Studies are among the many reports originally prepared for internal use as part of the continuing analysis by the Bank of the economic and related conditions of its developing member countries and of its dialogues with the governments. Some of the reports are published in this series with the least possible delay for the use of governments and the academic, business and financial, and development communities. The typescript of this paper has not therefore been prepared in accordance with the procedures appropriate to formal printed texts, and the World Bank accepts no responsibility for errors. Some sources cited in this paper may be informal documents that are not readily available.

ISBN: 0-8213-4382-3

ISSN: 0253-2123

Library of Congress Cataloging-in-Publication Data has been applied for.

CONTENTS

TEXT FIGURES

TEXT TABLES

TEXT BOXES

ACKNOWLEDGMENTS

This participatory economic study is based on the findings of a joint team of the World Bank and Ukrainian experts co-lead by John Hansen (Economic Advisor, World Bank Office in Ukraine), Ihor Shumylo (Deputy Minister of Economy of Ukraine) and Vira Nanivska (Director of International Center for Policy Studies). The participatory process in Ukraine benefited from the guidance of a CEM Advisory Board composed of Mr. Vasyl Rohovy, Minister of Economy and Chair of the CEM Advisory Board, Prof. Anatoliy Halchinskiy, Advisor on Macroeconomy to the President of Ukraine, and the three co-leaders of the CEM process. Most of the preparatory and review work was done between June 1998 and June 1999.

The analysis in this report draws on a series of policy studies that were prepared by Ukrainian teams of experts, including the following: *Agrarian Policy:* Mr. Sablouk (Director, Agrarian Policy Institute) and Mr. Fesina (Leading Research Fellow, Agrarian Policy Institute); *Energy Policy:* Mr. Vrublevsky (Deputy Minister of Economy), Mr. Kiriniachenko (Head of Department, Ministry of Economy), and Mr. Skarshevsky (Expert, Prime Minister Service); *Education Policy:* Mr. Vitrenko (Head of Department, Ministry of Economy); *Health Care Policy:* Mr. Vitrenko (Head of Department, Ministry of Economy), and Ms.Nagorna (Deputy Director, Ukrainian Institute of Public Health Care); *Fiscal Policy:* Mr. Chechetov (Deputy Minister of Economy), Mr. Skarshevsky (Expert, Prime Minister Service), Mr. Lomynoha (Head of Department, State Treasury of Ukraine), and Mr. Soldatenko (Head of Sector, State Tax Administration), *Industrial and Foreign Trade Policy*: Mr. Vrublevsky (Deputy Minister of Economy), Mr. Tryneev (Head of the Main Department, Ministry of Economy), and Mr. Yakubovsky (Deputy Director, Research Institute of Ministry of Economy); *Shadow Economy Policy:* Mr. Borodiuk (Doctor of Economics, Accounting Chamber of Ukraine), and Mr. Turchinov (Member of Parliament, Budget Committee, Verkhovna Rada); on *Social Protection Policies:* Mr. Yaremenko (Deputy Minister of Economy), Mr. Soldatenko (Head of the Main Department, Ministry of Economy), and Ms. Zinkevych (Deputy Head of the Main Department, Ministry of Economy).

World Bank and other experts who assisted and complemented the work of the Ukrainian teams included: *Foreign Trade and Commercial Policies*: Michael Michaely with Veronika Movchan; *Intergovernmental Fiscal Relations:* Deborah Wetzel, Thomas Cochran, Mark Davis, Sean O'Connel, Leonid Polishchuk and Lucan Way; *Public Expenditures on Education and Health:* Frederick Golladay, Galina Sotirova, Kate Schecter and Ghanaraj Chellaraj: *Legal Threats to Fiscal Sustainability:* Joachim Lippott (Legal Advisor, TACIS/UEPLAC); *Agriculture:* Csaba Csaki, Mark Lundell and Ian Shuker; *Banking Reform:* Angela Prigozhina and Alan Roe; *Coal Sector Policy:* Heinz Hendriks: *Shadow Economy:* Maxim Ljubinsky; *District Heating Policy:* Carolyn Gochenour: *Electricity Market Reform:* Laszlo Lovei, Istvan Dobozi and Sergey Milenky, *Environment:* Alexi Slenzak; *Education Finance:* Katerina Petrina; *Fiscal Reform:* Mark Davis; *Gas Sector Policy:* Laszlo Lovei and Konstantin Skorik; *Housing and Water Sectors:* Ihor Korablev; *International Trade*: Veronica Movchan; *Labor Market:* Arvo Kuddo; *Pension Reform:* Larisa Leshchenko and Katerina Petrina; *Private Sector Development:* Gregory Jedrzejczak and Vladimir Kreacic; *Prospects For Economic Reform* and *Debt Sustainability:* Andriy Storozhuk; *Social Assistance:* Galina Sotirova; and *Transport Sector:* Pedro Taborga.

Special credit goes to the International Center for Policy Studies, a leading NGO think-tank in Kyiv, for their support in this collaborative effort. A CEM facilitation team within ICPS comprising Sergiy Loboyko, Volodymyr Hnat, Andriy Bega, Vasyl Lashchivsky, Nazar Mahera, Larisa Romanenko and Christina Lashchenko handled the complex process of coordinating the work of the research teams, thereby making the participatory approach possible. A second team at ICPS headed by Hlib Vyshlinsky and Yevhenyia Yehorova handled publication of all reports produced by the CEM process. Special thanks are also due to Nadezhda Troyan and Tatiana Anderson for their dedicated work on document preparation, and to Victor Lukyanenko, Victoria Antoshchuk, Maria Korchynska and Oksana Burakovska for interpretation and translation.

This report was prepared under the guidance of Paul Siegelbaum (Country Director), Pradeep Mitra (PREM Director), Hafez Ghanem (Sector Leader), and Gregory Jedrzejczak (Resident Representative). The peer reviewers were William Easterly (PRDMG), Alex Sundakov (Economic Research Institute, New Zealand) and Marek Dabrowski (CASE, Poland).

The report draws significantly on the macroeconomic analysis and data prepared by the IMF, TACIS/UEPLAC, HIID, KPMG Barents Group and other donors.

In June 1999 the draft report was discussed in a joint Bank/Government conference in Kyiv attended by representatives of the Government of Ukraine, the World Bank, and a wide range of representatives from the academic, donor, NGO, domestic enterprise, and foreign investment communities in Ukraine. Special thanks are due to all of the key ministers and ministries of the Ukrainian Government for their excellent comments on the draft and for the opportunity to discuss in detail the findings and policy recommendations of the report. The current document reflects the many valuable comments that were received during the review process.

The views expressed here do not necessarily reflect those of the reviewers or of the organizations for which the authors work. The authors remain solely responsible for any errors that may remain in this paper.

ABSTRACT

Since independence, Ukraine has suffered one of the most severe economic declines of any country in this century. A decade of negative growth has left it with less than half of Soviet output levels. The decline in living standards has been less than the officially-reported GDP decline—a large share of output is in the shadow economy, and much of the Soviet-era output contributed little to the quality of life. But the sharply increased poverty now facing a major share of Ukrainians is clear from indicators of physical poverty such as falling life expectancy, rising infant mortality, and increased sickness.

The origins of this economic decline are much the same as in other transition countries—the twin shocks of collapsed trading relations and sharply higher energy prices following the breakup of the Soviet Union. As most Soviet-era products were not competitive on world markets, Ukraine's ability to shift exports to the West was limited. As the economy was heavily energy dependent, rising energy prices made it even harder to compete on world markets.

What has distinguished Ukraine from the other transition countries in the region that have more successfully replaced their old command economies with market economies has been the degree to which Ukraine tried to protect the loss-making enterprises from closure to preserve employment and income levels. To do this, the government lived far beyond its means, allowing subsidies and other privileges to push expenditures well beyond available resources. The difference was financed through hyperinflationary credit expansion during the early years of independence, then by heavy foreign and domestic borrowing.

The costs of these polices are now obvious. Today the Ukrainian government struggles to pay its bills on time and to meet its debt service obligations. Short of resources and faced with a large backlog of arrears in wage and social payments, the Government has put heavy pressure on profitable enterprises to pay taxes, leaving many with little for investment and growth. The combination of burdensome taxes and intrusive regulatory intervention has encouraged widespread tax evasion—putting even more pressure on firms remaining in the formal sector. Perhaps half of all economic activity now hides in the shadow economy, making it even harder for the Government to obtain the resources it needs to operate efficiently, to create a good business climate that attracts investment and growth, and to provide a good social system that develops and protects the people. The Government's high levels of domestic borrowing to cover its deficits and debt service costs has crowded out the enterprise sector from the capital market—with real interest rates exceeding 50 percent, few legitimate enterprises can afford to borrow.

Escaping the downward economic spiral requires a radical change in Government's role in the economy. Leading industrial enterprises from Soviet days are still owned by government, and at the local level government interference both with the sale and movement of agricultural products and with the operation of industrial enterprises causes serious economic problems. Although direct subsidies have been cut dramatically, the indirect cost of support to loss-making agricultural and industrial enterprises in terms of tax privileges and exemptions, preferential procurement, and politically directed lending from the commercial banks is not sustainable. This is widely known in Ukraine, but strong vested interests in the status quo, which provides widespread opportunities for corruption, have effectively blocked change.

Growth can be restored to Ukraine and poverty can be reduced only if the government moves quickly to a more market-oriented role. High priority actions include rapid privatization of virtually all large industrial enterprises including those in energy and telecommunications; a sharp and measurable decrease in the government's regulation of business; and fundamental changes in governmental organizational structures to encourage a shift from control to facilitation.

These changes could lay the foundations for Ukraine to raise living standards for all of its people based on internationally competitive production. It has abundant natural resources, highly trained human capital, strong industrial work ethic, and an excellent physical and geopolitical position. All it needs now is the necessary policies and institutions. This report outlines how Ukraine can accomplish this task.

UKRAINE: SELECTED INDICATORS TABLE

Indicators	1995	1996	1997	1998	1999F
GDP					
UAH billions (nominal)	54.5	81.5	93.4	103.9	130.6
Real GDP growth	-12.2%	-10.0%	-3.0%	-1.7%	-1.0%
US$ billions (PPP terms)	124.2	113.1	110.0	108.1	107.0
US$ billions (at market exchange rate)	37.0	44.6	50.2	42.7	31.9
GDP per capita based on market exchange rate (US$)	718	872	989	849	637
Atlas GNP per capita ($)	1,350	1,210	1,040	850	800
Gross domestic savings (% of GDP at market prices)	23%	20%	19%	18%	19%
Gross domestic investment (% of GDP at market prices)	27%	23%	21%	21%	20%
Agriculture and forestry (% of GDP at factor cost)	15%	14%	14%	14%	15%
Industry and construction (% of GDP at factor cost)	42%	38%	34%	36%	38%
Services (% of GDP at factor cost)	42%	48%	51%	50%	47%
MONETARY STATISTICS					
Monetary base growth	132%	38%	45%	22%	28%
Money supply (M3) growth	113%	35%	34%	25%	36%
Monetization ratio (M3/GDP)	13%	11%	13%	15%	16%
Exchange rate (UAH/US$, year end)	1.79	1.89	1.90	3.43	4.6
Inflation (CPI change, December on December)	181.7%	39.7%	10.1%	20.0%	17.0%
PUBLIC FINANCES (% GDP) [1]					
Consolidated budget revenues (including Pension Fund)	38%	37%	38%	36%	36%
Consolidated budget expenditures (including Pension Fund)	43%	40%	44%	38%	38%
Cash budget deficit	4.9%	3.2%	5.6%	2.7%	1.9%
Domestic financing[2]	3.9%	2.5%	5.3%	0.9%	0.6%
External financing	1.0%	0.7%	0.3%	1.8%	0.7%
Accrual budget deficit[3]	8.2%	8.4%	5.2%	3.0%	-0.6%
Total public debt (US$ billion)	8.2	10.1	14.2	15.2	15.0
Domestic	0	1.2	4.6	3.7	2.2
External	8.2	8.8	9.6	11.5	12.8

(continued on the next page)

UKRAINE: SELECTED INDICATORS TABLE (continued)

Indicators	1995	1996	1997	1998	1999F
BALANCE OF PAYMENTS (US$ billions)					
GNFS Exports [4]	17.1	20.3	20.4	17.6	15.8
Merchandise exports	14.2	15.5	15.4	13.7	12.3
% of GDP	46%	46%	41%	41%	50%
GNFS Imports [4]	18.3	21.5	21.9	18.8	16.1
Merchandise imports	16.9	19.8	19.6	16.3	13.6
Energy	7.8	8.9	8.3	6.2	5.9
Merchandise trade balance	-2.7	-4.3	-4.2	-2.6	-1.3
Current account balance	-1.2	-1.2	-1.3	-1.3	-0.5
% of GDP	-3.1%	-2.7%	-2.7%	-3.0%	-1.6%
Direct foreign investments [5]	0.27	0.52	0.62	0.74	0.45
Net international reserves (year end)	-0.4	-0.3	0	-2.0	-1.7
Gross foreign exchange reserves, excluding gold (year end)	1.1	2.0	2.3	1.0	1.6
weeks of GNFS imports	3.0	4.7	5.6	2.9	5.2
INTERNATIONAL DEBT (US$ billion)					
Total external debt (DOD)	8.4	9.1	10.0	12.2	13.6
Public	8.2	8.8	9.6	11.5	12.8
Private	0.2	0.3	0.5	0.7	0.8
% of GDP (Mod = 30%)	23%	20%	20%	29%	43%
Total external public debt service	1.5	1.2	1.2	1.8	2.0
% of GNFS Exports (Mod = 18%)	9%	6%	6%	10%	13%
ARREARS (UAH billion)					
Total wage arrears	0.6	3.7	4.9	6.5	5.5
Budget sphere	0	1.0	0.7	1.0	0.5
Pensions arrears	0.1	1.1	1.3	2.0	1.7
IBRD DEBT (US$ billion)					
IBRD DOD	0.5	0.9	1.2	1.6	2.1
IBRD debt service	0.01	0.03	0.06	0.06	0.10
IBRD debt service/External public debt service	0.5%	2.6%	4.7%	3.5%	5.2%
IBRD debt service/GNFS exports	0.0%	0.2%	0.3%	0.4%	0.7%
Share of IBRD portfolio	0.4%	0.8%	1.1%	1.4%	1.7%

[1] IMF GFS methodology
[2] Including privatization proceeds
[3] Negative—surplus
[4] GNFS—Goods & Non-Factor Services
[5] BOP definition

LIST OF ACRONYMS AND ABBREVIATIONS

CEE	Central and Eastern Europe
CIS	Commonwealth of Independent States
EBRD	European Bank for Reconstruction and Development
FSU	Former Soviet Union
UNDP	United Nations Development Programme
OECD	Organization for Economic Co-operation and Development
IBRD	International Bank for Reconstruction and Development
IFC	International Finance Corporation
MIGA	Multilateral Investment Guarantee Association
IDA	International Development Association
IMF	International Monetary Fund
EFF	Extended Fund Facility
NGO	Non Governmental Organization
NBU	National Bank of Ukraine
HDI	Human Development Index
VAT	value added tax
FDI	foreign direct investment
GDP	Gross Domestic Product
GNP	Gross National Product
PPP	Purchasing Power Parity
NAS	National Accounts System
GFS	Government Finance Statistics
GNFS	Goods & Non-Factor Services
NPV	Net present value
OVDP	State domestic bonds
FX, forex	Foreign Exchange

MONETARY UNITS

UAH = Ukrainian Hrivnya
USD = U.S. Dollar
USD 1.00 = UAH 4.50
(October 1999)

Vice President	: Johannes Linn
Director	: Pradeep K. Mitra
Sector Leader	: Hafez M. H. Ghanem
Principal Economist	: John Hansen

EXECUTIVE SUMMARY

This country economic memorandum—one of three reports produced jointly by the World Bank, the Ministry of Economy, and the International Center for Policy Studies through a highly participatory CEM process—defines a shared vision for a strategy that will allow Ukraine to halt its economic decline and move toward a more prosperous future.[1]

ECONOMIC DECLINE—AND GROWING POVERTY

Officially reported GDP is now less than 40 percent of its 1989 level—a decline twice as severe as that in the United States during the Great Depression, and worse than that in many other Central and Eastern European countries (figure 1). Many factors including initial conditions and external shocks, subsidies to failing enterprises, monetary expansion, and heavy borrowing have contributed to Ukraine's economic decline and growing poverty.

Initial conditions and external shocks

The most important initial conditions and external shocks have been:

- The breakdown in trade and payment relations that came with the collapse of the Soviet Union.

- The higher energy prices introduced by Russia after the collapse.

- The large scale of Ukraine's agricultural and industrial enterprises.

- A reluctance to impose hard budget constraints.

Trade and payments shock. Even during the Soviet era, Ukraine's economy was highly oriented to external trade, depending heavily on the markets of other republics in the former Soviet Union (FSU) and other communist bloc (COMECON) countries. This outward orientation was partly a reflection of real comparative advantage and partly the result of Soviet policies to foster the dispersion of economic activity throughout the FSU. When trade and payments relationships collapsed with the breakup of the Soviet Union, Ukraine lost markets that were vital to its enterprises, and after years of isolation from Western markets, its products could not compete in Western markets.

Energy price shock. As energy was available at negligible costs during the Soviet era, Ukrainian farms and factories were highly energy intensive. When Russia increased its energy prices by more than 10 times, many Ukrainian products became uncompetitive in cost as well as design.

Figure 1 Economic recovery in other former Soviet states outpaces that in Ukraine

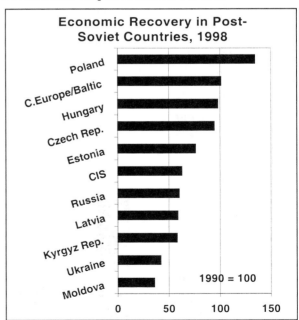

Source: World Bank 1998.

[1] John Hansen and Vira Nanivska (eds). 1999. *Economic Growth with Equity: Ukrainian Perspectives* (World Bank Discussion Paper No. 407). World Bank, Kiev and Washington, D.C.; and John Hansen and Diana Cook 1999. *Economic Growth with Equity: Which Strategy for Ukraine? (World Bank Discussion Paper No. 408).* World Bank, Kyiv and Washington, D.C.

Diseconomies of large scale. The exceptionally large scale of the farms and factories inherited from the Soviet era has made it difficult to restructure them. These "giants" created a politically and socially important concentration of people who could lobby effectively for subsidies that would delay real reforms.

Soft budgets. The Government's willingness to support failing enterprises with subsidies created a "soft budget" culture that helped put the Ukrainian economy onto its precipitous downward course.

Subsidies, money, and hyperinflation

Largely as a result of subsidizing enterprises and individuals, total deficits including directed credits exceeded 20 percent of GDP in 1992-93, and money supply expansion peaked at more than 1,000 percent in 1993. This, together with the monetary overhang from the Soviet era, lead to hyperinflation. Between the end of 1992 and the end of 1994, prices increased by almost 500 times. The public lost confidence in the domestic currency, producing sharp declines in real money balances. Today Ukraine has one of the smallest banking and monetary systems in the world relative to GDP, and much of the available credit has been absorbed by the government, crowding out the enterprises and making it hard for them to borrow the money they need for payments, investments, and growth (figure 2).

Figure 2 Government deficits exceeded total credit expansion

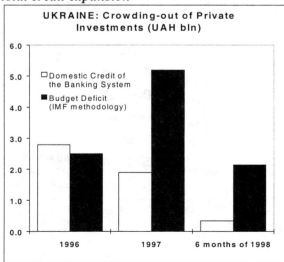

Source: World Bank staff estimates.

Indirect subsidies, deficits, and debt

Although government sharply reduced budgetary subsidies to enterprises, it now offers financially failing farms and factories tax privileges. Such largess has failed to revitalize these enterprises, and it has drained resources from other potentially viable firms. The full negative impact of these tax privileges has not yet become obvious in terms of overall tax revenues for three reasons.

First, to compensate for the loss of tax revenues, the government has increased the tax pressure on profitable firms through high rates and intensive inspections. This drives once-profitable enterprises into financial distress—and into the shadow economy. The combination of tax privileges for loss-making enterprises and tax pressure for profitable enterprises gradually reduces tax revenues, increases budget deficits, raises the burden of debt payments, and creates a need to put even more tax pressure on the remaining profitable enterprises.

Second, many enterprises do not receive tax privileges. This reduces the negative fiscal impact—but creates an uneven playing field, distorting the competitive conditions for enterprises. Since attaining privileges can be more profitable than improving production and marketing performance, managers allocate their time and resources accordingly, and corruption increases.

Third, a major share of taxes are being collected not in cash but as "mutual settlements." Although tax revenues were reported to be around 35 percent of GDP, actual tax collections in cash were less than 20 percent of GDP in 1998-99. By allowing failing enterprises to remain in operation and "pay" their taxes with barter—if they pay at all—the government has helped create a large virtual economy.

The illusion of stability

With the exception of the aftermath of the Russian crisis in late 1998, domestic price levels and the exchange rate have been relatively stable since 1995. This stability was supposed to provide the foundations for growth—but the economy continues to decline, albeit at a slower pace than before. The problem is that Ukraine's stability is based on the weak foundation of tight monetary policy and an artificially stable exchange rate rather than on deep structural reforms.

The debt crisis

After the August crisis in Russia, Ukraine found it difficult to roll over its billions of hryvnias of t-bill debt, much of which had been sold to foreign investors who became wary of all emerging markets in the aftermath of problems in Asia and Russia. Once the t-bill debt could no longer be rolled over, even at real annual yields exceeding 70 percent, Ukraine was forced to restructure this debt, making it almost impossible to borrow new money on private international capital markets.

The impact on growth

Ukraine's soft budget culture and the resulting high budget deficits have hurt economic growth in several ways. First, enterprises have remained inefficient. If the government instead had enforced bankruptcy, growth-supporting structural reforms would have taken place far more rapidly. Second, as noted above, budget deficits have crowded enterprises out of the capital market (figure 2). At barely 2 percent of GDP in 1998, Ukraine had the lowest ratio of bank credit to the private sector of any transition country other than the Kyrgyz Republic (the ratio for transition economies in general is about 40 percent). Third, commercial bank credit to enterprises is among the most expensive in the world, with real interest rates on commercial bank loans peaking at 100 percent in September 1998 and was still running at 30-40 percent in the fall of 1999.

The lack of structural reforms, a central theme of this report, has led both to continued economic decline and to high budget deficits, propelling the vicious circular relationship between them. If Ukraine had more quickly implemented fundamental structural reforms in enterprise ownership, market relations, the legal and juridical structure, and the role of government, the economy would not have collapsed as far as it has. And if the structural reforms had been put into place more quickly, the budget would have been supported by a larger tax base, lowering the deficits.

The impact on social conditions

Human suffering has been the greatest cost of Ukraine's slow structural reforms. Family incomes have dropped sharply. Health standards have deteriorated. And adult literacy and school enrollments have declined. Between 1991 and 1995 the UNDP human development index (HDI)[2] plummeted, moving Ukraine from 32nd to 95th among 175 countries (figure 3).

Figure 3 Economic decline has brought a sharp drop in Ukrainian living standards

Source: UNDP 1998.

TRANSFORMING THE ROLE OF GOVERNMENT

The government deficits that have played such a prominent role in Ukraine's continued economic decline reflect in large measure the fact that government has been slow to relinquish the role it played during the Soviet era.

---

[2] The Human Development Index is heavily influenced by per capita incomes and thus by official GDP. Since around 50 percent of total production in Ukraine may be in shadow economy and because much of this activity escapes the official measurements of GDP, the real decline in living standards may be considerably less than indicated by the dramatic decline in official data on per capita incomes. However, the physical indicators of the quality of life, particularly those related to health, indicate a sharp increase in the number of people living in real poverty.

Moving from a Soviet to a market role

Ukraine faced a major challenge when it attained independence in 1991—to replace its system of government that was designed to implement Moscow's directives with one that could design and implement the country's own market-oriented policies.

The government also had to undergo a fundamental change—from being responsible for the ownership, management, and control of essentially all economic activity to being responsible for facilitating economic activity in privately owned enterprises. This change has been difficult. As a result, many old administrative structures—such as the super-ministerial layer of the *apparat* between the ministers and the Prime Minister, and sector representatives in the Ministry of Economy and Ministry of Finance—are still in place.

High priority should be given to measures that will (a) reform the "Apparat" of the Cabinet of Ministers so that it focuses on policy coordination and support rather than on policy making; (b) consolidate the Cabinet so that it becomes a small collegial body focused on strategic policy making; (c) reform the civil service, clearly delimitating political and non-political posts, implementing pay reform, training of senior civil servants, and introducing merit-based promotion principles; and (d) reduce the number of business inspections and sharply limit the number of routine inspections by the State Tax Administration.

Mobilizing and using resources efficiently

With the total tax burden including pension fund contributions running at about 35 percent of GDP, Ukrainian enterprises and people are shouldering a burden comparable to that in countries with considerably higher levels of per capita income. Worse still, about half of all economic activity is hidden in the shadows and at least half of taxpaying enterprises are losing money. The full tax burden is effectively borne by only a small part of the country's economically active population.

By changing its role in the economy and in society, the government will be able to limit its resource requirements to only the highest-priority activities. At the same time, it needs to

find ways to increase its efficiency of resource use. For example, investments need to be made to increase the energy efficiency of hospitals. Also, better diagnostic equipment would allow shorter hospital stays, allowing Ukraine to consolidate unneeded facilities.

Moving shadow activity to the formal sector. The shadow economy—defined here as production that does not pay taxes—accounts for about half of all economic output in Ukraine. As a result, shadow economic activity is vitally important to a major share of the Ukrainian people, providing badly-needed jobs, goods, and services. As in other countries, the shadow economy is largely created by government policies—high taxes and a heavy regulatory burden. Barter also contributes to shadow activity by making it hard to monitor and tax financial flows. The very existence of the shadow economy leads to its expansion. A legitimate firm that pays its taxes has little hope of competing against enterprises in the same business that do not pay their taxes. The only choice is to cease production or move to the shadow economy.

Small firms remain small to avoid detection, stunting their growth. Large firms spend money on bribes so that they can continue avoiding taxes. Firms that thrive are often not the most efficient ones, but those with the best political connections. Since much of the economic activity in Ukraine goes untaxed, the government must tax even more heavily the firms in the formal economy, frequently leaving these firms with no choice but to cease production or join other enterprises in the shadow economy. As the resources available to government shrink, its ability to provide services to firms and their employees shrinks, making it even less attractive for the firms to remain in the formal sector. The downward spiral of revenues becomes self-perpetuating.

Given the economic and social importance of the shadow sector, the objective cannot be to suppress or control it. The objective must be to implement policies that will encourage this activity to move into the formal, tax-paying economy where it can grow openly with full protection of the law. Ukraine needs to move swiftly to reverse the shift of economic activity into the shadows. Otherwise the tax base will be eroded—leading to higher deficits, weaker government services, and the risk of financial and social strife (see chapter 2).

Fighting corruption. Tightly linked to Ukraine's large shadow economy is widespread corruption. In addition to corrupt enterprises that hide in the shadow economy to avoid taxation and to profit from non-transparent barter deals, an unfortunate number of government officials and functionaries at all levels seem to be corrupt, basing their decisions less on what is best for economic growth and the people's welfare, and more on what will be personally profitable. This shrinks the efficiency of government, dampening prospects for restoring real economic growth

Managing government debt

Ukraine's inability to move forward with structural reforms has limited its access to resources from the World Bank, the International Monetary Fund (IMF), and the European Bank for Reconstruction and Development. Faced with relatively large fiscal deficits of recent years, ranging from 3-6% of GDP, Ukraine has borrowed funds commercially at high interest rates and with short maturities. Although the ratio of debt to GDP in Ukraine has risen sharply in recent years and now stands at about 40 percent, the real problem is the terms on which the debt was contracted.

The key to reducing the debt service burden to more manageable levels is to implement the structural reforms needed to restore access to borrowing from international financial institutions. Such resources are available at much lower interest rates and for much longer maturities. The structural reforms needed to gain access to such funds will reduce deficits and the need for borrowing. They will also increase growth and thus the resources needed to repay old debts. Finally, accelerated reforms will rebuild the confidence of investors in Ukraine, gradually restoring access to private capital flows.

THE URGENCY OF STRUCTURAL REFORMS

Since independence Ukraine has made significant structural reforms in a number of areas. All small enterprises and about 80 percent of medium-size and large enterprises have been privatized. Although only about 15 percent of agricultural land is actually titled and held privately, most agricultural land is held collectively by private cooperatives. Nearly all export quotas and tariffs have been eliminated. Normal trading relations have been established with all major trading partners, including a partnership and cooperation agreement between Ukraine and the European Union. Ukraine has also signed a friendship treaty with Russia.

But some of the most crucial structural reforms have yet to be implemented. The lack of true structural reforms in large enterprises is the most serious problem facing Ukraine. The policy of protecting enterprises needs to be abandoned and replaced as quickly as possible by a policy of hard budget constraints. Faced with hard budget constraints and the threat of closure if they do not become self-financing, enterprises will seek out new investors (both domestic and foreign), new markets, new production technologies, and new management methods. They will also lease or sell underused space and equipment, paving the way for the creation of new enterprises that can employ the people who will be laid off when overstaffed state enterprises release redundant employees.

Although the design and implementation of improved bankruptcy procedures is absolutely essential if Ukraine is to break the heavy chain of non-payments that drags the economy down, bankruptcy must be implemented with care. In a normally functioning economy, only a small percentage of enterprises go bankrupt in any given year—but the threat that they might is enough to assure that most will do everything possible to avoid bankruptcy. In Ukraine, however, so many companies are already bankrupt *de facto* that rapid implementation of bankruptcy proceedings that forced all of these companies into immediate *de jure* bankruptcy could have a cataclysmic impact on the economy and on people. Many viable transactions would be frozen or delayed by the collapse of many banks and by bottlenecks in the nascent bankruptcy court system.

Major efforts will therefore be required to put in place an effective bankruptcy system that provides urgently needed incentives for payment discipline without creating an economic and social crisis. As demonstrated by Hungary and other formerly planned economies, this can be done.

The state also needs to create a business climate that is attractive to business development—one that stimulates investment, production, and growth by providing a level playing field where all competitors face clear, predictable, and equitable rules of the game. Such an environment would facilitate the structural transformation of old enterprises and would also stimulate the creation of new enterprises, the most important component in any program of structural reform.

Reviving agriculture

The situation in the agricultural sector today is calamitous. Ukraine, a country with a temperate climate and perhaps the world's best endowment of rich black soil, has seen its agricultural output fall year after year (figure 4). Equipment is worn out. Incomes are dropping. And the government is under constant pressure to provide tax privileges and write-offs of unpaid taxes and credits. The most pressing issues in the sector in terms of structural reforms are the lack of effective private owners and the lack of efficient markets for agricultural inputs and outputs.

Figure 4 Agricultural output continues to drop sharply despite rich agricultural resources

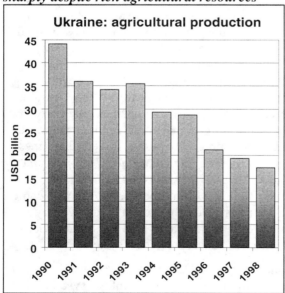

Source: TACIS/UEPLAC. *Ukrainian Economic Trends.*

Although most agricultural land is technically no longer held by the state, the collectives that control all but about 15 percent of the land are little more than a cosmetic reincarnation of the old state controls. Collective members generally operate as employees rather than as farmers—often under the control of directors from the Soviet era. Land ownership based on titles that can be mortgaged is essential so that farmers have collateral that can be used to secure loans for the investments needed to renew the equipment fleet and to provide working capital.

Access to banking system credit would help resolve the other big problem in agriculture—the continued state control of inputs and outputs through a system of commodity credits (credits of inputs like seeds and fertilizer that must be repaid with physical products like wheat). Cash credit would break the *de facto* state control over agricultural production and would introduce badly needed transparency in a shadowy environment dominated by physical transactions.

Reorienting manufacturing

Large-scale manufacturing is urgently in need of profound structural reforms. None of the industrial "giants"—enterprises with more than 750 million hryvnias in assets—have been privatized in a way that gives effective private ownership control. Many of these enterprises enjoy extensive tax privileges, making them a major source of budget deficits. State guarantees for loans to enterprises, in some cases involving millions of dollars, also create a burden when the enterprises, unable to repay the loans, leave the debts for the state to repay.

The key to structural reforms in manufacturing is hard budget constraints, reinforced by effective bankruptcy laws. Rapid privatization of enterprises of all sizes is also needed in all but a few exceptional areas. Such privatization should be done in a way that vests ownership control firmly in the hands of private investors without any blocking or "golden" shares held by the state. Privatization should be done in accordance with international standards, including a transparent, competitive process that advertises worldwide to find all potential, serious investors, especially those with good track records in the specific line of business.

Adjusting energy

Ukraine is one of the world's most energy-intensive countries. During the Soviet era, when energy was available at 5-10 percent of world prices, the wasted energy was mainly an environmental issue. Today energy intensity is a major economic issue. Energy accounts for nearly half of Ukraine's imports, creating a major drain on the balance of payments and diverting resources that could better be used to import the capital equipment needed to increase productivity, enhance international competitiveness, and provide new jobs.

Inefficiency is a constraint to economic growth and fiscal stability throughout the energy sector. In the coal sector, mines that have long been depleted continue to be operated for social reasons, creating a serious drain on the budget and raising the cost of coal to domestic energy users. District heating facilities waste massive amounts of energy in conversion to heat, in distribution, and in utilization. To correct this, extensive investments are needed in new boilers, distribution lines, heat meters, and building insulation. Here, as with gas and electricity, physical inefficiency is exacerbated by low cost recovery rates, low cash collection rates, and the lack of hard budget constraints.

As a result, all energy sectors are in bad financial shape, not even able to pay for inputs on time, much less make badly needed investments in improved efficiency. The lack of appropriate prices and payment discipline compounds the problem by failing to provide incentives for more efficient energy use by customers.

Bolstering banks

Ukraine's commercial banking system has suffered greatly because of the government's loose fiscal policy described above. As deficits increased, more and more of banking system capital was absorbed by the government (figure 5). Unable to appraise normal commercial risks and unwilling to buy more t-bills following the restructuring that took place in late 1998, banks began to place excess reserves in the central bank, creating an illusion of excess liquidity even though the money supply was extraordinarily small relative to GDP.

The excess reserves deposits were a reflection not of excess liquidity but of the profound institutional weaknesses of a commercial banking system that had grown content with arbitraging interest rates internationally, taking advantage of the implicit exchange rate guarantee of the stable hryvnia, and lending at extraordinarily high real interest rates to the government. The central bank is now working actively with the IMF and the World Bank to strengthen the commercial banking system so that it can begin to play the role that it should in providing credit on a normal commercial basis to Ukrainian enterprises.

ASSURING GROWTH WITH EQUITY

Under the Soviet system, income differences were minimized. In contrast, significant income differences are normal in a market-based system, providing essential incentives. Increased income disparities are therefore a common part of the transition process. At the same time, basic social justice—a key objective for the Government of Ukraine and for the World Bank—calls for reducing or eliminating absolute poverty. This can be done by ensuring jobs-oriented growth, providing access to human development services, and supplying a social safety net.

Figure 5 T-bill sales quickly absorbed all new credit

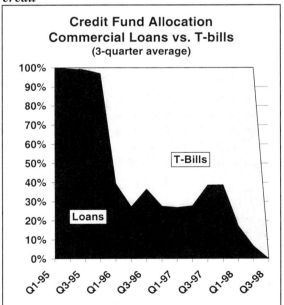

Source: Harvard Institute for International Development.

Jobs-oriented growth

The best way to ensure adequate incomes for all citizens is a jobs-oriented growth strategy—one that stimulates the creation of productive employment in profitable enterprises. Developing sound macroeconomic policies and a good investment climate are essential to this objective because this would allow Ukraine to exploit one of its strongest areas of comparative advantage—a low-cost, well-educated labor force with extensive industrial work experience. High payroll taxes, an artificially appreciated exchange rate, excessive minimum wages, barriers to labor mobility, and widespread unionization have all tended to increase the cost of labor, discouraging investments in labor-intensive activities. Such distortions also increase the demand for capital-intensive investments, resulting in higher-cost production that is less competitive, contributes less to economic growth, and generates fewer jobs.

A jobs-focused growth strategy does not mean that the government should require enterprises to hire or retain a certain number of workers. Nor does a jobs-focused strategy mean that the government should subsidize employment. Instead, a jobs-oriented strategy means that the government should introduce policies that stimulate the development of small and medium-size enterprises. Throughout the world, such enterprises are the leading source of employment. In the United States, for example, firms with fewer than 500 workers account for 80 percent of employment. In addition to providing incomes to hundreds of thousands of families, the job opportunities created by fostering the development of small and medium-size enterprises would make it much easier to undertake the urgently needed restructuring of state enterprises.

Supporting human development

Access to quality health and education services in Ukraine today is often severely limited because the government lacks the necessary financial resources. As Ukraine moves forward, all people will need affordable access to good health and education, regardless of their income. Steps need to be taken to assure the necessary financing. Health and education efficiency should be improved by cutting the

energy costs of schools and medical institutions, reducing under-used space, lowering excessive staff costs, improving the pay and professional preparation of those who remain in these sectors, and providing better equipment and supplies. Government spending should focus on the highest-priority needs in both sectors—particularly public health, and primary and secondary education. And user fees and other cost recovery mechanisms should be implemented more widely so that those who can afford services can openly contribute to the cost of their provision.

A social safety net

Much of the resistance to market reforms in Ukraine seems to come from the fear that introducing a market-oriented system will cause people to lose their jobs. As most Ukrainians are already poor by international standards, and many Soviet-era enterprises are heavily over-staffed, this fear is quite valid. An adequate social safety net must therefore be put into place if market reforms are to enjoy general support.

BARRIERS TO CHANGE

The participatory CEM process revealed a high degree of consensus on the policy recommendations summarized above. Given this consensus, we must ask why so much still remains to be done. Why has the reform process been so slow and incomplete? The main reasons appear to be inertia, vested interests in the status quo, and lack of institutional capacity.

Inertia

All political systems must deal with inertia when trying to bring about change, but the challenge has been particularly great in Ukraine. Ukraine was under the dominion of the Soviet Union much longer than, for example, the Baltic States—and was under the sway of the Russian tsars for centuries before that. The long tradition of following orders from Moscow has been hard to break.

The lack of a sharp economic and social crisis has also contributed to inertia. Countries with no way to avoid cold and hunger but through dramatic change will take the necessary actions. During the first bitter winter after independence, for example, Estonia was cut off by Russia from its traditional supplies of energy and food, and the government was making plans to evacuate Tallinn to the countryside where people would at least have wood stoves for warmth and cows for milk. In the event, Finland stepped in and made critical supplies available, but this dramatic crisis helped convince the Estonians that they had no alternative but to dramatically reform their economy in order to gain full access to the markets of Western Europe. Ukraine, a nation blessed with abundant natural resources including coal, gas, forests, exceptionally fertile soils, a relatively benign climate, and a well-developed physical infrastructure has been able to avoid a real crisis—the kind that leaves people demanding change at almost any cost.

Ukraine's ability to delay or avoid profound economic reforms also reflects its exceptionally favorable geopolitical position. Lying on the border between East and West, the major powers on both sides have actively sought to keep or attract Ukraine as an ally. As a result, Ukraine has enjoyed substantial resource inflows—primarily energy on concessional terms from the East and financial support on concessional terms from the West. With all this support, Ukraine has not faced the kind of crisis that forces profound reform.

Vested Interests

The inherent wealth of Ukraine has directly contributed to a second reason for slow reform —vested interests. If Ukraine had been a destitute country at independence, few individuals would have had selfish interests in preserving the status quo. Unfortunately, Ukraine's relative wealth has created vested interests. The longer the reforms needed to create a transparent, equitable, and efficient economic environment are delayed—the longer vested interests will be able work within the flawed post-Soviet system to appropriate as much of the nation's wealth for themselves as possible.

Vested interests also undermine economic progress by thwarting policy initiatives, sometimes leaving only the appearance of reform with little substance behind it. For example, when taxes are raised, vested interests arrange for exemptions and delayed payment schedules—or simply hide their activity in the shadow economy. When tariffs on utilities are raised, vested interests run up arrears. The Ukrainian economy will move forward again only when powerful interests develop an interest in reform. This can best be accomplished by engaging these groups in the dialogue—and by strict enforcement of hard budget constraints and anti-corruption measures.

Institutional Constraints

The policy reform debates in the parliaments of Europe demonstrate how slow, painful, and demanding the change process can be, even with top professional staff who can focus on a relatively limited range of issues. Imagine the problem facing Ukraine. The country must radically change its economic, human development, and social protection systems— and must do so after generations of living under a closed system that provided little opportunity to develop the necessary skills.

Even if well-designed policies could be copied directly from other countries without thought or discussion (an approach doomed to failure in most cases), Ukraine would still find it difficult to implement the policy reforms, for this often requires skills unknown under the Soviet system. This report has sought to help overcome some of the institutional barriers to reform in Ukraine by involving the broadest possible group of stakeholders in the process of preparing the analysis and recommendations presented here and in the two companion volumes (Hansen and Cook, 1999; and Hansen and Nanivska, 1999). But much remains to be done to develop a consensus for reform. Parliament and the public at large need to be brought into the policy debate and formulation, thus helping increase the quality and acceptability of laws.

OPTIONS FOR RESTORING GROWTH AND LIVING STANDARDS

The slow pace of structural reforms in Ukraine reflects the lack of consensus on an appropriate development path. Three basic alternatives are being actively debated in Ukraine today— *preservation* of the status quo, *protection* from competition, particularly from imports, and *competition* as in developed countries. Deciding which of these three paths to follow is crucial, for this will shape today's design of policies for the future. These three alternatives examined in detail in the "Vision" paper that was produced as part of the participatory CEM process (Hansen and Cook, 1999). The analysis there clearly demonstrated that a development path based on competitiveness is the only one likely to produce the sustainable improvement in Ukrainian living standards. This volume therefore focuses only on measures needed to establish a competitive market economy in Ukraine.

The competition-based growth strategy seeks to maximize enterprise efficiency—and thus overall economic growth and living standards—by creating an open, market-based economy within which enterprises must compete both internally and externally to remain profitable. Introducing such a strategy in the economic environment inherited from the Soviet era will require numerous changes. In the short run such changes will be disruptive— especially for those who temporarily lose their jobs. Based on world experience—and on that of nearby countries such as Poland, Hungary and Estonia that were part of the same Soviet system until just a few years ago—it is clear that a competitiveness strategy holds the best prospects for attaining the common goal of people from all parts of the political spectrum in Ukraine—maximizing living standards for all Ukrainians through sustainable growth. The challenge will be to find a way to handle the short-term disruptions in a way that makes adoption of this strategy politically and socially acceptable.

Creating a good investment climate. No fixed link exists between investment and growth. Well-developed countries facing a slump in demand can grow rapidly without significant investment simply by stimulating demand. Conversely, high investment may produce little or no growth if the investment is poorly targeted or the business environment is bad.

Given the dramatic collapse in demand for Ukraine's output since independence, substantial growth may be possible in certain areas without significant investment. But any significant recovery for the economy as a whole will depend for at least three reasons

on a substantial increase in the volume of investment —and on major improvements in its efficiency. First, the production infrastructure inherited from the Soviet era was massively decapitalized by the mid 1980s, a situation made even worse by the asset stripping that took place in the late 1980s and early 1990s with *perestroika*. Second, much of the inherited equipment was energy-intensive, a reflection of the low prices charged for energy under the Soviet regime. Third, the inherited equipment was generally designed to produce Soviet-style goods that are not competitive outside the former Soviet Union—or even within the region now that the newly independent states can import higher-quality goods from world markets.

If Ukraine is to attract the investments needed to become competitive and grow, it needs to establish a good business climate. Rather than using costly tax incentives and loan guarantees, the government should attract investment by creating an environment that *maximizes returns* and *minimizes risks* for investors. This should not be done through fiscal interventions, but by correcting problems that make inputs artificially expensive and that unnecessarily increase investor risk.

Increasing returns to investment. The key prices affecting returns to investment in Ukraine are those for capital, labor, materials, government services, and foreign exchange. Real interest rates on commercial loans are still running 30-40 percent—an extremely high rate that few legitimate enterprises can afford.

Labor costs are basically low in Ukraine, but high payroll taxes and barriers to labor mobility need to be reduced to restore Ukraine's comparative advantage in labor-intensive production. The cost to enterprises of maintaining "social assets," such as housing for workers, needs to be reduced. Material input prices are generally competitive, thanks to relatively low average tariffs, but this advantage for investors is being threatened by the current move to more protectionist policies.

Services provided by government—public safety, courts, infrastructure, education, health—are all vital to profitable enterprise activity. Such services are largely paid for with taxes. In Ukraine the burden of taxes, measured as a percentage of GDP, has been at least 25 percent higher than in countries at similar levels of per capita income. The burden for those who actually pay the taxes—those who are not hiding in the shadow economy—is even higher. The cost of government thus reduces the attractiveness of Ukraine to legitimate investors.

The price of foreign exchange is also critical to investment returns. An artificially low value for foreign exchange reduces the cost of imports and value of exports in local currency. As a result enterprises find it hard to compete with imports, and they may receive too little in local currency from the sale of exports to cover their cost of inputs. A realistic exchange rate, established by market forces free from administrative constraints, is thus vital to creating an attractive investment climate.

Reducing risks to investors. In addition to seeking maximum returns, investors seek minimum risks. In the past the government has sought to reduce risk by offering guarantees on private loans. This approach does nothing to reduce risk—it simply shifts the risk from the investor to the government. As a result, the government faces costly loan repayment obligations. A much better approach for government is to remove or mitigate the factors that increase risk. Unpredictable prices and exchange rates make it difficult for investors to estimate the future return on investments. Inflation and devaluation are usually driven by government deficit spending. Controlling budget deficits is therefore the most important step that can be taken to reduce the instability of prices and exchange rates.

Other major risks that the government could reduce through good policies, making Ukraine more attractive to investors, include non-enforcement of contracts; unpredictable changes in laws (especially tax laws); inadequate property rights protection; and regulatory intervention by government inspectors that is random, nontransparent, unpredictable, and often costly in terms of bribes that must be paid. The government should fix these problems—all of which it can control—rather than offering guarantees that simply shift the risk to the budget.

URGENT REFORMS FOR STABILITY

To avoid a serious economic crisis like Russia and various Asian countries have seen in recent years, Ukraine needs to maintain a sustainable budget deficit, a realistic exchange rate, and sound monetary policies. Without these, the restoration of growth would be virtually impossible, and the risk of a poverty-increasing crisis would be very high.

A sustainable budget deficit

Because of the adverse terms on which Ukraine borrowed to cover past budget deficits, attaining a sustainable balance between revenues and expenditures will require running a primary surplus (excluding interest on debt) of at least 2 percent of GDP. Ukraine cannot afford to borrow to cover interest costs. This is a sure road to debt pyramids and default.

A realistic exchange rate

The exchange rate needs to be allowed to balance the real underlying demand and supply for foreign exchange. Following the crisis in 1998, a broad range of implicit and explicit measures were introduced to control the demand and supply of foreign exchange in Ukraine. As a result it has been impossible for the market to reflect the true scarcity value of foreign exchange. The government should continue to lift these controls as quickly as possible. The devaluation resulting from lifting the controls would help ensure continued profitability for competitive exports and provide a reasonable degree of protection, allowing domestic producers to compete with imports in the local markets.

Sound monetary policy

Ukraine must walk a fine line with respect to monetary policy. If it were to follow a substantially looser monetary policy as some politicians are urging, the country could slide back into hyperinflation—with devastating consequences, especially for the poor. But if it continues to seek price and exchange rate stability by using tight monetary policy to compensate for loose fiscal policy, the formal economy will accelerate its downward course. With loose fiscal and tight monetary policies, producers would be crowded out of domestic capital markets by excessive government borrowing to cover the fiscal deficits and would be unable to find financing at reasonable costs. Under such conditions, monetary payments would increasingly be replaced by barter. Total production would shrink. An increasing share of economic activity would move into the shadow economy. And the government—without resources—would find it ever more difficult to provide essential human services and public safety

URGENT STRUCTURAL REFORMS

The urgent stabilization measures outlined in the previous section will help prevent a serious new economic crisis—but will do little to stimulate economic growth. To restore growth and higher living standards, Ukraine needs to implement deep structural reforms as soon as possible—reforms designed to fundamentally change the role of Government in the economy, to create a good business climate, and to protect people during the transition. A full list of the structural reforms suggested in the body of this report are given in Annex A. The top priority items from that list needing action within the next 6-12 months appear below.

Even this short list of priority structural reforms is fairly long and demanding, but trying to achieve sustainable results with a shorter list of reforms—or by implementing only some of the reforms—would almost certainly lead to failure since the reforms are closely inter-dependent. For example, the government might choose to focus on privatizing enterprises but not address the issues of deregulation, expenditure and deficit control, the enforcement of bankruptcy, or the "de-shadowization" of the economy, but this could easily lead to a worsening of an already bad environment. The newly privatized enterprises would find it difficult to make the decisions necessary for profitable operation because of excessive controls. Without effective measures to reduce budget expenditures and deficits, government borrowing in local financial markets would leave real interest rates for working and investment capital beyond the reach of legitimate enterprises. Without strong actions to enforce payments discipline—including an effective threat of bankruptcy—the privatized firms would continue to face a serious risk of failure because contracts for payment are not enforced. And without efforts

to bring firms from the shadow into the formal economy, the tax burden on firms in the formal economy would continue to drain away the resources urgently needed for investment and growth. The reforms clearly need to be treated as an integrated package.

Top three structural reform areas

Although virtually all of the structural reforms listed below are vital to Ukraine's future, one over-arching reform emerges from all this—changing the role of Government. This in turn can be broken down into:

- reforming the structure of government through administrative reform;

- reducing government control of production through deregulation; and

- reducing government ownership of production through privatization.

Attaining these objectives will require implementing many of the more detailed reforms listed below to succeed. For example, changing the administrative structure of government will have no impact if the policies of the past continue to be imposed. Likewise, transferring ownership from public to private hands is simple. If this were the only objective, the property could simply be given away. But to be successful, privatization requires a good process that optimizes benefits to Ukraine in terms of selling price, new investment, employment, and growth. Privatization also requires the reforms needed to assure that privatized enterprises can function in a normal market environment.

Implementing the following list of priority reforms in the next 12-18 months would help establish such an environment. The list looks first at the changes need in the structure and role of Government, then at the key changes required in policies for each of the main sectors of the economy.

Structure and role of government

- *Apparat:* Reform the "Apparat" of the Cabinet of Ministers so that it focuses on policy coordination rather than policy making.

- *Cabinet structure:* Consolidate the Cabinet so that it becomes a small collegial body focused on strategic policy formulation.

- *Deregulation:* Reduce the number of business inspections by half as measured by independent surveys; and sharply limit the number of routine tax inspections.

- *Tax privileges.* Reduce tax privileges so that all economic activity is subject to essentially the same rates of tax (aside from "sin" taxes on alcohol, tobacco and a limited list of luxury items).

- *Tax rates.* Apply a flat rate of VAT, somewhat lower than present levels across the board except for exports which, by international convention, are zero rated.

- *Enforcement of hard budget constraints.* Make enforcement of contracts, including through the implementation of an effective bankruptcy system, an important focus of government activity, thus establishing a badly-needed "hard budget" culture in Ukraine.

- *Inter-governmental fiscal relations.* Implement formula based intergovernmental transfers and clarify inter-governmental expenditure responsibilities.

- *Social protection.* Any budgetary support deemed necessary for poverty alleviation or other reasons should be budgeted explicitly and included in the overall budget deficit. Consolidate fragmented social assistance program under the housing support program so that it becomes a comprehensive, means-tested social safety net that is able to provide more adequate protection for the poor during the transition process.

Enterprise development

- *Tax policy, deregulation, contract enforcement, and bankruptcy.* Major changes in government's role in these areas are vital to creating a good business climate that fosters investment, especially in small and medium enterprises.

- *Privatization.* To help close the budget and BOP financing gap for 2000, and as a stimulus to creating a more favorable business climate, the government needs to privatize attractive enterprises (including firms in energy and telecom) through a transparent process consistent with international standards. New privatizations should total USD 1.0 billion by the end of the year 2000.

Agriculture

- *Bread of Ukraine.* Privatize 100 percent of all commercial grain storage capacity in Ukraine. Government can then issue competitive tenders for storage of state reserves, if such are still deemed necessary.

- *Input supply and output marketing.* Ban all "commodity credit" transactions. Allow free entry and operation of private sector businesses in supplying inputs and marketing outputs in the agricultural sector.

- *External trade policies in agriculture:* Remove all tariff and non-tariff barriers to export of agricultural products.

Energy

- *Electricity privatization:* Sell controlling blocks of shares of all oblenergos to strategic investors on a competitive basis through open international tenders with the assistance of internationally reputable privatization advisors.

- *Coal mine closures:* Transfer at least 20 additional mines to UDKR for closure in the next 6 months and provide UDKR with no less than UAH 25 million from the state budget every month to cover the costs of statutory benefits for laid-off miners and physical closure of mines.

- *Gas transmission privatization:* Award a long term concession for the operation and management of the entire gas transmission system to an international consortium of strategic investors through a competitive tender.

Banking system

- *Bank closures.* Initiate the closure of any major bank not showing any real prospects for recovery.

Shadow Economy

- ***Spread and lower tax burden.*** Reduce incentives to hide in shadows by lowering tax rates—and by simultaneously eliminating all tax privileges and enforcing tax payment—in cash.

- ***Reduce regulatory burden.*** A major, measurable reduction in the regulatory burden imposed on enterprises is urgently needed to encourage activity to shift to the formal sector.

- ***Enforce contracts***. Major improvements are needed in the nation's economic court system to improve contract enforcement.

PROSPECTS FOR THE FUTURE

If Ukraine pursues a competitiveness strategy, takes the crucial measures needed to avoid deficit spending, and implements essential structural reforms, it should be able to halt economic decline and restore growth within 12-18 months. The timing and speed of this growth will depend on the speed and quality of the necessary reforms. These, in turn, will affect the credibility of Ukraine as a location for investment, its ability to regain access to private international capital markets, and its access to increased support from international financial institutions.

If work on the full agenda of structural reforms summarized above (and detailed in Annex A) begins immediately, and if Ukraine completes most of the agenda within the next two or three years, it could attain its official target of doubling 1997 per capita GDP by 2010.

If the pace of reform is less rapid but still much faster than since independence, annual growth rates of at least 3-4 percent could be attained. At this pace, doubling GDP would take longer, but Ukraine might still recover its previous living standards more rapidly than the raw numbers would indicate. Adjusting for the over-statements of Soviet GDP figures, the large share of military and other non-consumable, non-productive output in Soviet GDP, and the widespread scarcity and low quality of consumer goods and services during that era, Ukraine could probably restore or even surpass the *real* living standards of the late 1980s within 8-12 years—or even earlier—even at this more modest pace of growth.

In short, as bad as the 1990s have been for Ukrainians, the future is promising if the country implements the necessary policies—and if Ukraine can, at the same time, preserve social solidarity and equity by implementing jobs-oriented policies supported by an adequate social safety net. With such policies, the children now becoming teenagers could be enjoying a standard of living better than what their parents enjoyed prior to the collapse of the Soviet system by the time they are having children of their own.

Ukraine's only viable path to restoring past living standards is to create a vibrant, export-oriented, internationally competitive economy based on private sector initiative. To make this possible, Ukraine will need to undertake far-reaching changes in the role of government, restructure production sectors, improve the investment climate, and provide high-quality education, health, and social protection. The challenge now is to reach a national consensus on the need for such changes, and then to implement the reforms as swiftly as possible—before more time is lost and the process becomes even more difficult. Fundamental structural change will indeed involve pain, but the pain of not reforming would be even worse. On the other hand, the gains from reforms will be very large. With the necessary policy changes in place, the future of Ukraine will indeed be bright.

1. THE LONG ROAD TO RESTORED PROSPERITY

All the countries that emerged from the former Soviet Union saw living standards fall and poverty rise. But Ukraine has found it particularly difficult to restore growth. Why? A large concentration of energy-intensive industries made initial conditions in Ukraine less favorable than in other countries. These initial difficulties were compounded by the deficits resulting from slow enterprise reform and by the government's tendency to live beyond its means. Although hyperinflation—fueled by printing money to cover the deficits—has ended, the deficits persist, and tight monetary policies together with loose fiscal policies have created a fragile stability that has brought stagnation, not growth. After years of economic decline, poverty is a growing problem. And limited financial resources have made it difficult to clean up environmental problems inherited from the Soviet era. Each of these obstacles is examined below.

STEADY ECONOMIC DECLINE

Although Ukraine's large shadow economy makes it hard to measure GDP, officially reported GDP is only about 40 percent of the level in 1989. Already, the economic decline in Ukraine has been twice as severe and lasted twice as long as the Great Depression in the United States.

Comparisons to the United State are flawed, however, because during the Soviet era Ukraine's GDP was overvalued. Moreover, a large share of output went to inefficient investment and military production. To the extent that output has fallen because of declines in such production, the impact on living standards is less than is shown by official GDP data. Still, Ukraine's economic decline has been severe (figure 1.1).

At independence Ukraine was widely believed to have excellent prospects. It was the most developed former Soviet republic, with considerable capacity in heavy industry (military-industrial complex, metallurgy, machine building, chemical industry). But this

heritage also helps to explain Ukraine's subsequent problems—large enterprises employing thousands of employees are much harder to downsize and restructure than small ones because of the concentration of political and economic power.

Other formerly Soviet countries—the Czech Republic, Estonia, Hungary, Poland—quickly imposed hard budget constraints on large public enterprises and privatized them. Ukraine, by contrast, propped up these enterprises with direct subsidies, directed credits, and tax concessions (Lunina 1999; Ilchuk 1999). These efforts were ostensibly made to prevent unemployment, but in retrospect it seems clear that other political forces played a major role.

Figure 1.1 Economic recovery in other former Soviet states outpaces that in Ukraine

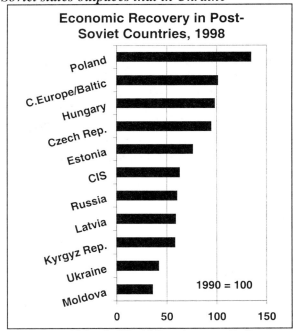

Source: World Bank, World Development Indicators.

Many enterprise managers made large profits by, for example, establishing private companies to buy and sell goods to state enterprises at artificially high prices. Thus profits moved from state-owned enterprises into private hands, and the government covered the losses with more subsidies and other support. Some of the gains from this system were shared with the government officials who made the transfers possible, assuring their interest in maintaining the system. These problems were compounded by the tendency to impose direct controls rather than competitive market solutions when problems arise.

High inflation

Many of Ukraine's economic problems can be traced to the hyperinflation of 1992-94. At its peak inflation reached nearly 10,000 percent (figure 1.2). Hyperinflation was partly triggered by the dramatic structural price adjustments that came with the breakup of the Soviet Union. The price of energy, a crucial input for Ukraine's farms and factories, increased about 10-fold. Inflation was also triggered by price adjustments in Russia in 1991-92.

A more important cause of hyperinflation, however, was the sharp expansion in the money supply in the first half of the 1990s (see figure 1.2). This growth was directly linked to the financing of government deficits during the early years of independence.

Some countries have achieved respectable economic growth despite inflation. In fact, when annual inflation is less than 25 percent, it has little correlation with growth (figure 1.3). Beyond that, however, growth generally drops quickly—and Ukraine is no exception. During 1992-94 its economy declined by more than 50 percent. Though other factors contributed to the decline, inflation was an important problem.

Ballooning deficits

Since independence budget deficits have averaged between 6 and 12 percent of GDP—two to four times the 3 percent maximum set by the Maastricht Treaty for EU countries (figure 1.4).[1] Even the EU limit may be high for a

country like Ukraine, given that it is not growing and generating a surplus that can be used to repay loans taken out to finance the deficit.

Figure 1.2 Financing of budget deficits led to high inflation

Source: National Bank and State Statistics Committee.

Figure 1.3 High inflation tends to stunt growth

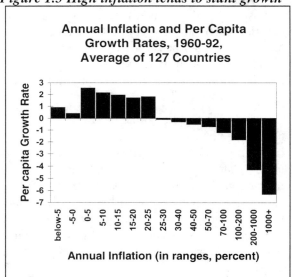

Source: Bruno and Easterly 1995.

---

[1] These official figures significantly understate the real magnitude of the deficit because they do not take into account the accumulation of arrears in the early years of independence, nor do they reflect the quasi-fiscal deficits represented by loans that the government directed the banking system to extend to enterprises instead of extending subsides from the budget. Deficits may have ranged from 25 to 30 percent of GDP in 1992 and 1993. Including quasi-fiscal operations, the deficit has been estimated at up to 33 percent of GDP (World Bank 1993, vol. 1, p. 4).

In the early years of independence these deficits were financed primarily by the central bank, which explains the sharp increase in the money supply. More recently, the deficits were financed by heavy foreign borrowing and then by treasury bills, many of which were sold to foreign investors. Slow reforms have been the main reason for high deficits. Of particular concern are the slow reforms in the role of government (see chapter 2) and in the reform of enterprises in banking and in agriculture, industry, and services—collectively, the "real" economy (see chapter 3).

The crisis of 1998

In recent years the Ukrainian government has cut budget deficits and limited the degree to which these deficits are financed by borrowing from the central bank. As a result inflation fell to 10 percent a year in 1997, helping to slow the economic decline (figure 1.5). In the second quarter of 1998 Ukraine experienced growth for the first time since independence, and prospects looked good for slight growth for the year as a whole. Then on August 17, 1998, the Russian crisis hit.

In the weeks that followed, Ukraine had extreme difficulty rolling over its debt obligations and would have fallen into default had it not been for an innovative "bail-in" arranged with its main creditors (see below). The exchange rate had already been under considerable pressure earlier in the year, and Ukraine borrowed heavily to support the currency—spending about $3 billion trying to defend the exchange rate. But after reserves dropped below $1 billion (about two weeks' worth of imports), Ukraine allowed the currency to adjust. On September 1, 1998, the exchange rate band was moved from 1.802.25 UAH/USD to 2.5-3.5 UAH/USD.

Administrative controls were introduced to prevent the enormous swings that had hit the Russian exchange rate, and over the next few weeks the rate was allowed to climb to the upper end of the new range. Although central bank intervention since September has been nominal, continued "short-term" controls on the foreign exchange market make it impossible to determine how close the current rate is to a true equilibrium rate. With the devaluation, inflation increased significantly, reaching about 20

percent for the year. And with economic uncertainty, output again turned down. Ukraine ended its ninth year of economic decline with a drop of 1.7 percent for the year, bringing the overall decline since 1989 to about 60 percent.

Figure 1.4 Budget deficits greatly exceed the EU limit

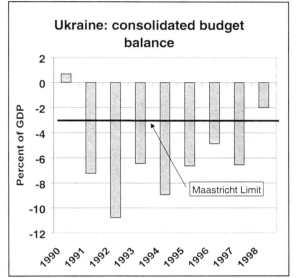

Source: Ministry of Finance.

Figure 1.5 The economy is stabilizing, but there is still no real growth

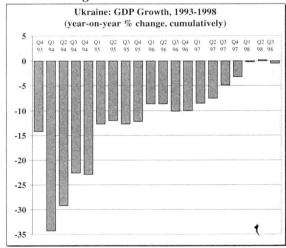

Source: State Statistics Committee.

Although some analysts blame the crisis in Russia for Ukraine's debt servicing crisis, devaluation, increased inflation, and economic decline, Ukraine's economic situation was the real source of the problem. Other countries in the region in close proximity and with substantial trading ties to Russia—the Baltic countries, Hungary, Poland, Turkey—escaped without major economic setbacks. The Russian crisis simply revealed the underlying weakness of Ukraine's slow structural reforms.

Ukraine's trade links with Russia contributed to its economic problems after the Russian crisis. Although Ukraine has diversified its exports and imports since the breakup of the Soviet Union, Russia remains an important trading partner (figure 1.6). More important than the initial Russian devaluation were the impact of the Russian default on global capital markets and the impact of the economic decline in Russia on its demand for imports from Ukraine. Largely because of the latter, Ukraine's imports dropped 14 percent and its exports, 13 percent.

Still, short-term public debt was at the heart of Ukraine's crisis. Although Ukraine's stock of t-bill debt had grown at an explosive pace in recent years (figure 1.7), the biggest problem was not the size of the debt—which was equal to about 10 percent of GDP—but the terms on which it was contracted. First, the average maturity of the debt was less than one year, which meant that the entire amount to be paid off or refinanced each year exceeded the stock of debt. Second, the interest rates that Ukraine had to pay to place this debt were extraordinarily high in real terms (see figure 1.7). As a result monthly debt service exceeded monthly cash revenues during much of 1998. Had it not been for debt restructuring at the end of the year, debt servicing would have exceeded budgetary revenues by the end of 1998.

Until the East Asian crisis much of the foreign money to buy t-bills was coming from Russia, because yields on Ukraine's t-bills were up to 600 basis points higher than Russia's, and the stable hryvnia gave investors a false sense of security. Once the East Asian crisis hit Russia and investors began to shy away from emerging markets, interest rates in Moscow increased and Russian investors took their money back to Moscow. And once the Russian crisis erupted, international investors began to stay away from all emerging markets in the region.

Figure 1.6 Ukraine's dependence on Russia as a trading partner has declined but is still significant

Source: National Bank of Ukraine.

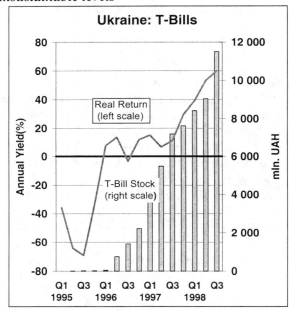

Figure 1.7 T-Bill volumes and costs quickly rose to unsustainable levels

Source: World Bank data.

If Ukraine had been in a strong position, it would have been able to replace local currency borrowing with expanded borrowing in European markets. In fact, during the first half of 1998, Ukraine borrowed about USD 1.1 billion there through a series of Eurobonds denominated in deutsche marks and in European currency units at interest rates of 15 percent or higher in hard currency. But aside from a $155 million t-bill placement through ING-Barings in August 1998—a placement made possible only by offering a 55 percent coupon in hryvnias and a guarantee of 17.5 percent in dollars—the government was unable to mobilize resources from abroad during the second half of 1998. And on September 9 Moody's downgraded Ukraine's credit rating to B3, placing it in the middle of the "lower non-investment grade" category along with Romania and Russia.

With international credit markets effectively closed, Ukraine looked internally to refinance its debt. But this was not feasible for three reasons. First, the government's gross financing requirements (the primary deficit plus interest and amortization) greatly exceeded new credit creation in the domestic economy. Second, asking the central bank to increase the money supply to cover the government's borrowing requirements could have triggered a surge in inflation. Third, a substantial share of t-bills and other short-term government obligations had been sold to foreign investors, and when those investors wanted to liquidate their positions in Ukraine after the Russian crisis, Ukraine had trouble providing the necessary foreign exchange.

In the end Ukraine worked with its creditors to restructure most of its debt, reducing the debt servicing burden to more sustainable levels, at least for 1999. In doing so, Ukraine became one of the first countries to have a "bail-in" instead of a bailout. By this time international lenders of last resort—such as IMF—had become cautious about bailing out international investors who had made risky investments. Thus in Ukraine the investors were asked to bail in—to contribute through a restructuring of the outstanding liabilities to the resolution of the debt servicing crisis.

THE IMPACT ON SOCIAL CONDITIONS

Human suffering has been the greatest cost of slow structural reforms in Ukraine. Family incomes have declined, and health standards have deteriorated. The sharp decline in Ukraine's human development index—which reflects life expectancy at birth, adult literacy rates, gross school enrollment, and real GDP per capita—provides dramatic evidence of the

pain that slow structural reform has caused (figure 1.8).

Figure 1.8 Ukraine's human development index has plummeted

Source: UNDP 1997, Human Development Report for Ukraine.

In 1991 Ukraine's human development index placed it at 32nd place among 175 countries, but by 1995 it had dropped to 95th in this same group. During this same period Ukraine has had to deal with a variety of environmental problems, including the aftermath of the 1986 Chernobyl disaster.

Falling incomes

With an average income of $2,760 per person in 1990, Ukraine enjoyed the third highest standard of living among current members of the Commonwealth of Independent States (excluding the Baltic's).[2] At the time Ukraine was richer than two-thirds of the countries in the world, at least according to official statistics.[3] Life expectancy at birth was more than 70 years,

---

[2] Yuri Dikhanov, "Decomposition of Inequality Based on Incomplete Information," World Bank, 1996, p. 22.

[3] Living standards were overstated by official statistics for at least two reasons. First, although the incomes were paid, long queues were mute evidence of the fact that the money exceeded what was actually available to buy, and thus money incomes did not reflect real incomes. Second, the exchange rates used to convert rubles into dollars were artificially established by the Soviet authorities.

and the gross enrollment ratio of 76 percent was on par with that in Japan and Switzerland.[4]

But slow structural reforms since 1990 and the loss of energy subsidies from Russia have taken a heavy toll on the average Ukrainian family.[5] Per capita incomes had fallen by 1998 to just $1,040 at market exchange rates, placing Ukraine in the 40th percentile in terms of per capita income. Many Ukrainians had substantial savings at the beginning of independence, but these were largely wiped out by the hyperinflation of 1992-94.[6]

Increasing poverty

Of even greater concern than income levels is the 40 percent of Ukrainians now estimated to be living below the poverty line (figure 1.9). Estimates of household expenditures from a 1996 World Bank study paint a brighter picture, showing only 30 percent of people living below the official poverty line.[7] But the official Ukrainian poverty line at the time, equivalent to about $0.80 a day, was certainly set too low, and so understates the incidence of poverty.

The World Bank normally uses poverty lines of $1 and $2 a day to measure destitution and simple poverty in its low-income member countries, which generally lie in temperate or tropical climates. For transition economies, which tend to be more urbanized and have colder climates (thus requiring more spending

on public transportation and heating), the cutoff is normally $4 a day. By this criterion, about 75 percent of Ukrainians were living below the poverty line (on a purchasing power parity basis) in 1997.

Figure 1.9 Many Ukrainians have fallen below the poverty line

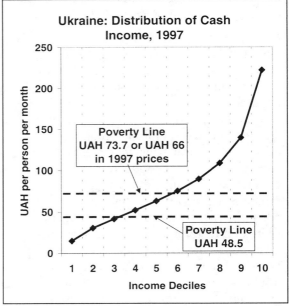

Source: State Statistics Committee.

Growing income inequality also creates social and economic concerns. During the Soviet era Ukraine (and Belarus) had the most equal income distribution of any republic, as measured by the Gini coefficient. This common measure of inequality stood at 22 for Ukraine and 26 for the Soviet Union as a whole. Similarly, the richest 10 percent of Ukrainians earned 3.88 times as much as the poorest 10 percent, compared with 5.66 for the Soviet Union as a whole.

By 1997 income inequality had increased significantly. Such a change is normal, even desirable, as a country moves to a system where income differentials provide incentives for people to get more education, work harder, and take on more responsibility in exchange for higher incomes. Today the situation in Ukraine is similar to that in advanced market economies. For example, Ukraine's Gini coefficient of 38 compares with 25 for Sweden, 33 for France,

---

[4] The gross enrollment ratio is the number of students enrolled in primary, secondary, and college education expressed as a percentage of the population in the relevant age group for these levels of education.

[5] This Soviet-era subsidy and related price distortions have been estimated to have added 2-3 percent to Ukraine's GDP (World Bank, 1993).

[6] Since around 50 percent of total production in Ukraine may be in the shadow economy, the real decline in living standards is probably considerably less than indicated by the dramatic decline in official per capita income data, but the physical indicators of the quality of life, particularly those related to health, indicate a sharp increase in the number of people living in real poverty.

[7] Expenditures are a much better indicator of living standards than cash income for two reasons. First, people tend to underreport income for tax and other reasons. Second, at the lower income levels in Ukraine, income in kind—the form of food from household garden plots—adds substantially to the cash income of households.

Chapter 1

and 40 for the United States.[8] Thus the solution to Ukraine's growing poverty problem does not lie in reducing income inequality. Rather, it lies in implementing the policies needed to accelerate growth sharply so that even poor families have enough income to avoid absolute poverty.

A final area of concern is the incidence of poverty across population groups. From a policy perspective this pattern is important because it suggests the social protection measures that would have the greatest impact on reducing poverty at the least possible cost. The most vulnerable group in Ukraine is families with more than three children—especially if the family is headed by a single parent, usually a woman (table 1.1). The policy implications of such findings, in terms of designing an appropriate social safety net, are spelled out in chapter 5.

Deteriorating health

Sharp increases in sickness and death since 1990 demonstrate the devastating impact of Ukraine's depression on the lives of ordinary people. Spending on health services is one of the largest categories in the government budget, yet the system is deeply in debt and failing to deliver urgently needed care. Even radical reforms will bring results only gradually because of entrenched inefficiencies. Still, it is essential for financial stability—and even more important, for the health and welfare of the people—that these reforms be launched immediately.

Population decline. Since independence Ukraine has experienced a sharp drop in population growth—so sharp that the resulting increase in dependency ratios (the number of non working to working persons) may undermine the financial sustainability of various social programs. The threat to the pension system is significant because, under the current pay-as-you-go system, today's workers pay the pensions of today's pensioners rather than saving for their own retirement. If current trends persist, by 2056, there will be only 0.5 workers supporting each pensioner, compared with 1.6

Table 1.1 Families with many children or elderly are the most likely to be poor

Poverty incidence in Ukraine	
Indicator	Poverty headcount index
Average	30
Number of children	
0	27
1	32
2	34
3 or more	48
Number of people over 65	
0	23
1	34
2 or more	49
Dependency ratio (children and elderly)	
0	16
0.25-1.0	31
1.25-2.00	44
2.25 +	67
No active adults	39
Rural/urban	
Rural	27
Semi-urban	28
Urban	33
Regional distribution	
South	26
West	28
Central	29
East	35
Education	
Primary or less	37
Secondary	31
Special. Sec.	27
Higher	20

Source: World Bank (1996), Poverty in Ukraine.

today and 2.0 in 1990, imposing an impossible burden on the working population.

Why has the population declined? Higher mortality and lower life expectancy are important factors. Among the leading causes of adult deaths are heart failure, lung cancer, alcohol-related problems, suicide, and other forms of violent death, including accidents.

Migration has also played a role in Ukraine's declining population. During 1991-92 more people were moving into Ukraine than were leaving, with particularly large inflows from the Baltic states, the Trans Caucasian region, and Kazakhstan. But since 1994 migration has reversed, as continued economic decline has forced people to seek economic opportunities

---

[8] World Bank, *World Development Indicators*, pp. 68-70

elsewhere. On a net basis, more than 400,000 people left Ukraine between 1990 and 1997.

Low birth rates are the final factor explaining the population decline in Ukraine. Birth rates fell from 15.0 per 10,000 in 1985 to 12.7 in 1990 and 9.0 in 1997. The decline in the 1980s probably reflects the disintegration of the economy prior to the collapse of the Soviet Union and, perhaps more important, the reluctance of couples to raise children in post-Chernobyl Ukraine. The decline in birth rates since 1990 is almost certainly linked to Ukraine's difficult transition to a market economy.

As Ukraine restores economic growth and as the large cohort of today's teenagers reaches child-bearing age, there is every reason to believe that the population will stabilize or even grow—greatly reducing the risk of labor shortages and dangerously high dependency ratios in the pension system.

Morbidity and mortality. Slow structural reforms have contributed to high rates of sickness and death in Ukraine. The average death rate rose from 13.4 per 100,000 people in 1992 to 15.4 in 1995, and is now more than 50 percent higher than in the European Union. In 1995 life expectancy at birth was just 67 years in Ukraine, compared with more than 77 years in the European Union. And infant mortality, at 15 per 1,000 births, is more than twice the rate in the European Union.

The death rate from heart attacks and other circulatory failures is running three times the level in EU countries. Over the past five years deaths from heart attacks and related problems have increased 40 percent. Other leading killers are "external" factors, including accidents, homicides, and suicides. The stress of the difficult transition to a market economy is seen in all of these indicators—especially in the suicide rate, which for men rose from 41 per 100,000 in 1993 to 52 in 1997, compared with about 20 in Europe.

Despite the horrors of the Chernobyl disaster in 1986, the death rate from cancer today is the same as the European average. In fact, cancer has fallen sharply as a cause of death (from 16.5 percent of all deaths in 1989 to 12.8 percent in 1996). This is a credit to the success of the

Ukrainian authorities in moving people from the contaminated areas and in treating those who suffered exposure. This also confirms the experience in Belarus—which received a major share of the fallout from Chernobyl—that the loss of life and rate of illness due to the disaster are much lower than is commonly believed. In fact, the psychological trauma of the accident seems to have been worse than the physical damage.

Other leading causes of illness in Ukraine include diseases of the circulatory, respiratory, and digestive systems. In part because of its large number of intravenous drug users, Ukraine has one of the highest and fastest growing rates of HIV infection in Europe, with a growing number of full-blown AIDS cases. Syphilis is also on the rise, increasing by nearly 8 times since 1992 and now 74 times the rate of infection in the European Union. Tuberculosis cases are increasing as well, and waterborne diseases (including cholera) are a major source of illness.

In short, Ukraine is in the midst of a health care crisis. The solution is not more money, because the government is already spending more than it can afford unless major savings are realized elsewhere in the budget. Instead, major structural reforms are required (see chapter 5).

Education needs

Ukraine's education system is relatively good, and the problems that do exist will likely be easier to fix than those in the health system. Education standards have been high for many years and show no significant signs of deterioration. Nearly 100 percent of Ukrainians are literate, and with an average of 11 years of schooling completed, Ukrainian standards are consistent with those of the European Union. Still, the quality and focus of the education system need substantial improvements to meet the demands of an industrial, modern market economy (see chapter 4).

Environmental problems— and possible solutions

Ukraine is blessed with one of the world's largest areas of fertile black soil, Europe's third longest river, abundant forests in the southwest, a long coastline along the once-fertile Black

Sea, and hydrocarbon reserves that could make the country largely self-sufficient in gas within a few years. But Ukraine is also burdened with serious ecological problems—the result not only of the Chernobyl disaster but also of more than 70 years of Soviet exploitation and ecological abuse. There is a massive backlog of environmental cleanup, especially for water pollution and solid waste disposal. There is one bright spot, however: the economic decline has actually reduced air and water pollution.

Chernobyl and other nuclear contamination. The Chernobyl disaster and its effects have overshadowed other environmental issues in Ukraine. The accident was truly of epic proportions—it was the world's first major meltdown of a nuclear reactor core. An estimated 26 people died almost immediately of radiation poisoning, most of them the "liquidators" who contained the fire after the initial explosion and cleaned up the site afterwards. About 3.25 million people were exposed to the radiation, with about 300,000 forced to move out of the "exclusion zone" surrounding the plant. The entire town of Prypyat, where Chernobyl workers lived, had to be relocated to Slavutych. Some 4–6 million hectares of land have been closed to human habitation in Ukraine, of which 3–5 million hectares is agricultural land. Overall, about 6 percent of Ukraine's population and 11 percent of its agricultural land were affected by the accident.

With the breakup of the Soviet Union, which originally helped pay the costs of the Chernobyl accident, Ukraine must now handle them largely on its own. The sarcophagus covering the burned-out Unit 4 at Chernobyl urgently needs $760 million in repairs. Replacing the generating capacity of the three remaining reactors and shutting them down permanently—a high priority not only for Ukraine but also for its European neighbors— would cost an estimated $130 billion, or 12 times the consolidated government budget for 1998.

Although the areas directly affected by Chernobyl are the common focus of attention and concern regarding atomic waste, the most unfavorable ecological situation is in Zhovty Vody city in Dnipropetrovsk Oblast, where raw uranium is processed and a dump for radioactive waste is located. More broadly, tens of tons of used nuclear fuel, tens of thousands of cubic meters of solid radioactive waste, and tens of millions of tons of liquid radioactive matter have piled up at Ukrainian nuclear power stations, creating a massive environmental liability for which there is no known affordable solution.

Industrial pollution. Industry in Ukraine adversely affects both the general environment and the work environment for industrial employees. Despite the drop in industrial output noted above, industrial air and water pollution remain highly detrimental to human health. Economic losses from health-related problems have not been calculated at the national level, but visits to individual plants show that workers often do not wear protective gear and that there are serious occupational health hazards in mining, chemical, and metallurgical industries. Such problems were largely underreported in the past, but in the early 1990s reporting began to improve.

Working conditions are particularly unsafe in heavily industrialized areas such as Donetsk, home to many of Ukraine's mining, chemical, and metallurgical industries. Of 1.2 million workers in Donetsk, 45 percent work in environments that are not up to sanitary and health standards. Major workplace problems include unacceptable air quality (affecting 28 percent of workers), high noise levels (16 percent), and high vibration levels (5 percent). During 1993-96 some 6,860 new cases of occupational disease were registered in Donetsk, nearly all of them associated with coal mining. During this same period 23,200 occupational injuries resulted in more than 550,000 lost work days. The exceptionally low life expectancy in heavily industrialized areas reflects the severity of these problems—men are expected to live just 60 years.

Several immediate, inexpensive actions at the plant level could improve safety and reduce pollution:

- Introducing better safety procedures and equipment to reduce industrial accidents.

- Strengthening cleaning, housekeeping, and materials handling programs to reduce fugitive emissions.

- Repairing and maintaining process and pollution control equipment.

- Attending to operating performance generally—including that of utilities—to increase efficiency and reduce emissions.

- Installing minimum instrumentation and controls.

- Implementing energy- and other resource-saving measures.

Freshwater and drinking water. The quality of freshwater and drinking water is increasingly being undermined by industrial, agricultural, and municipal pollution. Over the past few decades communal water supply and wastewater treatment infrastructure have deteriorated, creating significant health risks for urban populations. About 70 percent of Ukrainians depend on the Dnieper River for water supplies. Water pollution is a concern along the southern segments of the river, especially near the cities of Dnipropetrovsk and Kamiansk, because of a concentration of industrial and municipal activities and large volume of wastewater discharges. Eutrophication is a serious problem for the entire river.

Groundwater is a source of drinking water for about 15 percent of the population. Problems result from major chemical, metallurgical, and mining activities. Rural areas also suffer problems because of poor sanitary practices and poor waste management related to livestock production.

Municipal water and sewage treatment utilities are good candidates for economic reform. These utilities should operate on a commercial basis and be given operating and financial autonomy—including the ability to set rates for water and wastewater treatment that reflect the true costs of these operations and create a self-financing capability.

Municipal waste management. Many municipal landfills do not meet sanitary standards, and some have exhausted their capacity. Since the early 1990s the number of landfill users (mainly small businesses) has increased considerably, altering the municipal waste management situation. In many cities the municipal solid waste system has effectively collapsed, with infrequent residential collection, extensive illegal dumping, co-disposal of hazardous industrial waste, and extremely poor landfill operations and uncontrolled landfill access.

Over the short term a lack of capital financing impedes system improvements. Over the long term the barrier to system sustainability is an inability to recover costs and provide for capital renewal. Still, some steps should be taken. Wastes should be separated, and landfills should be managed better. In addition, institutional and fiscal actions are required to place municipal solid waste on a sustainable financial footing in terms of cost recovery and capacity to meet future investment needs.

Environmental funds. Environmental funds have been set up in Ukraine to fine polluters, discouraging pollution and increasing the financial resources available to fight pollution. Payments by polluting enterprises split up, with 30 percent going to the national budget, 50 percent to the oblast budget, and 20 percent to the local budget. Fines are paid for pollutants emitted into the atmosphere by stationary and mobile sources; pollutants discharged into surface waters, territorial and internal sea waters, and underground waters (including wastes disposed through communal sewerage systems); and wastes disposed in the environment.

Resource pricing. Low prices for energy, water, and raw materials and a lack of accountability among enterprises have encouraged excessive resource use and sustained energy-inefficient industrial activity. These factors have also discouraged the adoption of more efficient technologies. The consequent pressure on the government and the environment to supply these resources has exacerbated environmental pressures.

Water consumption is particularly high in both industry and agriculture. Yet water charges, a means of encouraging conservation, are insignificant. Although water and wastewater charges have been raised in recent years, they are still low in real terms.

2. TRANSFORMING GOVERNMENT FOR GROWTH

As noted in chapter 1, budget deficits have been a key factor leading to the inflation, devaluation, high interest rates, shortage of working capital and investment, and economic decline that have plagued Ukraine since independence. Government spending has not been kept in line with revenues, and the government continues to impose a much heavier burden on economic activity than is typical in other countries at similar stages of development. Reforming government will require changing the level and focus of government spending so that services that cannot be provided by the private sector can be provided at high quality and low cost by the public sector, leaving all other activities to the private sector.

Major reforms are also needed to improve the equity, efficiency, and transparency of the tax system. The revenues needed to finance government spending should be mobilized in ways that do not undermine investment, growth, and family incomes. Similarly, reforms are needed in the way Ukraine manages its debt, both internal and external, with a focus on reducing the total level of financing and securing funds at lower interest rates and longer maturities. Finally, reforms in intergovernmental fiscal relations should provide adequate resources to sub-national authorities and ensure that these resources are used efficiently.

This chapter concludes with a section on the shadow economy, defined as the estimated half of economic activity in Ukraine that does not pay taxes. This topic is included here because the shadow economy is very much the result of government policies. Those operating in the shadow economy do so primarily to escape burdensome taxes and regulations. This problem can be solved by reducing government spending, thus limiting the amount of taxes that need to be collected; spreading taxes more widely to reduce the burden of taxes on individuals and companies; and easing the burdens of regulatory compliance.

ADAPTING GOVERNMENT TO A MARKET ECONOMY

The role of government in Ukraine has not changed sufficiently since Soviet days. The government is still heavily involved in production and marketing in key economic areas such as large-scale manufacturing and agriculture. Although most small nonagricultural enterprises have been privatized, the "giants" generally remain under government control. Agricultural production operates largely on the basis of collectives, not private farms, and the government actively intervenes in the marketing of agricultural output through state orders and controls on the storage and movement of grain. Even privatized enterprises are closely controlled by government inspectors enforcing tax, health, fire, antimonopoly, and other laws and regulations.

The structure and size of government has also changed little. Government remains highly centralized and bureaucratic. Though centralized, however, the system is also fragmented. For example, people with responsibility for the sectors like agriculture are found not only in the Ministry of Agriculture, but also in the Ministries of Economy and Finance, and in the Ministry of the Cabinet of Ministers—the "Apparat." The decision-making process is bureaucratic and the responsibility for policy decisions is ambiguous. government decision-making is presently subject to widespread criticism on the basis that decisions are: (a) taken without strategic oversight and are not always consistent with the reform agenda; (b) can quickly be reversed; (c) are non-transparent because responsibilities within government overlap, and lines of accountability are unclear; (d) are taken, in many cases, on the basis of private, rather than public interest; and finally (e) are frequently delayed. For these reasons, government often fails to address serious economic and social reform issues, and/or does not address problems effectively.

Moreover, the institutional capacity of the key government agencies is weak. Due to the limited history of policy making in Ukraine, few competent policy analysts or policy change managers can be found in Government, and the experience of the few who exist is based mainly on Soviet rather than market model. A mechanism of getting input from stakeholders and for building consensus in the development and implementation of policy reforms is absent. As a result, government policy decisions are not made on the basis of a thorough analysis of available choices with the selection of the most appropriate ones.

These institutional problems within the Government are compounded by political and economic uncertainties. Bad past policy decisions have created crisis environment where much of the government attention is focused on fighting the short term problems instead of building the foundations for long-term growth. Moreover, the lack of clear rules and failures to enforce the rules effectively as well as distortions created by bad regulations have enriched a small part of the population, whose strong vested interests in status quo present a serious barrier to further reform.

All these have created a seriously defective policy framework which imposes major constraints on the economic reform program and growth in Ukraine. As a result, economic activity remains weak—even though officially recorded GDP contraction has slowed down, a further decline of 1-2 percent is expected in 1999; excessive government regulation and the uncertainties over the legal framework have discouraged external investment and hindered employment; protection by branch ministries of state enterprises under their control has delayed privatization and hindered private sector development; high rates of taxation have encouraged growth of the black economy; and public sector corruption is perceived to be a serious problem.

Administrative and regulatory reform should bring the role, structure, and size of government in line with the needs of a market economy. To promote growth and raise living standards, the government should focus on creating a good business climate rather than directly regulating economic activity and on providing human development support services. Enhancing government capacity for reform design and implementation is central to reform success.

A new role for government

Major reforms in the role of government are needed to improve the management of the economy and ensure growth. Four areas deserve particular attention. First, the government urgently needs to move from own-and-control to market-based regulations and incentives. Such policies could replace many of the current legions of inspectors and enterprise managers would become focus on investing and producing rather than on negotiating with the inspection. This would stimulate economic growth, increase the tax base, and reduce corruption.

Second, organizational reform of the government ministries and the Apparat is required to streamline the decision making process and to enhance accountability. Ministries should be empowered with decision making responsibilities and be fully accountable for the results[9]. The physical structure and administrative procedures of government must be reformed to refocus its efforts on the needs of a market economy.

Simplifying the structure of the central government is a necessary but not sufficient condition for improved government performance. The capacity to carry out ministerial core functions also depends on the existence of a professional and motivated civil service[10]. Similarly, the efficient delivery of public services depends on the existence of a well-paid workforce matched to requirements. Civil servants should be trained in policy making techniques, as well as new management procedures and schemes of delegation should be developed. The civil service competitiveness should be improved in relation to pay levels in other sectors. However, the reform of the central

---

[9] An important precondition for an efficiently functioning Cabinet is a clear distinction of powers between the existing three branches of power - Parliament, President and Cabinet, which is not the case today. This is a constitutional problem, but it could be resolved within the existing constitutional framework.

[10] Average civil service wages are 0.7 times per capita GDP in Ukraine. The corresponding figures for ECA and OECD are 1.3 and 1.6 respectively.

---

civil service is not likely to include any downsizing, as it is very small by international standards[11].

Third, the rule of law should be strengthened. A major government function in a market economy is to establish stable laws and a judicial system that ensures equitable enforcement of these laws. Currently the legislation is very unstable and the judiciary system is weak and is not trusted by the public.

A smaller size

In principle, there are two options for cutting government deficits—increasing revenues or decreasing expenditures. Only the second option is viable if Ukraine wants to restore prosperity. The government is large for a country at Ukraine's income level, placing a heavy burden on resources needed for private investment and household consumption.

In other middle-income countries government spending averages 25–30 percent of GDP. In Ukraine spending (including special funds) is about 45 percent of GDP. Under the Soviet system a large government was possible because the government delivered many necessities to workers at low or no cost—a major share of household income came in kind rather than in cash. But under a market system the government can no longer play this direct distributional role. As a result people need real money in their pockets to buy enough food, clothing, and shelter to survive.

A government that is too large relative to its economy reduces living standards in two ways. First, it takes money from people that they need to meet normal living expenses. Second, it takes money from enterprises needed to finance expansion and growth. Both effects are evident in Ukraine. Agricultural and industrial enterprises are severely decapitalized. Investment and working capital are scarce, and investment rates are low. There is clear evidence of redundant employment in many areas of government. And family incomes are low. In the end the decision on the appropriate size of government is a political one. Still, it seems

clear that the balance between government revenues and expenditures should be restored not by further increasing the tax burden, but by reducing government expenditures. Priorities for public spending are discussed below.

A key problem facing Ukraine today is that key ministries lack the capacity to analyze policy options, designing policies, and assuring their implementation. The existing institutional structures of the state are still highly oriented to the old Soviet command and control mode. Critically important bodies such as the Ministries of Finance and Economy that should be taking the lead in defining strategic objectives for the future and designing the policies needed to attain these objectives are bogged down in details of economic micro-administration. Although the situation is expected to change shortly, an important share of the staff in both of these ministries is still located in the "branch departments" responsible for controlling the enterprises in the key sectors of the economy including agriculture, energy, manufacturing, health, education, and the like. As noted above, the "apparat" of the Cabinet of Ministers forms yet another layer of administrative controls between the Prime Minister and the ministries actually responsible for economic progress in these critical sectors of the economy. The focus and abilities of the professionals talented in the Apparat need to be redirected towards jobs that are consistent with the needs of a market economy.

Other countries such as those in Central Europe and the Baltic States moved quickly after the breakup of the Soviet Union to reform their administrative structures to meet the challenge of supporting the development of a market-based economy. The World Bank and the IMF are working closely with reformers in the Government of Ukraine to bring about the necessary changes and are willing to provide substantial financial support to this end, but so far the combination of inertia, vested interests in the status quo, and lack of adequate institutions have prevented meaningful change.

The need for institutional change is by no means limited to CabMin, the central ministry offices in Kyiv. Improvements in structure and policy skills are needed in all sectoral ministries;

---

[11] About to 0.45% of the total population, compared to an average of 1.95% in ECA and 4.3% in OECD.

regulatory agencies need to develop greater skills and authority; a strong system of economic courts should be developed to handle the enforcement of contracts (through bankruptcy where necessary); a better police and criminal court system is needed to protect those operating legally from criminal activity; and more needs to be done to develop a system for large scale privatization that is consistent with international standards. Further parliamentary reforms may also be needed to encourage the formation of larger, more stable parties with a longer term, less populist outlook.

The need for fiscal adjustment

Fiscal adjustment in Ukraine has been slow and unsuccessful. Government has hardly adjusted to the role that it needs to play if Ukraine is to have a viable market-based economy. Limited progress has been made in modernizing budget and tax practices, improving the legal and regulatory framework, and strengthening fiscal institutions. Prohibitively high taxes impede economic development and foster tax arrears, tax offsets, and the shadow economy, eroding the tax base. Falling revenues combined with poor commitment control and bad spending policies have generated consistent budget arrears and fiscal deficits (table 2.1).

Table 2.1 Government revenues in the former Soviet block countries (percentage of GDP)

Country	1993	1994	1995	1996	1997	1997
Czech Rep	42	43	42	31	30	30
Lithuania	25	27	27	21	27	27
Ukraine	71	51	46	45	39	36
FSU average	36	35	29	26	—	—

Source: IMF data

Fiscal deficits contribute to stagnation by crowding out private investment (figure 2.1) The government is facing a liquidity crisis—set off by the financial crisis abroad but exacerbated by Ukraine's lack of fiscal and economic adjustment—and the central bank will likely have to finance any new deficit spending by printing money. Unless the budget is balanced, inflation, currency depreciation, and

economic instability will worsen. Even if short-term liquidity problems are overcome, debt levels are quickly becoming unsustainable, and the structural and institutional changes needed for growth have not been made. Parliament and government must make the difficult political decisions needed to break the cycle of overspending, overtaxing, and economic stagnation.

Figure 2.1 Government deficits have exceeded total credit expansion

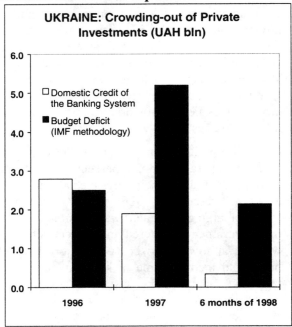

Source: World Bank staff estimates.

Efforts to rationalize spending, broaden the tax base, and control the deficit have moderated the government's role in the economy and shrunk the budget deficit (figure 2.2). But more needs to be done. During 1992-94 the government printed money. In 1995-96 it clamped down on monetary policy to reduce inflation and stabilize the currency. To reduce monetary emissions, it cut the cash deficit. But the cash deficit was contained by postponing spending and running up arrears, making the fiscal situation appear better than it was. In 1997 the government began slowing the growth of arrears, but it did so by reverting to large cash deficits, paid for by issuing government securities to domestic and foreign commercial banks and by selling Eurobonds. In 1998 cash deficits and arrears again rebounded, accompanied by a rapid increase in tax arrears. In sum, relative to GDP, little real fiscal adjustment took place between 1994 and 1998.

Underlying these developments is the lack of a strong fiscal authority that can manage and direct change while dealing with Parliament and other forces. Disagreements between political forces and interest groups have stalled reform. Reform-minded interest groups remain weak, and those who are in a position to break the deadlock lack sufficient incentives or political will to do so. The government in particular has failed to identify its constituency or obtain a strong coalition to back reforms. The resulting slow pace of reform risks bringing the entire process to a halt as the expected benefits do not materialize, either with better policies or the emergence of an economic supply response.

Figure 2.2 The consolidated budget balance is improving, but deficit are still unsupportable

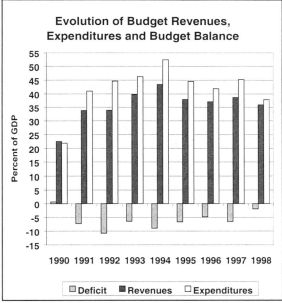

Source: World Bank staff estimates.

The government's track record, combined with the continuing economic crisis, makes fiscal adjustment more difficult now than it was in the past. Yet the solutions have not changed. Taxes need to be reduced and realigned, and tax administration improved. Spending needs to be cut and rationalized to allow for lower taxes and to reposition the government in a market-oriented economy. These actions need to be

sufficiently deep to reduce the deficit and reverse rapidly expanding debt and debt service. Time is running short, and Ukraine must act before it finds itself in a debt service trap that deprives it of domestic and foreign investment for years to come. Though the measures outlined in this section can make a big difference, they will only be possible with a strong government commitment to break from the past, make politically difficult decisions, and follow through with persistence

REFORMING PUBLIC SPENDING

Ukraine has rationalized spending by curtailing industrial, agricultural, and commercial support. Between 1992 and 1994 spending on the "national economy" was cut 70 percent in real terms, or from 24 percent of GDP to 15 percent (figure 2.3).[12] The bulk of this cut was achieved by reducing directed credits to state enterprises, which by 1996 were eliminated. Between 1994 and 1997 direct industrial support was reduced, and by 1997 national economy expenditures were down to 3.2 percent of GDP. These cuts were crucial to reform—efficient resource allocation requires that the private sector make most decisions about commercial activities. But the reduction in commercial support (to state-owned enterprises and agricultural cooperatives) was done in the absence of broader market liberalization and reform (such as mass privatization, a serious commitment to bankruptcy, and the implementation of tight budget constraints). Without a mechanism to stimulate cost-efficient production, the official economy could not—and has not—responded.

In mid-1994 the Kuchma administration initiated reforms that have touched on nearly every budget program (see figure 2.3). Between 1994 and 1997 spending fell by 27 percent in real terms, and by 12.5 percent relative to GDP.[13] Capital expenditures, which were

---

[12] The national economy is defined here to include industrial and agricultural support, the State Reserve Fund, and directed credits to state enterprises from the central bank.

[13] Unless otherwise stated, changes in expenditures are reported on a real, accrual basis (that is, the nominal figures are augmented by the change in arrears over the

already low (3.6 percent of GDP), were cut to negligible levels. As noted, national economy expenditures were cut from 15 percent of GDP to 3.2 percent. Universal subsidies were reduced and are now to be eliminated. Privileges and entitlements have not been honored, but in the past few years expenditures on benefits have increased anyway. Social spending has been cut by more than a quarter. Chernobyl Fund expenditures have remained constant, while defense spending has increased as a share of GDP and spending on administration and justice have actually increased in real terms.

Thus the composition of expenditures has changed dramatically since independence and has generally moved in a direction consistent with the role of government in a market-oriented economy. More recently, however, with the government facing cash shortages and high barriers to borrowing, changes are being driven by short-term cash management imperatives and political pressures rather than by a strategy to reduce the fiscal burden and improve the structure of expenditures. This approach has led to an unsustainable fiscal balance and a poor allocation of public resources. There is now an urgent need for a clear, comprehensive, multiyear strategy. Toward that goal, the government should:

- Improve budget formulation and implementation.

- Encourage more efficient energy use in budget institutions.

- Rationalize and target social spending.

- Remove privileges.

- Introduce a modern treasury system to control public resource flows.

- Control or remove special funds.

- Increase capital expenditures according to well-designed priorities.

Budgeting for efficient spending

Today the budget is not an effective tool for formulating and implementing government spending policy. Budget formulation is an open-ended request process that emphasizes needs over availability, and ultimately ends up being a bargaining process rather than a priority-setting exercise (see World Bank, 1997) Moreover, administrative control is fragmented and the assignment of responsibility for commitment control is not clear. Because tradeoffs are not made explicitly at the outset and because administrative control is weak, cash rationing becomes the mechanism for allocating spending, for controlling expenditures, and, ultimately, for meeting deficit targets.

Figure 2.3 Spending is down sharply

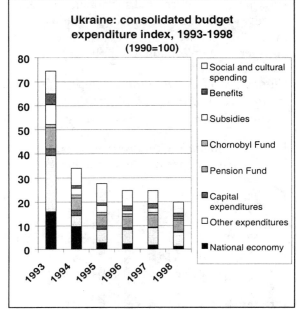

Source: Government data and World Bank staff estimates.

Budgets should be made more realistic, with appropriations that accurately reflect national objectives. Budget implementation should then be executed according to strict rules of control and responsibility. Three steps are needed to achieve these goals.

First, a new budget system law should be passed that provides for aggregate fiscal control. Any Parliamentarian suggesting to increase spending or decrease revenues should be obligated to offer compensating measures so that the overall budget deficit is not increased. And except for the Budget Law and its amendments, laws should not increase spending or decrease

---

measurement period and deflated by the consumer price index).

revenues unless they are presented jointly with the Ministry of Finance.

Second, the budget preparation process should prioritize spending programs, and budget execution should comply with these priorities. Once spending limits have been assigned to spending agencies, the agencies should not be allowed to contest the limits, only the priorities within the aggregate limits. This procedure would lead to the final allocation of resources and better align commitments with available resources.

Finally, once the budget has been formulated, budget execution should be controlled at each stage of the spending cycle—commitment, verification, and payment. There should be clear rules for control (including the responsibilities of the officers in charge of controls within line ministries and the Ministry of Finance), accounting and reporting requirements, and inspections and audits. Procedures for managing and monitoring personnel should also be reviewed. Finally, the Ministry of Finance should be able to issue sanctions in cases of mismanagement.

Boosting energy efficiency

Energy—including gas, electricity, and heating—is one of the largest spending categories for most budget institutions. Substantial arrears have accumulated, particularly in local health and education institutions. Nearly all budget institutions have electricity meters and at least 75 percent have gas meters, but heat meters are almost nonexistent. In the absence of metering, energy charges are based on square meters of floor space. This approach favors energy distributors over budget institutions and destroys incentives to conserve heat and gas.

An obvious solution to this problem is to meter all, or nearly all, budget institutions. Gas meters can be installed for about $100, so all budget institutions should be fitted with them. Heat meters are very expensive, particularly if they are capable of regulating heat flow. Still, installing heat meters can have a high payoff, and a plan should be developed to install heat meters in budget institutions on a cost-benefit basis. The plan should identify which institutions should receive meters with regulatory control, which should receive basic meters, and which (if any) do not warrant meter installations. Thought should be given to sharing the costs of meters with the energy providers.

Another way to increase energy efficiency would be to abandon norms-based budgeting, which tends to allocate money in terms of space to be heated, for example, and move toward budgeting by strategic objective. Under this approach the spending ministries would submit proposals to the Ministry of Finance on the programs and services they plan to deliver (rather than a list of proposed expenses). The list would be subject to an ex ante ceiling imposed by the Cabinet of Ministers based on the importance of programs in different areas. Ministers would then be judged on their ability to deliver results under tight budget constraints, providing them with an incentive to conserve energy.

Rationalizing and targeting social spending

Quality health and education services are essential for growth and prosperity. With shrinking public resources, these expenditures must be rationalized to maintain quality. Since 1992 real expenditures on health have dropped 55 percent and on education, 46 percent (about in line with the fall in GDP). Moreover, there has been a shift in expenditures toward wages and benefits—at the expense of capital expenditures and other recurrent expenditures such as books, school lunches, and energy. Between 1992 and 1995 employment in these sectors actually increased, most likely because the authority for employment decisions was transferred from the state to local managers.

Expenditures for social protection have changed in recent years, with less spending on subsidies and more spending on benefits. Cuts in universal subsidies have been offset by increases for housing and communal service programs. This positive development should be duplicated in other areas of social protection. But a number of untargeted subsidies remain, including child birth support and burial assistance funded out of Social Insurance Fund, and support for single mothers, monthly child care allowance till the child is three years old funded out of local budgets and Pension Fund. (In the case of aid for families with children, the Pension Fund is responsible for delivering the support). Pensions to servicemen and internal agency personnel, as well as transfers from the budget to the Pension Fund for military pensions, have increased dramatically since 1995. Finally, outlays for privilege entitlements that are traditionally funded (including privileges to veterans and invalids of World War II, "labor veterans," and other elderly people) have also risen.

High-quality health, education, and social protection services should be a priority for any government that wants an efficient market economy. Chapter 4 of this study discusses how the government can increase the quality and efficiency of human services in Ukraine.

Removing privileges

Various population groups are entitled to a variety of low- or no-cost goods and services at the expense of the budget or special earmarked funds. A number of these privileges have been carried over from Soviet times; others have been introduced since independence. In 1997 the government estimated that if all privilege entitlements were fully funded, about 17 million of Ukraine's 51 million people would receive 81 million privilege "hits." (A hit is defined as the entitlement of a single person to a single privilege, allowing for multiple hits per person.) The theoretical budgetary cost was estimated at 15.6 billion hryvnias for 1997—almost 20 percent of GDP. Since funding these entitlements would rapidly lead to hyperinflation, the government has distinguished between entitlements provided by law, entitlements committed in the budget, and entitlements that are actually funded (Lippott, 1999). The difference between the second and third categories becomes payment arrears.

Privileges are not an efficient method of compensating the population, whether for labor, heroism, personal ailments, or natural or human-made catastrophes. Where compensation is appropriate, cash payments are a more efficient way to improve welfare and decrease wasteful exploitation. But given the current fiscal crisis such expenditures must be weighed against other alternatives. Despite the need for deep

budget cuts, expenditures on some privileges have been increasing. Further, unfunded entitlements erode public confidence in laws, government resolutions, and stated intents, in return for often short-term political gain.

Table 2.2 Social Insurance Fund expenditures (percent)

Function	Share
Temporary disability allowance	55.0
Sanatorium treatment	31.6
Allowance for pregnancy and birth	9.5
Staffing	2.5
Onetime assistance for childbirth	1.3
Burial assistance	0.5

Source: 1998 draft budget of Ukraine.

In 1997 the Ministry of Finance prepared a list of privileges established by administrative authority as a precursor to the Rada introducing a draft law to remove privileges established by legislation. The administration and the Rada should agree to eliminate privileges in the near future.

Introducing a modern treasury system

The government regularly restricts the release of funds to spending units according to incoming revenues, effectively rewriting the budget without Parliament's approval. This causes serious disruptions within the economy, hurting prospects for restoring growth. Sequestration leads to arrears, a particular problem in the case of civil servant wages and pensions because funds have implicitly been committed for such expenditures before sequestration.[14] Government arrears impede private sector development, increase shadow economy, impose high social costs, and breed cynicism about government and market reforms in general.

Instead of using sequestration to control cash flows, the government needs to move quickly to

---

[14] In theory sequestration prevents the commitment of funds. However, as practiced in Ukraine and many other countries, it is applied to expenditure categories such as salaries of regular employees, which are a *de facto* ongoing commitment. In such cases, the term "expenditure arrears" would technically be more correct, especially when the "sequestration" is applied after the goods or services have already been delivered.

a modern treasury that can control public revenues and spending, manage budget cash flows, monitor debt service, and forecast budget expenditures. A consolidated treasury can greatly reduce the inefficiencies, informational problems, and losses associated with having budget funds managed in a variety of different commercial bank accounts. The Treasury should advise Cabinet when formal changes need to be made in tax or expenditure policy to correct emerging payments problems before they reach crisis level and force day-by-day cash management and sequestration. The government is currently working closely with the World Bank and other donors to implement a project to this end.

Controlling special budget and off-budget funds

Pension Fund. Pension Fund expenditures have remained stable in real terms, but individual contributions have fallen dramatically, and the fund no longer provides the assurance of a comfortable retirement that it did in the Soviet era. It has become, at best, a minimalist social safety net.

Several steps can be taken to transform the Pension Fund into a system that is both financially sustainable and capable of providing a decent retirement (see chapter 4). From the fiscal perspective of this chapter, the government needs to ensure that no bailout of the Pension Fund is needed or undertaken, either from the general budget or from an increase in payroll taxes.

Chernobyl Fund. Chernobyl Fund expenditures are not sufficiently targeted toward victims and cleanup of the disaster. Privileges, compensations, capital expenditures, housing construction, and resettlement account for an astounding 79 percent of the fund's expenditures, while environmental cleanup and medical support make up only 9 percent. Privileges and compensations alone eat up 44 percent, yet many certified recipients have not been seriously affected by radiation. And many of the capital projects are inconsistent with the government's role in a market economy. Since the early 1990s the fund's expenditures have hovered around 2 percent of GDP.

A lot of money has thus been wasted. The payroll tax for the fund is being eliminated—a welcome move. The government should also limit future fund expenditures to medical support, compensation for losses, and capital and recurrent expenditures directly related to cleanup. In addition, it should audit the Chernobyl Fund and make the results publicly available, and amend the law on Chernobyl to remove privileges and other entitlements.

Social Insurance Fund. The Social Insurance Fund relies on a 4 percent payroll tax to provide welfare, disability, and health insurance (table 2.2). Under current arrangements for temporary disability, neither employees nor employers have any incentive to economize on sick leave because sick leave payments are made entirely from the fund. Changes to disability payments are being made as part of the Government's program of economic reforms that is being supported by the International Monetary Fund (IMF) under an Extended Fund Facility (EFF). Also, the payroll tax is to be reduced by 1 percentage point in the 1999 budget.

Other Social Insurance Fund expenditures still need to be rationalized, however. Payments for sanatorium treatment are effectively subsidies to state sanatoriums that enable them to attract patients through lower charges. This has encouraged widespread abuse of these facilities in the form of "sanatorium vacations," crowding out private providers. Pregnancy allowances and burial and childbirth assistance are allocated to all workers regardless of their economic situation. These kinds of payments should be targeted only to the most needy, preferably through direct budget support.

Several steps are needed to reform the Social Insurance Fund. To prevent abuse and ensure that payments are merited, part of sick leave payments—say, the first two weeks—should be transferred to employers. Sanatorium benefits should be removed, and sanatoriums privatized. Overly generous and untargeted maternity leave payments should also be pruned. Onetime assistance for child birth and burial should be targeted to poor families through the general budget. And the payroll tax should be reduced by an amount commensurate with the savings from these steps (about 1.75 percentage points, including the 1 point cut already proposed by the IMF).

State Reserve Fund. The State Reserve Fund has traditionally been involved in a complex mix of activities involving material reserves and agricultural reserves. Although designed to balance annually, the fund has systematically run an annual deficit of 1–2 percent of GDP, primarily by not recovering budget loans to the agricultural sector. In 1998 the State Reserve Fund was taken almost entirely off budget and was required to be budget neutral. At the same time, two new off-budget funds were created: the Price Stabilization Fund and the Leasing Fund. There has been no indication that past practices have been altered, and the need for a bailout remains a distinct possibility.

The Government should provide no further direct or indirect support to the State Reserve Fund. If it fails to balance, it should be allowed to dissolve. The Price Stabilization Fund has been abolished and should remain so. The Leasing Fund should be privatized.

Road Fund. Not all the extra-budgetary funds should be eliminated and financed through the consolidated funds of the budget. This is particularly true when the resources result from a user charge and are employed by the extra-budgetary fund to improve services to those paying the fees. An earmarked budgetary fund effectively seals the relationship between fees and services, making the activity much like that of any private company which provides goods or services in exchange for payments—payments no one would suggest be co-mingled with the government's ordinary budgetary funds.

Road infrastructure is a good example. The fuel taxes and tolls that usually finance road funds are clearly paid by the users of the facilities, and these resources are used to provide better roads—and to finance related services such as public transport which, by taking cars off the road, provides better circulation for vehicles on the roads.

Even for roads, however, an earmarked extra-budgetary fund is not without risks. Because of inelastic nature of demand for fuel and the somewhat progressive nature of a tax on fuel

(the rich spend more on fuel than do the poor), fuel taxes can be raised to the point that they become a major and valuable source of revenues as in some European countries. Under such conditions, when the taxes collected exceed what is needed to maintain adequate roads, two risks develop because of earmarking. First, more of the people's money may be spent on roads than is justified simply because the money is there, making it hard to finance more urgent needs such as public health. Second, if the money is not spend of excessive road infrastructure but is allowed to accumulate, the pool of resources becomes a popular focus of raiding parties looking for resources to "borrow" to finance unbudgeted expenditures, and may even become a focus of corruption.

If the Road Fund in Ukraine is to be kept as an extra-budgetary fund, the following principles should be applied:

- road users pay for roads through an explicit road tariff that is clearly separated from the government's tax revenues;

- the road tariff is designed to ensure it does not drain revenues from other sectors;

- the road fund is managed by a separate road fund administration overseen by a board that includes representatives of road users and the business community;

- there are published legal regulations governing the way the funds are managed, and periodic independent audits are held to assure that these regulations are followed.

Increasing public investment

Public investment has fallen dramatically. During 1992–95 capital expenditures averaged 3.3 percent of GDP—quite low by international standards (World Bank 1997). In addition, allocations were spread over many projects, some of which have dragged on uncompleted for years. Capital expenditures are politically and bureaucratically easier to cut than other recurrent expenditures, which helps explain why by 1998 they had been eliminated as a budget item (though some recurrent maintenance expenditures are probably really capital expenditures).

In some sense this has been a positive development. Eliminating "white elephant" projects is an important step in transition. But the depth and length of the expenditure moratorium have been extreme, and a serious deterioration of the public assets will have long-term consequences for public services. Advisable reforms include bringing the level of public expenditures (relative to GDP) closer to world levels and developing public expenditure projects on a qualitative basis, in a multiyear setting, to meet explicitly stated policy priorities.

UPGRADING THE TAX SYSTEM

Significant efforts have been made to modernize the tax system, but these efforts have not proceeded smoothly, and the job is incomplete. Constant revisions have generated uncertainty and considerable adjustment costs for the government and taxpayers. News laws and procedures are often poorly planned, and special interest groups distort initial designs. To raise Ukraine's tax system to international standards, the tax burden should be lowered. Taxes should be restructured to promote efficient use of available resources. The tax base should be broadened. And the costs of compliance should be cut, while tax administration should be improved.

A high tax burden

The share of tax (and contribution) revenues in GDP dropped 7 percentage points between 1994 and 1997—from 51 percent to 44 percent—but remains high relative to countries in the region with similar income levels. Although the tax rates for each of the main taxes are within international ranges, the overall level is high because each tax is at the high end of the spectrum. Revenues are also high because there are more than 100 taxes and contributions. The government should eliminate the myriad small taxes that yield limited revenue and are a nuisance for taxpayers as part of reducing overall tax rates.

The structure of tax rates does not favor the efficient use of available resources. Taxes on labor, which is abundant, are high. Taxes on energy, which is scarce, are low. If the Chernobyl Fund tax is eliminated as planned for

the 1999 budget, payroll taxes will have fallen from 53 percent of salaries in 1996 to 37.5 percent in 1999. While this is a positive development, the burden on workers is still too high. Moreover, the structure of excise taxes is not optimal—excises on petroleum products, for example, are too low. Raising taxes on such products could yield the revenues needed to offset cuts in the payroll tax and the personal income tax (which should be no more than 30 percent, with no exemptions but with a higher minimum threshold), easing the tax burden on workers.

An uneven incidence of taxation

The tax base is shrinking as economic activity moves from the formal to the informal economy and as new economic activity emerges outside the formal sector (see the section on the shadow economy, below). These developments undermine the government's ability to collect taxes and lead to a more unequal distribution of the tax burden—effectively punishing those who remain in the formal economy. Efforts to meet revenue targets through drastic enforcement practices induce economic agents to leave the formal tax system. Moreover, substantial exemptions favor some sectors over others and erode the overall tax base. The tax base should be broadened by strengthening compliance and enforcement practices, reducing overall tax rates, and eliminating tax exemptions.

High compliance costs for taxpayers

Myriad taxes and surcharges, a rapidly changing tax environment, and largely unregulated enforcement practices imply high costs for taxpayers. Because large firms can often use their connections to avoid taxes, small and medium-size entrepreneurs suffer, inhibiting the emergence of a strong, competitive, formal private sector.

In the past revenue collection was highly decentralized and essentially automatic; the center had little information on local performance. Now the central administration is struggling to ensure a uniform application of the tax law nationwide—no small task given the system's obsolete administrative and organizational methods. Further, a lack of internal control creates opportunities for corruption. Efforts have been made to strengthen revenue agencies and to limit contact between taxpayers and tax agents, but the results have yet to be felt.

With falling compliance and weak revenue collections, tax arrears are growing rapidly, especially in heavy industry and agriculture (Ilchuk 1999). State enterprises withhold personal income tax and pay enterprise profit tax, a value added tax, and a host of other contributions. As the economic situation of these enterprises has deteriorated, so has their ability to pay taxes.

Tax administration practices should be improved to lower the costs of compliance, reduce corruption, and make collections more efficient. A modernization strategy should be implemented for the entire revenue collection system. All tax legislation should be compiled in a code to ensure consistency and streamline procedures. Legislation on the value added tax should take into account the major deficiencies and allow time for implementation in the tax agency and among taxpayers. Different agencies with revenue collection responsibilities—the State Tax Administration, Pension Fund, and Customs—should cooperate with one another and be placed under the clear authority of the Ministry of Finance.[15] Flat taxes for small entrepreneurs should extend to cover the personal income tax and value added tax. And opportunities for corruption should be eliminated, with integrity guidelines introduced for tax agents.

MANAGING GOVERNMENT DEBT

The debt owed by the government has been rising dramatically (figure 2.4). The highly unfavorable terms on which this debt was secured have forced the government to borrow ever-larger amounts to finance the primary budget deficit as well as interest and amortization payments on previous debt— leading Ukraine into a classic debt trap. By the time the market collapsed in August 1998, real yields on domestic debt exceeded 60 percent. Such high yields are clear evidence that prices and the domestic currency were fundamentally unstable and unsustainable.

The unfavorable terms for debt reflect Ukraine's falling access to official credits, which offer lower spreads over benchmark rates. Countries pursuing sound monetary and fiscal policies and implementing structural reforms can usually depend on international financial institutions— such as the World Bank and IMF—to cover a large part of their financing requirements at modest cost.[16] But during 1996–97 both institutions reduced their lending to Ukraine because reforms were not implemented as agreed. Ukraine received just $1 billion from the

Figure 2.4 Foreign debt is rising sharply

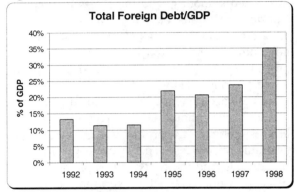

Source: World Bank data.

Figure 2.5 Debt Service could soon become unsustainable

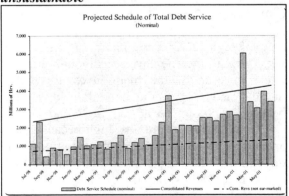

Source: World Bank data.

---

[15] As implementing departments rather than policymaking bodies, they could retain considerable operating autonomy within clear policy guidelines.

IMF and $600 million from the Bank in budget support during these two years.

Until last fall Ukraine's stock of foreign debt was well within sustainable levels. But the recent devaluation significantly increased the ratio of external debt and of debt service to GDP. As a result Ukraine faces a rising debt service burden that will leave it little room for maneuver in the event of another balance of payments shock or domestic economic downturn. World Bank esti-mates show that even in a high-case scenario in which the primary deficit is held to zero over the next three years and inflation and exchange rates are relatively stable, foreign and domestic debt service will all but overwhelm Ukraine's ability to pay (figure 2.5).[17] Under this scenarios at an annual rate of 40 percents per year, interest payments will reach 25 percent of government revenues by the end of 2000, interest to cash revenues will reach 80 percent, and debt service to GDP will reach 18 percent—or 2.9 billion hryvnias a month.

Setting debt management priorities

Reducing the budget deficit is the most important step that Ukraine can take to reduce the risk of future debt service problems. In fact, to avoid borrowing to pay interest on past loans, Ukraine needs to run a primary budget surplus of at least 2 percent of GDP. A surplus would allow Ukraine to begin reducing the stock of debt and would facilitate restructuring it on more favorable terms.

Ukraine also needs to significantly improve the entire debt management system. Accounting systems should allow more reliable and timely information to be shared among the Ministry of Finance, Ministry of Economy, and central bank. Moreover, better training and debt management techniques are needed by those who plan the debt strategy and those who arrange the placement of debts. Such actions

---

[16] World Bank loans to Ukraine, for example, have a maturity of up to 20 years, with up to 5 years' grace, and carry a floating interest rate that is currently 6 to 7 percent.

[17] These estimates were generated by a Debt Service Sensitivity Model which was created for Ukraine by the World Bank under the guidance of the Deputy Minister of Economy, Mr. Igor Shumilo.

would have a high financial return—as debt systems and management improved, Ukraine's creditworthiness and access to international capital markets would increase, lowering the cost of borrowing.

IMPROVING INTERGOVERNMENTAL FISCAL RELATIONS

Reforms are also needed in the fiscal relations between national and sub-national governments. On the macroeconomic side, intergovernmental fiscal relations have a direct impact on fiscal sustainability and on growth. On the microeconomic side, they affect the efficiency of resource use, the delivery of services, and the development of private activity. Intergovernmental fiscal relations also play an important role in redistributing resources to promote social equity.

Over the past three years about one-third of government expenditures took place at the sub-national level, and most social expenditures are made at the local level. The bulk of taxes are collected by State Tax Administration authorities, then shared between national and sub-national governments through tax sharing or transfers. The current system lacks transparency, is unstable in terms of revenue-sharing formulas and ratios, and does not encourage the most effective use of resources

Priorities for reform at the subnational level include defining the appropriate degree of decentralization, matching the responsibilities of lower governments to their decision-making authority, building local sources of revenue, strengthening budget processes and implementation, creating a regulatory framework for subnational borrowing, promoting a "hard credit" culture, and strengthening the institutional and legal framework for intergovernmental finance.

SHRINKING THE SHADOW ECONOMY

The shadow economy is not really another sector in the economy. Most activities in the shadow economy are identical to those in the formal economy—the only difference being tax evasion. True, Ukraine's shadow economy has a more sinister side—with illegal activities like drug dealing, prostitution, and extortion—and, as in almost any country, special police work is needed to control these crimes. But such activities are not within the World Bank's area of expertise. The focus here is on why such a large share of productive activity in Ukraine is not paying its fair share of taxes, the impact this tax evasion has on economic and financial stability, and measures that can be taken to control it.

A broad consensus exists among government, donors, honest businesspeople, and the general public that the shadow economy has benefits and drawbacks. The shadow economy creates jobs, raises family incomes, and spurs economic growth—without it, living standards would be intolerably low. But the shadow economy also drains the strength of the economy. And if the shadow economy spreads much further, it could destroy civilized Ukraine by:

- Further reducing the flow of tax revenues to finance the budget deficit, exacerbating financial and economic crises.

- Undermining the government's ability to provide essential services such as education, health, public safety, and environmental quality.

- Raising taxes for legitimate businesspeople, eroding their ability to provide jobs and forcing them to choose between the shadow economy and bankruptcy.

- Increasing lawlessness.

Efforts to stamp out the shadow economy could create a social disaster, destroying the production that is providing a basic living to millions of Ukrainians. The objective should not be to destroy the shadow economy but to help those working in the shadows to move into the formal sector and to produce jobs and output while paying taxes.

Controlling the shadow economy and bringing otherwise legitimate activities back into the formal sector can be exceedingly difficult because of the vicious circle that the shadow economy sets in motion, a vortex that sucks more and more economic activity into its grip. The government, short of tax revenues needed to provide services to legitimate businesses, raises taxes. High taxes plus the lack of good

public services make it attractive for businesses to move to the shadow economy where they can escape taxation. Tax revenues fall further, making it even more difficult for the government to maintain services.

Figure 2.6 Regulatory discretion is excessive in Ukraine, creating opportunities for corruption

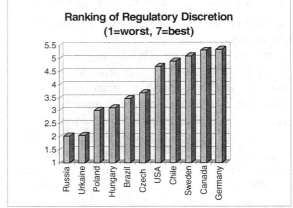

Source: World Economic Forum 1997.

The force of this vicious circle is multiplied by competitive pressures among enterprises. Those who pay taxes cannot compete with those who do not, leaving them with two options close their doors, or go into the shadows. Many have taken the latter road, and more will follow unless the government implements radical reforms that provide greatly improved incentives to stay in the formal sector such as regulatory controls and taxes that are transparent, equitable and predictable; taxes that are lower, and public services that attract them to remain in the formal sector. The latter includes services to the enterprises such as enforcement of contracts, protection from Mafia elements, as well as services to their employees such as the promise of decent pensions that are linked to contributions and are paid on time.

Experience elsewhere indicates that the most successful strategies for bringing shadow activity into the formal economy focus on lowering high tax rates and easing intrusive regulatory controls. Less important but also essential is seeking out and publicly punishing major tax evaders. The following sections draw on a rich collection of recent analytical work (see Kaufmann 1997; Kaufmann and Kaliberda 1996; and Novitsky, Novitskaya and Stone 1995). In addition, a major study on the shadow economy was carried out for this report by Ukrainian colleagues (see Borodiuk and Turchynov 1998).

The shadow economy—definition and background

Ukraine's informal economy encompasses at least three types of activities:

- Illegal activities such as drug dealing, prostitution, protection rackets, and theft from state enterprises.

- Marginal subsistence activities of micro enterprises that employ individuals and their family members.

- Legal activities that are hidden from taxation, regulation, or other public scrutiny and official records.

The third area of activity is both the largest part of the shadow economy and of the most concern. It suggests that Ukraine's economy is highly distorted, motivating massive covert behavior that does not exist in well-functioning market economies. That distortion is rooted in excessive government intervention in the economy.

The shadow economy is nothing new in Ukraine. It is not a result of market reforms—in fact, it reflects Ukraine's slow progress in achieving those reforms. During the Soviet era the central government created many economic regions. Few efforts were made to minimize production costs, including transportation. In addition, draconian restrictions on trade, currency transactions, and private property and business made people reluctant to obey legislation and trust the government to protect their savings, investments, and property. These conditions created a shadow economy.

During the 1980s the typical shadow economy businessman produced goods in state-owned plants at night for his own benefit or made unaccounted extra output and disguised its sale through doctored accounts. In the early 1990s he colluded with those in power to appropriate public property, materials, and tools for private use. Today he is a member of the Ukrainian nouveau riche, having accumulated substantial capital by acting unlawfully but with the protection of corrupt state authorities.

Causes and consequences of shadow activity

The shadow economy is exceptionally large and growing. In an efficient market economy, businesses choose to operate in the formal sector because the benefits they receive—legal protections, public services, the psychological benefits of being good citizens—exceed the costs of taxes, regulatory scrutiny, and legal compliance. But in Ukraine the costs of being formal are excessively high, and the benefits doubtful.

Low benefits and high costs induce businesses to operate informally, reducing revenues to the state and undermining its ability to provide services that might attract businesses into the formal economy. The key cost encouraging shadow activity is the burden of regulations and taxes as they are implemented. If rules look fine on paper but officials have considerable discretion in implementing them—as in Ukraine—the result is a higher effective burden on business, more corruption, and a stronger incentive to move to the unofficial economy (figure 2.6).

Burdensome regulation. The regulatory burden can be measured in a number of ways. A simple measure often used in World Bank enterprise surveys—the time required for senior managers to comply with regulation—shows that Ukraine has one of the most burdensome environments in the world, with regulatory compliance consuming 29 percent of managers' time (Novitsky, Novitskaya, and Stone 1995). A 1997 survey by the International Center for Policy Studies (ICPS) found that in Kyiv managers of private enterprises meet with tax, customs, licensing, and other officials 103 days of the year. Similarly, a recent International Finance Corporation (IFC) study found that small businesses endure an average of 78 inspections for year, requiring 68 written responses, consuming 2 days a week of the manager's time, and requiring a cash outlay of 4,200 hryvnias (about $2,100) a year.[18] A

---

[18] The IFC survey was carried out in late 1997 and interviewed 200 small businesses in four Ukrainian cities. The survey was carried out by the Ukrainian Marketing Group Formula. Amanda Leness and Kyiv staff Nils Andreas Masvie and Thomas Rader were involved in its design, implementation, and analysis.

survey by the State Committee on Entrepreneurship Development and the ICPS of market venders in Kyiv suggested that officials inspected them nearly every day: 25 times a month. Bureaucrats are vested with the discretion to investigate every transaction and contract, and rarely refrain from exercising this discretion.[19]

Bureaucratic discretion. International evaluations of administrative discretion confirm this problem. The survey of corporate executives underlying the 1997 *Global Competitiveness Report* assigns Ukraine a rank of 2 (next to worst) on a 6-point evaluation scale of regulatory discretion, roughly equal to Russia (World Economic Forum 1997). Canada and Chile rate 5 on this scale, while other Eastern European nations (the Czech Republic, Hungary, Poland) rank between 3 and 4.

Figure 2.7 Heavy taxes make Ukraine unattractive to investors and stimulate the shadow economy

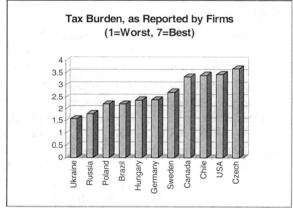

Source: World Economic Forum 1997.

Effective tax burden. Businesses in Ukraine frequently complain that, while marginal tax rates are not unusually high, the way they are assessed and the cumulative effect of multiple taxes make effective rates far higher, while the administrative burden is exceptional. The ICPS

survey found that the average business faced seven annual tax inspections. The average inspection lasted more than 10 days and required more than 80 percent of enterprises to provide the inspectors with office space, computers, telephones, and other equipment (often purchased only to satisfy the inspector). So the total financial burden of taxes goes well beyond actual collections. The 1997 *Global Competitiveness Report* rates the tax burden from the firm's standpoint on a scale of 1 to 7; a low score indicates that the tax system hinders competitiveness, a high score indicates the tax system enhances competitiveness (World Economic Forum 1997). Among the countries evaluated, Ukraine had the worst score at 1.58, compared with 1.80 for Russia, 2.22 for Brazil, and 3.50 for the United States (figure 2.7). The effective tax burden has a much larger impact on the size of the shadow economy than do official tax rates. A one-point increase in this index reduces the share of the unofficial economy by 6.5 percentage points, controlling for differences in national income.

Public services and corruption. Public services take a number of forms. One crucial state service is to ensure property rights for land, tangible assets, and intangible assets (such as intellectual property). The Heritage Foundation evaluates the security of property rights on a scale of 1 (most secure) to 5 (least secure). Chile scores a perfect 1 on this scale, along with Canada, Germany, and the United States. By contrast, Ukraine shares the lowest rank, 4, with three other former communist countries—Azerbaijan, Georgia, and Romania. The Czech Republic, Hungary, and Poland score a 2, while Brazil and Russia score 3.

Another measure of public service quality involves public integrity—official corruption is generally associated with bad services and less fairness in the delivery of those services. Ukraine's problems with corruption are well documented by enterprise and citizen surveys. A 1996 World Bank business survey found that many regulatory procedures and permits—for loans, imports, border crossings, fire and health inspections, telephone line installations, and the like—required bribes (table 2.3). The costs of such bribes fall disproportionately on small firms, deterring new firms from starting up and

---

[19] This paper draws on three ICPS surveys, two of which were carried out on 300 firms in four oblasts in 1997 as part of the Quarterly Rapid Enterprise Survey. For the latter, see ICPS (1998). The third survey was carried out in cooperation with the State Committee on Entrepreneurship Development in a single rayon in Kiev and is referred to as the SCED-ICPS survey.

Table 2.3 Unofficial payments by enterprises for official permits and favors, 1996

Type of license, service, or favor	Average fee (USD)	Enterprises admitting need to pay (percent)
Visit by fire or health inspector	42	81
Visit by tax inspector	87	51
Lease in state space (sq. meter per month)	7	66
Export license/registration	123	61
Import license/ registration	278	71
Border crossing (lump sum)	211	100
Border crossing (% of value)	3%	57
Domestic currency loan from bank on preferential terms (% of value)	4%	81
Hard currency loan on preferential terms (% of value)	4%	85

Source: Kaufmann 1997.

informal firms from joining the formal economy (Rose-Ackerman and Stone forthcoming).

A 1997 survey found that half of all Ukrainians blame the government for recent negative economic conditions (GLS Research and others 1997). Moreover, corruption was the leading cause cited for negative economic conditions. About 70 percent of respondents described government decision-making and lawmaking as corrupt and unfair. Transparency International rates corruption in a large number of countries from 0 (most corrupt) to 10 (no corruption). Russia and Ukraine rate poorly, the Czech Republic, Hungary, and Poland are in the middle, and wealthy OECD countries rate very well (figure 2.8). A 1 point increase in this integrity measure is associated with a 3.5 percentage point drop in the shadow economy (Johnson, Kaufmann, and Shleifer 1997).

The consequences .The high costs and small benefits of participating in the formal economy create an enormous informal sector. The World Bank estimates that half of Ukraine's economy is in the shadow. Much of this shadow activity is happening in mainstream enterprises. For example, a 1997 survey by the IFC found that 69 percent of Ukrainian small businesses fail to report at least 30 percent of their profits. Thus Ukraine's malfunctioning tax, regulatory, legal,

and service delivery systems have driven mainstream businessmen to commit illegal acts in order to survive. Continuing this system will encourage a downward spiral of revenues, public services, and the rule of law.

How can shadow activity be reduced?

Current efforts. The government pursues a variety of antishadow actions. For example, it enforces tax collection by introducing new taxes, using more sophisticated methods for accounting, calculating, paying, and auditing taxes, expanding the mandate of the tax administration, and investigating and punishing tax dodgers based on special normative acts rather than usually applied ones.

Similarly, the government has strengthened budget revenues by increasing luxury taxes, requiring collateral against tax liabilities, sequestering funds (refusing to allow obligations against authorized budgetary funds), requiring local authorities and managers of large enterprises to repay debts to the budget, Pension Fund, and the like, and it is accelerating bankruptcy procedures against companies in default on tax payments. The government has also introduced incentives that encourage companies not to engage in barter, and the authorities are relying on various tools such as indirect methods to reveal shadow incomes based on ownership of cars, houses, bank accounts, and other valuable assets, as well as on expenditures for luxuries such as foreign travel.

A new approach. Excessive state intervention and weak governance have stimulated the growth of Ukraine's shadow economy. The solutions are simple but difficult to achieve: reversing the downward spiral and reducing the shadow economy. Ukraine should ease state intervention in the economy, limiting bureaucratic discretion and reducing the burden of taxes and regulations for businesses. In addition, public services should be strengthened, starting with better legal protections of property and contract rights and a systematic attack on corruption, and extending to improving the accountability and performance of civil servants.

Figure 2.8 Corruption is high in Ukraine

Source: Transparency International 1997; Lambsdorff 1998.

The government can combat corruption through a four-pronged strategy. First, by boosting the benefits of honest behavior through civil service and judicial reform, increasing the probability of detection and punishment, and imposing stiffer penalties. The probability of detection increases with better budget and financial systems, as well as with special oversight and investigative efforts. Anticorruption activities must not become an uncontrolled witch-hunt, however, and initial efforts should focus on increasing incentives for honesty, educating bureaucrats and private citizens through awareness campaigns, and punishing a few major receivers and payers of bribes.

Second, the most promising anticorruption reforms reduce the benefits that are subject to the discretion of public officials. Some public activities can be eliminated (or privatized), others subjected to competition and market forces, and others redesigned with clear rules and simple processes. Where rules and procedures are widely known, opportunities for corruption are reduced. Reorganization within government to consolidate and rationalize responsibilities and lines of authority can also increase accountability and transparency, and facilitate systems of budget and financial control.

Third, government and private citizens must move quickly to stem the culture of illegality. One approach is to wage a public education campaign, beginning with integrity pledges and personal financial disclosure by top officials.

Finally, there would be less temptation to accept bribes if the government reduced the number of government employees and paid the remaining employees higher wages.

Through the policy changes envisioned in the World Bank's adjustment programs, the public sector improvements under the Public Administration Reform Loan, and ongoing Economic Development Institute integrity-oriented activities involving government and civil society, the Bank is helping the government enhance its efforts to create a more favorable and normal business climate in Ukraine.

3. THE REAL SECTORS AND STRUCTURAL REFORMS

As noted in chapter 2, major efforts are needed to make the government a positive force for economic growth and higher living standards. But in the end, raising living standards and achieving financial stability depend directly on restoring real economic growth. For this, urgent structural reforms are needed in Ukraine's real economy, which has shrunk by more than 60 percent since 1989.

Ukraine is blessed with one of the world's most fertile environments—yet agricultural output has dropped to less than 45 percent of the level in 1990, bringing poverty to millions. Agriculture suffers from stalled reforms in land ownership and from government intrusion in the marketing of agricultural inputs and outputs, discouraging private investment. From the Soviet era, Ukraine inherited a large and sophisticated industrial sector, and it remains the world's eighth largest producer of steel and an important international source of airplanes, rockets, and weapons. But though privatization is proceeding for small and medium-size enterprises, the "giants"—which account for a sizable share of industrial assets and employment—remain firmly under state control. Moreover, industry must cope with heavy tax and regulatory burdens.

Energy plays a leading role, supporting all other productive activity. Financially and physically, however, the sector is on its knees. Low tariffs, low collection rates, and even lower cash payments have made it impossible for the sector to supply better, more reliable services at lower cost. Finally, agriculture, industry, and energy all need better access to high-quality, cost-effective financial services. But the banking sector is weak, and excessive deficit financing makes new loans hard to come by and very expensive.

REVIVING AGRICULTURE

The food and agriculture sector has greater economic potential in Ukraine than in any other country of the former Soviet Union. Agro-climatic conditions are well suited to the production of grains, oilseeds, livestock, root and fiber crops, and fruits and vegetables. In terms of production costs, Ukraine's greatest absolute advantages are in wheat and sunflower, closely followed by corn and sugar beets.

Ukraine contains about 25 percent of the world's rich black soil, as well as 27 percent of Europe's tilled soil—giving it 0.64 hectares of tilled soil per capita, compared with 0.25 hectares for Europe as a whole (UNDP 1997). Yet agricultural output has been falling for years (figure 3.1). The country's fertile land is producing only a fraction of its potential, robbing Ukraine of the food that it needs for its people—and for exports that could earn the foreign exchange required for modern agricultural equipment and technology. The land is basically as good today as it was 100 years ago. What has changed is the ownership and structure of farming enterprises and the policies under which these enterprises operate.

Figure 3.1 Agricultural output has declined steadily

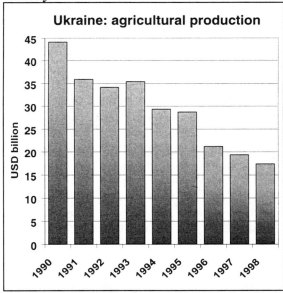

Source: Tacis/UEPLAC, Ukraine Economic Trends.

Agricultural exports. Ukraine traditionally was a net exporter of food and a major supplier of grain, sugar and livestock products to the rest of the former Soviet Union. Ukrainian agricultural and food product exports decreased significantly in 1992-1994, mainly as a result of the breakdown of traditional trade links with the FSU countries. Falling incomes in countries to which Ukraine previously exported further reduced exports to those markets, and a combination of energy inefficiency in Ukrainian farming, sharply rising cost of livestock production, and trade barriers in western markets made it difficult to replace the markets lost in the FSU.

With liberalization of foreign trade in 1995-1996, agriculture and food exports began to recover, reaching 21% of the total merchandise exports from Ukraine in 1996. But in 1997-1998, the exports of agriculture and food products declined again, reflecting the continuing decline in agricultural production and increasing inefficiencies in the sector.

Despite the low grain harvest in 1998, grain exports during 1998/1999 season increased to more than 6.2 mln tons, nearly 25 percent of domestic grain production. Sunflower exports also increased in 1998, reflecting Ukraine's comparative advantage in production of this crop. At the same time, sugar exports declined to the lowest level in the last ten years – to only 154 thousand tons during the 1998/1999 season. The sugarbeet decline reflected low productivity at the farm level—the average sugarbeet yield in 1998 was 17.4 tons per hectare, the lowest in more than 30 years, large inefficiencies at the majority of sugar refineries, and on the external side, low international prices and import barriers imposed by Russia. Agricultural exports today are mainly directed to Russia and other FSU countries and are dominated by grain, sunflower seeds and a few dairy products., and significant interference of the government in the sector during the recent period.

Production trends. With falling demand for exports in traditional markets FSU and higher energy prices after independence, Ukraine's energy-dependent agricultural sector found it difficult to pay for the inputs and capital equipment needed to maintain production. The output decline since independence was far more acute in herds than in crops. Livestock production is considerably more energy intensive than crop production, so when energy costs rose, grain production fell, and feed became scarce, animals were slaughtered. Among crops, the greatest declines between 1990 and 1998 were seen in flax and soy (-80%), sugar beets (-60%) and grain (-40%).

On the other hand, the production of potatoes and vegetables has been fairly steady, and sunflower seed production has actually increased by over 20%.[1]

Ownership trends and impacts. The relatively stable production of potatoes and vegetables reflects the importance of private smallholder agricultural production in Ukraine, which accounts for a major share of non-technical crops even though only 14 percent of all agricultural land in Ukraine is truly in private holdings (including the 3 percent privatized since independence). In fact, although the increase in privately held agricultural land in Ukraine since independence has been marginal, total production has actually risen on private land while falling by over 40 percent in the "social sector" of farming. The latter includes collective farms that, while private in name, continue to function largely as before with a heavy degree of governmental control, particularly from local authorities (table 3.1). The production of potatoes and vegetables has become the domain of private plots and private farmers. The large-scale collective enterprises remain the main producers of grain, sunflower and sugarbeet.

Shadow economic activity. Agriculture is heavily influenced by shadow economic activity—the direct result of widespread discretionary government intervention in the operation of agricultural markets both for inputs and outputs. Such controls provide widespread opportunities for corruption including non-transparent barter deals, siphoning profits from cooperatives and other entities either owned or effectively controlled by the local political structures, and provision of goods at favorable prices in exchange for various favors. Official output figures on the farm sector are almost certainly understated because a substantial share of output is not being recorded in the official statistics. Worse yet, by distorting resource allocation decisions and reducing economic efficiency, this pervasive shadow economic activity also reduces real output for Ukraine and income to the farmers, one of the poorest groups

---

[1] Sablouk and Fesina, 1999

Table 3.1 Indices of the gross output of the agriculture sector, 1990-1998 (1990 = 100)

Year	All farms			Social sector			Private sector		
	Total	*Crop*	*Herd*	*Total*	*Crop*	*Herd*	*Total*	*Crop*	*Herd*
1990	100	100	100	100	100	100	100	100	100
1991	87	83	90	83	79	87	97	97	97
1992	80	84	76	68	69	67	107	129	91
1993	81	93	69	66	74	57	116	149	91
1994	68	72	63	53	56	49	103	121	90
1995	65	74	56	48	54	41	106	134	86
1996	59	67	51	38	43	32	109	141	86
1997	58	71	44	36	48	23	110	143	86
1998	53	61	45	31	38	23	105	129	88

Source: State Committee of Ukraine

in Ukraine despite the country's rich soil and good climate.

Recent reforms

March 1999 marked the eighth anniversary of land reform in Ukraine and of attempts to make the food and agriculture sector more efficient and productive. In addition to land reform and restructuring of collective and state farms, agricultural reforms have included liberalizing the market environment, privatizing agro processing and trade, and creating a new institutional framework.

Though some reforms have been achieved, progress has been neither smooth nor universal—the result of a continuous struggle between supporters and opponents of reform. Faced with these tensions, the government has been unable to implement the policies required to address critical reform issues. Significant progress in some areas has been circumvented by reversals elsewhere.

Land reform and farm restructuring. Moderate progress has been made in land reform and farm restructuring. Land share certificates have been issued to 80 percent of Ukraine's large farms, with the number rising from just over 3,300 in early 1997 to 8,500 in mid-1998. Nearly 150 of these farms have been fundamentally restructured, and by January 1998 land sharing

plans had been worked out for about 1,250 other farms.

Experience shows that only those FSU countries which managed to privatize agriculture *de facto* (Estonia, Latvia, Lithuania, Kyrgyzstan, Armenia, and Georgia) managed to overcome output decline and restore economic growth. Ukraine is one of the less advanced in effective agriculture/land reforms. Collective farming still dominates in the agriculture sector of Ukraine, bringing continuous output decline, fiscal tensions, and serious social and political stress. Therefore, radical de-collectivization program must become the principal direction of the agriculture policy in the coming years, along with a radical reduction in government intervention in the markets for agricultural inputs and outputs, thus assuring that all farms, privatized or not, have full access to well-functioning markets.

Despite eight years of reform, only 17 percent of agricultural land is cultivated by the private sector (family farms and household plots), and most Ukrainian agriculture remains effectively collectivized. Moreover, the growth of private farming has slowed considerably since 1994. The number of private family farms has stagnated around 35485, accounting for only 2 percent of agricultural land and production. In 1998, about 93 percent of large farms reported losses, and most have accumulated significant debt. The government needs to make every possible effort to renew land reform and farm restructuring.

Land markets. Shortly after independence, a moratorium was placed on the sale of agricultural land, even if privately owned. The government argues that various decrees and normative acts since then, including Presidential Decree 666 of 1994, have made the moratorium applicable only to land that was given to farmers by local municipalities. Parliament, however, continues to declare that there is a moratorium on the sale of land. The government has responded by enacting joint normative acts by the State Committee on Land Reform and Ministry of Justice. These acts:

- Give a right to two or more members of a collective agricultural enterprise, joint stock agricultural company, or agricultural cooperative to withdraw adjacent land plots from the farm enterprise.

- Limit to three months the period within which a farm members' council of a collective agricultural enterprise has to give its consent to one or more members who file an application to withdraw land plots.

- Limit to one year the period within which the withdrawing member must be given possession of the plot in question.

The obstacles to direct private ownership have led the land market in the direction of leasing plots of land. In 1998 private farmers and new corporate-style farms began leasing land plots withdrawn from collectives and plots still in collective agricultural enterprises but not being farmed. This positive development shows that collective agricultural enterprises can supply land to the lease market. As members of collective agricultural enterprises see their enterprises leasing land, they may become more willing to withdraw the land they are entitled to from their enterprises and lease it. Some fear that leases will be given at unreasonably low rates, but the State Committee on Land Reform plans an information campaign to inform farm members about lease options and payments.

Privatization in agro processing. Agro-industrial privatization has proceeded reasonably well. The number of agro-industrial enterprises that have been privatized to a depth of 70 percent increased from 2,200 in 1997 to 3,900 in 1998 (out of a total of 4,800). Demonopolization of agro-industrial enterprises has been promoted aggressively by the Anti-Monopoly Committee, which has broken up more than 60 percent of the monopolists identified in the agro-industrial sector. But privatization with ownership by managers, workers, and raw material suppliers has not resulted in restructured or more efficient enterprises. Most agro processing is operating with low capacity utilization, weak corporate governance, and outdated equipment. Consequently it is unable to produce products that are competitive even on domestic markets. Foreign investment is minimal.

Market and price liberalization. Moderate progress has been made in liberalizing agricultural markets and prices. Price and margin controls on grain have been eliminated. Most foreign trade restrictions have been removed and few additional barriers imposed. As a result, the implicit taxation of agriculture has been reversed. Yet farms have been unable to respond to higher prices and expand output because they lack access to investment and working capital, and corporate governance remains essentially unchanged. Government intervention in domestic grain markets inhibits foreign investment. By requiring in-kind repayment of inputs, credits, and tax/pension arrears, the government has placed itself first in line among creditors, seriously restricting farms' access to commercial loans.

In 1995 and early 1996 the government appeared to be committed to refraining from intervening in agricultural import and export markets. But in mid-1996 Parliament imposed duties on exports of live animals and hides. Then in October 1997 it adopted the *Law on Regulation of Agricultural Imports.* This law, which sets quotas for imports of certain animals and meat products, would effectively increase agro-industrial protection from about 21 percent to nearly 30 percent if implemented in full. Protective measures contributed to the 1998 decline in agricultural imports by 11 percent. During the same year, government convinced Parliament to grant exemptions for export of skins that are processed abroad and re-imported as semi-finished goods, easing the negative impact of the export taxes on primary agricultural producers. The government has also resisted pressures to impose export taxes on sunflower seeds and other primary agricultural products.

Although it passed regulations for the Law of Agricultural Imports, the Cabinet of Ministers has not authorized any import quotas. Moreover, in 1998 the government submitted to Parliament amendments to the law that cut a number of unusually high tariffs (from rates of more than 50 percent to 30 percent). The government has also asked that tariffs on livestock feed be cut to no more than 50 European currency units per ton.

The government has sent mixed signals to the private sector on domestic market development. A number of budget and off-budget programs have been created to channel inputs—machinery, fertilizer, seeds—to farms and to accept payment in grain. This is basically a slightly disguised way of allowing the state to barter inputs for grain through state-owned grain elevators and state-owned or -controlled input supply enterprises. In 1998 these programs cost about $400 million, and the system creates a substantial risk that—as in the past—the government will try to collect outstanding debts by requiring farmers to deliver grain. This approach seriously impedes private grain markets and, because it involves multiple levels of government, creates opportunities for corruption.

The Government plans to privatize 445 of Ukraine's 545 grain elevators and storage facilities, and by the end of 1998 had privatized 165. Although privatization is proceeding well, the grain storage units being privatized are often the less important ones. Moreover, it appears that even after privatization of all but 100 units, the state will still control a major share of grain storage capacity. By some estimates the state, through marketing arrangements and commodity loans, will maintain effective control or at least influence more than 90 percent of trade in agricultural commodities.

In February 1997 the Cabinet of Ministers issued Resolution 124 requiring competitive procurement procedures for state grain purchases. Nevertheless, most state purchase contracts for agricultural products in 1997 were not awarded on a tender basis or through commodity exchanges (which would allow transparent private participation). Through Resolution 1417 of December 1997, the Cabinet of Ministers stated that procurement of agricultural commodities for state reserves must go through commodity exchanges. In addition, the 1998 budget eliminated resources for direct procurement of agricultural commodities (including grain), and the government issued decrees to limit state purchases and channel them through commodity exchanges. These are encouraging developments.

An agenda for agriculture reforms

The most difficult agricultural reforms are those involving the liberalization of domestic and international trade in agricultural products and the introduction of meaningful reforms in the ownership of agricultural land. For agricultural growth to recover:

- Government intervention in the sector must be limited. The state must stay out of commodity markets and focus on developing the institutional framework required for market-based agriculture.

- Farm restructuring must increase, with genuine privatization of farms, improvements in corporate governance, and creation of hard budget constraints.

- Agro processing must be facilitated by creating secondary markets for enterprise shares and developing a climate conducive to foreign direct investment.

- Open and competitive factor markets must be created in the sector—including a market for agricultural land.

Implementing this agenda would encourage domestic and foreign investors to supply the capital needed to improve the supply of primary agricultural inputs, storage handling, and processing.

FOSTERING PRIVATE SECTOR DEVELOPMENT

During the Soviet era, Ukraine's heavy industrialization—especially in iron and steel,

Table 3.2 Industrial output indexes by branch, %

1990=100	1995	1996	1997	1998	1997 to 1996	1998 to 1997
Industry—Total	52	50	49	49	98	99
Electricity	70	65	63	63	97	100
Fuel	44	41	44	43	105	99
Ferrous metallurgy	41	46	50	46	108	93
Chemical and oil-chemical	41	40	41	41	99	101
Machine-building and metal works	50	37	37	35	96	96
Wood, woodworking and pulp-and-paper	56	46	45	50	95	111
Construction materials	38	25	22	23	92	104
Light industry	32	24	24	25	95	102
Food	47	43	39	39	85	100

Source: State Statistics Committee

aerospace and transport aircraft, and other military equipment—underpinned relatively high living standards. Yet today Ukraine's strong industry is one of i0ts greatest sources of weakness. These sectors depend on energy, on markets that have collapsed, and on a management style that is not suited to a modern market economy.

Privatization has helped, but many privatized factories are still run by their old managers, following outdated traditions. In many enterprises the absence of strategic or lead investors and the broadly based nature of share ownership have created serious problems with corporate governance. As a result of all these factors, industrial output has dropped at least 60 percent, and only in late 1996 did the situation begin to stabilize (figure 3.2).[2]

The Soviet legacy

Production. A large industrial complex based on strong centralized management dominated the economic landscape in Ukraine prior to the disintegration of the USSR. Today this complex needs radical restructuring. For reasons noted

earlier, its losses are destabilizing the entire economy. Most of these old Soviet enterprises cannot operate efficiently without the economies of scale associated with access to foreign markets. In fact, their current crisis stems largely from the collapse of the trading relations formed over many decades among the USSR and Council for Mutual Economic Assistance countries.

The military industrial complex (MIC) in particular has suffered from these problems. The

Figure 3.2 The industrial collapse since 1990 is coming to an end

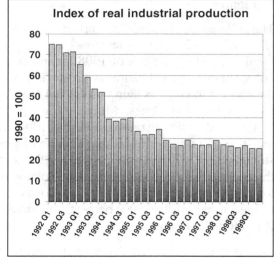

Source: TACIS/UEPLAC, Ukraine Economic Trends, adjusted by UEPLAC.

---

[2] Based on an adjusted index of industrial output that resolves some of the index number problems inherent in the traditional way of calculating industrial output, TACIS/UEPLAC estimates the decline at 73 percent to the third quarter of 1996, when the decline bottoms out.

number of MIC enterprises and organizations dropped by about 80 percent between 1990 and 1999, and the number of workers fell by 85 percent. By 1999 the volume of armaments and war materiel production was only about five percent of 1990/91 levels.

Many of these old defense industry plants tried to convert to civilian products, but most of their "conversion products" were non-competitive, not only in foreign markets, but in domestic markets as well. Warehouses filled with unmarketable goods, dragging down working capital and leaving the plants with no money to replace and upgrade their antiquated fixed capital stock. With non-competitive final products, Ukraine has turned increasingly to the production of primary products such as basic iron and steel with little downstream value added—and thus shrinking demand for the nation's substantial corps of well-educated scientists and engineers.

Radical reforms of the MIC is needed to make its products again competitive on domestic and international markets. The restructuring should focus creating a business climate that provides market-based incentives for reform and a legal framework that makes it easy for enterprises to respond to such incentives without excessive government intervention. Privatization of much of the sector is still needed to assure that the managers have the incentives to become more efficient, subject of course to normal governmental controls over any industry such as armaments that has the potential to jeopardize national security and social welfare.

Most industrial activity in the Soviet Union was highly energy-intensive—especially in iron and steel. It made little sense to invest in energy-saving technology because energy inputs were priced at 5-10 percent of world levels. But once the energy prices charged by Russia moved to world market levels, broad swaths of Ukraine's energy-intensive industrial output became non competitive in world markets.

Outside of military equipment, product design and quality were generally poor, so Ukraine found it very difficult to start exporting to Western markets. Restoring exports to former Soviet countries holds little hope of providing the engine of growth that Ukraine needs to

restore living standards. Russian markets are in turmoil and will likely stay that way for quite some time. And even as the Russian economy improves, preferences will almost certainly shift

Figure 3.3 Heavy industry increases while other manufacturing declines

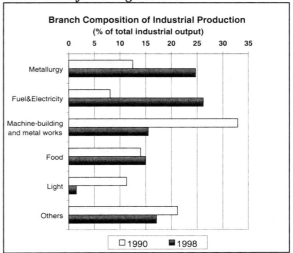

Source: State Statistics Committee

to developing new domestic sources of supply rather than depending on scattered external sources.

Industrial production dynamics. The share of heavy industries such as metallurgy, electricity, and fuel has risen since 1993 at the expense of other manufacturing industries (figure 3.3). Machine-building and metal works have experienced most severe contraction. The sector's key problems have been a lack of political will to privatize leading companies in a transparent manner to strategic foreign investors, a generally hostile business environment that discourages investors from market economies in taking larger positions in Ukrainian machine-building and metal works, and the combined shortage and high cost of domestic capital.

Despite Ukraine's comparative advantage in agriculture, the food processing sector's share in total industrial output actually declined between 1993 and 1998 (from 14.4% to 12.7%). In 1997-98, however, this sub-sector attracted more foreign direct investment than any other sector. This plus the incentive of increased competition from imports brings hope that the sector may begin to realize its intrinsic potential (table 3.3).

Ferrous and non-ferrous metallurgy has shown the fastest exports growth and one the smallest contraction of output since independence (figure 3.4). However, the relative competitiveness of this sub-sector is based more on barter transactions and non-payment of its bills for energy and raw material than on efficiency.

The Russian crises negatively affected industry, including the exports of ferrous and non-ferrous metal. Reluctance or inability of Ukrainian

Table 3.3 Foreign direct investment in Ukraine by industry (share to total, %)

	1994	1995	1996	1997	1998
Total	100	100	100	100	100
Food	14	15	12	21	21
Domestic trade	10	22	29	16	16
Machine building	23	13	10	8	13
Chemical and oil-chemical	6	4	3	7	6
Fuel	...	1	1	1	3
Metallurgy	5	5	3	2	4
Light	6	4	2	2	2

Source: State Statistics Committee

companies to substitute suppliers from the CIS with suppliers in the West – even in cases when they do have the cash to do so, leaves them highly exposed to up and downs of CIS markets. *Problems.* Inherited Soviet behaviors, visible at the enterprise and administration levels, are a major constraint to private sector growth in Ukraine. Many bureaucrats live off a growing number of licenses, permits, and controls. As this expanding class becomes entrenched and learns how to protect its interests, the Ukrainian economy risks stabilizing at a low level of efficiency and output. Indeed, bureaucratic interference at the oblast level appears to be worse than in Soviet times, and is certainly more chaotic with the newly decentralized decision-making system. Bureaucrats with a vested interest in resisting deregulation are supported by "unreformed" owner-managers who abuse the perverse regulatory system. This symbiotic relationship between bureaucrats and managers contributes directly to the poor performance of state enterprises. Bureaucrats do not want enterprises to be highly profitable because that would make them more independent. Managers

find it much easier to bribe bureaucrats than to become competitive.

The main challenge for private sector development in Ukraine differs from that in former Soviet republics that started enterprise reforms earlier. For example, in Moldova the constraints to privatization had more to do with ideology than with vested interests. In Ukraine enterprise reform is hindered by residual ideology but also by the untaxed incomes that an influential portion of the population draws from the current system.

The challenges facing the industrial sector today as the result of its Soviet past and the slow pace of reform since independence are greatly compounded by pervasive shadow economy activity. Overall an estimated 50 percent of GDP is produced in the shadow; in the industrial sector, the share is probably considerably higher, particularly among small- and medium-sized firms where entire enterprises hide in the shadows. But the problem also prevails among large scale enterprises which, though operating as registered, tax-paying firms, buy inputs at inflated prices from and sell outputs below cost

Figure 3.4 Industrial Products play a large role in Ukrainian exports

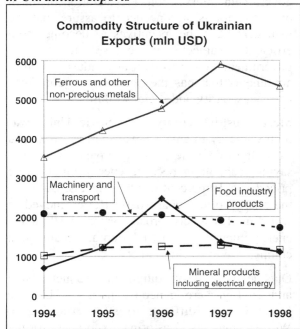

Source: State Statistics Committee

to parallel "daughter" enterprises in the shadow economy, thereby transferring profits into the shadows beyond the reach of the tax authorities. By showing losses as a result of such transfer pricing, some firms are able to get tax privileges and even direct subsidies from the government, further draining the government coffers.

Such practices are problematic for both the government and the enterprise sector—the gains to the latter being at best short term and precluding the long term growth which is frequently potentially possible. Shadow economy activity thus poses a serious threat to industrial growth—to say nothing of the government's ability to operate in a normal manner and to provide the services needed for economic growth and human development. First, small firms are encouraged to stay small to avoid detection, discouraging growth. Second, serious investors are hesitant to enter sectors dominated by shadow activity, knowing that they will either face unfair competition from those not paying their taxes, or will have to go into the shadows, exposing themselves to multiple risks. Third, firms operating in the shadow find it dangerous to become profitable, for this exposes them to exploitation by tax collectors, who extract bribes in exchange for privileged tax treatment, and by criminal elements who take advantage of the fact that firms operating outside the law cannot turn to the law for protection. Fourth, managers of shadow enterprises have to spend a lot of time and money defending themselves from such exploitation—or paying off the exploiters, and this reduces the human and capital resources available for economic growth. In short, the dominance of shadow economic activity in Ukraine is a major reason for the continued economic decline.[3]

Prospects. To succeed, Ukrainian industry must penetrate European and global markets with high-quality, energy-efficient products. Doing so will require intense private sector development efforts. Experience from around the globe shows that state-owned plants tend to be much less efficient than private plants—and the situation is not likely to be different in Ukraine. And in today's global economy, it would be impossible for the government to mobilize the billions of dollars of investment required to modernize industry. Private investment, domestic and foreign, must take the lead. Though the following recommendations focus on reforming manufacturing enterprises, they are equally applicable to enterprises in agriculture, infrastructure, and trade.

The challenges ahead

As noted, privatization of small enterprises is essentially complete, and privatization of medium-size and large enterprises has proceeded well (figure 3.5). Between 1995 and 1998 more than 9,500 medium-size and large enterprises transferred at least 70 percent of their shares to private ownership. The state still employs more than half the work force,[4] but as

Figure 3.5 Privatization of medium-size and large enterprises is nearly complete

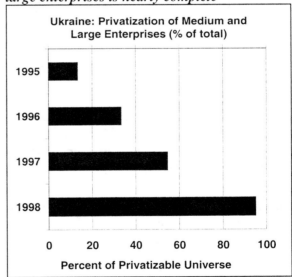

Source: PricewaterhouseCoopers/U.S. Agency for International Development.

---

[3] Again it should be noted that the economic decline is probably overstated by official figures. While these figures are derived on a different basis than those of the tax authorities and thus more fully reflect total economic activity in Ukraine, significant parts of GDP still appear to remain outside the official figures.

[4] According to Vrubelvsky, Tryneev, and Yakubovsky (1998, p. 23), "even though about 75% of all enterprises have changed their form of ownership, the share of working population employed in privatized enterprises does not exceed 20%." Further clarification is needed, however, on the definition of "private."

with much of the data on Ukraine, this has to be qualified: as much as one quarter of these jobs are in name only—people are not paid and do not work. Problems remain in cash privatization of the largest industrial enterprises and utilities.

New companies emerging from privatized state enterprises have better ownership structures than, for example, in Russia. During mass privatization Ukraine auctioned more shares of privatized companies to the general public. Independent shareholder registrars and public disclosure requirements, introduced in the reform program, make managers more accountable to shareholders. And in enterprises privatized by "buyout-through-leasing," managers are more accountable to employees than in other former Soviet republics. Still, the situation is far from ideal; regulatory enforcement and corporate culture remain weak.

The development of new small and medium-size enterprises has been comparable to the results achieved in other former Soviet republics but much slower than in Central European countries. More than 600,000 private firms have been registered, but only 100,000 have become registered taxpayers. Among the rest, some hide in the shadow economy and some never really existed as operating companies. In 1996 small and medium-size enterprises accounted for just 2.5 percent of overall industrial output. Even in the most advanced regions, these enterprises accounted for less than 10 percent of GDP and employment. These data should be viewed with caution, however, because most new private businesses operate in the shadow economy.

Corporate restructuring and liquidation. Though the decline in industrial output was even more severe than the drop in GDP, the decline in industry has not been all bad. The service sector has grown from 43 percent of output in 1994 to 50 percent in 1997, at the expense of industry, agriculture, and construction. Base industries—coal, energy, metallurgy—have done better than machine-building and light industries; many obsolete products have been eliminated. But while there have been changes at the sectoral level, structural reforms have not resulted in serious restructuring at the enterprise level.

One problem is that bankruptcy laws do not provide for restructuring and liquidation. The Bankruptcy Law prefers straight liquidation to Chapter 11-type restructuring based on an agreement between creditors and owners. Creditors' rights are further hampered by the priority given to collecting taxes—including through seizure of assets and freezing of bank accounts.

Vested interests of new owners and institutional weakness make bankruptcy or restructuring through liquidation even more difficult. The government has even tried to discourage bankruptcy—the Agency to Prevent Bankruptcy was only recently renamed the Bankruptcy Agency. No medium-size and large enterprises have been declared bankrupt, though many are technically so. The second World Bank–financed Enterprise Development Adjustment Loan calls for three pilot liquidations of large enterprises and for making the current Bankruptcy Law operational. A new bankruptcy law is being discussed by Parliament, but the outcome is unlikely to be consistent with the draft prepared by the government with the help of international financial institutions and other donors.

The few isolated cases of enterprise restructuring have been initiated by new outside owners (investment funds, banks, individuals), inside owners (primarily new managers), foreign investors, and donors (including the World Bank). The objectives and scope of restructuring differ in each case. Restructuring by external owners often includes searching for new investments, reorienting production, and reducing the labor force. Insider reorganization is usually oriented toward survival and preserving jobs, and is achieved by rebuilding old networks of cooperation, spinning off technological units and cost centers. Searching for foreign investors is a part of the agenda, but fear of losing control is a serious limitation. Externally supported projects are mostly designed as demonstration efforts, to train local consultants and disseminate best practices— with mixed results. Among some 50 enterprises interviewed by World Bank staff in March 1998, most had started some type of restructuring, and about half of those had achieved short-term viability. But restructuring has not yet produced significant macroeconomic benefits—hidden unemployment remains at 20-30 percent (though official unemployment is still around 4 percent)

Competitiveness and foreign investment. The considerable control retained by line ministries and other government agencies is perhaps the most important reason for the slow development of the formal private sector. This control, combined with complex and outdated regulations, has provided the breeding grounds for corrupt practices and bureaucratic inefficiencies. The Anti-Monopoly Office is one of the best-organized parts of government, but its enforcement powers are limited. A new agency promoting entrepreneurship is only starting to develop its capacity.

Cumbersome customs practices inhibit competition. In addition, small businesses face numerous fees, bribes, rackets, and red tape. The costs of regulatory compliance for Ukrainian enterprises have been estimated at more than 2.6 billion hrivnyas a year, or 2.9 percent of 1997 GDP. And the government continues to intervene in the daily operations of enterprises (even privatized ones), limiting competition and interfering in the rights of owners and creditors.

Since independence, cumulative foreign direct investment in Ukraine has been less than $3 billion, compared with $8.4 billion in Poland and $15 billion in Hungary (figure 3.6). As a result foreign direct investment has played a negligible role in restructuring the Ukrainian economy. Foreign portfolio investment is a slowly growing part of the securities market—most (some $2 billion) was invested in high-yielding treasury bills prior to the 1998 crisis. But Ukraine is a less attractive destination for foreign portfolio investment than its neighbors—it has neither the attractive resource-based enterprises of Russia nor the transparent and well-regulated equity markets of Poland. There is also slow-growing investment in equity by specialized funds and Western institutional investors (pension funds, insurance companies).

State intervention and the behavior of enterprise managers. Only by working directly with enterprise managers is it possible to understand how wasteful and unproductive the Soviet system was, and how little has been done to develop market skills and incentives. More than half the time of managers and their core teams is spent complying with the requirements of central, oblast, and municipal authorities. This does not include the considerable time managers spend in Kyiv lobbying the Cabinet of Ministers, line ministries, and Parliament for valuable state benefits. Nearly all firms expect privileges, even if the odds of receiving them are small. Efforts to win the "lottery" for privileges divert managers from the daily work needed to make their enterprises more competitive.

Figure 3.6 Foreign direct investment is minimal

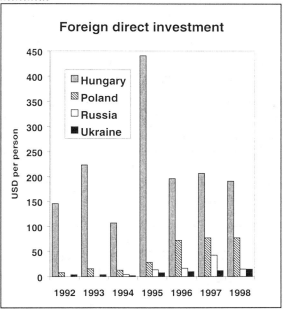

Source: World Bank 1998.

The permits, licenses, and certifications that enterprises need to operate border on the bizarre. Three examples illustrate the problem:

- Local administrations must register each export order, regardless of its size.

- Ukraine does not recognize even the most valuable Western product certificates (including ISO 9000), so enterprises have to secure a Ukrainian quality certificate.

In Kyiv and Lviv the average private firm faces more than 60 inspections a year, and in other oblasts the average ranges from 25-50 a year. Perhaps worse than the frequency of inspections is the well-known tendency of inspectors to harass companies, collect bribes, and exercise political vendettas.

Managers and owners of privatized enterprises have no incentive to sell unused assets. Because the land under buildings has not been privatized, managers prefer to wait rather than to act. Moreover, enterprises require permission from the State Property Fund to sell assets if the state has retained even 1 percent of shares. And even completely private enterprises are not allowed to sell their (obsolete) equipment if it is on the "mobilization reserve" list—which may not have changed since the peak of the Cold War.

Ukrainian firms have faced much stronger resistance to possible labor force reductions than was encountered in other former Soviet republics. Regulations, severance payments, and concern for workers are the three main reasons quoted by managers and local authorities.

Finally, all the negative behaviors observed at the firm level in the Soviet Union are present in Ukraine, including mistrust, lack of entrepreneurship, and disregard for institutions, law, and quality. To try to survive in this environment, managers have come up with their own solutions:

- Barter is dominant, accounting for up to 80-90 percent of transactions, with the usual sub optimal effects. Prices are lower for outputs and higher for inputs. Deals are nontransparent. It is impossible to switch to cheaper and better-quality raw materials from the West due to lack of cash. And inequalities are rampant— employees are paid in food and shareholders receive sugar instead of dividends while managers have nice cars.

- Daughter companies are created with the official task of providing inputs and selling goods. But many daughter companies collect profits because, as entirely private companies, they have more flexibility in "rewarding" employees and have not thousands but only a few owners. Most of the privatized firms surveyed relied on this approach.

- Daughter companies also allow parent companies to show losses, thus

positioning to obtain subsidies and privileges from the government.

Despite these problems, Ukrainian enterprises are in some ways better off than enterprises in other former Soviet republics. Many enterprises appear to have a better-developed industrial culture and steeper learning curve. Almost everyone interviewed by the World Bank— oblast officials, managers, consultants—seemed interested in learning about experience in other countries of Central and Eastern Europe, particularly about restructuring results and the business environment. Divestment of social assets to municipalities is well under way (though all the enterprises visited retain many social assets due to the limited absorptive capacity of municipalities). And a surprising number of small consulting companies have come on the scene, almost all of them inspired by mass privatization, as have well-developed training facilities offering MBAs programs jointly with Western universities.

Table 3.4 The energy sector has shrunk dramatically

PRIMARY ENERGY SUPPLY AND CONSUMPTION					
Year	1990	1995	1996	1997	1998
Primary Energy Production					
Washed coal (mt)	130.7	65.6	54.3	56.7	57.7
Crude oil & condensate (mt)	5.3	4.0	4.1	4.1	3.9
Natural gas (bcm)	27.8	18.1	18.4	18.1	18.0
Peat & wood (mt)	4.3	3.9	3.8	3.7	3.5
Nuclear power (TWh)	76.2	70.5	79.6	79.4	75.2
Hydro power (TWh)	10.3	10.1	8.8	10.0	15.9
Total Production (mtoe)*	**116.8**	**73.1**	**69.8**	**70.9**	**71.5**
Primary Energy Import					
Coal (mt)	21.1	16.0	11.0	9.0	8.2
Crude oil (mt)	54.3	13.3	9.2	8.9	9.9
Natural gas (bcm)	87.3	66.3	71.0	62.4	53.5
Petroleum products (mt)	11.5	9.5	6.0	5.9	5.0
Total Import (mtoe)	**150.6**	**87.2**	**81.1**	**72.3**	**64.5**
Primary Energy Export					
Coal (mt)	20.0	2.4	2.0	2.2	1.7
Petroleum products (mt)	11.3	1.4	1.4	1.3	1.7
Electricity (TWh)	28.0	4.1	4.4	4.3	3.6
Total Export (mtoe)	**28.3**	**3.6**	**3.5**	**3.5**	**3.5**
Primary Energy Consumption (mtoe)	**239.0**	**156.6**	**147.3**	**139.8**	**132.6**
Annual Percentage Change		-1.7%	-6.0%	-5.1%	-5.2%
Efficiency Indicators					
Primary Energy Consumption per					
USD of GDP	0.9	1.3	1.3	1.3	1.2
person	4.6	3.0	2.9	2.8	2.6

Source: World Bank staff estimates.

An agenda for enterprise reform

Several steps should be taken to build sound entrepreneurial and fiscal foundations for future growth. First, transaction costs—including numerous fees, bribes, rackets, wasted time, red tape, and noncommercial risks—have to be slashed to attract domestic and foreign entrepreneurs to Ukraine.

Second, enterprise managers and employees need to obtain better skills, knowledge, and incentives to function in a competitive environment. In this way Ukraine can also better exploit the comparative advantage of its relatively cheap labor.

Third, the rights of owners and creditors have to be secure enough to make enterprises an attractive investment. These include the rights of shareholders to engage in secondary trading of shares and to use voting rights to influence company managers and the rights of creditors to register and execute collateral and to force bankruptcy.

Fourth, corporate governance needs to be improved and will remain a challenge during the transition to privatized industry. In enterprises that are not fully privatized, it is often unclear who should represent the interests of the state—or even what those interests should be. In such circumstances the rights of minority shareholders are often unclear. A national agency on corporate rights has been established, but it remains to be seen how it will function. The state maintains involvement even in enterprises where it holds only a minority share, making it difficult for the real owners to operate the enterprise in a normal manner. In fact, intrusive regulation ensures that the heavy hand of government is felt even in enterprises without state equity ownership.

Finally, the government needs to take strong action to reduce its budget deficit and to stop crowding enterprises out of the domestic capital market. T-bills offered yields in excess of 70 percent in the summer of 1998, creating a powerful incentive for banks and other investors to invest in this relatively risk-free government paper rather than lend money at lower interest rates to riskier enterprises. Various tricks of financial engineering based on guarantees, external funding, earmarked accounts, and directed lending could possibly be used to create a parallel market that would make investment and working capital funds available to enterprises at rates that would allow them to compete in world markets. But such financial devices would create distortions of their own and could easily lead to an even more severe crisis. The only viable solution is for the government to stop living beyond its means and start living within a budget that minimizes its need for deficit financing.

RESTRUCTURING ENERGY RESOURCES

Ukraine's energy intensity is about six times the level typically found in nations at similar income levels. For a country that must import over 50 percent of its of energy consumption at world prices, this creates an extremely heavy burden on the balance of payments, on production costs in every sector (especially industry, agriculture, transport, and energy), on residential utilities, and on the budget, which usually ends up subsidizing the consumption—and often the nonpayment—of energy by all of these sectors. If the energy sector is to meet the needs of the Ukrainian economy, it must increase cost recovery so that it can pay for imported and domestic fuels and invest in more efficient energy production and distribution.

Energy and Shadow Sector

The Ukrainian energy sector has gone through a tumultuous period since the beginning of the 1990s. Total energy consumption today is only about 60 percent of what it was before independence (table 3.4). A major decline—but considerably less than the reported decline in GDP, resulting in the decreased energy efficiency per dollar of GDP shown in table 3.1. The structure of the sector has changed dramatically during·this period, with most of the change concentrated in the period between 1990 and 1995. Despite a dramatic decline in domestic coal production, Ukraine has become somewhat more self-sufficient in primary energy production over the period, with imports falling from over 60 percent of domestic consumption to only 50 percent. Aside from natural gas production, which dropped by about 30 percent, domestic production of other energy sources stayed fairly stable, and nuclear power output actually rose.

In terms of international trade in energy, imports have dropped by over half with the sharpest declines being in the import of crude oil (down over 80 percent), a reflection in part of the fact that Ukraine no longer plays a major role in refining petroleum from Russia for shipment to COMECON states. Another dramatic change has been the decline in Ukraine's energy exports by nearly 90 percent, with roughly similar percentage declines in coal, petroleum products, and electricity.

The transition in Ukraine to a market-based energy sector has been seriously hindered by widespread corruption, vested interests, and institutional weaknesses. Under the Soviet regime, energy resources had a much lower value in the FSU than in the rest of the world, and the government tightly controlled their distribution. When the FSU collapsed, so did the control system. At the same time, the value of energy imported from the FSU went up roughly ten-fold as prices moved toward world levels. The opportunities for corruption were massive, and opportunists quickly stepped forward. So far little has been proven in court, so it would be inappropriate to expand further on this point here. But we can say with little doubt that corruption and shady dealings in the distribution of Ukrainian energy supplies have created fortunes—and that much of the resulting wealth is now outside the country.

Some market-oriented institutional structures such as auction-based markets for gas and electricity have been developed since independence, in part with assistance from the World Bank and other donors. But serious institutional barriers to reform remain in all energy sub-sectors. Of these, perhaps the three most important are the lack of real ownership, the lack of an environment relatively free from corruption, and the lack of payments discipline. At independence the energy companies became more or less independent fiefdoms with control over vast wealth and little effective oversight from central or local governments. Corruption was inevitable in such an environment. Opportunists stepped into this vacuum and took control, often treating public assets like private. Only a limited number of energy companies across the various sub sectors have been privatized, and of these, few if any serious private investors with an established track record in the sector have been allowed to purchase a majority interest.

The willingness of such investors to come into the sector is now jeopardized not only by the blocking or majority shares still held by government in energy companies, but also by the lack of payments discipline. With cash collections in electricity averaging only about 10 percent of total amount billed, for example, serious investors would find it almost impossible to make a profit that can be reinvested to improve efficiency.

The lack of payments discipline is compounded by extreme under-pricing. For example, the cost of generating electricity cost from fossil fuels in July 1999 was 2.95 US cents/kwh, but the energy distribution companies sold it for only 1.86 US cents/kwh. Leaving the energy sector with shrinking working capital stocks and nothing for investments in improved efficiency, under-pricing and non-payments are destroying the financial viability of the energy sector and jeopardizing the future of the entire economy.

A crisis in coal

Ukraine's coal sector is in a calamitous situation: output has declined rapidly, the demand for subsidies is rising steadily, and the prospects for improvement are diminishing. The sector, which accounts for 2 percent of employment and 6 percent of GDP, supplies a mere 50 million tons to the market (down from 130 million tons in 1990). Of this, about 30 percent is waste rock. Moreover, much of the coal produced is of extremely poor quality.

Annual budget subsidies to the coal sector total $750 million—about 7 percent of budget revenues and 40 percent of the budget deficit for 1997. In addition, in 1997 payment arrears increased by $600 million. And productivity is among the lowest in the world—in 1997 the 500,000 people engaged in coal production produced just 8 tons a man per month, compared with 40 tons in Poland and 60 tons per man-month in western Europe.

Geology, history, governance, management, and misguided policies explain the industry's decline. Due to poor geology (with thin coal seams at great depth), the coal sector is largely uneconomic and will generally remain that way, though some mines could operate profitably if they shed labor and social assets. Policies have long emphasized the social and economic status of miners, leading to high wages, employment numbers, and political power for miners. Scarce funds, combined with strong pressures to finance overdue wages, mean that no resources are available to invest in better mines. As a result the entire sector is in rapid decline.

In a liberalized and functioning energy market, local coal would quickly lose market share because it cannot compete with imported coal and alternative fuels. And because there are no budget funds to compensate mines for their competitive disadvantage, conditions in the sector will inevitably worsen. Without bold action, nearly all mines will stop production, leaving behind a social and environmental disaster. These developments are obvious—yet many Ukrainians still believe that coal has a strong future because domestic oil and gas deposits are thought to be depleting and coal is the only major source of local energy.

The government should be actively involved in restructuring the coal industry and privatizing viable mines. Instead the line ministry for coal is demanding more public support to produce coal and to modernize mines. Ukraine can develop a new, more efficient industry where well-paid workers produce high-quality coal at internationally competitive prices and meet an important share of domestic energy demand. But doing so will require hard work, courage, and social sensitivity. Several issues inhibit successful reform.

Lack of a realistic long-term development plan. Sector reform has not proceeded because the government has failed to develop a widely accepted long-term development plan taking into account the coal industry's prospects and the country's financial capabilities. As part of the World Bank's Coal Sector Adjustment Loan, the government placed all mines into one of three categories: viable mines, uneconomic mines, and mines with uncertain status that could eventually go to either of the first two categories. Viable mines were to be grouped into commercial holding companies, uneconomic mines were to be closed, and mines in the third category were to receive temporary operating subsidies under strict rules and conditions. But this model has failed, at least

temporarily, and the World Bank's Coal Adjustment Loan that was approved in 1996 had not been disbursed by early 1999.

To generate cash for mines, stakeholders such as the Ministry of Coal Industry want to return to old policies—including centralizing coal marketing and consolidating mines into a small number of large state holding companies. But this strategy would have disastrous consequences for the economy. The state would have to make large up-front investments in mine development and modernization and provide additional support by imposing import quotas and duties—policies that would be unbearably costly for the budget and for energy consumers. Advocates of such policies claim, among other things, that Western countries want to force Ukraine out of world coal markets, that this goal is supported by the International Monetary Fund (IMF) and World Bank, and that the loss of central control is a root cause of the industry's misery. Such claims reflect the profound lack of knowledge about the true status and prospects for coal mining in Ukraine today.

The government should undertake public information campaigns to disseminate knowledge on the coal industry's real long-term prospects. The general public should know that the future Ukrainian coal sector should consist of a much smaller number of viable mines that operate under commercial rules and, as much as possible, under private ownership. At the same time, coal mining regions should try to diversify into new economic activities, creating a cleaner, viable, and more prosperous environment. About 50 million tons a year—the same output as today—could be produced with just 50 mines, not the 250 operating today. Uneconomic and redundant mines need to be closed, the best mines need to be separated and commercialized, and uneconomic mines that cannot be closed immediately for political and social reasons need to be run under tight investment, recruitment, and wage constraints.

Regionally concentrated unemployment. Regional unemployment is one of the main reasons that the government has not adopted a realistic long-term development plan for the coal industry. Powerful political forces want to slow down mine closures because of inadequate alternative job opportunities—and given the economic decline and poor investment climate in Ukraine, this is a valid concern. But creating sustainable new jobs is a slow and cumbersome process that risks arresting the mine closure process. At the same time, slowing down mine closures would have serious adverse effects on Ukraine's growth because of the drain on resources created by unprofitable mines.

The government is reluctant to implement low-cost measures that create jobs, such as micro credit programs to establish new small-scale enterprises and programs to make underused public buildings, factory sheds, and warehouses available for new businesses. As a result the Ministry of Coal Industry and other stakeholders often refer to the lack of financial resources for employment creation as a reason not to close mines. It is also cited that in western Europe the adjustment of coal industries took 40 years and required huge sums of money, under a much better economic environment. These are well-placed concerns, and the World Bank is seeking with the Ukrainian authorities to learn from the problems in other countries in order to design a viable program for coal restructuring in Ukraine.

The government needs to actively support, through regulations and financial aid, a major program for closing uneconomic mines and promoting regional development and job creation. Some unemployment is unavoidable, however. Initiative, flexibility, and innovation are needed to identify new employment opportunities, provide financing, and follow through on project execution. Without mine closures, the sector will weaken, the need for subsidies will increase, and sustainable economic development of coal regions—as well as of the country at large—will be delayed. For political and practical reasons, the restructuring and privatization program could be broken into phases. The first phase could, for example, aim at closing about 60 uneconomic mines over three years.

Weak laws, regulations, and institutions. The political and social reasons for not closing mines are often mixed with unclear or contradictory regulations, exacerbated by institutions that lack the motivation and capability to address these problems. Procedures for creating new private

enterprises are cumbersome. The social and safety requirements associated with layoffs cause considerable debate, confusion, and inefficiency. And the Ministry of Coal Industry acts more as a lobbyist for the industry than as a state body for policy execution.

The government needs to provide a clear mandate for restructuring and to have efficient institutions in place for its execution. A new energy ministry may have to be established to promote economic efficiency and fiscal sustainability throughout the energy sector, including coal. Alternatively, such capacity could be developed within the Ministry of Economy. The state's highest coal policymaking body needs to fully support government reforms. A special agency for mine closures (UKDR), created as part of the Bank-financed Coal Pilot Project, initially closed some mines, but restructuring funds for mining associations have been misused. This agency must be maintained and strengthened.

Nonpayment for coal shipped and cross-subsidies between mines. The decline of the best mines is mainly caused by nonpayment for coal shipped and by cross-subsidies to non performing mines. Nonpayment is widespread, making true commercialization of mines impossible. Mines supplying coal to power plants receive less than 10 percent of its value in the form of cash payments—too little even to cover wages. Nonpayment causes wage arrears, discourages workers, and leads to excessive dealer profits and shortages of essential supplies. Closely linked with nonpayment are cross-subsidies from profitable to unprofitable mines, causing lack of funds for investments and improvements at the better mines and artificially extending the lives of the unprofitable mines.

Potentially viable mines need to receive the cash they earn and so should be taken out of mine groups, which drain their revenues. These mines must implement high-return investments to prevent their further decline, secure their production capability, and increase profits. Apart from good management and worker education, the government should offer several support measures to help these mines escape from their financial trap. The state reserve system should buy coal only from the best mines. The state should provide cash support for social services that are still provided by mines, as well as compensation for labor redundancies. And support should focus on mines that execute cost-cutting plans and prepare high-return investments financed by commercial credits.

Such mines would either have to be independent or, preferably, belong to a company that has only viable mines. Because such companies do not exist and probably cannot be created within a short period, it may be necessary to create a temporary agency that provides managerial assistance to mines implementing a cost reduction and investment program. This agency could also support the formation of viable mining companies and the privatization of profitable mines, distributing grants for social activities and labor redundancies. Credits for investments would preferably be provided by commercial banks. But if banks perceive the risk of lending to the coal industry as too high, a special credit facility controlled by the agency could be developed.

In the medium term, the best possible solution would be to privatize the coal mines, selling concessions to private companies to extract the coal under agreements that would assure substantial royalty payments to the budget in line with international practice. Of the coal mines in Ukraine today, only a relatively small share would have adequate high-quality reserves be attractive to private investors. Furthermore, the investors would have to be allowed to adjust employment levels in line with economic realities. But the effort would be well worthwhile for privatizing the mines would de-politicize the sector, leading to more normal operations and relationships. Because of the political ramifications, this process needs to be done according to high standards of consultation and compliance with legal norms to avoid social backlash that could set reforms in the sector back by many years.

Prospects for power

After years of slow developments, reform in the power (electricity) sector has recently been moving forward, with progress in the sector's structure, legal and regulatory environment, and in privatization. But slow movement or even reversals have occurred in other areas, with high

non payments and low cash collections, limited capital for new investment, government interference that makes it difficult to recover costs, limited competitiveness in the power pool market, and sluggish corporate restructuring.

Areas of advances. Essential components of a competitive power market structure—called the Energomarket—are in place, and the wholesale market is functioning. Generator scheduling, dispatch, and settlement operations comply with the Energomarket Members Agreement, and in September 1998 the National Electricity Regulatory Commission lifted the cap on generators' price bids.

Progress has also been made on another pillar of the Energomarket—the Market Funds Procedure—with major improvements in the way the procedure allocates cash revenues. All non cash payments are now taken into account to reduce incentives for barter. Excessive offsets are penalized. And companies that are owed large debts receive more cash.

Most tariff irregularities have been removed. Thermal power plants are paid according to market rules. The wholesale price now includes a subsidy to compensate distribution companies for having to serve, under existing law, privileged customers at prices that do not recover costs. Following a significant real increase in 1998, wholesale tariffs for generators are at market levels. The transition to market-based retail tariffs for nonresidential customers started in October 1998 and was expected to be completed by the end of 1998. However, this process was delayed by Parliament, which passed a law prohibiting government from increasing tariffs, but after a protracted legal battle that went to the Constitutional Court, the government began to take the necessary steps in March 1999. These measures will also help raise residential tariffs (set in hrivnya), which fell below industrial tariffs (set in dollars) with the accelerated exchange rate depreciation starting in late 1998.

Payment collections for distributors were 97 percent in April-August 1998, compared with 89 percent in the same period of 1997. The improvement was smaller for generators: from 86 percent to 89 percent. Cash collections continue to be low—18 percent for distributors and 7 percent for generators. Though customer debt for electricity fell in 1998, it is still unsustainable high ($1.5 billion in August 1998). Further reductions are needed through a vigorously applied disconnection policy.

Areas of slow or no progress. The power sector's financial distress has persisted due to rampant nonpayment, causing financial losses for power companies. The result is a deteriorating electrical system, occasional fuel shortages, poor customer service, rotating power outages, and constrained ability to privatize power companies.

The culture of nonpayment for electricity is condoned and even aggravated by the government. Government agencies are responsible for two-thirds of unpaid electricity bills. On occasion the government interferes with the National Electricity Regulatory Commission's jurisdiction to set market-based tariffs and issue licenses to distributors. By abusing the financial viability of the power sector, the government is able to delay the inevitable structural reforms needed in the sector's role and in state enterprises. Unpaid consumption—whether through privileges, subsidies, unauthorized connections, or non reporting or misreporting of consumption—absorbs 20 percent of generated electricity.

Cash collections are low because customers and distributors lack incentives to increase cash payments. Some taxation policies and aspects of the Market Fund Procedure make it beneficial to accept barter payments, offsets, and other cash surrogates in lieu of collecting and forwarding cash to the Energomarket clearing accounts. As a result power companies find it almost impossible to raise new funds for much-needed modernization and expansion programs. Payments problems are not limited to final consumers. Private distribution companies have been ignoring the Energomarket procedures which demand that all money collected by distributors should be sent directly to the Energomarket transit account. Instead, they are retaining the cash collected for their own purposes.

As a result, all four generating companies are experiencing severe shortages of cash, leaving them without adequate funds to maintain fuel inventories. Their problems are compounded by interference in tariff policy by Parliament and the government, particularly the Ministry of Energy. In addition, the Presidential administration, local authorities and Government frequently prevent electricity companies from switching off some categories of customers who do not pay for the electricity. In fact, in the period prior to the Presidential elections, oblenergos were not allowed to switch off anyone. These problems make it clear that the National Electricity Regulatory Commission (NERC) is not truly independent of political pressures as originally intended. Its independence needs to be established if investors are to have confidence that the regulation of the sector will create a good investment climate.

Because of nonpayment and fuel inventories that are low and unevenly distributed, competition among generation companies has been limited. As a result generation and distribution costs continue above normal levels. Rampant barter increases effective fuel costs by 20-30 percent, power companies are overstaffed and saddled with social assets, and deferred maintenance and modernization hurt technical efficiency.

About 40 percent of the shares of distribution companies have been sold. Successful and sustainable sector reform ultimately hinges on the depth and quality of the privatization program, which is managed by the State Property Fund. In this regard, the absence of strategic investors and reputable investment advisers in recent privatizations raises serious concerns. Foreign strategic investors seem to have little faith in the constantly changing privatization procedures. Thus implementation of a transparent process consistent with internationally accepted practices—including appointment of foreign advisers—should be a top priority.

Financial and technical assistance. In its efforts to design and implement power reforms, the government is working with key donors, including the World Bank, European Commission, European Bank for Reconstruction and Development, U.S. Agency for International Development, and donor countries. Technical assistance seeks to:

- Implement market-based retail tariffs without government interference.

- Achieve effective collection of retail tariffs and make credible arrangements to collect all arrears within three years.

- Ensure rule-based operation of the wholesale electricity market, with a comprehensive and transparent Market Funds Procedure.

- Facilitate privatization of a controlling share in all four generators and all 27 oblenergos.

Goals for gas

In 1990 Ukraine consumed 115 billion cubic meters of natural gas, representing about 40 percent of primary energy consumption. Domestic wells provided 28 billion cubic meters; the remainder came from Russia and Turkmenistan. By 1996-97 gas consumption has dropped to 80-85 billion cubic meters a year. This decline did not reflect major energy conservation measures, but rather the collapse of economic output since the 1980s. In fact, given Ukraine's economic contraction, the energy intensity of the economy in terms of gas consumption has actually risen. The share of gas in primary energy consumption has surpassed 50 percent, making Ukraine one of the world's most gas-intensive economies.

Ukraine has significant proven and probable gas deposits, both onshore and offshore. Domestic gas fields now produce about 18 billion cubic meters a year. Imports from Russia provide 60-65 billion cubic meters a year, including 30 billion cubic meters that Ukraine receives from RAO Gazprom as payment in kind for transit of Russian gas across Ukraine to Europe. Ukraine has large gas storage facilities, a well-developed transmission system, and an extensive distribution system.

The main challenges for gas are to privatize the sector without creating exploitative private monopolies, place gas sales on a solid commercial foundation, encourage energy conservation, and, perhaps most important, increase collection rates, particularly cash payments.

Initial reforms. In 1994 Parliament banned the privatization of transmission and distribution pipelines and related infrastructure, so these belong to the State Property Fund and are not among the assets of gas companies. Gas production, transmission, and storage functions were assigned to Ukrgazprom. Ukrnafta produced most crude oil. In addition, there were several smaller, partially privatized oil and gas producers.

Until 1996 Ukrgazprom was solely responsible for importing gas. But then, facing a massive buildup of payment arrears, the government took a radical step: it eliminated government guarantees for gas imports and gave private gas traders exclusive rights to import and sell gas to customers in certain oblasts. With this move, Ukraine became one of the first countries to unbundled gas transmission and distribution from gas import and supply.

Another important reform was made in gas exploration and production. Domestic gas output has the potential to increase to 30 billion cubic meters a year with large but economically justified investments over a period of three to five years. Recognizing that these investments would have to come from abroad, the State Geology Committee started awarding exploration and production licenses to private—mostly foreign—companies.

Competing reform concepts. These two steps—the transfer of responsibility for gas imports to private traders and the award of exploration and production licenses to foreign companies—have had mixed results. Gas traders have improved payment discipline among industrial customers; the government stopped accumulating additional debt to Russia and Turkmenistan; and foreign direct investment started to flow to the upstream gas industry. But payment discipline remains low among households, budget entities, district heating companies, and power plants. The frequent redistribution of supply franchises among traders has led to occasional violence and charges of corruption. And no major multinational oil and gas company has found Ukraine's legal and regulatory framework attractive enough to make large-scale investments in gas exploration and production. Even with respect to external debt, success was only partial: RAO Gazprom claimed that the Ukrainian government was responsible for the arrears accumulated by private traders because the traders were pressured by government officials to maintain supplies to politically important customers.

Although the system was left largely intact in 1997, the need for additional reforms was widely acknowledged. Even Ukrgazprom, a company that once defended the status quo, now argues that it cannot ensure a reliable transmission system unless privileged customers (households, budget entities) are made to pay for domestically produced and transit-fee gas. All shippers (RAO Gazprom, traders, and private gas producers) have complained that the metering and control of gas flows in the transmission and distribution networks are inadequate. Potential foreign investors in the upstream gas industry want assurances that they can access the gas transmission and distribution networks and freely market their gas. A commission set up by Parliament has demanded that territorial supply monopolies be abolished and a properly functioning gas market be established.

Two very different reform concepts emerged in the debate. The first, put forward by Ukrgazprom and the State Oil and Gas Committee (SOGC), favored vertical integration of the oil and gas industry to increase the flow of revenue from consumers to producers and transporters, and to facilitate the reallocation of profits to fund priority investments. The second reform concept—recommended by foreign investors, the World Bank, and the European Bank for Reconstruction and Development and supported by the Anti-Monopoly Committee and the deputy prime minister for economic reform—argued for the separation and privatization of Ukrgazprom's production, transmission, and marketing activities, the elimination of exclusive supply franchises, the privatization of gas distribution companies, the liberalization of gas prices, and the establishment of an independent regulatory body to ensure open access to the transmission and distribution networks.

The change of government at the cabinet level in mid-1997 opened a window of opportunity for those who wanted to eliminate regional gas import and supply monopolies. The new cabinet decided that the import and supply of gas to industrial consumers should be liberalized in 1998; that traders should be allowed to import and sell gas to industrial consumers at freely negotiated prices; and that gas distribution companies should be given exclusive rights to sell Ukrgazprom's domestically produced and transit-fee gas to households, budget organizations, and district heating companies.

Meanwhile, the State Property Fund sold the majority of shares of several gas distribution companies to company managers and employees at very low prices. The newly privatized distribution companies kept enough revenue to cover their wages and other recurrent costs, and only sent the remainder to Ukrgazprom. As a result Ukrgazprom's financial situation continued to deteriorate.

Recent developments. In early 1998 supporters of vertical integration focused on establishing Naftogaz, a company whose assets include everything that the state owned in the oil and gas industry. Establishing Naftogaz, it was argued, would solve several problems:

- Low payment collection, because Naftogaz could take away the right to operate the distribution system from distribution companies whose performance was not satisfactory.

- Limited foreign direct investment in oil and gas production, because Naftogaz could enter into joint ventures.

- Underfunding of priority investments, because Naftogaz could reallocate profits among its subsidiaries.

A February 1998 presidential decree ordered the government to establish Naftogaz. The decree also ordered steps to unbundled gas production, transmission, and distribution functions—but this unbundling was to take place within the framework of Naftogaz. A government resolution issued in June 1998 approved the charter of Naftogaz and appointed its chairman and supervisory board.

In April 1998 another presidential decree ordered the transfer of responsibility for the regulation of the gas industry from the Ministry of Economy and the SOGC to the National Electricity Regulatory Commission. Given the time required to recruit gas specialists and implement necessary organizational changes, the National Electricity Regulatory Commission had not begun to function by late 1998.

In August 1998 Ukrgazprom was abolished and its production, transmission and distribution, and trading functions were formally separated by establishing three companies—Ukrgazproduction, Uktransgaz, and Trading House Gaz Ukraine. The newly created companies were subordinated to the state-owned Naftogaz. Naftogaz also received 50 percent plus one share of Ukrnafta, 100 percent of state shares of the oil pipelines in Druzba and Pridneprovska, and state shares of the offshore gas producer Chernomornaftogas and smaller gas companies.

Required reforms. Though important gas reforms have occurred, much remains to be done. The following steps, if implemented within two to three years, could help restore the financial health of the gas industry, increase budget revenues, address the complaints of investors in gas exploration and production, and ensure the reliable transit of gas from Russia to central, southern, and western Europe:

- Developing the legal and regulatory framework for the sector, including approval of production sharing arrangements for oil and gas and establishment of two independent regulators for downstream and upstream operations.

- Organizing regular gas auctions where gas traders and large consumers can pay cash for gas—based on freely negotiated prices—from gas producers and Ukrgazprom's successor.

- Establishing a state-owned joint stock company to operate the transmission network and appointing a consortium of domestic and foreign companies to manage the shares of this company for at least 15 years. Ukrainian state ownership in the consortium should be limited to 25 percent plus one share.

- Separating and privatizing the gas production activities of Ukrgazprom and the gas exploration activities of the State Geology Committee.

- Introducing incentives and criteria to improve the collections of gas distribution companies and, in cases of poor performance, transferring to other entities (domestic or foreign) the rights to operate the distribution system and supply gas to non industrial customers.

- Improving the metering, tracking, and balancing of gas flows, including the introduction of contractual arrangements for the settlement of differences on a daily and monthly basis.

- Introducing a distance-dependent transmission tariff, a two-part distribution tariff, and a storage fee.

These reforms may adversely affect several well-connected actors in the sector. Private traders may lose their best customers if financially liquid industrial companies purchase their gas at auctions. Central and local governments' ability to provide gas to insolvent industrial and agricultural companies and cash-strapped budget entities will be greatly reduced. Managers who cannot adapt to a market environment and workers who are redundant will lose their jobs. Government officials who benefit from nontransparent gas trading will also be worse off. In summary, advocates of centralized, vertically integrated, and opaque structures represent the greatest threat to successful reforms.

A new design for district heating

District heating tariffs force industrial consumers to cross-subsidize household consumers. Consequently, in cities outside Kyiv—which has resolved this problem—households pay less than 80 percent of the cost of service. The government has declared that district heating tariffs (as well as other utility tariffs) will be raised to cover 100 percent of costs, but it has been unable to introduce this final jump in tariffs. This move should be made as soon as possible, but Parliament has been moving in the opposite direction: in 1998 it passed a law banning increases in tariffs for domestic utility services.

In late 1998, as noted above, the president of Ukraine appealed to the Constitutional Court to prevent Parliament from intervening in the administrative details of government, such as the setting of tariffs to ensure full cost recovery for commercial operations. The court reversal of the law in March 1999 among other things, helped avoid derailing the government's Extended Fund Facility (EFF) program with the IMF. Because household consumers are more expensive to supply with heat than large industrial consumers, substantial prices are still required in residential tariffs, but initial steps have been taken towards establishing more equitable district heating tariffs.

District heating tariffs also need to be revised to address a number of other issues:

- Depreciation is based on historical values—which are far below current replacement costs and so do not allow for future replacement of assets.

- Depreciation rates are based on unrealistic-ally long economic lives (about 75 years on average)—which makes it difficult for district heating enterprises to renew their assets on a self-financing basis.

- The district heating tariff structure contains only an energy charge—a two-tier structure with fixed and variable components would allow for more transparent information about the marginal cost of heat supply.

Billing for heating and hot water is typically based on norms (that is, on square meters and numbers of persons, respectively) rather than on actual consumption, because most residential buildings are not metered. While this system of billing provides an incentive for consumers to install heat meters (since heat losses are paid by non metered consumers), few residential consumers can afford them. The same holds true for budgetary consumers, which are also often not metered, although industrial consumers are typically metered. Incentives are needed to improve the metering of household and budgetary consumers.

As in all energy sectors, late payments and non-payments are a serious problem in district heating. Incentives are needed to improve the collection of heating bills—including disconnections, formal rescheduling of arrears, and public awareness campaigns. To promote energy efficiency, proper pricing signals should be sent to consumers through tariff levels and structures. These reforms would make it easier for lenders to finance needed investments. In addition, international accounting standards must be introduced so that district heating enterprises can follow commercial practices.

Most district heating enterprises are municipal enterprises, which allows munici–palities to interfere in their activities. Converting municipal district heating enterprises into joint stock companies with supervisory boards would allow for greater commercialization and independence and should be encouraged.

Finally, the district heating sector maintains a system of privileges that applies discounts of 25 percent, 50 percent, 75 percent, or 100 percent to the heating bills of various groups (military personnel, war veterans, Chernobyl victims, and so on). A large portion of households exploit such privileges. These jeopardize the financial sustainability of heating companies because municipalities do not adequately compensate them for the discounts. Such privileges should be phased out, replaced by a comprehensive social safety net program targeted to assure that no family falls into absolute poverty (see chapter 4).

ADVANCING BANKING AND FINANCE

Without a strong banking sector to intermediate capital—mobilizing savings and extending credit on commercial terms to enterprises that will use it well—Ukrainian enterprises will continue to suffer crippling shortages of working and fixed capital, preventing them from investing in the plant and equipment needed to produce high-quality goods that can compete with imports in the domestic market and as exports in the global market.

Some of the capital required by Ukrainian firms can and should come from foreign sources as loans, portfolio investments, and foreign direct investments. But aside from some small

Table 3.5 Basic data on Ukraine's banking system, 1998, end of period

Indicator	Millions of hrivnyas	As % of total banking assets	As % of estimated 1998 GDP
Total banking sector assets	19,918		19.2
Total bank lending to the economy	8,855	44.5	8.5
Government securities holdings of commercial banks	2,096	10.5	
Total deposits in banking sector	8,278		8.0
Total households deposits in the banking sector	3,089		3.0
Total deposits in State Oshchadnyi (Savings) Bank	811		0.8

Source: IMF data.

countries with great mineral or petroleum wealth, foreign savings rarely equals more than 3 percent of GDP, and in most cases much of that small amount goes for consumption rather than investment. Although Ukraine can and should seek to sharply increase foreign direct investment in local production, it will have to mobilize most of the savings needed for investment in fixed and working capital from domestic resources.

The reforms discussed in chapter 2—reforms that would sharply reduce the government's tendency to crowd private investors out of domestic capital markets—are an essential precondition to accelerated investment and growth. But major improvements are also needed in the banking sector so that it can mobilize savings efficiently and make wise lending decisions. Given the current status of the domestic banking system, this will be a major challenge.

A downward spiral

The contours of Ukraine's banking system—comprising some 180 banks—remain poorly defined. The sector still has a long way to go before it can mobilize significant savings and allocate those resources to the most productive sectors to promote economic growth. In recent years Ukraine's banks, like those in other former Soviet countries, have failed to foster public confidence (which would increase resource mobilization through banks) or improve their capacity and service (which would support economic development through better resource allocation).

Public confidence in banks was undermined by the hyperinflation of 1992-94. Though confidence recovered through early 1998, it has suffered again from the recent financial crisis (tables 3.5-3.7).

Previous Bank documents have analyzed the weaknesses of the banking sector in considerable detail (World Bank 1995). Recent events have largely confirmed the variety and depth of these weaknesses, as well as aggravating many long-standing problems: undercapitalization, weak corporate governance and management, poor asset quality, limited capacity to manage and cope with risk, excessive political intervention in some banks—the list is long.

One of the institutional factors contributing to the painful decline of the Ukrainian banking sector has been "kartoteka 2," a system retained from the Soviet days that forces commercial banks to serve as collection agent for the State Tax Administration (STA). When the tax authorities determine that an enterprise is in arrears, they have the right to demand that the commercial bank place a note in *Kartoteka II* (Ukrainian for "Card File Number 2") indicating that any money entering the account of that enterprise must immediately be removed and given to the tax authorities. Due process, which is routine in all developed countries for attachment of assets, is not required of the STA, nor do enterprises have an effective right of appeal. Consequently, enterprises tend to minimize their use of commercial banks because cash flow management and prioritization among creditors becomes impossible. Firms have been

Table 3.6 Depth of Ukrainian financial system
(percentage of GDP)

	1992	1993	1994	1995	1996	1997	1998
Currency	10	9	7	5	5	7	7
Domestic currency deposits	36	17	12	5	4	5	4
Foreign exchange deposits	4	7	9	3	2	2	5
Total money (M2)	50	33	27	13	11	13	15
Forex deposits/total bank deposits	10	28	42	37	34	26	42
Currency/M2 (domestic currency)	22	34	36	50	55	57	59

Source: National Bank of Ukraine, Ukrainian Economic Trends, and EU TACIS publications.

destroyed because kartoteka takes their cash, making it impossible for them to purchase the inputs required to stay in operation and earn the resources needed to repay creditors. By discouraging firms from keeping their money in the banking system, *kartoteka* weakens the banking system, depriving it of the deposits that it needs to become an effective financial intermediary. This in turn increases the cost and scarcity of capital in Ukraine, further reducing the prospects for restoring growth.

In a sense, *kartoteka* is the Soviet equivalent of a bankruptcy and arbitration system, and it has been retained in Ukraine partly because an effective market-based analogue is not yet in place. The best solution would be for Ukraine to develop a good system of economic courts capable of handling, with full due process and right of appeal, the full range of normal bankruptcy work. This institutional development is essential. As long as banks instead of courts keep the card file and extract money from accounts upon instructions from the tax administration, the prospects for restored economic growth based on a strong banking sector will be dim indeed.

The current crisis—quiet but serious

Long-standing structural problems in the Ukrainian banks have been intensified by the recent turbulence in international and local financial markets. Above all, the real economy—and so the banks—has faced interest rates that have been unsustainable high in real terms. These high interest rates have led to even worse shortages of credit for productive sectors, to an intensified lack of profitable lending opportunities for banks, and to an increased volume of non performing loans. The blame for these adverse developments can be laid squarely at the door of the huge fiscal imbalances analyzed elsewhere in this report. At various stages in the past year, the fiscal situation has created additional problems for banks by:

- Depriving them of profitable lending opportunities.

- Pushing many into an excessive exposure to T-bills.

- Imposing direct losses through the T-bill restructurings initiated in August 1998.

- Contributing to the buildup of bad loans as a result of continued high real interest rates.

- Leaving the Central Bank little choice but to apply emergency restrictions on banking activities (in the interests of macroeconomic stability), with further negative consequences for bank profitability.

Ukrainian bankers are justified in arguing that there is an ongoing banking crisis layered on top of the structural problems that they have faced for some time. But this crisis is unlikely to be as dramatic as recent crises in other parts of the world—including Russia, where banking systems are generally much larger and more fully developed. The payments system, though under threat, has proved reasonably robust. Despite of a brief run on deposits in August 1998, the situation recovered remarkably quickly after the announcement of the IMF program in early September. And while the large depreciation of the national currency caused a 30 percent erosion of banking capital, that capital was too small to allow most banks to expand their activities and increase lending.

Still, the situation is serious. There can be no real recovery in banking until real interest rates return to more sustainable levels—and that will require deep fiscal adjustment, which itself will hurt many bank clients. Problems have become more evident for large banks, and at least two of the five largest banks are thought to be insolvent. The situation has become truly dreadful for many small and medium-size banks. For the moment, and in the absence of serious policy decisions about structural reform in the sector, the Central Bank believes that it has little short-term choice but to support the system with "liquidity loans"—many of which are actually bailout loans—but at the expense of further pressure on inflation, to say nothing of its own financial viability.

The five specialized banks that constituted the banking system in Soviet Ukraine were used to move money back and forth between the state budget and the state enterprises, filling gaps when financial balances did not quite match the material balances. Competition between the five banks was almost unknown.

The banking system continued to play a highly politicized role after independence. The government used the banks to channel budget funds to favored enterprises. During the early years of independence, the banks got special benefits from the Government such as free access to budget funds, state procurement contracts, and government guarantees for trade finance deals. But they also accumulated a heavy burden of bad loans and equity investments. The dominance of public enterprise assets in the portfolio of banks led to abusive insider lending, reflecting the influence that

state and local authorities had on the banks.

With new private commercial banks coming into the market, improved supervision, increased transparency in market operations, and access to new profitable instruments such as government securities (t-bills) during the past few years, the influence of government in the banking sector has been lessening. The sale of t-bills carrying interest rates peaking at over 80 percent allowed banks to enjoy yields which in the past would have been allowed only to a few privileged banks.

The right to manage state budget funds has been one of the important remaining privileges sought by banks, but this system is being brought to a close with the implementation of a professional treasury system and unified budgetary accounts. Though the commercial banking system in Ukraine is far more professional today, it is still far from de-politicized—as seen by the highly political discussions in Parliament about the Law and Banks and Banking and the Law on the National Bank, laws which seek to decrease the degree of political control over these institutions.

Strategies for the future

Although the normal tendency is to focus on the short-term problems of the banking system, which are certainly serious, the temporizing measures likely to be taken from this perspective could easily make the situation worse. Thus it is important to look first at a long-term strategy for the sector, then decide what actions can be taken in the short run to advance toward the long-term objectives.

Long-term strategy. At the macroeconomic level, it will be difficult to achieve progress and improvements without substantially rectifying fiscal policies. First and foremost, measures are

Table 3.7 Depth of financial systems in regions of world, 1994
(percentage of GDP)

Item	OECD	Latin America	C.E.E.	NIS	Ukraine
Total money (M2)	73	23	42	20	13
Bank deposits	67	18	25	12	7
Currency	6	5	17	8	5

Source: National Bank of Ukraine.

required to justify lower real interest rates—the reforms to do this being mainly fiscal in nature. The economy cannot function efficiently with the real interest rate well above 20 percent There is also a more general need to improve the operating environment for banks and their clients. It is not possible to have sound banks in an unhealthy economy. In the absence of good borrowers, banks will either disappear as traditional lenders or engage in risky lending to nonviable private and state enterprises that are hoping for future government bailouts. Required measures include better corporate legislation, a new bankruptcy law, streamlined collateral evaluation, repossession and realization procedures, establishment of registries for movable and immovable property, and restructuring of inter-enterprise arrears.

Within the banking sector, the main challenge is to use a more effective mix of carrots and sticks. The previous strategy relied very much on sticks—a problem when some banks are politically more powerful then the regulator. The future mix should intensify measures such as those already incorporated in the World Bank's Financial Sector Adjustment Loan (FSAL):

- Adjusting the legal framework to give the regulator the tools to rehabilitate troubled banks and liquidate failed banks (for example, by rapidly promulgating the draft Law on Banks and Banking Activity).

- Upgrading the quality and organization of bank supervision (by eliminating all but the most liquid collateral deductions in loan loss provisioning, temporarily skewing the foreign exchange exposure rule to allow long but not short open foreign exchange positions, and upgrading offsite analysis and internal communications between the offsite, onsite, and licensing departments in the central bank).

- Creating incentives for banks to strengthen their institutional capabilities, especially their risk management abilities, including borrowing for this purpose (for example, through the Bank's proposed Financial Services Project).

- Central bank interventions in individual banks could be structured more toward building risk management systems than toward the simplistic penalty-based approach currently being pursued. Licensing could also be used more effectively (for example, by not providing foreign exchange licenses for banks that do not have proper foreign exchange risk management systems in place), as could access to credit lines from international financial institutions and grant-funded technical assistance.

- Encouraging the flow of long-term resources to the banking system through foreign direct investment and funding from international financial institutions.

Short-term strategy. Earlier analysis and experiences of other countries suggest that there is no short-term solution for systemic malaise. Issues such as corporate governance, management skills, and public confidence need to be addressed as soon as possible, but the desired results will be achieved only in the long run. Nonetheless, the authorities should continue to:

- Rationalize central bank support to banks so that financial and human resources are not wasted on revitalizing dead banks; this will in any case be crucial for attracting donor support to bank restructuring.

- Rationalize and encourage increased bank capitalization through consolidations, mergers, and liquidations.

- Support operation of the payments system.

- Impose stricter prudential requirements and higher qualitative criteria for bank owners and managers.

- Strengthen banking supervision.

4. CAN UKRAINE ACHIEVE GROWTH—AND SOCIAL EQUITY?

Growth is vital if all Ukrainians are to enjoy higher living standards. But growth is not enough. Without the right policies, growth may benefit primarily the rich and do little to help the poor. Some may argue that growth and equity are mutually exclusive—that consumption by the lower classes reduces the savings available for investing in growth. But even very poor people save and invest, and income provides customers for products and thus the basis for investment and growth. While it may not be possible to maximize growth and equity simultaneously, it is possible to increase both of them at the same time. This should be Ukraine's primary goal.

Social equity has long been of great importance in Ukraine. But the Soviet approach to equity must be replaced by market-friendly approaches if Ukraine is to halt its economic decline and restore living standards. Most important are policies that create new jobs by encouraging investment, particularly in new small and medium-size enterprise, and facilitating labor mobility, helping workers in depressed regions move to areas where jobs are opening up. The government must also ensure universal access to basic education and health. Finally, to prevent people from falling into absolute poverty, the government needs to put in place a basic social safety net for families that have lost their incomes due to unemployment, age, or infirmity.[1]

OLD AND NEW APPROACHES TO SOCIAL EQUITY

During the Soviet era there was little difference between minimum and maximum wage rates in Ukraine. Aside from the privileged *apparatchik* classes, differences in living standards were also minimized. Workers received a large share of their incomes in the form of food, housing, education, communal services, medical care, access to recreational facilities, and other goods and services—either at no cost or at prices that recovered only part of the cost of supply.

This system allowed the government to minimize income differentials, but it also destroyed the incentives for individuals to invest in their education and to work harder. Thus, as Ukraine moves to a market-based economic system, it is entirely normal—even desirable—that income distribution will become somewhat less equal. Some people will always have less than others, and some people will always be living in relative poverty. But the efficiency gains from a market system will ensure that, while some people will have less than others, they will have far higher incomes than they do today.

As Ukraine moves toward a market economy, the challenge will be to prevent absolute poverty. No household should have an income so low that it cannot afford the food, shelter, clothing, medical care, and education needed for survival and health, for basic human decency, and for raising children to become solid, productive citizens. Access to these basic human needs for all Ukrainians is the definition of "social equity" used in this report.

Ukraine is seeking market-based mechanisms that ensure that no citizen has to live in absolute poverty. Some political parties want to attain this goal using the Soviet approach—by expanding government spending and by extending already widespread privileges. Such parties may block privatization and restructuring so that agricultural and industrial enterprises can continue to play the redistributive role they played in the Soviet era.

But as this report has demonstrated, continued reliance on Soviet methods has been a key reason for Ukraine's economic decline. The methods are responsible for the tax pressures on enterprises, the pyramid of debt that the country is struggling to repay, and the failure of large

---

[1] This chapter draws heavily on the work of Olexandr Yaremenko and Mykola Soldatenko (1998), and on the work of World Bank Staff including Arvo Kuddo (labor policy), Galina Sotirova (social protection), Larisa Leschenko (health policy), Katerina Petrina (education policy), and Frederick Golladay and his colleagues (see bibliography for details)

enterprises to restructure and become efficient. These policies simply make poverty worse. The burden that they inflict on the budget has also made it impossible for the government to alleviate inherited environmental problems. Market-friendly approaches to social equity are urgently needed.

NEW JOBS—THE BEST POSSIBLE SOCIAL SAFETY NET

Tensions in Ukraine's labor market are rapidly increasing. Between January and August 1998 state employment centers had 1.5 million registered job seekers, of whom 1.2 million were officially unemployed. Relative to the same period in 1997, the number of applicants was 39 percent higher and officially unemployed persons, 52 percent higher. And by the end of 1998 at least 2.4 million job seekers were registered at state employment centers.

Despite the sharp increase during 1998, unemployment in Ukraine was just 3.7 percent of the able-bodied population, compared with 2.1 percent a year earlier. This is still a very low rate relative to many other transition economies, especially those in Central Europe. But a labor force survey in October 1997 found that only 27 percent of active job seekers registered at employment offices—the lowest share among 13 transition countries in Central and Eastern Europe and the former Soviet Union. Weak employment services, small unemployment benefits, and limited job offers make Ukraine's employment centers unattractive to job seekers.

Hidden unemployment and underemployment are considerably higher. In the first half of 1998, 2.2 million workers—accounting for 17 percent of formal sector employment—were on administrative leave. And 1.8 million workers— 14 percent of the workforce—were engaged in part-time employment.

There has been a major shift in employment from the secondary to the tertiary sector, and labor retrenchment has been especially severe in the industrial sector. Between late 1996 and mid-1998 the number of industrial workers dropped from 4.3 million to 3.7 million. Employment in services is on the rise, however, reflecting the horizontal mobility of the labor force to more productive sectors.

One of the most serious problems in the labor market is the accumulation of wage arrears. In September 1998 wage arrears equaled 6.4 billion hrivnyas (about 6.5 percent of GDP). More than three-quarters of the wage debt was more than three months overdue—one of the highest levels among transition countries.

Because many transactions are still based on barter and cash payments are delayed or even nonexistent, part of wages are paid in kind, and there is no meaningful methodology to recalculate or tax such wages. In August 1998, however, in-kind payment of wages was estimated at 14 percent of total wages, including 63 percent in agriculture and 10 percent in industry and construction.

Strengthening macroeconomic and sector policies

During transition the best way to minimize unemployment and poverty is to restructure enterprises as quickly and vigorously as possible. This may sound illogical given the many redundant workers who will have to be laid off during the restructuring of public enterprises. But as it is, many of these workers are not being paid, and so will not suffer financially from being laid off. Furthermore, the longer failing enterprises are allowed to stay in production—consuming inputs that are worth more than the goods produced—the greater will be the economic decline, and the more costly and lengthy will be the recovery process. Instead of protecting enterprises, the government should focus on protecting people by providing a solid social safety net in cases where extended unemployment threatens families with poverty (see below).

Job-focused growth strategies. Ukraine's best hope for minimizing unemployment is to follow a growth strategy that quickly creates productive new jobs. An open, competitive economic environment favors small over large enterprises, and small businesses tend to create more jobs per million dollars of investment than large ones do, because small firms are generally much less capital-intensive. Small enterprises also tend to be more flexible and thus better able to seek out opportunities that create new jobs. A competitive environment encourages the efficient use of resources, generating more value added—which means that more money can be paid to workers. A competitive environment also brings rapid closure to bankrupt companies, allowing banking and budget resources to be used to create new jobs and to support workers delayed in moving from one job to another. Finally, a competitive environment encourages new exports to profitable new markets, generating foreign exchange that can be used to create additional jobs, pay higher wages, and import products of higher quality and lower cost than domestically produced equivalents.

Though it may create more short-term unemployment, a jobs-oriented competitiveness strategy will sharply reduce long-term unemployment, create more new jobs, and increase wage payments far in excess of what can be attained with a preservationist or protectionist strategy.[2] Valuable years have been lost in Ukraine. But with a firm commitment to a competitive, jobs-oriented growth strategy, Ukraine can expect excellent results within one to three years given its many advantages—including a strong work ethic, well-educated population, extensive natural resources, and good trading relations with important markets.

Labor market flexibility. Countries that are the most successful in maintaining low unemployment maintain low barriers to the movement of workers from one job to another. Without labor market flexibility, enterprises that need to downsize will remain burdened with too many workers. Policies that limit labor mobility also make labor more scarce and costly for growing enterprises, reducing their competitiveness and their ability to grow, employ more workers, and generate higher standards of living.

The largest barriers to labor market flexibility in Ukraine are laws and regulations that prevent enterprises from laying off workers and prevent or discourage workers from seeking alternative employment. Political pressures are also important in state enterprises—which is one of the strong arguments for privatization. Common barriers to workers seeking new jobs include a

lack of satisfactory housing in new locations (particularly rental housing) and large discrepancies in housing costs across regions.

The Ukrainian Constitution also may inhibit labor market flexibility. Article 22 states that actions should not be taken that would worsen people's living conditions. Thus amendments to existing laws regarding social guarantees to workers could be interpreted as violating the Constitution. But Article 22 is discussing civil rights and liberties, not living standards and benefit levels, and so should not be taken as a barrier to reforms that will, in the end, greatly improve the living standards of workers (Kuddo 1998; Lippott 1999).

Though Ukraine has adopted a number of new laws on employment, the 1972 Labor Code is still in effect. Individual labor contracts are the major missing element needed in a market economy. Written labor contracts are rare, and when their rights are violated, workers have a weak institutional basis to complain. Thus a group of experts should develop a new, market-oriented labor code or new labor laws. Labor laws are not as elegant, but they are technically less complicated than labor codes. Ukraine also needs to improve institutional mechanisms for implementing and enforcing labor laws and regulations.

Developing active employment policies

Job-oriented macroeconomic policies that promote competitiveness should be supported by active employment programs—including job search assistance, small business development, and public works programs for temporary employment.

Job search and training assistance. State employment centers provide services that could be considered active support measures, including job search assistance, job counseling, and psychological and adaptation support. But between January and August 1998, of 1.5 million registered job seekers, these centers were able to place only 17 percent in jobs. During this period 25 percent of job seekers left the roster of registered unemployed without finding jobs through the system. And during 1998 only 4 percent of unemployed workers participated in training programs.

---

[2] See World Bank and ICPS (1999) "Economic Growth with Equity: Which Strategy for Ukraine" for a discussion of these strategies .

Small business development programs. To help establish more favorable conditions for the development of small business in Ukraine, small business development programs were developed in 1997-98 at the national and regional levels. These programs envisage the number of jobs in small businesses increasing from 1.18 million in 1997 to 1.25 million in 1998, to 1.33 million in 1999 (Yaremenko and Soldatenko 1998, p. 29).

Public works programs. The state employment centers support labor-intensive public works programs as a form of emergency job creation. During 1998 an estimated 4 percent of job seekers participated in public works programs. Participation in public works programs is limited by the fact that the enterprises and local communities that are supposed to run these programs often cannot afford to pay even their own workers. Moreover, international experience with public works schemes has generally not been favorable. Small programs at the local level may, however, have political and economic benefits that help compensate for the costs.

HUMAN RESOURCE DEVELOPMENT

Next to social protection (discussed later in this chapter), education and health are the largest categories of budget expenditures, each accounting for 10 percent of the consolidated government budget in 1998. Though major areas of activity can be devolved to the private sector, the government will need to retain an important role in certain areas—one of the most important being the development of human resources. Communicable diseases and uneducated people impose high social costs. Conversely, a healthy, well-educated population has benefits that reach far beyond the individuals concerned. Government involvement can ensure that market-based economic development is accompanied by high standards of education and health care.

This is not to say that the government should be the sole or even primary provider of education and health services. In fact, if done well, increasing the private sector's role in providing these services will reduce the burden on government—lowering taxes, stimulating economic growth, and increasing consumer choices (Vitrenko and Lukovenko 1998; Golladay and others 1998).

Increasing the formal role of the private sector in health and education will also help reduce the role of shadow economic activity in these sectors. Corruption in the form of under-the-table payments is a particular problem in the health sector where doctors, painfully short of funds to purchase the medicines and other supplies that they need to do their job—and often living on salaries approaching poverty levels—take informal payments in exchange for preferential treatment. Expanding private sector involvement in providing medical services

---

Box 4.1 Non-governmental financing for public schools

In Ukraine education used to be provided exclusively by the state, but now private schools are permitted. Under the fiscal pressure the government has realized that education should involve a partnership among the government, parents, and communities.

Such a partnership in Ukraine is developing in the form of school boards that raise financial support from parents and sometimes from the communities. For example in Kiev, a secondary school was established in 1991 as an experimental school-laboratory of the Pedagogical University. In early 1992 parents in each class held the meetings and decided to establish a school fund managed by a School Board, which each year decides on the size of levies per child.

Originally the amount of the contribution was equal to the price of the bottle of vodka. Using this symbolic amount of money parents, have demonstrated their willingness to pay for the high quality education of their kids rather than spending this money on alcohol. The revenues of the fund also include donations from physical and legal entities and fees for additional courses. The levy per student now averages 5 UAH per month.

The funds raised are mainly used for renovating the building, paying for communal services, and providing bonuses for the best teachers and pupils. With the additional funds mobilized through private contributions the school is now able to provide classes in computer science, three foreign languages, and early education services.

Source: Bank staff interview

would provide a legitimate outlet for this obvious demand and willingness to pay for better services. At the same time, this would reduce the burden on the public health services, allowing them to focus their scarce resources on supporting those who cannot afford to pay for private services. Other reforms as outlined below would simultaneously improve the financial strength of the public sector health-care providers.

Figure 4.1 Relative public spending on education and health have been fairly stable

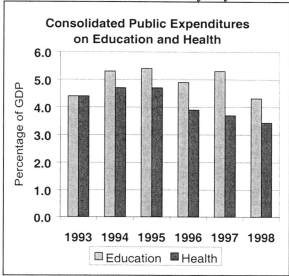

Consolidated Public Expenditures on Education and Health

Source: Ministry of Finance.

Shadow economic activity appears to be less of a problem in the education sector. Informal payments are regularly made by parents for extra services such as better supplies, special classes, and access to computer training, but in most cases, because of the transparency and direct accountability of the relationship between teachers and parents, these payments are not a source of personal enrichment but simply a payment for services that cannot be supplied by the government. Such payments are normal in every country and should not be sent through the formal budgetary process. The payments are small and putting them through the budget would be inefficient, destroying the direct link between payments and services that keeps this relationship transparent and voluntary. The only substantial problem in terms of corruption and shadow activity in education that this study has identified is informal payments to school

authorities to get preferential treatment for the admission of students into select schools and occasionally to assure certification of those who would otherwise fail.

Adjusting the approach to education

Ukraine has a remarkably well-developed education system. But the system also places a heavy burden on the budget, and in several areas the curriculum has not kept pace with the needs of the emerging market economy.

Accomplishments Ukrainians are well educated. Adult literacy is about 98 percent, and gross enrollment ratios compare favorably with those in upper-middle-income and high-income countries (table 4.1). In 1997 total enrollment was nearly 9.2 million, or 18 percent of the population—a ratio that has remained unchanged since 1990.

Issues. Ukraine's pattern of education is still influenced by the Soviet past, both in terms of curriculum and physical structures. Soviet education sought to prepare people for specific, lifelong roles in the economy rather than to develop individuals' talents or prepare them to adapt to changes in the economic environment. Soviet education placed strong emphasis on training scientists, engineers, and other technical specialists, and the teaching methods stressed memorization of facts rather than methods of analyzing and solving problems. As a result

Table 4.1 Gross enrollment ratios in Ukraine and other countries by income, 1990-93

	Primary	*Secondary*	*Tertiary*
Ukraine	**86**	**88**	**46**
Low income	76	28	6
Lower middle income	101	55	21
Upper middle income	98	76	17
High income OECD	102	98	42

Source: Ministry of Education.

Ukraine has a shortage of specialists in business management, economics, international relations, the social sciences, and the humanities. In 1992, 60 percent of certificates and degrees awarded by higher-education institutions were for the study of engineering. Only 6 percent were for management or economics. As a result Ukraine has a serious shortage of well-trained policy analysts who can guide the country into a market-based future. At the same time, skilled engineers are having trouble finding work.

The physical inefficiency of the education sector is also imbedded in the inherited system. School buildings are not energy efficient, imposing high energy costs on school budgets (box 4.2). The low density of building usage leads to high maintenance costs. Teaching staff and education institutions are fragmented because of the specialization inherited from the Soviet system.

Financing. As a share of GDP, government spending on education has been steady or even rising since independence (figure 4.1). But in terms of real expenditures, funding has dropped dramatically in line with GDP (figure 4.2). Today the largest blocks of government spending arrears are in the education and health sectors. These arrears are concentrated at subnational levels of government, which are responsible for all but some technical education through the secondary level.

As noted, arrears in payments for the energy consumed by schools and universities are a serious problem. These cannot be allowed to continue growing without even more serious effects on educators and their families and on the financial viability of energy companies. Yet the budget resources allocated to education cannot be increased without worsening the budget deficit or creating problems elsewhere in the economy. The only viable solution is to introduce structural reforms in education that sharply increase the sector's efficiency.

Preschool education. Since 1991 preschool institutions have absorbed about 16 percent of the education budget. But the number of kindergartners has dropped 43 percent since 1992, while the cost per student has fallen by just 26 percent (table 4.2). As a result the ratio of students to teachers fell from 11:1 in 1985 in 6:1 in 1997. In 1997 only 36 percent of the relevant age group was enrolled in preschool; rates were far lower in rural areas (19 percent) than in cities (43 percent).

Only part of the dramatic decline in preschool enrollments can be explained by falling birth rates. The rest appears to be linked to Ukraine's economic collapse. A large share of preschool education was provided by factories, and factory failures together with the withdrawal of women from the labor force appear to account for a major share of the decline in preschool enrollments. In 1997 the cost per student in kindergartens was higher then in vocational and higher education—an extraordinary relationship by international standards. Given the high lifetime returns to preschool education, care should be exercised in making major cuts in this area. Still, some adjustments would be justified.

Figure 4.2 Health and education spending have fallen faster than GDP

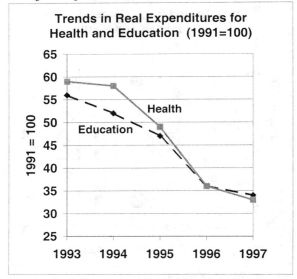

Source: Golladay and others 1998, p. 9.

Parents finance only 15-20 percent of preschool education costs, and many parents are exempted from this payment by various privileges. Requiring parents to cover more costs, together with the following additional measures, could rationalize preschool spending, increasing economic efficiency and sustainability:

- Increasing the ratio of students to teachers.

- Establishing a standard for per child costs that includes only spending on teachers' salaries and site maintenance, then allocating central financing according to this norm. All other expenses should be covered by parents or communities.

- Leasing preschool space that is not needed or used effectively.

Box 4.2 Local budget financing of schools

The financing provided by local authorities is barely sufficient to cover teachers' salaries, leaving almost nothing to cover the remaining costs of education. With sharply higher prices for heating, many schools face a crisis situation. This problem is highlighted by the financing of a secondary school in Kiev.

With help from donors, the school installed a new, more efficient heating system that reduced the cost of heating by about 25%. Even so, budget resources fell about 60% short of needs. Contributions from parents in the form of fees for special classes, books, and other materials helped cover the shortfall. By leasing part of the building, the school managed to cover all expenditures on electricity and water supply. Nevertheless, the school accumulated arrears on heating costs amounting to nearly 40% of revenues.

School budget for 1999, thousands UAH

Consumption	**729**
Goods and services	717
Wages, salaries, benefits	408
Materials and office supplies, repairs and maintenance	93
Communal services	217
Heating	208
Water supply	4
Electricity	5
Others	12
Revenues	**526**
Local budget financing	433
Parents financing and leasing space in building	93
Balance	**-204**
Arrears on heating	204

Increased heating costs due to the higher price of energy compared to Soviet days have raised total school costs by over 30 percent. This increase is equal to about 90 percent of the deficit.

In short, school financing has not kept up with the rising cost of energy, and even with energy saving measures in place, the schools do not have enough resources to cover costs. More will have to be done on the one hand to increase efficiency—through better use of building space, energy and staff, and on the other, to provide more adequate funding. The latter will require measures to bring the shadow economy into the tax net and to reduce lower priority expenditures.

Source: Bank staff interview with school.

- Encouraging private preschools.

- Transferring responsibility for preschool education to local budgets and giving localities the taxation and user charge rights needed to raise the required revenues.

- Using proceeds from the divestiture and privatization of social assets to help cover costs.

General primary and secondary education. During 1991-97 financing for general primary and secondary schools averaged about 65 percent of the education budget.[3] In 1997 secondary schools contained 7.1 million students and 571,000 teachers. Between 1985 and 1997 the ratio of students to teachers dropped from 14:1 to 12:1—low by international standards.

High staffing levels are caused by the perception that employing large numbers of teachers ensures better education. But three additional factors play major roles. First, many rural schools are very small—enrolling, on average, just 30 students per age cohort. Urban schools, by contrast, have about 100 children per age cohort. Second, highly specialized teachers are often employed only part time. Teachers in grades 5-11 are required to have been trained in the subjects that they teach, and while many have been trained in two related subjects, some are prepared to teach only one. Thus teachers of specialized subjects often cannot be employed full time, even in large urban schools. Finally, specialized classes at the upper secondary level have small enrollments. This problem is especially pronounced in schools that allow students to specialize in the sciences, arts, business, or agriculture.

The financial savings from reducing high staffing intensity are smaller than might be expected, however, because Ukrainian teachers' salaries are quite low—averaging 121 hrivnyas a month (about $60) during the first quarter of

---

[3] In Ukraine, the term "secondary" generally applies to what would be known in the US as primary and secondary. Thus, when the term "secondary" is used in this chapter, it should be taken to apply to all education from grades 1-11 (ages 6 to 17).

1997, or 55 percent of average GDP per capita. In 1996 teacher salaries and payroll taxes accounted for just 54 percent of the budget for basic education—compared with 60-70 percent in Western education systems. And even if the average ratio of students to teachers were increased, it is unlikely that the additional workload could be imposed without providing additional compensation to teachers. In addition, increasing workloads would often require that teachers receive additional training. This cost, along with the cost of increased unemployment support for out-of-work teachers, would have to be included in any assessment of the net benefits of increasing class size. Finally, secondary schools have a number of other pressing (and pricey) concerns—including a dire shortage of textbooks and computers (Vitrenko and Lukovenko, p. 7).

Table 4.2 Preschool education, 1992-97

Indicator	1992	1995	1996	1997
Number of children (thousands)	2,063	1,536	1,342	1,171
Share of total students (percent)	18	14	13	11
Cost per student (1997 hrivnya per year)	863	646	501	636

Source: Ministry of Education.

Article 53 of the Ukrainian Constitution speaks of free access to a complete general secondary education. But careful legal analysis seems to indicate that this is a general social objective, not a specifically guaranteed right that everything associated with secondary education will be free. Though most parents want all services provided by public schools to be free of charge, parents end up paying sizable fees for extracurricular tutorials and voluntary and forced assistance. Money also comes from corporate and other sponsors. Total non-budget financing—whether private, shadow, or unofficial—totals 500 million hrivnyas, or about one-quarter of budget allocations to education. More private support for both public and private secondary education, a widespread practice in most modern economies, could greatly improve both the quality and the fiscal sustainability of Ukraine's education system.

There are no quick fixes for the poor financial position of Ukraine's education system. The three major areas of potential savings—staff reduction, school consolidation, and energy conservation—will require short-term expenditures to realize long-term gains. The following measures would help rationalize spending on secondary education:

- Raise the ratio of students to teachers.

- Lower heating and lighting costs through new engineering designs and construction standards for schools.

- Remodel interiors to improve space use, reducing the operating cost of buildings.

- Consolidate rural schools and small urban schools, lowering administrative costs.

- Involve communities, through parent-teacher associations, to help schools and teachers compensate for the limited resources of regional and central governments. Such organizations, which can respond quickly to problems, are widespread in Western schools.

- Sell or rent textbooks rather than providing them free of charge.

Attention should also be given to raising and revising teacher salaries, to retaining highly qualified teachers, and to funding schools based on line-item allocations for specific inputs such as salaries, books, and overhead. The exact mix of expenditures can then be optimized to maximize efficiency in line with local realities.

Vocational education. During Soviet times vocational and technical schools were established to meet enterprises' demands for skilled technicians, and graduates were automatically employed. Today many enterprises are being forced to cut costs and retrench staff—reducing the demand for vocational school graduates. Moreover, studies in a number of countries show that general education yields higher rates of return than vocational education. Strong cognitive skills developed in grades 9-11 improve the on-the-job trainability of students, whereas narrow vocational training does not. Vocational education should be reconfigured to the needs of market-oriented enterprises, and vocational and technical programs that have seen enrollments fall should be phased out.

Higher education. Ukraine spends more money on higher education—18 percent of the national education budget in 1997—than on any level other than secondary education. During 1990-97 the number of university students remained roughly unchanged, while the number of tutors and professors grew by 10 percent. Between 1985 and 1997 the number of higher education institutions grew by 6 percent, mainly because of private sector development.

Higher education is expensive in all countries. But even if part of the cost is borne directly by students, every possibility for lowering costs should be explored. Several areas need to be examined in Ukraine for possible savings. First, are there too many separate institutions? Second, are the schools operated efficiently? Third, are curriculums aligned with the needs of a market economy? Fourth, are too many Ukrainians enrolled in higher education? Higher education is clearly desirable. But if it means less money for other critical social needs tradeoffs will have to be made.

Regarding consolidation, higher education institutions should probably be cut to no more than three to five universities and five to eight colleges in every regional center (Vitrenko and Lukovenko 1998, p. 10). The number of higher education institutions in the regions today is extremely high and cannot be economically justified.

As to cost recovery, higher education institutions have started to charge tuition fees—which in 1997 were equal to 20 percent of budget expenditures on higher education. Additional efforts for strengthening higher education could include further promoting cost recovery (and limiting state subventions), establishing student loans, expanding merit scholarships to top students who show a financial need, and encouraging private provision, which tends to be more responsive to changing skill requirements in the labor market. Taking into account the development of private higher institutions in 1998 the government has

established the accreditation system for private entities to ensure quality educational programs.

The role of private resources. The government should not attempt to provide the entire range of education services from its budget. Rather, it should ensure more equitable access through subsidies, insurance schemes, voucher systems, and tax credits that make secondary education affordable to all and higher education affordable to a reasonable number, with merit scholarships for outstanding students from poor families. The public sector can partner with the private sector through one of several schemes:

Public funding for private schools. In the Netherlands two-thirds of students attend publicly funded private schools. Experience has shown that where the private sector works side by side with the public sector, the private sector is usually more efficient and effective.

Public schools, private management. In Bolivia the partnership between the government and a religious non-governmental organization has been so successful that the government is studying it as a possible model for education reform.

Providing students with a choice. In the United States vouchers have been proposed as a solution to weak schools. Students would be given vouchers, funded by public tax dollars but redeemable in private or public schools. Schools would then have to compete for students.

Excessive state support for private schools, however, will encourage children from affluent families to attend elite private schools, leaving public schools to children from underprivileged homes. The mix of backgrounds that prevails in public schools has considerable social benefits, promoting a broader sense of society. Thus Ukrainian policymakers will have to strike the appropriate balance, which may well consist of supporting private education without providing direct public financing for it.

Reviving health care

Ukrainians have excellent access to a publicly funded, Soviet-style health care system. Primary care is provided through a dense network of modest hospitals and simple primary care facilities. In rural areas a rudimentary network of first-aid stations provides first-line care. But except for headaches, indigestion, minor abrasions, insect bites, and the like, the paramedics stationed at these facilities must refer patients to district or oblast hospitals for care. In urban areas polyclinics, staffed with physicians and often attached to a hospital, provide outpatient services. In 1996 there were about 29,200 primary health care facilities—one for every 1,800 people.[4]

Secondary and tertiary care is offered by referral hospitals and research institutes. There were 1,035 hospitals in 1996, equipped with 528,000 inpatient beds—one for every 96 persons. But many of these facilities are not well equipped, and most are poorly supplied with diagnostic materials, drugs, and dressings. As a result, staff time and inpatient care are often substituted for material inputs. Diagnoses could usually be made quickly on an outpatient basis if better laboratory and imaging facilities were available. Moreover, conservative treatment plans are adopted, with patients kept in hospitals for long periods to allow doctors to monitor recovery. As a result the average hospital stay is nearly 17 days—roughly twice as long as in the West.

The health care system is in crisis. As noted in chapter 1, the overall health of Ukrainians is deteriorating. The death rate is climbing. Birth rates are falling. Life expectancy has dropped sharply. And the incidence of preventable communicable diseases—including tuberculosis—is rising rapidly. This deterioration has set in despite the fact that the system spends far more than it receives. Unable to pay its bills, the system has trouble heating its buildings, keeping the lights turned on, retaining its highly trained staff, purchasing modern equipment for diagnosis and treatment, and providing patients with the medicines and even the food that they need to live.

The share of GDP allocated to health care has been fairly steady, at close to 4 percent (figure 4.1 above). Still, the collapse in economic output since independence has sharply reduced available resources to the sector, a decline only partially offset by the substantial inflows of humanitarian aid. However, increasing spending on health care in the absence of restored economic growth would almost certainly worsen the government deficit—further exacerbating economic decline and lowering living standards.

Thus the main challenge for the health care sector is to improve quality while cutting costs. This will require major efforts to increase the efficiency of health care operations, focus on preventative rather than curative services, move from the Soviet specialist system toward a more generalist approach, establish a better expenditure balance between staff, facilities, and supplies, and increase private funding for health care (figure 4.3).

Physical efficiency. The health care system suffers from many of the Soviet-era problems afflicting the education sector—including buildings that are neither space- nor energy-efficient, an excessive number of specialized institutions, and general excess capacity.

The number of hospital beds per 1,000 people is very high by Western standards. In 1996 there were 580,400 hospital beds in operation—about 12 beds for every 1,000 people. International best practice is to have 2 beds per 1,000 people. In 1996 Denmark, Ireland, Mexico, Portugal, Spain, the United Kingdom, and the United States had fewer than 5 beds per 1,000 people (OECD data).

Enormous resources are wasted, particularly given the low average occupancy rate for the beds by patients who actually need to be in hospitals. Changes in diagnostic and treatment facilities and techniques could sharply reduce the need for hospitalization and the average hospital stay. The inefficient use of beds is particularly costly given that hospitals are expensive to heat because of large amounts of wasted space, the low energy efficiency of the buildings, and the cold Ukrainian climate.

---

[4] This section on health draws heavily on work done for the CEM by Ukrainian and World Bank researchers. The notes prepared include Yuriy Vitrenko and Antonina Nagorna (1998). *Health System.* Kyiv: ICPS and World Bank; Frederick Golladay et. al. (1998). *Review of Public Expenditures on Health and Education in Ukraine.* Washington: World Bank.; and Katerina Petrina. (1998). *Ukraine: Financing education during economic transition.* Kyiv: World Bank, processed.

About one-third of all bed-days of care provided by Ukrainian hospitals are used by persons who do not have a medical problem. These "social" patients include the homeless, elderly, orphaned, and indigent. As a result of the large number of social admissions, the occupancy rate for hospital beds is highly seasonal, with fewer than a third of beds occupied during the warm summer months and most hospitals being full during the coldest months of winter. The social cases do not place a significant burden on the medical staff, but they account for a large portion of the costs of food, linens, and housekeeping.

Figure 4.3 The financing gap in Ukrainian healthcare results from the small private contribution

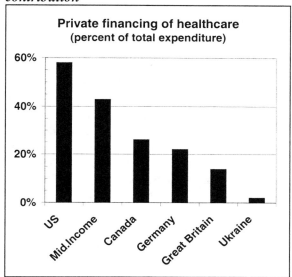

Source: Vitrenko and Nagorna (1998), p. 8, and World Development Indicators, World Bank.

Efforts are being made to reduce the ratio to 8 beds per 1,000 people by 2000. To meet that target, more than 200,000 beds will have to be closed. But even then, Ukraine will still have twice as many beds per 1,000 people as the wealthiest industrial countries. Moreover, the closure of beds will not result in significant savings because the design of buildings generally does not allow administrators to close wards in order to reduce heating and maintenance costs. Mechanical systems—heating, and plumbing—are not zoned or separately regulated, so closing a unit may not affect operating costs.

Preventative and curative care. Preventable sources of sickness and death have become a critical problem largely because the Soviet-era public health system focused not on preventing disease and death, but on delivering specialized, expensive curative care. The incidence of most illnesses could be reduced markedly through a good public health program that emphasized healthier lifestyles, more extensive inoculation campaigns, and better water and sanitation facilities.

Controlling communicable diseases is a public responsibility because the spread of disease cannot be controlled by individuals or even neighborhoods acting alone—control requires collective effort. The breakdown of public health programs since the collapse of the Soviet Union—particularly immunizations and sanitary inspections—has increased the incidence of preventable and communicable diseases. In addition, the social disruption that has accompanied the economic collapse has contributed to a growth in violence and in antisocial behavior, making violent death a leading factor in mortality. The spread of intravenous drug use and the explosive growth of a commercial sex industry have contributed to a serious increase in sexually transmitted diseases, including AIDS. Drug use and prostitution are poorly documented in all countries, and the relatively recent emergence of these problems in Ukraine has meant that programs for monitoring and controlling them are not well developed. For these reasons, experts believe that drug abuse and sexually transmitted diseases are much larger problems than official statistics suggest. Dramatic actions should be taken now to combat the spread of AIDS in Ukraine. AIDS is particularly dangerous because it spreads rapidly and quietly. Experience in Africa and elsewhere demonstrates that a major share of the population can become infected with HIV without visible symptoms, then begin developing full-blown AIDS before the authorities fully realize what is happening or are prepared to handle the crisis. Experience from countries seriously afflicted by AIDS indicates numerous negative impacts on economic performance including (a) sharp falls in average labor productivity, (b) large percentage increases in health outlays both private and public resulting in lower domestic savings and aggravated fiscal deficits, and (c) lower investment in both physical and human capital because of the other effects and a consequent decline in actual and potential growth rates. Investing now to prevent these serious economic problems later would bring a very high rate of return. If necessary, funds should be borrowed from the World Bank or other comparable sources to combat the disease now while the cost would still be relatively modest, thus avoiding an economic and social cataclysm later that could seriously derail economic progress.

Preventing sickness is much cheaper than treating it. Switching approaches would involve retraining medical staff and launching public inoculation and information campaigns. Though such efforts have costs, the move to a more preventative approach should start immediately. Besides being more cost-effective, everyone finds it much more pleasant to be well than to get well.

Specialist and generalist care. As with education, the Soviet approach to medicine emphasized a specialist approach, both in medical staff and in medical institutions. In Western countries the family doctor or general practitioner is the cornerstone of the health care delivery system. Priority is given to public health care in the form of "First Medical-Sanitary Aid" because it is the most economic way to meet most of the health needs of the largest share of the population. In Ukraine, however, the medical system has become highly overspecialized. For example, barely more than 10 percent of the doctors treating adults in urban areas are generalists, but they have to handle about 40 percent of initial patient referrals and care. World experience shows that family doctors can provide full medical help to 70-90 percent of the patients. Ukrainian authorities have estimated that the share of general practitioners in the health protection budget should be increased to about 40 percent (Vitrenko and Nagorna 1998).

Overspecialization is also a problem in medical education. Curriculums tend to slot individuals into narrow specialties, and institutions tend to focus on specializations—contributing to the high cost of the Ukrainian health care system. Given the deep institutional roots of the current structure, several years of institutional reform and re-education will be required to create a more efficient structure. Thus immediate cost savings will be difficult to generate in this area.

Staffing levels, facilities, and supplies. A key reason for declining health care in Ukraine is that financial resources, already in short supply, are not allocated to the highest priority uses. Since 1992 the share of budget resources going to staff has risen from less than 50 percent to more then 60 percent, reflecting the system's tendency to retain staff at the cost of other crucial inputs—even though the number of medical personnel per 1,000 people is already quite high by international standards.

Expenses for building maintenance, especially for energy costs, also absorb a large share of the budget. Energy alone eats up 20-30 percent of the budget of the typical urban hospital, a sharp increase from the situation in 1990 when energy was heavily subsidized. Partly as a result of increased heating costs, the hospitals and clinics cannot buy the modern diagnostic and treatment equipment needed to improve the quality of medical care and to reduce its costs. Modern equipment and techniques—such as imaging equipment and micro-surgery—is far less invasive than traditional diagnostic and treatment techniques, thus saving money by reducing the length of hospital stays. And with modern equipment, many operative procedures can be done on an outpatient basis. Less invasive techniques also result in less pain and faster recovery.

An externally financed investment project is needed that would allow Ukraine to invest in the equipment and training required for modern techniques. Over the long term the project would be self-financing through savings on energy and on shorter hospital stays.

Staffing levels and patterns. Ukraine has 4.5 doctors per 1,000 people—compared with 2.0 in Germany, 1.6 in Sweden, and 1.3 in Poland. Ukrainian authorities claim that these ratios should not be compared directly with Western ratios because Ukraine uses a more inclusive definition of "doctor," including administrative personnel who have been trained as physicians but who do not actually work with patients. But a similar problem emerges in assistant-level staffing in the health care system. In 1996 the Ukrainian health care system employed about 583,000 trained assistants (nurses, laboratory technicians, medical assistants, and so on). This implies 95 patients per assistant in Ukraine, compared with 715 in the United Kingdom and 435 in the United States. Thus the number of physicians and assistants is much higher than would be needed in an efficient, well-equipped health care system.

The high ratios of doctors and health care assistants to patients served reflects the Soviet approach to medical education and health care delivery. Low retirement age and the possibility of receiving both pension benefits and wages encourage doctors who have achieved retirement age to continue working. Even the Soviet government did not pay pension benefits to working pensioners in health and education; given the current fiscal crisis, Ukraine is excessively generous to pay both. Pension policies may therefore be another major reason the ratios of doctors and of health care assistants to patients has increased since independence and is now high by international standards. This may also help explain why graduates of medical universities have trouble finding jobs.

Public and private financing. Government spending on health care in Ukraine is slightly larger as a share of GDP than in the average middle-income country (figure 4.4). From this we can conclude that the health care crisis is not the result of a lack of effort on the part of the government to finance the sector. In fact, a slight reduction might even be possible relative to GDP.

On the other hand, total expenditures on health as a share of GDP are significantly lower than in comparable countries. This reflects the heavy dependence in Ukraine on state-provided medical care and thus the sharply lower contribution of individuals to their health care needs. Only 2 percent of health care expenditures are covered by individuals, compared with much higher levels in the average middle-income country (see figure 4.4). If Ukrainians want better health care along the

lines available in other countries, they will have to pay more out of their own pockets.

Figure 4.4 Ukraine lags comparator countries in total health expenditures despite strong public contributions

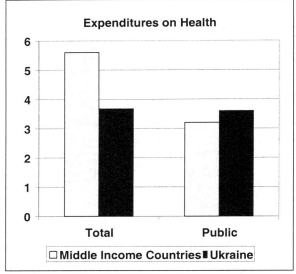

Source: World Bank 1998; government data; World Bank staff estimates.

Although there is a strong resistance in Ukraine to formally asking people to pay a larger share of their health care costs directly, a clear willingness and ability to pay exists in Ukraine. Individuals are spending substantial sums on medical insurance in private companies, informal payments in health care system, purchases of prescribed drugs and the like.

The concept of free medical care is embedded in Article 49 of Constitution. This does not mean that the Constitution guarantees the maintenance of all existing medical institutions. It rather obliges the state to maintain adequate networks at a standard not worse that now. The structural reforms of the existing medical networks that could bring more efficiency in health care will be in compliance with the Constitution. The Constitution also does not ban private networks for medical care or cost recovery for services rendered. To the contrary, it encourages the state to develop networks of different kinds of ownership (Art.49, para.3 of the Constitution). The Constitution also expressively envisages introduction of medical insurance.

Medical services always have cost, and in the end, the people of Ukraine have to pay—either directly or through their taxes. The main question is the balance between private and tax-based state financing and the impact that this balance has on the efficiency with which health care services are delivered. World experience indicates that, if people have to pay at least a significant part of their medical costs directly, they will take a greater personal interest in the cost-effectiveness of the services received, thus increasing the efficiency of the healthcare system. Also, when people have to share in the cost of medical service, they take better care of themselves, and they avoid bothering doctors with minor ailments that could be cured with nonprescription medicine and other remedies. The reduced burden on clinics and hospitals would make it possible for these institutions to spend the resources saved on better facilities, equipment, and supplies for those who actually need help.

In addition to easing the burden on the budget and increasing the quantity and quality of medical services, a greater role for paid medical services in Ukraine would lead to greater efficiency. When people have to share in the cost of medical service, they take better care of themselves, and they avoid bothering doctors with minor ailments that could be cured with nonprescription medicine and other remedies. The reduced burden on clinics and hospitals would make it possible for these institutions to spend the resources saved on better facilities, equipment, and supplies for those who actually need help.

To improve its health care system by increasing access to paid medical services, Ukraine should:

- Introduce a nominal fee for each visit to a doctor, clinic, or hospital.

- Place a cap on the value of medical services that any family can receive in a given year without payment.

- Introduce a national health insurance system that would allow individuals to pool risks and help pay for future medical costs that exceed the annual cap through low, stable monthly payments.

- Introduce a safety-net scheme that would assure that no Ukrainian would ever be denied necessary medical treatment for lack of income.

- Reduce barriers to the establishment of private medical practices.

The human environment—water, sanitation, and housing

Access to safe water, sanitation, and adequate shelter often prevents families from sliding into absolute poverty even though incomes are low. The government has a role to play in providing water and sanitation, especially in developing countries such as Ukraine, because of the externalities involved. Modest investments in providing access to clear drinking water and sanitation improve the health and thus the quality of life for the individuals directly affected. Such access can also prevent the spread of communicable diseases, preventing major economic losses for society as a whole. Major investments are needed to increase the quality, accessibility, and efficiency of Ukraine's water and sanitation.

Water and Sanitation Background. Ukraine's slow transition to a market economy has hurt municipal water and wastewater services. Artificially low tariffs, poor payments collection, and limited financial support from the national government have left negligible funds for maintenance and investment, placing many water and wastewater systems in danger of physical failure. Inadequate water treatment has brought an increase in water-related diseases. The population has become increasingly dissatisfied with the quality of services and is worried about the safety of the water supply. If the country's water and wastewater infrastructure is allowed to continue deteriorating, the quality of life for many Ukrainians will decline further.

The old Soviet command and control system together with the current subsidy policies create severe disincentives and distortions that make the sector inefficient: (a) poorly managed water companies lack incentives and tools to turn themselves into more efficient institutions; (b) water and wastewater systems are poorly constructed and maintained, many of them now on the brink of collapse and hampered poor plant performance, excessive water consumption, large network losses and high energy consumption; and (c) investment policies are poorly focused, emphasizing new capacity at the expense of potentially more cost effective investments in system rehabilitation and efficiency enhancements. The financial problems and inability to raise resources are exacerbated by falling household incomes, which limits the capacity of many to pay significantly higher water and wastewater tariffs.

Agenda for policy change. The Government's response to these problems has evolved slowly. Some reform principles have been endorsed, but implementation is limited especially at the local level. Water companies continue to be poorly managed institutions desperate for cash, neglecting maintenance and unable to undertake urgent rehabilitation of plants and networks.

The prime objective of reforms today is to strengthen these companies so that they can improve accessibility and quality of the water supply and wastewater services at affordable levels, thus restoring public confidence. For this, water companies must become independent, well managed and financially viable utilities. Efforts have been made to turn water companies into autonomous and well-managed water utilities by turning them into private joint stock companies, but political and legal obstacles—such as the restriction that municipal governments cannot own stocks—have prevented this approach from moving forward. Government is now developing legislation to allow the privatization and concession of water utilities.

Investing in the future. Future reforms in the water supply sector should include the following key elements: (a) promoting private sector activity (b) transforming present water companies into independent "corporatized" utilities regulated by local governments; (c) gradually turning water companies into financially self-sufficient institutions through tariff reform and better revenue collection; (d) introducing least-cost strategies for selecting investments that give preference to plant and network rehabilitation and efficiency enhancements; (e) bringing in the consumer as a participating party in water company decision making and assuring social sustainability of the transition; (f) restructuring remaining public sector operations; and (g) ensuring environmental sustainability.

Successfully implementing a strategy along these lines would have a highly positive impact on the quality and reliability of water supply and sanitation services throughout Ukraine, thus reducing physical poverty even when monetary incomes are still low.

*Housing. Background. Be*cause the Soviet housing system was not able to provide adequate housing for the population, the average Ukrainian today in urban areas has about 18 sq. m. of housing space about one third the average in Western European countries. Furthermore, factory-based standardization lead to a limited choice in housing design. Despite the shortage of housing space, homelessness is still a relatively rare problem in Ukraine, partly because of a housing subsidy program that protects the very poor, and partly because beds in medical facilities are commonly used during cold weather to provide shelter.

In the Soviet era, energy efficiency was not an important design consideration because of low energy prices. Consequently, buildings were constructed with poorly insulated exterior walls and roofs, exposed metal joints, and leaky windows. The existing housing stock is largely old and in poor condition, requiring extensive deferred maintenance, capital improvement, and in some cases, demolition and replacement. The economic recession since independence has reduced the government funds allocated to housing construction, and most municipal, state enterprise and cooperative housing construction has stopped. The shortage of funds and poor collection of payments have increased maintenance problems of the existing housing stock.

Housing privatization was one of the early priority areas for Government, which sought through policy changes to develop a private housing market and to gradually eliminate government controls other than those required for public safety. The *Law on the Privatization of the State Owned Housing in Ukraine* became operational in early 1993. The housing sector in Ukraine since then has been going through a gradual process of transformation as government control of the sector decreases and a market-based housing system slowly begins to emerge.

Today over 50 percent of all apartments targeted for privatization have been privatized. This process has resulted in state-owned and private apartments co-existing in the same buildings, creating problems for the maintenance of building shells, mechanical systems, and common spaces. Municipal housing maintenance companies commonly continue to be responsible for the management and maintenance of the buildings.

Policy reforms in housing. Since 1994, the Government's program of economic reforms has a direct impact on the housing sector, especially through the phase-out of subsidies for housing, heating, hot water, drinking water, sewerage, and gas. While representing a major accomplishment, this process is far from complete. Current cost recovery levels for residential services only average about 60 percent today, compared to the 80 percent set as a target in 1997. Prospects deteriorated further in 1998 for attaining reasonable levels of cost recovery when Parliament passed a law on July 23, 1998 banning increases in tariffs for domestic utility services. The battle over communal tariff rates continued at time of writing,[5] and few expect to see significant

progress until after the Presidential election in late 1999.

Agenda for action. The government needs to take action in the following areas to strengthen the financial sustainability and raise the quality of housing in Ukraine:

- improve availability of financing for households for home purchases and for developers for housing construction;

- encourage local governments to release land in the urban areas for private real estate development to enterprises and other groups interested in utilizing specific sites;

- replace current burdensome local government land and building regulations, which act as a disincentive to real estate development, with a modern, development-friendly set of regulations consistent with international best practices; and

- implement cost recovery measures to improve the financial viability of housing remaining in the public sector and of the public utility (communal) services provided to the housing sector by the public sector.

Rapid implementation of reforms along these lines would not only contribute directly to improved living environments for the people of Ukraine, but would also stimulate jobs and economic growth. Because housing is labor intensive and depends primarily on locally-produced materials, it can be an excellent tool for employment generation and for stimulating domestic economic activity. With the World Bank and USAID assistance, reform-oriented city administrations have accelerated the privatization process, have created private housing maintenance utility companies, and have worked to strengthen related communal services, thus helping create the conditions needed for a strong housing sector in Ukraine.

If the government simply establishes an appropriate legal environment and makes public land and housing available for sale to private developers, the private sector can mobilize the investments needed to improve the housing

---

[5] The President twice vetoed Parliaments law of July 1998, but Parliament twice over-rode the veto, a measure that endangered lending from the IMF and the World Bank. In late 1998, the Constitutional Court began to review an appeal by the President's administration that Parliament did not have the constitutional right to pass such a law, which infringes on the domain of the executive branch and directly imperils the integrity of the national budget. The Court decided at the beginning of 1999 that the Parliament decision to ban the tariff increase was not legitimate. According to the decision of the President in May 1999, all oblast administrations declared the increase of local communal tariffs to 100% of the cost of services with different terms of effectiveness mainly during May – June 99. But in June 1999 the Parliament has decided again to ban the tariff increase and the case is forwarded again by the President to the Court.

stock and to provide new housing at prices accessible to all but the very poor. For these people, the government does have a special role to play—providing subsidies that allow the very poor to have minimum shelter while still being able to afford the other necessities such as food and clothing. Ukraine is exceptionally well positioned in this regard, having worked with an external donor to establish a well-run program that provides support to families so that they do not have to spend more than 15 percent of their income on housing.

The financial viability of the program could be improved and its burden reduced if those with incomes at the higher end of the range of those eligible were to pay 25 percent instead of 15 percent of their income. The efficiency of the other social safety net programs described in the next section could also be improved if they were combined with the means-tested housing program.

THE SOCIAL SAFETY NET

Politicians and government officials often argue that a slow pace of reform in Ukraine is needed to preserve social peace. The Ukrainian authorities are not alone—countries around the world share this concern when faced with making profound changes in economic and social structures. A good social safety net is thus vital to the success—and even the feasibility—of reforms. Ukraine has a social safety net, but spending in real terms on social protection has dropped even more dramatically than overall budget expenditures since 1993, a period when more, not less, social protection was needed (figure 4.5). More importantly, the system leaves important segments of the population in poverty while supporting some who are not impoverished. The current approach, which depends on a system of unemployment insurance, is fragile and likely to fail in the face of the substantially higher unemployment that is likely to come with the enterprise reform effort needed to restore efficiency and growth.

Protecting the sick, the elderly, and the unemployed

Sickness and old-age are insurable risks. Everyone is likely to suffer these debilities at some point in their lives. These risks are statistically predictable, and the common way to protect individuals is to share the risk though insurance. Everyone, young and old, contributes to the insurance fund for health and old age in sickness and in health. When sickness strikes or old age arrives, those who suffer can draw resources from the fund to cover the cost of sickness and the loss of income that comes with old age.

Ukrainians need to examine the following questions when considering ways to improve the effectiveness and financial sustainability of health care and pension systems:

- Who pays for the insurance against sickness and old age?

- How do they pay?

- How much do they need to pay?

- How can these costs be minimized?

- How can the services provided under these programs be improved without increasing costs?

Health insurance. As noted, Ukrainians pay a small share of the cost of the medical services that they use. The dramatic declines in personal incomes resulting from the economic collapse make it difficult to implement major changes in this area immediately. A few simple steps, however, would greatly facilitate the transition to a good health insurance program.

First, Ukraine already has a health insurance program—one that is fully funded by the government with no direct contributions by patients. As taxpayers, however, patients are already paying the full cost of this health insurance program. Patients need to see a more direct link between what they pay and what they use. A health insurance program could be created by reducing the taxes paid or by asking citizens to pay part of this money into a health insurance fund and the rest directly to health care providers as services are used.

Health care providers, who could be state or private, would recover their costs from two sources—the health insurance program and the citizen. In line with practice elsewhere, roughly 80-90 percent of costs would be covered by the insurance program, with the remainder coming directly from the patient as a copayment. The amount that each household had to contribute to the cost of health care (including both insurance premiums and copayments for services received) could be limited to a maximum percentage of income—much as housing costs are capped. With such a program, users could be "charged" the full cost of services, helping to establish the principle of cost recovery.

At the outset the program could begin with the state funding out of tax revenues a major share of the insurance premium and the citizens paying the rest. This balance could gradually be reversed by lowering payroll and other taxes while raising the share of the premium to be paid directly by citizens.

Mechanisms could be established whereby the health insurance program would be recognized by private physicians, who would be able to recover part of their cost of providing services through the program. This would provide a voucher-type mechanism by which the government could support the development of the private health care system, thus reducing the burden on the government health care system.

Developing a full proposal for a national health care scheme is beyond the scope of this report. But the above points provide an idea of how such a system—which would gradually revolutionize the financing and quality of the Ukrainian medical system—could be introduced with minimal social disruption.

Pensions. Insurance against the loss of income in old age is commonly believed to come largely from the Ukrainian government—and to be hopelessly inadequate. Critics claim that the average monthly pension forces old people to live in poverty. In late 1998, for example, the official poverty line was 73.7 hrivnyas per person, but the average pension was only 54 hrivnyas—less than a third of the average monthly wage. But the situation is both better and worse than the data would indicate.

On the positive side, most Ukrainians insure against loss of income in old age not only with pensions, but also in many other ways—including working for pay after normal retirement age, developing and maintaining family networks that will support them in old age, and growing their own food in family garden plots. Given that the retirement age is 55 for women and 60 for men, most retirees still have at least 5-10 years of useful working years (by international retirement standards)—especially since the average Ukrainian woman who retires at the official age can expect to live for another 22.1 years, and the average man for another 14.3 years. Moreover, early retirement schemes reduce the average retirement age to 54 for women and 58 for men. It is not surprising that about 15 percent of "young" pensioners continue to work after retirement.

On the negative side, the pension system is not financially sustainable and is running up large arrears—2.1 billion hrivnyas as of November 1, 1998. Some pensioners are not even receiving the meager pensions to which they are entitled. Despite numerous attempts to raise additional funds, there is no sign that the buildup of arrears is about to be controlled.

The Ukrainian pension system is based on the pay-as-you-go approach, which means that current payments into the system are used to meet current benefit obligations. Like pay-as-you-go pension systems all over the world, the Ukrainian system is in crisis. In fact, it faces even more severe problems than other countries because of Ukraine's low retirement age, numerous early retirement schemes, and unfavorable demographic situation—the dependency ratio is rising rapidly because birth rates are low and the population is aging rapidly.

Ukraine's pension system lacks some features of an ordinary insurance system because there is practically no link between contributions and benefits. Today's pension benefits are little more than a minimal social safety net. Yet despite very low pensions, the pension system is not sustainable because of massive wage arrears and tax evasion.

The Ukrainian system is highly redistributive to pensioners who have contributed little or nothing and to members of certain groups who are legally eligible for higher pension benefits (civil servants, prosecutors, military officers, war veterans, Chernobyl victims). The Pension Fund has to finance not only old age, disability, survival, service, and social pensions, but other benefits such as military pensions, Chernobyl benefits, and other allowances that, in theory at least, are covered through transfers to the Pension Fund from state and local budgets. Shifting these non insurance payments directly to state and local budgets would allow moving to a real system of pension insurance that offered higher benefits to elderly Ukrainians.

In response to the need for pension reform, a three-tier system has been proposed. The first tier would maintain the pay-as-you-go system as a defined benefit scheme—but it would gradually be downsized and restructured. The second tier, a mandatory defined contribution, fully-funded program, would be financed with gradually increasing payroll contributions. The third tier, which would be voluntary, would offer supplementary protection through tax-advantaged occupational pension and personal saving plans for people who want more income in old age.

Pension reform should proceed in stages, with gradual introduction of a three tier system. The most urgent task is to reform the basic pay-as-you-go tier to make it more financially sustainable, and the government has already made proposals to this end. Political pressures so far have forced it to avoid increasing the retirement age directly. Instead, rules have been changed so that, to be eligible for pensions, 30 years of service will be required for men and 25 years for women by 2000. By 2010 it will be 35 years for both men and women. In place of the current fictitious replacement rate of 55-75 percent of last earnings, which the government can no longer provide, the new proposal establishes a much more realistic replacement rate of 35 percent for the pay-as-you-go tier. After the presidential elections, further efforts should be made to raise the pension age as has been done in other countries, thus helping assure the longer-term financial viability of this important program.

Successful pension reform will require establishing supervision capacity for investment funds, banks, and insurance companies, implementing huge administrative changes in the collection of both first- and second-tier contributions, and developing modern management information and computer systems.

This will take time, and a lot of technical assistance will be needed. Until the institutional reforms needed to assure the integrity of the financial sector are in place, the government should be cautious about introducing a mandatory pension program where private financial institutions play a major role.

Establishing a personified record-keeping system where records are kept by individual worker rather than by enterprise is already under way, and this is a good first step toward a sound system of contribution management. The remaining elements of the future pension system should be introduced gradually to ensure the security of the system while minimizing the transition costs.

Unemployment insurance. Ukraine's employment services are under severe pressure. The budgets of state employment centers are very limited, and the number of unemployed is increasing steadily. Employment tax compliance rate is only about 66 percent—which means that, of the planned revenues of 634 million hrivnyas for 1998, state employment centers expect to collect just 420 million hrivnyas. As a result the centers have had to reduce its active employment programs and divert a major part of revenues to paying unemployment benefits. The average duration of registered unemployment is increasing (averaging 8.5 months per job seeker in 1997), further increasing the costs of benefit payments per unemployed worker.

Unemployment benefits in Ukraine are relatively high: 100 percent of average wages at the last job for the first two months, 75 percent for the next three months, and 50 percent for the next seven months. The average benefit replacement rate began increasing in 1996. At that time the ratio of the average benefit to the average wage was 16 percent; in 1997 it was 25 percent; and in the first half of 1998, it was 27 percent. Despite inflation, the minimum monthly unemployment benefit has been held at 16.6 hrivnyas (less than US$ 5)—a level far below the poverty line (73.7 hrivnyas).

A draft law on compulsory social insurance for the unemployed, which is with the Cabinet of Ministers, is designed to reconfigure unemployment benefits. The new system will require that workers have recorded contributions to the unemployment insurance fund and unemployment benefits will be set as a percentage of the average salary during the last two months of work. But even with the new law, the insurance principle is not fully followed. The draft law also proposes partial unemployment benefits to workers who lose salary due to administrative leave or temporarily reduced working hours. The introduction of temporary benefits responds to the massive unpaid administrative leave in the country today.

Introducing temporary unemployment benefits will almost certainly delay the restructuring of enterprises, and if state employment centers have to pay such expenditures, this will further limit employment programs for those who have already registered as unemployed. In addition, since temporarily unemployed or partially employed workers will still be on enterprise payrolls, the state employment centers will not be able to offer other employment services, including job placement.

In 1999 the financial obligations of the state employment centers will increase significantly, primarily because of the November 1997 amendments (effective January 1999) to the Law on Employment regarding severance pay and unemployment benefits. Under the amended law the state employment centers are obligated to pay two out of the three months of severance payment entitlement. Although this amendment might facilitate retrenchment of excess labor, it will significantly deplete revenues of the employment fund. The government is worried about the consequences of this measure for state budgets and has suggested postponing implementation for one year. Strengthening public employment services and their finances remains a key issue for labor market policies.

The deep restructuring needed in the economy, particularly in the old Soviet-era enterprises, also indicates the need for caution in unemployment insurance schemes. Today there is widespread hidden unemployment in the large-scale enterprises of Ukraine caused by attempts to preserve the status quo through lower wages, unpaid leave, short working weeks and similar schemes. As the unavoidable restructuring of Ukrainian companies moves forward, sharply higher official unemployment rates are inevitable. This will put pressures on a fully adequate system that could destroy the budget, creating deficits that, as in the past, would lead to macroeconomic problems like capital shortages and inflation that would ruin prospects for economic growth, making long-term unemployment inevitable and creating even more pressures on the budget. Under such circumstances it is very difficult to design unemployment insurance systems that would not bring the worst possible results—financial ruin of the government, shattered expectations for the workers, and a vicious circle of deficits, economic stagnation, and continuing unemployment. To avoid such a no-growth, high-unemployment trap, a full-scale unemployment program should be deployed very carefully, making certain that it is properly sequenced with respect to the pace of industrial restructuring and the availability of government resources. Since those who are officially unemployed may in fact have other quite adequate sources of income including jobs in the informal sector, employment of other household members, and extended family support, a better strategy would be to make certain that a fully adequate income-tested social assistance program is in place to assure that households have enough income to avoid absolute poverty.

Housing Subsidies. Ukraine introduced a housing subsidy program in 1995 under which families are eligible for support if their payments for housing and communal services exceed 20 percent of household income (or 15 percent for the poorest strata of population). Numerous abuses by applicants, calculation mistakes by housing subsidy office employees, late transfers of subsidy funds by local budgets and misuse of budget funds over the years led to creating an audit program, which has improved the integrity of the system. Substantial changes since the program began have also improved eligibility criteria, procedures for assigning subsidies, and mechanisms for making the payments. Procedures are in place that require repayment of overpaid subsidies and impose disciplinary, financial and criminal liability in the case of abuse.

Today about 20 percent of the population receives subsidies, a number that increases to about 15 percent during the heating season. The estimated targeting accuracy is high, with relatively few non-poor receiving support; conversely, relatively few poor fail to receive support. The program now appears to be a model upon which a more comprehensive program of family assistance could be constructed, reducing the fragmentation and overlap among existing programs (see PADCO, 1999). Unification of targeted social assistance programs will, however, require significant investment in information technology including hardware, software development, communications systems, financial reporting and auditing systems, and a widespread upgrading of the information technology skills. This work should be accompanied by the development of a new methodology for establishing the poverty level, which in turn should be linked to eligibility for social assistance. Now that Ukraine has decentralized tariff setting and has moved in principle to 100 percent cost recovery, reforms should also focus on privatizing housing, creating condominium associations, and restructuring locally owned utilities. Such reforms could greatly improve the well-being of low income families, reducing the need for assistance programs.

Other social safety net issues

Targeting. Ukraine has a large informal sector that makes it hard to find any indicator that would provide an accurate measure of household income and consumption level. Official information on individual household income rarely reflects the real wellbeing of the family and thus their need for government support. In providing social services and benefits it is possible to use three broad classes of targeting mechanisms.

Individual assessment mechanisms. This mechanism requires that program managers make decisions based on the eligibility of individual applicants. Examples of individual assessments options in Ukraine are mean tests (in housing subsidy program and some family childcare assistance programs the eligibility criteria is household income that is below the cut-off point) and using characteristics of household as the criterion (e.g. single mothers).

Group or geographic mechanisms. Here groups of candidates are granted eligibility on the basis of some easily identifiable shared characteristics. For example, in Ukraine single pensioners receive pension supplements. However, the lack of a poverty map and reliable regional poverty assessment does not allow the use of geographical targeting.

Self-targeted programs. Some services and programs are ostensibly available to all, but are designed in a way that discourages the non-poor from using them. Three factors usually discourage non-poor from participating - time, stigma, and low quality. Self-targeting can be accomplished, for example, by requiring participants to work. This may involve helping to deliver the service, for example by helping in community kitchens. It may also involve providing a more general service such as trash collecting or helping to maintain community infrastructure. Or it may be a full job in construction, as in public employment programs. Time, as we know, has an opportunity cost. The opportunity costs in terms of time taken away from other activities as well as the energy expenditures may discourage the leakage of benefits to persons who are poor according to the declared income but who in reality are non poor because of informal sources of income. The time costs are highest in the work fare schemes. Care must be taken, however, to assure that the work time required is limited so that participants are not locked into the welfare scheme—they must be given adequate time to search for regular employment. In fact, the program should be designed to assist participants in the job search process. The program may even include a training component, though this is usually best done in cooperation with potential private sector employers.

Based on the above, it is clear that self-targeting should be pursued wherever possible in designing social assistance programs in Ukraine, for they involve the lowest administrative costs, leaving more resources available to help the poor, and they are least subject to abuse and corruption.

Fragmented and overlapping programs. As part of its efforts to establish a market economy, the Ukrainian government has moved the social protection system away from the provision of non targeted subsidies for foods and services to targeted programs for groups with low incomes or specific needs. Programs have developed in a haphazard way and as a continuation of the pre-transition tradition of privileges. As a result the current system is fragmented in its approaches to targeting, financing, and administration.

Different programs use the family, the individual, or the household as the unit of assistance. Programs differ in the eligibility criteria they use in certifying individual needs based on circumstances such as disability, old age, having a child, single parenthood, or household income (the housing benefit). Some programs simply follow the political logic of providing additional assistance to privileged groups such as war veterans. This fragmentation of targeting approaches is compounded by a similarly fragmented administration of programs. Programs are administered by a variety of governmental and non-governmental agencies—including central government institutions, employers, local social protection offices, and local authorities.

Weak and fragmented financing. Social assistance programs are financed from a variety of sources. For example, pension supplements to pensioners with low pension levels or with special personal circumstances are paid out of the Pension Fund. Special central funds, such as the Chernobyl Fund, pay benefits under some programs. Other programs are entirely or partly financed out of local budgets. Data show that in aggregate, while poverty has been increasing, social protection spending has suffered a harder hit during the economic crisis than consolidated government expenditures as a whole, dropping from 14 percent in 1995 to 10 percent in 1998 of the total expenditures.

In addition, a comparison of oblast expenditure on social protection, health, and education during 1992-98 shows that the largest fluctuations have occurred in social protection expenditures, indicating the uncertainty and unpredictability of social protection funding. In general the lack of stability of financing for these programs at the subnational level has mainly contributed to the buildup of arrears. In 1998 arrears at local level on education, health and social protection funding were 90, 61 and 44 percent of total arrears on these programs respectively.

The fragmentation and duplication of programs and the use of different targeting approaches can lead to significant errors of inclusion and exclusion, jeopardizing the effectiveness of programs in reaching the needy. It can also reduce overall efficiency in using scarce social protection resources. Fragmentation and duplication also appear to keep administrative costs higher than necessary. The complexity of program financing makes it difficult for the government to analyze and plan the use of scarce resources. The inadequately defined division of responsibilities between local and central governments in areas such as defining eligibility and financing and administering assistance programs has resulted in maintaining unfunded mandates and entitlements to assistance (arrears on payments), leaving vulnerable populations without assistance and diminishing confidence in the ability of the system to deliver on its promises.

The social assistance system should be restructured in a way that ensures effective programs and efficient use of scarce funds. This goal could be achieved by consolidating programs, introducing unified targeting approaches, and streamlining financing and administration responsibilities. A unified targeting approach could use a guaranteed minimum income to define program eligibility. The unit of assessment could be the family or the household, and the guaranteed income could be differentiated for household or family size and structure and for additional needs stemming from specific family or household circumstances (single parenthood, disability). In developing such a program and defining benefit levels, careful consideration should be given to work incentives. Work already done to create a means-tested, household-based assistance program for housing costs provides an excellent foundation for further work. (e.g. PADCO 1999).

5. RESTORING GROWTH AND LIVING STANDARDS

Restoring living standards in Ukraine will be a major challenge. Complex structural reforms are needed to create a business climate favorable to investment. Perhaps even more important, such investment must be used efficiently.

Increasing investment from domestic and foreign sources will require raising returns and reducing risks. Many countries, including Ukraine, have tried to increase investor profitability through tax holidays and direct subsidies, but such policies are not sustainable and can easily make the investment climate worse. A far more effective and sustainable strategy is to remove distortions that artificially inflate the cost of critical inputs (capital, labor, materials) and that reduce the effective selling price of outputs. This would stimulate increased private sector investment in the "best" areas-those with the greatest potential for efficient competitive production.

Equally important are policies that minimize the risks facing investors. The government should avoid using loan guarantees or other mechanisms which only compensate for commercial risks. Such policies increase moral hazard, encouraging enterprises to undertake risky investments that they would otherwise avoid. Total risk actually increases. Instead, government can and should reduce specific risks such as frequent changes in the tax code, unclear property rights, costly and inconsistent regulations, lack of juridical enforcement of contracts, and lack of adequate protection from extortion and other Mafia activities.

If Ukraine can design and implement the policies needed to increase the volume and efficiency of investment, prospects for restoring growth are excellent. But if the government retains its current intrusive role in production, lets deficits return to higher levels, finances the deficits through increased borrowing, and begins printing money in a doomed effort to stimulate growth, it might achieve a year or two of positive growth—but a crisis situation would quickly return. Another crisis would be far worse than the one of late 1998. Having

exhausted the patience of its creditors, the government would find it almost impossible to borrow domestically or abroad, and enterprises would face extreme shortages and high costs for fixed and working capital. Under such circumstances, sharp declines in living standards would be inevitable—and could easily lead to social conflict.

UKRAINE HAS INVESTMENT— WHY NOT GROWTH?

Official national accounts statistics indicate gross investment rates of 25-35 percent of GDP during 1989-95, with a drop to 18 percent in 1997. While well below the 35-40 percent seen in East Asia before the 1997 crisis, these rates are similar to those for other middle income countries. The combination of modest but sustained investment and continued economic decline indicate that Ukraine's problems lie not in the level of investment, but in its nature and efficiency.

During 1993-94, a large share of available capital went into the accumulation of inventories that could not be sold, raising the annual share of inventories to more than 10 percent of GDP and significantly lowering the share of fixed capital formation in total investment. Even so, fixed capital formation did not fall as much as might have been expected in a highly inflationary environment. Nor do the substantial rates of investment seem consistent with the continuing economic decline since then.

The disconnect between reported investment and economic decline is perhaps because investment is captured more accurately than output, and output is relatively underreported. Authorities can track the import of capital equipment and other large-scale purchases for investment more easily than output, much of which is hidden in the shadow economy. In addition, investment may be overstated in enterprise accounts to increase reported costs, thus reducing taxable profits. But even after all the necessary statistical adjustments are made, an obvious question remains: if investment has been relatively high in Ukraine, why is the economy still shrinking?

The investment puzzle has several solutions. First, the enterprises that Ukraine inherited from the Soviet era were heavily decapitalized. Second, much of the capital stock that was still functioning was designed for a world that no longer exists. Third, policies do not foster efficient production.

Massive decapitalization during the Soviet era

Ukraine inherited an impressive capital stock from the former Soviet Union. But capital productivity in the Soviet Union began declining steadily in the 1950s and by the 1970s was close to zero (figure 5.1). Capital productivity in Ukraine followed a similar trend, and by the time of independence Ukrainian farms and factories were economically decapitalized even though they had a fairly large physical stock of capital. The modest investment that has taken place since independence has not been enough to reverse a generation of effective decapitalization.

Existing capital stock was for a different world

Even the capital stock in place at independence was designed for a world that disappeared with the Soviet Union. The low-price energy of the Soviet era vanished, making energy-intensive farms and factories uneconomical to operate. Changing the energy efficiency of an entire production system requires a far higher rate of investment than is required simply to replace worn-out capital. Investment has fallen far short of the required levels, leaving Ukrainian goods costly because they are energy inefficient and uncompetitive in all but basic raw and intermediate materials — and a few exceptional products such as weapons.

Ukraine's traditional export markets collapsed along with the Soviet Union (figure 5.2). Partly because of the energy intensity of its Soviet-era factories—but also because these factories could not produce modern goods—Ukraine was unable to redirect its output to other markets, especially to the European Union. Output plummeted in 1993-94, and more than 10

percent of the output in these years was produced "for the warehouse."

Figure 5.1 The Soviet system collapsed because of gross inefficiency in using capital

Source: Easterly and Fischer 1995.

Figure 5.2 Trade dependence on Russia has dropped significantly since independence

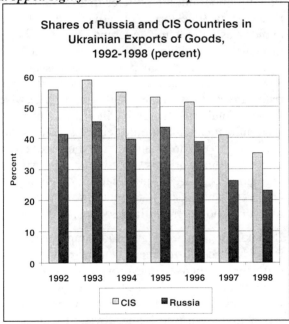

Source: Ministry of Statistics.

Ukraine is still struggling to retool its factories. It needs to emulate the successful economies of Central Europe and the Baltics in improving the physical and operational efficiency of its enterprises so that it can increase its production and export of high-quality, high-profit products to rich markets in Europe and the rest of the world. Progress has been made in redirecting markets. As seen in figure 5.2, the share of Ukrainian exports going to markets outside Russia jumped from about 60 percent in 1992 to nearly 80 percent in 1997, with comparable reductions in the share going to Russia and other members of the CIS.

But more progress is needed if Ukraine is to become a truly prosperous country. Otherwise a major share of its industrial goods will be low-profit products—like basic iron and steel and basic chemicals—many of which are shipped to low-profit markets like Russia, often on a barter basis. This is a trap—the low profits from these products and markets make it difficult for Ukrainian producers to finance the investments needed to break into larger, more profitable markets.[1]

Ukraine needs to increase not only the quantity but also the quality of investment. The number of dollars or hryvnias spent is a misleading measure of investment unless the capital is invested in ways that maximize the efficiency and rate of return on investment. The quality and marketability of the goods produced by the investment is vitally important. Ukraine needs to attract technology and design skills, production methods, plant management techniques and marketing expertise, and access to foreign markets.

The need for policies that balance returns and risks

Global experience shows that the best way to gain all these ingredients vital for the efficient production of high-quality, internationally competitive goods is to attract foreign direct investment. A strong correlation exists between economic growth and foreign direct investment.

---

[1] Although Russia is one of the largest markets in the world from a geographic perspective, it is relatively small from an economic perspective, with a total 1995 GDP smaller than that of the Netherlands. In terms of per capita income, and thus ability to purchase higher-quality, higher-profit goods, Russia ranks on par with Belize and Costa Rica based on 1997 World Bank data. Furthermore, Russia's geographic dispersion increases both selling and transport costs, further reducing its profitability as a market.

Limited foreign investment in Ukraine, in fact, helps account for its continued economic decline (figure 5.3).

Figure 5.3 Foreign direct investment in Ukraine is low relative to other countries

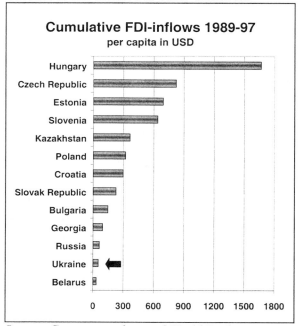

Source: Government data and World Bank estimates.

The importance of investment, including the strong role of foreign direct investment, brings us to the focus of the rest of this chapter—the measures that Ukraine must take to create an investment climate that will attract much higher foreign and domestic investment. What the average investor seeks in an investment climate is very simple—the highest possible returns with the lowest possible risks. Ukraine's task is therefore very straightforward—maximize living standards by creating a more productive economic environment that stimulates investment and growth.

LOWER COSTS MEAN HIGHER RETURNS

Some countries try to increase investment returns by providing tax holidays and even direct subsidies to investors. But this approach is dangerous because it involves high fiscal risk. The revenue losses and budgetary expenditures are usually up-front costs—while the returns (in the form of higher tax revenues) may never come. Investors are often suspicious of *ad hoc* subsidies because these can be taken away as easily as they are given. The removal of special privileges for foreign investors in Ukraine in 1997 shows how easily this can happen.

The recent decision to establish "free economic zones" in Ukraine is another example of a policy based on tax privileges that fails to address the underlying problems of greatest concern to investors. Furthermore, the zones jeopardize the government's revenue base, placing an even heavier tax burden on all the enterprises that do not receive these special privileges.

A far safer and more effective approach would be to take steps that, by removing market distortions, reduce the costs of inputs for producers. The most important costs for any investor are capital, labor, domestic material inputs, imported inputs, infrastructure services (such as public utilities), and government services (most of which are paid through taxes). Most of these key inputs cost more than is economically warranted in Ukraine today.

Capital costs

The extraordinarily high cost of capital in Ukraine is the key factor driving up costs and discouraging investment. This high cost is the direct result of excessive government deficits, which have had to be financed on highly unfavorable terms because, with faltering economic reforms, Ukraine has not had full access to credit from international financial institutions (including the IMF and the World Bank). Credit from these institutions would have been available at a fraction of the interest rates and for maturity periods at least 10-20 times longer than the short-term t-bill debt used instead to finance government deficits.

The extraordinarily high cost of capital has been examined in earlier sections of this report. Real interest rates that still exceed 50 percent a year make investment impossible not only for domestic investors, but for foreign investors as well. Investors in Ukraine must compete both in export markets and with imports in the domestic market. The foreign producers of these goods generally pay, at most, 5-10 percent in real terms for their capital.

The cost of capital is an obvious problem for domestic producers. But three closely related problems arise for foreign investors as well. First, although foreign investors usually bring in substantial amounts of reasonably priced capital from abroad, most also seek to finance part of their domestic costs with local currency to reduce foreign exchange conversion risks. High domestic interest rates make such financing impossible. Second, a large share of foreign investments involve some form of partnership with a local investor. High local interest rates make it extremely difficult to find a local investors who are able to finance their share of the deal at a reasonable cost. Third, high interest rates are almost always a sign of potential or actual financial and economic instability—driving away investors.

To lower the cost of capital, the government needs to eliminate its budget deficit, pay obligations on time, stop running up arrears, repay or restructure the most costly portions of its debt, and establish a strong record of economic reforms. It is especially important for Ukraine to take the measures needed to restore and enhance the flow of funds from the IMF. This move will make it easier for the World Bank and the European Bank for Reconstruction and Development to provide financing for small and medium-size enterprise development, financial sector development, and activities that increase the overall productivity of investment and of workers. Efforts are also needed to gain access to the full facilities of IFC and the Multilateral Investment Guarantee Association (MIGA), both of which are designed to encourage foreign investment in countries like Ukraine. The ratification of the establishment agreement with IFC was a most welcome development in this respect.

Labor costs

Dollar wages in Ukraine have risen sharply since independence when trading relations collapsed and the dollar became highly priced relative to the domestic currency (figure 5.4). With the devaluation of about 45 percent between early 1998 and April 1999, the upward trend in wages has been arrested, and wages are now slightly more competitive. Direct labor costs have been competitive relative to real wages in neighboring countries in Central Europe. These wage rates should make a variety of products internationally competitive. "Give and take" contract manufacturing operations such as the sewing and export of garments based on imported materials should also be as profitable for Ukraine as it has been for a number of other countries in the region. Still, several problems need to be addressed:

Figure 5.4 Dollar wages have risen sharply, but devaluation will make them more competitive

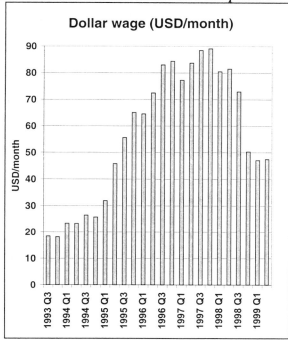

Source: UEPLAC, Ukrainian Economic Trends.

- Regulations and political pressures for enterprise-financed severance obligations force firms to retain unnecessarily large work forces, and can quickly offset the advantages of low individual wage rates, making investment unprofitable. The government should establish an adequate social safety net, then remove most limitations on the release of workers (see chapter 4).

- Payroll taxes, currently equal to 37.5 percent of the payroll, need to be reduced to make the employment of workers more attractive (see chapter 2).

- For some enterprises, maintaining social assets such as day-care centers, clinics, housing, and resort facilities is a substantial indirect cost of labor. In most cases such social assets should be put on a cost recovery basis and turned over to municipal governments, NGOs, or the private sector.

Domestic materials and services

The monetary cost of domestic inputs generally does not seem to be a barrier to achieving good returns on investments in Ukraine. Producers generally face domestic competition, and average tariffs are still relatively low. But the low quality of many locally produced inputs creates high costs for domestic producers. And in the longer term, investors' biggest concern is that Ukraine may pursue an increasingly protectionist strategy, creating sharply higher costs for the protected domestic goods needed as inputs.

Imported materials

The direct cost of imported materials is not a barrier to investors because average tariffs are still quite low—about 15 percent (Michaely/Movchan 1998). In fact, some investors (such as Daewoo/AvtoZAZ) enjoy duty-free imports, creating undesirable distortions. On the other hand, if current protectionist tendencies develop further, the high cost of imported goods is likely to become a barrier to investment.

Of greater concern are the indirect costs that distort the real price of imported goods, discouraging investment activity. In early 1999 the biggest problem was obtaining foreign exchange for purchasing materials. In a continuing effort to artificially support the exchange rate, the government imposed a range of administrative controls for access to foreign exchange. Another cost-raising barrier to imports is the government's quality and standards inspection system. Ukraine generally does not accept goods just because they meet, for example, European standards—and insists on subjecting even products widely sold in Europe to its own costly laboratory inspections. The fees, reportedly up to $250,000 for one widely reported case involving standard household cleaning products, seem designed to cover more than the cost of inspection, and the delays are costly. Similar problems arise with the customs service. All these barriers to imports and the opportunities they create for corruption are also barriers to the investment so urgently needed for restoring growth. Fixing these problems would not require significant time or money—it is basically a matter of political will.

One approach that has worked well in other countries such as Indonesia is to put customs and quality inspection on a commercial basis, engaging one of the world's private companies that offer pre-shipment inspection services. Once goods have passed quality certification by the inspection company at the point of origin, they are automatically cleared in the country of destination. The pre-shipment inspection company also handles all customs revenues, passing them directly to the national treasury. In other countries the increased customs revenues that result from reduced corruption have more than paid for these services.

Infrastructure services

Several potential and actual barriers to investment exist in public utilities and other infrastructure services.

- *Energy.* Enterprises commonly must pay more than the economic cost for energy supplies as a result of government efforts to cross-subsidize households. With the support of World Bank energy loans, Ukraine has made commitments to correct the pricing and cost recovery problems in the energy sector. But progress has been slow.

- *Telecommunications.* This sector is still relatively underdeveloped in terms of coverage and service quality. Poor communications services significantly increase costs to investors. But there is a bright side. The telecom sector could be one of the most promising sectors for privatization and investment once the government establishes an appropriate policy framework for the privatization and subsequent operation of the national telephone system.

- *Transportation* Transportation costs in Ukraine are higher than they should be not only because of physical inefficiencies, but also because of problems in policies, especially those related to delays in border crossings. Noncompetitive transportation costs deter investment, especially for export-oriented projects—the kind of projects that should be of highest priority to Ukraine.

Government services

Including government services as an input to production and treating them as a factor of concern to potential investors may not be conventional. But this approach is entirely appropriate. In market economies, governments play a critical role in assuring efficient, profitable production and low risks. For example, governments provide law and order, register contracts and third-party claims, enforce the rules of the game through effective courts, and run programs for health, education, and transport that are vitally important to workers, their families, and their employers.

Enterprises pay for most of these services through taxes, and the tax cost of these inputs is an important factor in deciding whether to invest. Serious problems exist on this front in Ukraine that serve as a major deterrent to investors:

- Many services are of low quality. For example, small and medium-size entrepreneurs often fall prey to protection rackets because the government is not providing an adequate system of law and order. In addition, contract enforcement services, including bankruptcy proceedings, are unsatisfactory.

- Services cost too much, as measured by the taxes that must be paid to obtain them. The problems of high tax rates, large government structures, and a small tax base because of the large shadow economy were discussed in chapter 2.

- The regulatory burden is excessive. Regulatory provisions are numerous and nontransparent. Too many inspectors administer flawed rules and regulations in an *ad hoc* manner. Complying with regulators costs time and money, both directly and in the form of bribes. All these costs discourage investment (again, see chapter 2).

Fixing these problems should be a top priority for the government in its search for investment and renewed economic growth.

REDUCING RISK

Much can be done in Ukraine to improve returns to investors by implementing the measures just noted. But it is not just low returns that keep away investors. In fact, rewards to investing in Ukraine can be high, especially for enterprises operating in the shadow economy. But so can the risks. The government has the power to reduce these risks in concrete, sustainable ways.

Government guaranteed loans are not the way to reduce risks. Such guarantees are dangerous, as the Ukrainian government is now learning. Guarantees create a serious risk that budget resources may have to be used cover the repayment of tens of millions of dollars of loans. Guarantees do not reduce risk—they simply shift risk from the enterprise to the government. In fact, because guarantees create moral hazard that encourages enterprises to assume more risk than they otherwise would, state guarantees for loans can actually increase the total amount of risk and thus the danger of a new financial crisis.

Real, sustainable risk reduction must instead come through measures that fundamentally change the level of risk. These measures include establishing basic law and order, judicial enforcement of contracts, a transparent and predictable legal framework, clear property rights, and a level playing field.

Basic law and order

In an environment of lawlessness and criminality, the enterprises most likely to thrive are lawless and criminal—hardly the kind that Ukraine wants to encourage. The emergence of a large shadow economy and the associated Mafia-type activities—including protection rackets, extortion, theft, and even murder—make it hard for honest businesses to be successful. In fact, these law and order problems create a strong incentive for enterprises to stay small and hide in the shadows so that they do not become attractive targets for Mafia thugs. But staying small reduces economic growth, and enterprises that hide in the shadows create fiscal problems for the government. They depend on government services but do not contribute to the cost of providing them. Much needs to be done to create better law and order if Ukraine wants an environment in which competitive activity flourishes and generates higher living standards.

Juridical enforcement of contracts

The problems of law and order in Ukraine with respect to criminal activity will be left to studies by experts in that field. This report, however, must highlight the need for better law and order in civil and commercial law, especially in the enforcement of contracts. Failure to honor contracts destroys the foundations of a market economy—and of society. Widespread failure to honor contracts is one of the most serious complaints of investors about the local business climate. As highlighted by the large and growing stock of inter-enterprise arrears in Ukraine, the failure of contracting parties to deliver and pay according to contract is the most frequent problem. Inter-enterprise arrears, for example, amount to 85 percent of GDP, up from 65 percent in 1996 and much higher than is typical for well-functioning market economies. By focusing on the resolution of conflicts rather than the enforcement of contracts, the court system is biased against those who stand to lose when contracts are not carried out as written. This problem is driving away millions of dollars of potential investment that could give average Ukrainians a better life.

The actual frequency of bankruptcy may be low, but all enterprise owners and managers should feel that, if they do not honor contracts for delivery and payment, the other party could take them to court, where they could lose ownership of their assets. Ukraine needs to complete the reform of its bankruptcy law and improve the institutional framework of economic courts to handle arbitration and bankruptcy. Abundant technical assistance has been provided on the legal front, and a good draft law is available. Time will be required to develop an institutional network sufficient to handle a large number of bankruptcy cases, but technical assistance could readily be mobilized to asset in this process as well. Furthermore, only a fraction of the "bankrupt" firms would actually have to be taken into court. Faced with a credible threat of bankruptcy, most firms would almost certainly find a way to solve their problems. Once it has created a credible threat of bankruptcy, Ukraine can begin the second phase of transition— moving from the transfer of ownership from public to private hands to the consolidation of ownership and control needed for effective enterprise management.

A transparent and predictable legal framework

Another major risk facing Ukrainian enterprises is that the rules of the game are not clear. Less than a decade ago, Ukraine did not have its own laws, and many of the laws that it inherited from the Soviet era worked against the development of a normally functioning market-based economy. Even today the civil laws of Ukraine make repeated reference to the legal codes of the Soviet Union. The process of changing these laws has created great confusion, increasing costs and risk for investors.

Formal codification of civil, commercial, criminal, and tax law has not been completed, making it difficult to assure consistency. The haste with which laws have been written— combined with the lack of well-established procedures, the shortage of good law libraries, and the dearth of people trained in this work— has produced a jumble of often contradictory legislation. The absence of a system for publishing court decisions in a legal gazette further complicates the jobs of lawyers, judges, and investors who are trying to understand how written laws should be interpreted.

Contradictions and lack of transparency in the legal environment create serious risks for investors. If those in charge of drafting legislation cannot create a consistent set of rules, investors have no way of knowing how the rules will apply. One of the biggest problem areas is taxation. Tax legislation has become an impenetrable briar patch of contradictions waiting to snag the unsuspecting businessperson. The only guide—and often the final authority—is the tax inspector. But the

degree to which the inspector selects and interprets the legislation in a manner favorable to the investor may depend on how much of the resulting tax savings are shared with the inspector. The process is predictable, but the results are not.

The lack of equity in current laws also creates risks for investors and distortions in the allocation of investment resources. The biggest problem is tax concessions. These exemptions and privileged rates, which can be granted (and removed) on an *ad hoc* basis, make the tax system highly inequitable and create serious risks for investors, both directly and indirectly. Directly, an investor may invest on the basis of various tax concessions, then, after the money has been locked up in fixed assets, discover that the government has removed the concessions, destroying the profitability of the investments. Indirectly, the investor may be harmed if a local competitor is given tax concessions and he or she is not. This is a particular risk for enterprises competing in the same line of business with large state-owned enterprises.

Efforts to clarify conflicting tax laws and regulations, remove special concessions, and establish a transparent, predictable, and equitable tax code are under way. Many donors—including the European Union, the U.S. Agency for International Development, and the World Bank—are assisting. If done well, the resulting tax code will greatly reduce risk by increasing transparency and predictability, and by reducing regulatory discretion and corruption—stimulating investment and economic growth.

Property rights, privatization, and enterprise reform

The lack of clear property rights in Ukraine also creates an unnecessarily high level of risk for investors, both directly and indirectly. Directly, the most serious problems lie with the privatization process. Small enterprises in trade and manufacturing face many potential threats to their ownership rights because of the poorly defined and often intrusive regulatory and tax system. But the most serious problems arise with medium-size and large manufacturing enterprises, public utilities, and agrarian enterprises.

Small enterprises. The privatization of small enterprises (largely shops) has gone well and is considered complete. Real owners have been created in almost all cases, and many small, privatized enterprises are now thriving. In agriculture, a large number of Ukrainian families own "*dacha* plots"—small plots of land, usually in rural areas and often associated with a small cottage or *dacha*, where a significant share of household vegetables and fruits are grown, especially among low-income families. Some family farms have also been created, but here success has been more limited. And as discussed in chapter 3, most "private" land is still held collectively without individual titles, creating serious issues of ownership.

Medium-size and large enterprises. The privatization of medium-size and large enterprises (and farmland) has involved significant ownership problems. Enterprise privatization has depended on certificate privatization, which allowed individuals to purchase shares in enterprises using certificates that were distributed to all Ukrainian citizens, who were compensated for the value of savings lost during the hyperinflation of 1992-93. This process effectively transferred legal ownership of the majority of shares in more than 8,000—or nearly 80 percent of—medium-size and large enterprises in this group.

But certificate privatization has not created effective owners in the sense of individuals or small group of individuals who can actually assert control over enterprise operations. The expected consolidation of ownership through sales of certificates and shares in the secondary market has not taken place—a reflection in large measure of the unfavorable investment climate that has discouraged investments of all kinds, both direct and in portfolio ownership. The depth of malaise in the local investment scene is shown by the local stock market value index (figure 5.5). Without "real" owners, enterprises have tended to remain under the control of the old "Red directors" and employees of these enterprises.

Because many of the enterprises that have been privatized through the certificate process remain under the control of enterprise managers and workers from the Soviet era—including many

who are redundant and lack modern management skills—it is difficult for this relatively close community of "owners" to fire themselves. It is much easier for them to continue trying to operate the enterprises with the full complement of workers, staying afloat with special concessions from the government and banks, and by running up arrears on taxes, loans, wages, and supplier credits.

Figure 5.5 Wood Index of share values

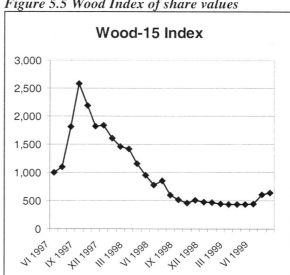

Source: Wood/Eastern Economist.

Solving this problem will not be easy. But it is crucial to establishing a productive, growing economy where investors can become real owners—owners who are free to manage enterprises to maximize profitability. At the sectoral and enterprise levels, the most important strategy will be for the government to impose a hard budget constraint on all enterprises, regardless of sector, location, or ownership. As has been seen in Estonia and Hungary, enterprises faced with a true hard budget constraint:

- Lease or sell unused or underutilized buildings, equipment and land

- Buy out worker shares.

- Find new investment partners, domestic or foreign.

- Develop new designs, products, markets, and management techniques.

- Invest in more efficient production equipment and technologies.

- Adjust staffing levels in line with production requirements and efficiency.

In addition, although the privatization of small and medium-size enterprises that were once state-owned is well advanced, Ukraine lags behind comparable and more advanced countries in terms of developing new small and medium-size enterprises. This reflects the adverse climate that small and medium-size enterprises face in terms of burdensome taxes and regulations, lack of predictability and transparency in laws, and inadequate enforcement of contracts. The numbers of small and medium-sized enterprises in Ukraine are almost certainly understated because many hide in the shadows, escaping not only taxation but even registration. But even if the total was doubled or tripled, it would still be clear that Ukraine is missing a major opportunity to expand employment and output by not creating an environment that stimulates the development of small and medium-size enterprises.

The giants. The process of transferring ownership from public to private hands for the large enterprises—the country's crown jewels—has barely begun. Of an estimated 277 enterprises with assets exceeding 170 million hryvnias, about half have minority private participation, often in the form of workers and managers. But it appears that none of these has been successfully privatized to a depth of at least 70 percent.

From the perspective of developing a good investment climate and attracting large-scale foreign investment, priority should be given to privatizing the giants—most of which are in the metal, machine building, and chemicals sectors. This situation reflects major problems—and major opportunities. These large enterprises account for a substantial share of all employees in public enterprises and the majority of capital (as measured by book value). The stakes for privatization are therefore high, both for workers and for the economy. Given the key role of these enterprises in the economic and social life of Ukraine, it is important that the much-delayed privatization be launched as quickly as possible.

Such privatization should at the same time be done very carefully. Experience in Russia, Nigeria, and many other countries demonstrates that hasty privatizations done without due attention to best-practice standards open the door to rampant corruption, making it possible for privileged insiders to grab valuable public assets at little or no cost. Depending on local conditions, a variety of different techniques can assure good privatization, but privatizing large-scale enterprises will almost involve: (a) advertising the privatization offerings as widely as possible, both internationally and domestically, to assure that the best potential investors are aware of the possibilities and openly compete for the enterprises, (b) preparation of detailed information on the companies to be privatized, (c) making this information readily to all seriously interested investors, (d) allowing interested parties do come in and do their own "due diligence" on the enterprises, and (e) assuring that the bid evaluation and award process is as fully transparent and equitable as possible.

These measures greatly reduce the risk that corruption will rob the country of benefits that it should have received from the privatization process. They will also reduce the risk of a public backlash in response to perceived corruption that could lead to the re-nationalization of certain enterprises. Such might be justified in the case of serious corruption or incompetence of the process, but such actions seriously undermine investor confidence and interest in future privatizations. It is also desirable to fix at least the most serious defects in the business climate prior to the sale of the "crown jewels," thus increasing the probability that the best investors will come forward and bid.

Ukraine is making progress in establishing the rules of the game for large scale privatization—a process that needs to take place largely on a competitive, case-by-case basis with a single lead investor or consortium of investors winning the competition and taking a controlling interest. Internationally acceptable procedures for selecting the adviser that will conduct each trade sale have been developed for Ukraine. The list of enterprises subject to trade sale privatization is known, and priorities have been established, with the highest priority going to the privatization of UkrTelcom, the national telephone company, and to the regional (oblast-level) electricity distribution companies (the oblenergos).[2]

A substantial portion of the shares of electricity distribution companies have already been diffused to private holders through certificate auctions and similar measures, and this will make it harder for lead investors to attain a controlling interest—something that most serious investors will insist on. Because the government has declared its intention to retain a minority blocking position (25 percent of shares plus one share) to give it a veto on any major decisions of the private owners, many of these enterprises, particularly the electricity companies, will likely be relatively unattractive to private investors. Thus it is important to move forward with trade sale privatizations before even more enterprises find their shareholdings diluted to the point that they are no longer attractive to serious investors.

A level playing field

The problems that a distorted playing field can create for enterprise profitability and returns on investments were discussed above. An uneven playing field also increases risks for investors, particularly when competition from other domestic producers is involved.

The presence of government as an active producer creates risks for private competitors who generally cannot depend on the government for fiscal and financial concessions that will help them compete if they are too inefficient to compete on their own. Although Ukraine may have privatized more than 80 percent of industrial enterprises, and close to 100 percent of agricultural enterprises, the government still

[2] Unfortunately, on 15 December 1998 Parliament rejected the government's draft law that would have launched privatization of UkrTelcom, saying that it would undermine the nation's economic security. A compromise approach involving stage-wise privatization looks possible, but it seems doubtful that serious lead investors willing not only to purchase shares but also to make major new investments of their own funds would be attracted to a company where control still rested firmly with the government.

directly or indirectly controls much of the activity in both agriculture and industry.

Because the government directly controls the assets of the "giants," private investment in subsectors dominated these enterprises is more risky. By privatizing its interests, the government would gain, receiving privatization proceeds and reducing its fiscal responsibility for supporting these enterprises. It would also gain because such privatization would level the playing field, making it interesting for other enterprises to begin operating in these sectors. This would increase the government's tax base, raise living standards, and reduce social protection payments.

Government exit from the giants would also stimulate investment in new small and medium-size enterprises that would serve as suppliers to the giants. In industrial countries small and medium-size enterprises are by far the most dynamic source of new jobs and job growth—but especially in the manufacturing sector, many of these enterprises depend on profitable, large-scale enterprises as customers for their products. Conversely, small and medium-size enterprises often depend on the large enterprises for key material inputs. But these small and medium-size enterprises cannot be healthy if the large-scale enterprises on which they depend for sales or inputs are sick. Restoring the giants of Ukraine to health through privatization and restructuring is thus vital to the economic success of the small and medium-size enterprises where most of the jobs will be created to absorb redundant workers from overstaffed public enterprises.

Indirect government control comes not only from its powers of taxation and regulation, but also through its ownership of enterprises that play an important role in the life of private enterprises. On numerous occasions Ukrainian government, often at the sub-national level, has used its control over vital inputs and outputs to reduce the profitability of individual farms and transfer the rents to the state—or to individuals operating under the umbrella of the state. Until the risk of such state intervention is removed—a key objective of the World Bank's proposed Pre-Export Guarantee Facility project—private investment in the potentially rich and productive agricultural sector will remain too risky to attract any but a few intrepid investors. Unfortunately, this project was rejected by Parliament in December 1998.

The principle of establishing a level playing field is also being undermined by measures to promote industrial development. One of the best-known examples in Ukraine is the package of incentives to the passenger car industry. In addition to being potentially costly to the budget and to consumers, these preferential tax measures distort investment incentives, drawing investment resources into lines of production that may be competitive only if given exceptional tax treatment, or creating opportunities for artificially high private profits (rents) at the expense of the public in areas were Ukraine can be competitive. In the absence of such a policy-induced bias, investment would almost certainly go into lines of activity—such as production of vehicle components—where low-wage, high-skill countries like Ukraine can be highly competitive.

PROSPECTS FOR ECONOMIC REFORM

Ukraine faces a choice between three fundamentally different economic strategies for the future. First, it could seek to preserve the status quo, as is being done in Belarus. Second, it could try to protect domestic producers from international competition with high external tariffs and other barriers to trade, as was done throughout Latin America in the 1960s and 1970s. Finally, it could undertake the structural reforms outlined in this report to create a vibrant, market-based economy that can compete internationally—taking care at the same time to ensure that low-income groups are protected by a government that focuses not on business but on people.

Those who have collaborated in preparing this report—including professional analysts from the government, from a leading Ukrainian NGO, and from the World Bank—strongly agree that the competitiveness approach is the only one capable of producing the permanently rising living standards that are desired by all Ukrainians, regardless of their political affiliation. Questions may arise regarding the sequencing, the feasible pace, and the speed with which these reforms will yield higher living standards. The path chosen by Ukraine for future growth will almost certainly involve elements from each of these three strategic options. The country will probably chose to sacrifice competitiveness and growth in certain areas to preserve specific elements of the status quo for cultural and political reasons. It may protect certain activities from the full force of competition today in hopes that these activities may become internationally competitive tomorrow.

But there can be no doubt regarding the necessary direction. The policy compass must point to a competitive future for Ukraine.

This final section of the report quantifies the results that could be attained with different rates of reform and progress towards the goal of establishing a competitive economy — as well as the consequences of deviating from this strategic goal.

The actual pace of reform described in this report must be decided by the people of Ukraine., and this will become the main determinant of whether Ukraine follows an optimistic High Case or a Base Case Scenario. The fiscal and monetary policies listed as "essential reforms" in previous chapters must be implemented rigorously under either scenario. Provided that these minimum requirements for stability are attained, the exact pace of reform and thus of economic growth can be a matter of political judgment. As a sovereign nation, Ukraine must decide where to strike the balance between the desire to avoid change and the desire for higher income. The purpose of this section is simply to quantify some of these implications so that good policy decisions can be made based on a full analysis of the probable consequences of the two high case alternatives.

The following projections provide a strong case for an immediate acceleration in the pace of reforms—almost a shock treatment like Estonia and Poland used to get the sharply higher living standards that they are enjoying today. If nearly all of the structural reforms examined in this study were implemented with the next 12-18 months, Ukraine could possibly attain the growth rates shown in the high-case scenario below—and thus the growth rates targeted in the government's program through 2010. The Base Case Scenario quantified below assumes a slower pace of reform with correspondingly less favorable results. Finally, the Low Case assumes that macroeconomic and structural reforms move seriously off track, with grave consequences to economic growth and living standards.

The High Case

In its *Program Ukraine—2010*, the government sets as a goal the doubling of 1997 per capita GDP by 2010. Prospects for significant growth through 2000 are limited by the aftershocks of the 1998 crisis in Russia and by the fact that fundamental structural reforms—even if implemented immediately—will take time to bear fruit in the form of higher growth rates. The government therefore anticipates most of the growth taking place during 2001–10, when growth would have to average 7-8 percent a year to attain the targeted doubling. With exceptionally strong policy performance, including immediate and full implementation of most of the measures discussed in this report, Ukraine might be able to attain these goals.

Other countries that started from a low initial base—China, Vietnam—have attained comparable growth rates. Such rates were approached by the East Asian tigers before the recent reversals. Further evidence that such growth rates might be possible for Ukraine is found in the fact that the World Bank is projecting close to 5 percent growth for 2001-07 for Europe and Central Asia as a whole, and Ukraine could possibly average growth 2 percentage points higher than this regional average given its strong basic endowments— including low wage rates for well-educated workers, good basic infrastructure, and close proximity to rich Western markets.

But attaining the high rates of growth projected in the 2010 document would require extraordinary efforts. Fewer than 5 percent of the world's countries have managed to sustain growth rates in excess of 5 percent since 1961 (figure 5.6). And among all middle-income countries, only six maintained annual rates of growth averaging more than 7 percent for 10 years between 1970 and 1995. All these countries (Botswana, China, Indonesia, Oman,

Thailand, and Solomon Islands) operated under special circumstances, and in several cases the growth proved to have been built on weak foundations.

Figure 5.6 Few countries grow by more than five percent a year over a sustained period

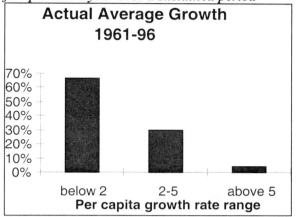

Source: World Bank staff estimates.

Part of the increase in GDP growth projected in the 2010 document is assumed to come from the integration of shadow economic activity into the formal sector. About 10-15 percent is already added to formal sector GDP in calculating total GDP, but moving shadow activity into the formal sector would increase reported GDP. On this basis, and with strong reforms, the ambitious targets of the 2010 program could be realized. Under this scenario, increased tax revenue from activity now in the shadow economy would make it possible for the government to lower tax rates, stimulating real economic growth elsewhere. The increased revenues would also make it easier for the government to maintain programs that would increase the real and monetary incomes of the poor. However, it should be remembered that a shift of business activity from shadow economy into an official sector does not per se produce any new income or wealth. Shadow economy already provides a living for a significant share of the population, and covering more of the informal sector in official statistics, does not increase prosperity. Therefore, reforms that improve the economic growth fundamentals— investment-savings balance, productivity and technological innovation—should be implemented vigorously to ensure a real longer-

Table 5.1 High Case Scenario

	1997	1998	1999	2000	2001	2002-05	2006-09
Growth Rates (%)							
GDP	-3.0	-1.7	0.0	2.0	4.0	6.5	8.0
GNFS Exports[1,2]	0.0	-13.4	-7.5	4.0	4.1	7.3	9.9
GNFS Imports[1,2]	2.0	-14.0	-12.5	2.9	4.5	9.1	9.7
Prices[3]	17.3	13.2	25.0	18.0	12.0	9.0	8.0
Percent of GDP							
GNFS Exports[1]	40.6	41.6	51.5	54.3	53.3	50.8	48.7
GNFS Imports[1]	43.7	44.4	52.0	54.3	53.5	53.7	52.3
Current Account Balance	-2.7	-3.1	-1.1	-0.4	-0.5	-3.0	-4.0
Gross Investment[4]	21.4	20.7	21.0	21.4	22.0	24.7	29.2
Consolidated Government Expenditure	43.6	38.9	37.5	35.9	35.7	34.0	33.3
Consolidated Budget Deficit[5]	-5.6	-2.6	-1.8	-1.3	-1.4	-1.3	-1.6
External Debt Indicators[6]							
Debt Service/GNFS Exports (%)	6.6	14.2	15.4	20.2	17.8	13.0	13.4
Debt/GDP (%)	21.7	30.1	41.7	41.4	38.3	36.0	28.9
Interest/GNFS Exports (%)	3.3	5.2	5.1	5.3	4.9	4.5	3.9
Net Foreign Direct Investment Infows (mln. USD)	581	747	550	900	1100	1404	2055
As a percentage of GDP	1.2	1.8	1.7	2.9	3.3	3.4	3.4

[1] GNFS – Goods & Non-Factor Services
[2] Value growth
[3] GDP deflator
[4] Including inventories accumulation and net acquisition of valuables
[5] IMF GFS methodology
[6] Including public and private debt. At annual average exchange rates
Source: World Bank staff estimates.

term improvement in welfare—even after shadow economy source of growth is exhausted. If Ukraine does attain the goals set out in the 2010 program, it can expect to see the economy evolve as indicated in table 5.1.

Policy measures that improve the efficiency of capital use are one of the most critical requirements for the success of the 2010 program. But measures that increase investment in the economy are also vitally important. Due to high level of neglect during the final years of the Soviet era and since independence, more than 60 percent of the capital stock in industry is now estimated to be obsolescent. Major investments will be needed in capital repair and technological upgrading for industry and agriculture to restore growth and living standards. Ukraine also needs investments in supporting physical and institutional infrastructure, including a good system of economic courts. Restoring economic growth quickly enough to revive living standards within the next generation will depend heavily on implementing profound structural reforms as rapidly as possible—but these will need to be supported by raising gross domestic investment significantly.

International experience indicates that rapidly growing countries commonly invest 25 percent or more of GDP. Despite the substantial physical and social infrastructure inherited from the Soviet era, Ukraine will almost certainly need similar levels (at a minimum) to attain the desired rates of growth because of the energy inefficiency and low technical quality of much of this equipment—especially in the sphere of consumer goods production. While public capital expenditures will also rise slightly as a percentage of GDP to provide adequate social infrastructure, the locomotive of growth must be private investment in a business-friendly environment if Ukraine is to realize the full potential of the high-case 2010 scenario.

Eliminating the government's budget deficit (negative savings) will significantly increase total savings in the economy, freeing resources for far more productive private sector investment. Under the high case scenario, the investment-savings gap would be closed through foreign savings of 2-4 percent of GDP. A major share of this will need to come in as foreign direct investment because such capital tends to be far more stable than portfolio investment and would significantly reduce Ukraine's external debt service burden.

The success of the High Case Scenario will be closely linked to exports. If a good business climate is created in Ukraine, this will attract investment (especially foreign direct investment) that is interested in using Ukraine's low-cost, high-skill labor force for manufacturing internationally competitive products for export. The resulting export boom would provide the foreign exchange needed to purchase additional capital equipment and the inputs to produce more goods, both for export and for domestic consumption, thus raising domestic living standards. The strong inflow of foreign exchange generated by export success would provide a real foundation for a stable exchange rate, contributing to domestic price stability and thus to even higher rates of investment and growth.

In short, the strategy that lies behind the High Case Scenario, which is similar to that in the government's 2010 program, is to implement as quickly as possible the fundamental policy changes needed to create an upward spiral where investment, production, and exports work together to create higher living standards.

Base Case Scenario

The strategic development objectives and fundamental policies assumed for the Base Case Scenario are identical to those for the High Case Scenario. International competitiveness remains the means of attaining sustainably higher living standards. The only difference is the rate of policy reform—and thus the rate of economic growth. The Base Case Scenario requires all of

the "urgent reforms" needed in the High Case to prevent another financial crisis including a lower the budget deficit, controls on government borrowing, prudent monetary policy, and a realistic exchange rate. The other high case reforms—such as changing the role of government from Soviet to market models, privatizing, and establishing real markets for agriculture—are also required to attain the Base Case Scenario. In no way is the Base Case Scenario a "muddling through" scenario. However, taking into account the experience of the past decade and the strength of Ukraine's left-wing political parties that oppose rapid market-oriented reforms, the base case assumptions are less optimistic than those in high case regarding the feasible pace and consistency of the reform process.

Under the Base Case Scenario it should be possible to achieve growth rates of 3-4 percent a year. Though considerably lower than those in the High Case Scenario, these growth rates are higher than those attained by about 70 percent of the world's countries on a sustained basis over the past 25 years. And while the rate of improvement in living standards would not be as fast, 4 percent growth over 12 years would increase average incomes by 60 percent. The increase would be far greater for Ukraine's poor families, many of whom would go from receiving almost no wage income to getting a good paycheck that arrived on time.

A 60 percent nominal increase in GDP based on internationally competitive production might even bring many Ukrainians ahead of where they were in 1990, taking into account the fact that much of what was produced during the Soviet era was either of very low quality or designed for military use (and thus did nothing directly to raise real living standards). The degree to which nominal incomes during that period overstated real incomes is seen in the massive buildup of savings accounts in banks—not because Ukrainians suddenly became exceptionally thrifty, but because it was hard to find anything to buy. A savings account sufficient to buy several cars is not particularly valuable if there are no cars for sale. If GDP figures for 1990 are discounted by, say, 20 percent to account for military production that could be neither consumed nor invested to

Table 5.2 Base Case Scenario

	1997	1998	1999	2000	2001	2002-05	2006-09
Growth Rates (%)							
GDP	-3.0	-1.7	-1.0	1.0	2.0	3.9	4.5
GNFS Exports[1,2]	0.0	-13.4	-10.5	4.8	3.1	4.3	5.5
GNFS Imports[1,2]	2.0	-14.0	-14.5	3.1	3.4	5.3	5.7
Prices[3]	17.3	13.2	27.0	20.0	17.0	10.5	10.0
Percent of GDP							
GNFS Exports[1]	40.6	41.6	49.5	52.2	54.2	51.7	48.2
GNFS Imports[1]	43.7	44.4	50.5	52.4	54.5	53.3	50.7
Current Account Balance	-2.7	-3.1	-1.5	-0.9	-1.1	-2.0	-2.9
Gross Investment[4]	21.4	20.7	20.1	20.3	20.8	22.1	24.3
Consolidated Government Expenditure	43.6	38.9	37.6	36.6	35.4	34.8	34.8
Consolidated Budget Deficit[5]	-5.6	-2.6	-1.9	-1.6	-1.3	-1.0	-1.1
External Debt Indicators[6]							
Debt Service/GNFS Exports (%)	6.6	14.2	15.9	20.6	18.9	14.5	13.5
Debt/GDP (%)	21.7	30.1	41.4	40.6	40.4	37.4	31.4
Interest/GNFS Exports (%)	3.3	5.2	5.3	5.3	5.0	4.3	3.8
Net Foreign Direct Investment Infows (mln. USD)	581	747	500	750	900	1031	1463
As a percentage of GDP	1.2	1.8	1.6	2.4	2.9	2.8	3.0

[1] GNFS – Goods & Non-Factor Services
[2] Value growth
[3] GDP deflator
[4] Including inventories accumulation and net acquisition of valuables
[5] IMF GFS methodology
[6] Including public and private debt. At annual average exchange rates
Source: Official data and World Bank staff estimates.

produce consumption goods, and by another 20 percent to account for shortages of consumer goods, 4 percent annual GDP growth over the next 10 years or so might be sufficient to restore the average real living standards that prevailed at the end of the Soviet era.

If the Base Case Scenario is realized, the macroeconomy can be expected to evolve along the lines shown in table 5.2. Economic growth is brought about by an increase in investment, just as in the High Case Scenario. Similarly, exports play a vital role. But because structural reforms take place more slowly in the Base Case Scenario, investment and export growth do not increase as much as in the High Case Scenario. Even more important, the investment that does take place is less efficient in generating output

and growth because the measures taken to curb the burden of government and to develop an attractive investment climate are not as adequate. As a result private investment plays a less prominent role than in the High Case Scenario.

Even though investment under the Base Case Scenario is lower than under the High Case Scenario, finding financing for this investment will be more difficult given the less favorable investment climate. Foreign direct investment, a non-debt way of financing foreign savings, will not be forthcoming to the same degree because the business climate will be less attractive. As a result the government will have to resort to larger foreign borrowing to obtain the foreign savings needed to achieve the investment required to produce the target average growth (see table 5.2).

Low Case Scenario—a surge, then muddling through to disaster

Some groups in Ukraine, while recognizing that a return to the Soviet Union is not an option, find a third way somewhere between a system where responsibility for production lies squarely with the state and one where responsibility lies squarely with private business will almost certainly lead to failure. In short, the third way leads to the third world.[3]

As shown in table 5.3, any attempt to continue

Table 5.3 Low Case Scenario

	1997	1998	1999	2000	2001	2002-05	2006-09
Growth Rates (%)							
GDP	-3.0	-1.7	-1.0	6.0	4.0	-0.9	-2.5
GNFS Exports[1,2]	0	-13.4	-10.5	4.7	2.9	-0.3	-3.2
GNFS Imports[1,2]	2.0	-14.0	-14.5	6.5	2.0	-0.7	-3.0
Prices[3]	17.3	13.2	27.0	45.0	90.0	110.0	100.0
Percent of GDP							
GNFS Exports[1]	40.6	41.6	49.5	47.7	46.1	44.2	39.5
GNFS Imports[1]	43.7	44.4	50.5	49.5	47.4	44.8	40.2
Current Account Balance	-2.7	-3.1	-1.5	-2.6	-2.3	-1.0	-1.0
Gross Investment[4]	21.4	20.7	20.1	22.0	24.0	24.9	23.1
Consolidated Government Expenditure	43.6	38.9	37.6	39.5	39.8	41.9	47.5
Consolidated Budget Deficit[5]	-5.6	-2.6	-1.8	-8.8	-10.0	-11.3	-10.0
External Debt Indicators[6]							
Debt Service/GNFS Exports (%)	6.6	14.2	15.8	20.5	22.6	17.9	15.1
Debt/GDP (%)	21.7	30.1	39.8	37.7	37.1	34.8	33.8
Interest/GNFS Exports (%)	3.3	5.2	5.2	5.0	5.2	3.3	2.8
Net Foreign Direct Investment Inflows (mln. USD)	581	747	500	500	450	348	228
As a percentage of GDP	1.2	1.8	1.6	1.4	1.2	0.9	0.6

[1] GNFS – Goods & Non-Factor Services
[2] Value growth
[3] GDP deflator
[4] Including inventories accumulation and net acquisition of valuables
[5] IMF GFS methodology
[6] Including public and private debt. At annual average exchange rates
Source: Official data and World Bank staff estimates.

nevertheless want to preserve as much of the Soviet past as possible. They claim that the changes made over the past decade are proof that rapid market reforms are not a viable solution because of the "special conditions" of Ukraine. The emotional appeal of this position is understandable. Few people prefer change to stability, and many lived much better under the Soviet regime than they do today. But a return to the Soviet past is impossible—and efforts to

[3] This statement, which has been attributed to Vaclav Klaus, rings all too true for Ukraine. After years of hesitant reforms that have left much of the old Soviet system in place, GDP has declined so severely that Ukraine could soon be eligible to join the group of the world's poorest nations that are eligible to borrow from the World Bank's affiliate, the International Development Association. Another widely-cited aphorism is relevant here: "Those who do not long for the benefits of the Soviet system have no heart—and those who think that the Soviet system can be restored have no head."

muddling through with partial reforms would leave Ukraine dangling between the Soviet and market economic systems—producing dire consequences. With a surge of monetary expansion, Ukraine might be able to enjoy 12-18 months of accelerated economic growth, like Belarus did. But as now shown by the Belarussian experience, this growth would not be sustainable and would inflict high costs on Ukrainians in the form of high inflation, growing scarcities, and reduced investment for long-term growth. Without the incentives and freedom of action that come with private ownership of agricultural and industrial assets, productive efficiency would decline, a trend that would be compounded by continued government intervention. Under such conditions, neither foreigners nor residents would be particularly interested in investing in Ukraine, slowing investment and growth. Slow government reforms regarding its role and size would make high budget deficits likely, increasing the pressures to borrow at high costs in unfavorable capital markets. Faced with limited investor interest in its t-bills, the government would put pressure on the central bank to increase monetary emission, rekindling the fires of inflation that burned Ukraine so badly during the early years of its independence.

Of the three generic policy alternatives, only one—competitiveness through economic and structural reform—will put Ukraine on the path of long-term, sustainable growth needed to restore living standards. Implementing the necessary reforms will require difficult decisions and sustained efforts over many years. Quick results are unlikely. Some of the necessary reforms—especially the restructuring or closing of loss-making enterprises—will cause temporary unemployment. Two measures are therefore urgently needed to sustain social consensus during the transition:

First, Ukraine needs to develop a business-friendly environment that stimulates the creation of new jobs, especially in small and medium-size enterprises. Second, Ukraine needs to design and implement a social safety net that protects families from absolute poverty and helps them find new jobs.

These reforms will be difficult. But the alternatives—high debt and high inflation, muddling through, or protectionism—would lead to far more serious social problems. High debt and inflation would lead to artificial economic growth, followed by a crash with social consequences far worse than the crash of late 1998. A strong program of rapid structural change and the development of a strong market economy is the only way to meet the aspirations of the Ukrainian people for sustained higher living standards, as reflected in the government's program for 2010.

In short, doing nothing means going backwards. Failing to push forward from the current status with a strong program of reforms will inevitably lead to higher deficits, more inflation, and further economic decline.

Financing the future

Given the severe financial crisis of late 1998 and continuing debt service pressures, how is Ukraine going to be able to find the necessary financing to cover the budget deficit, the current account deficit and repay foreign debts? The longer-term financing prospects, as outlined above, look good under the Base Case and High Case Scenarios. But will the country be able to get through the next two to three years?

For the next two to three years, the financing requirements for the High Case Scenario would be very similar to those for the Base Case Scenario. It will take some time for Ukraine to reap the benefits of structural reforms before it launches into the sharply higher growth of the High Case Scenario. After takeoff, the more buoyant economic growth and better investment climate of the High Case Scenario would make financing even easier to obtain than in the base case scenario, so a detailed discussion is not needed here of that alternative.

This section demonstrates that under either scenario there is no room for error or backsliding in reforms, but the situation will be sustainable if reforms move forward quickly. On the other hand, the Low Case Scenario is not sustainable from any perspective and will not be discussed further here.

Ukraine faces financing challenges on two fronts over the next few years—financing government borrowing requirements and financing the balance of payments.[4]

Table 5.4 Budget financing requirements and availabilities, 1999

Requirements	Billions of USD
Primary budget deficit (excl. interest)	(0.5)
Interest	1.2
External	0.7
Domestic	0.6
Amortization	2.5
External	1.3
Internal	1.2
IMF quota increase	0.5
Total budget financing required	*3.8*
Availabilities	
External financing	1.8
World Bank (adjustment lending)	0.7
IMF	0.8
Other	0.3
Domestic financing	0.3
T-bills (excl. central bank)	0.1
Central bank (incl. t-bills)	0.3
Privatization	0.1
Total budget financing available	**2.3**
Roll-over of NBU-held T-bills	1.5
Total (including roll-over of NBU-held T-bills)	*3.8*

Source: World Bank staff estimates

Financing the budget. The financial crisis of late 1998 highlighted the importance of sound fiscal management. The base case and high case scenarios assume that the government will vigorously implement the program of fiscal and financial prudence that it has worked out with the IMF in the context of the Extended Fund Facility. The government faces a gross

financing requirement in 1999 of $3.8 billion. In round numbers, the main components of this requirement are as shown in the upper half of table 5.4.

Assuming that policy performance is sufficiently strong to keep the IMF program on track, thus making additional financing possible from other sources such as the World Bank, about $2.3 billion equivalent of financing could become available without further debt renegotiation or restructuring (see bottom half of table 5.4). The budget financing gap of about $1.5 billion for 1999 could be met as follows. The local currency portion of the gap, equivalent to about $1.2 billion, could be more than filled if the central bank were to roll over the $1.5 billion equivalent that it holds in t-bills maturing in 1999.

Filling the $0.3 billion foreign currency component of the budget financing gap could be more difficult but could be handled as follows given the reasonably solid external payments situation anticipated under both the Base and High Case Scenarios. If the government were to roll over the entire stock of t-bills held by the central bank with no payment of interest in 1999, it could use the surplus over domestic financing requirements to purchase about $0.3 billion of foreign exchange from the central bank, thus covering the gap. A far better approach, however, would be to accelerate the privatization of state-owned enterprises to foreign investors, thereby generating the additional foreign exchange needed and preserving the nation's minimal external reserves. In fact, strong efforts to increase privatization—especially of the 200 industrial "giants"—could also have a strong positive influence on the performance of these companies in terms of investment, job creation, productivity, and exports, leading to higher living standards on a sustainable basis.

Financing the balance of payments. Ukraine's external financing requirements also appear in the top half of table 5.5, which shows medium- and long-term external debt repayment as part of the external financing requirements. In fact, the budget financing and the external accounts financing tables are closely linked from this perspective. As shown in the lower part of table

---

[4] The borrowing requirements discussed here are similar to the better-known public sector borrowing requirement, but here we include only borrowing of the consolidated government (including the central bank); the borrowing of public enterprises is excluded.

Table 5.5: Balance of payments financing requirements and availabilities, 1999

Requirements	Billions of USD
Goods and non factor services trade deficit	0.3
Medium- and long-term external debt service	2.0
International reserves increase	0.9
Total financing required	*3.2*
Availabilities	
Medium and long-term external borrowing	2.0
World Bank (adj. and project)	0.7
IMF	0.8
Other multilateral	0.2
Other	0.3
Net current transfers	0.6
FDI and portfolio investment	0.6
Total financing available	*3.2*

Source: World Bank staff estimates

5.5, balance of payments will be fully financed in 1999 if Ukraine implements the EFF as planned (thus maintaining access to IMF and World Bank funding) and maintains a competitive exchange rate and free current account convertibility (thus ensuring that enterprises have access to the resources they need for production and that exporting is profitable). A good foreign currency regime is also vital to ensuring that imports are not underpriced through an overvalued domestic currency. If the domestic market were flooded with imports, the resulting balance of payments deficit could be very difficult to finance.

Risks for future budgetary financing

Risks in 1999. This analysis indicates that, while fiscal situation is sustainable in principle, avoiding another major financial crisis depends heavily on the following assumptions:

- The government controls spending and maintains revenue efforts sufficient to assure a primary budget surplus of at least 1.5-2.0 percent of GDP.

- Arrangements can be worked out with the central bank regarding a rollover or refinancing of the large stock of t-bills that it holds.

- The government sharply accelerates structural reforms, enabling it to gain and retain full access to IMF and World Bank financing.

- Net current transfers are sustained at historic levels. These transfers, which include current grant financing from the donors and transfers of funds from Ukrainians abroad, depend heavily on a domestic environment of stability and progress.

- Foreign direct investment flows are sustained.

Developments and risks in 2000. The following developments and risks can be seen for internal and external financing for the year 2000.

- The burden of foreign debt amortization doubles between 1999 and 2000, rising from $1.3 billion to $2.2 billion, largely as the result of about $1.0 billion in fiduciary loans and Eurobonds that will fall due in 2000.

- Although World Bank and IMF amortization shows large percentage increases—especially for the World Bank as grace periods on its loans begin to expire—the absolute burden of World Bank and IMF amortization is modest (less than 30 percent of the total).

- The interest payment burden can be stable if Ukraine avoids taking on new high-cost t-bill debt.

- Despite the assumed increase in the primary budget surplus from 1.6 percent to 2.0 percent of GDP, gross financing requirements in 2000 will remain unchanged at about $3.8 billion.

- In 2000 the total budget financing requirements ($3.8 billion) and availabilities ($2.3 billion) will be similar to the levels of 1999, But with a falling stock of central bank–held t-bills falling due, the potential for rollover is less, and the financing gap will climb from about $100 million to about

$500 million, making increased efforts to accelerate privatization even more urgent to cover the budget deficit in 2000.

Risks in 2001. If debts are repaid as scheduled rather than rescheduled in 2000, the financing picture in 2001 does improve with residual budget financing requirements dropping from $3.9 billion to around $3 billion, but this is not enough to resolve the problem. Privatization and continued market reforms will therefore remain crucial to avoiding a balance of payments crisis in 2001. The estimated $2.0 bn of financing this would bring into the country would make a major contribution to alleviating external debt repayment pressures and supporting the fledgling economic growth.

Risks for future balance of payments financing

To minimize future balance of payments problems, Ukraine needs to move as quickly as possible to implement policies sufficient to assure the following:

- a primary budget surplus equal to at least 2% of GDP, which would reduce the risk of high-cost foreign financing for the budget deficit (as in 1996-98).

- a flexible exchange rate that compensates for domestic inflation, thereby helping ensure the international competitiveness of Ukraine's goods and the profitability of enterprises producing these goods.

- liberalized internal markets to ensure growing supplies of internationally competitive goods.

However, even if all of these important measures are put into place, Ukraine still faces a potentially serious balance of payments financing problem in the year 2000—one driven almost entirely by the $1.0 billion of restructured T-bills and Eurobonds that will fall due that year. These payments push estimated external financing requirements from $3.2 billion in 1999 to almost $4.0 billion in 2000. Even after all other feasible sources of financing are taken into account, a gap of up to $1.0 billion remains.

Given that Ukraine's access to international capital markets is likely to remain negligible during 2000, and given that the external lenders who rescheduled debts in 1998 are unlikely to be willing to reschedule the same debts again in 2000, the only viable source of financing appears to be a sharp increase in privatization proceeds. The World Bank is working with the government to agree on a plan to generate roughly $1.0 billion in cash privatization proceeds, largely from investors who would pay in foreign exchange. Meeting these targets would also significantly expand the resources available from the multilateral lending agencies.

Without such privatization revenues, it is hard to see how Ukraine could escape a major balance of payments crisis in 2000. Such a crisis could be triggered by new economic problems in Russia, a refusal by Russia to provide energy resources to Ukraine without full payment in cash at world prices, a failure to roll over a debt obligation, problems in the energy sector triggered by Y2K glitches, or a number of other factors, any of which have a significant probability. Once a crisis started, people would flee from the hrivnya into dollars. As foreign exchange reserves ran low and NBU could no longer defend the currency, the exchange rate would depreciate precipitously, triggering panic and leaving the government little option but to clamp on exchange controls and trade restrictions. The resulting shortages of imports would push down production in import-dependent factories, resulting in further economic decline and job losses. Shortages of important consumer goods including energy could also develop, causing widespread suffering and even unrest. Without major and rapid improvements in the nation's economic policies and management, such a highly undesirable scenario cannot be dismissed.

But if Ukraine establishes the favorable business climate needed to attain a dramatic increase in the pace of privatization, it will generate the resources needed to avoid serious economic and social problems—and it will create a market-oriented environment that would attract investments that go far beyond the privatization of existing enterprises, thus creating jobs, economic growth, and higher living standards for all.

BIBLIOGRAPHY

Companion volumes from the Country Economic Memorandum Project

Hansen, John, and Vira Nanivska (eds). 1999. *Economic Growth with Equity: Ukrainian Perspectives* (World Bank Discussion Paper No. 407). World Bank, Kiev and Washington, D.C.

Hansen, John and Diana Cook. 1999. *Economic Growth with Equity: Which Strategy for Ukraine?* (World Bank Discussion Paper No. 408). World Bank, Kiev and Washington, D.C.

Analytical reports for the Country Economic Memorandum Project

Borodiuk, Volodymyr, and Oleksandr Turchinov. 1998. *Shadow Economy*. Kyiv: International Center for Policy Studies and World Bank.

Golladay, Frederick, Galina Sotirova, Kate Schecter, and Gnanaraj Chellaraj. 1998. "Review of Public Expenditures on Health and Education in Ukraine." World Bank, Washington, D.C.

Hansen, John and Diana Cook. 1999. "Economic Growth with Equity: Which Strategy for Ukraine," *Policy Studies #3*, March 1999.

Kuddo, Arvo. 1998. "Institutional Changes in the Ukrainian Labor Market." World Bank, Washington, D.C.

Lippott, Joachim. 1999. "Legal Challenges to Fiscal Sustainability in Ukraine." TACIS and the Ukrainian-European Policy and Legal Advice Center, Kyiv.

Lomynoha V.Y., A.A. Maksiuta., V.G. Skarchevsky, and M.V. Chechetov. 1998. *Fiscal Policy*. Kyiv: International Center for Policy Studies and World Bank.

Sabluk, Petro, and Anatoly Fesyna. 1998. *Agricultural Policy*. Kyiv: International Center for Policy Studies and World Bank.

Siedenberg, Axel and Lutz Hoffmann (editors), *Ukraine at the crossroads. Economic reforms in international perspective*. Heidelberg, New York, 1999.

Vitrenko, Yury, and V. Lukovenko. 1998. *Education: Economic Aspects*. Kyiv: International Center for Policy Studies and World Bank.

Vitrenko, Yury, and Antonina Nagorna. 1998. *Health System*. Kyiv: International Center for Policy Studies and World Bank.

Vrublevsky, Vitaly, and Valeriy Kiriachenko. 1998. *Energy Policy*. Kyiv: International Center for Policy Studies and World Bank.

Vrublevsky, Vitaly, Gennady Tryneev, and M. Yakubovsky. 1998. *Industry and Trade Policy*. Kyiv: International Center for Policy Studies and World Bank.

Yaremenko, Oleksandr, and Mykola Soldatenko. 1998. *Social Protection*. Kyiv: International Center for Policy Studies and World Bank

Other sources

Aiyar, S.S.A. 1998. "Lessons in designing safety nets," *PREM Notes, #2-4/98*. Washington, DC:: World Bank.

Bermingham, Paul. 1998. *Telecommunications Strategy*. Washington, DC: World Bank.

Bobadilla, Jose Luis, Christine A. Costello, and Faith Mitchell, eds. 1997. *Premature Death in the New Independent States*. Washington, D.C: National Academy Press.

Bruno, Michael, and William Easterly. 1995. "Could Inflation Stabilization Be Expansionary?" *Transition* 7 (7-8): 1-3.

Caprio, Gerard Jr. 1998. "Banking on Crises: Expensive Lessons from Recent Financial Crises." World Bank, Washington, D.C.

Dikhanov, Yuri. 1996. "Decomposition of Inequality Based on Incomplete Information." World Bank, Washington, D.C.

Easterly, William. 1997. "The Ghosts of Financing Gap." Policy Research Working Paper 1807. World Bank, Development Research Group, Washington, D.C.

Easterly, William, and Stanley D. Fischer. 1995. "The Soviet Economic Decline." *The World Bank Economic Review* 9(3): 341-71.

EBRD (European Bank for Reconstruction and Development). 1998. *Transition Report 1998.* London.

Frye, Timothy, and Andrei Shleifer. 1997. "The Invisible Hand and the Grabbing Hand." *American Economic Review Papers and Proceedings* 87: 354–58.

Gaddy, Clifford, and Barry Ickes. 1998. "Beyond a Bailout: Time to Face reality about Russia's 'Virtual Economy.'" *Foreign Affairs* 77: 53–67.

GLS Research, GA-PBN, UFE Foundation, Government of Ukraine, and USAID. "The Economic Reforms in Ukraine: Opinion Survey of 1,600 Ukrainian Citizens April/May 1997." Kyiv.

Graham, Edward M. Forthcoming. "Investment Incentives to Foreign Direct Investors: Are They Effective and Should They Be Subject to Multilateral Control?" World Bank, Washington, D.C.

Hansen, John. 1978. *Guide to practical project appraisal – social benefit-cost analysis in developing countries.* United Nations Industrial Development Organization, Vienna and New York.

Hendley, Kathryn, Barry Ickes, and Randi Ryterman. 1998. "Remonitizing the Russian Economy." http://econ.la.psu.edu/~bickes/barter.pdf.

Hoopengardner, Tom. 1996. *Poverty in Ukraine.* World Bank (Report No. 15602-UA), Washington, D.C.

Hufbauer, Gary Clyde, and Kimberly Ann Elliott. 1993. *Measuring the Costs of protection in the United States.* Washington, DC: Institute for International Economics.

ICPS (International Center for Policy Studies). 1998. "Quarterly Rapid Enterprise Survey: Regulatory Environment (February)" Kyiv.

Ilchuk, Serhy. 1999. "The Government Creates Bad Debts in Ukraine." *Policy Studies.* Kyiv: International Center for Policy Studies

Johnson, Simon, Daniel Kaufmann, and Andrei Shleifer. 1997. "The Unofficial Economy in Transition." *Brookings Papers on Economic Activity 2.* Washington, DC: Brookings Institution.

Kaminsiy, Graciela, Salul Lizondo and Carmen M. Reinhart. 1997. *Leading Indicators of Currency Crises.* World Bank, Washington, D.C.

Karatnycky, Adrian, Alexander Motyl, and Boris Shor. 1998. *Nations in Transit, 1997.* New York: Freedom House.

Kaufmann, Daniel. 1997. "Desperately Seeking Economic Recovery: Why is Ukraine's Economy—and Russia's—Not Growing?" *Transition* (April): 5–8.

Kaufmann, Daniel, and Aleksander Kaliberda. 1996. "Integrating the Unofficial Economy into the Dynamics of Post-Socialist Economies." In Bartlomiej Kaminski, ed., *Economic Transition in Russia and the New States of Eurasia*. Armonk, New York: M.E. Sharpe.

Kuddo, Arvo. 1999. "Labor Market Developments in the FSU Region." World Bank, Washington, D.C.

Lambsdorff, Johan G. Forthcoming. "Corruption Perceptions around the World." Institute for Development Studies, Sussex University, UK.

Lunina, Inna. 1999. "Insolvent Enterprises Unbalance the Budget." *Policy Studies*. Kyiv: International Center for Policy Studies

Michaely, Michael. 1998. *Ukraine: Foreign Trade and Commercial Policies*. World Bank, Kyiv, processed.

Novitsky, V., I. Novitskaya, and A. Stone. 1995. "Ukrainian Private Enterprises: Getting Down to Business." World Bank, Washington, D.C.

PADCO. 1999. *A Guaranteed Minimum Income Program in Ukraine: Its Design and Implementation.* PADCO (Policy Report No. 29, 2/99), Kyiv.

Petrina, Katerina. 1998. "Ukraine: Financing Education during Economic Transition." World Bank, Kyiv.

Polackova, Hana. 1998. "Contingent Liabilities—A Threat to Fiscal Stability." *PREM Note* 9. World Bank, Poverty Reduction and Economic Management Network, Washington, D.C.

Policy Development and Review Department, IMF, Washington, D.C. (April 1999). "Involving the Private Sector in Forestalling and Resolving Financial Crises".

Pomerleano, Michael. 1998. "Corporate Finance Lessons from the East Asian Crisis." Viewpoint 155. World Bank, Finance, Private Sector, and Infrastructure Network, Washington, D.C.

Ravallion, Martin. 1999. "Protecting the Poor in a Crisis—and Beyond." *PREM Note* 12. World Bank, Poverty Reduction and Economic Management Network, Washington, D.C.

Rose-Ackerman, Susan, and Andrew Stone. Forthcoming. "The Burden of Bribery on Private Business: Evidence from World Bank Surveys" Business Environment Group Discussion Paper.

Shah, Anwar, ed.. 1995. *Fiscal Incentives for Investment and Innovation*. New York: Oxford University Press.

Treisman, Daniel. 1996. "The Politics of Intergovernmental Transfers in Post-Soviet Russia." *British Journal of Political Science* 26: 299–335.

Ukrainian State Company for Credits and Investments. 1998. "Investment Climate: Commentaries of Reputed Experts." *Monitoring Investment Activities in Ukraine:* 7–28.

UNDP (United Nations Development Programme). 1997. *Human Development Report for Ukraine*. Kyiv.

Valdes, Alberto. 1997. *Agricultural Production, Pricing, and Marketing Structures in Ukraine (EC4NR Agriculture Policy Note #11). Washington: World Bank.*

Vennen, Thomas. 1998. *Impediments to Foreign Investment in Ukraine*. TACIS/UEPLAC, Kyiv, processed, March 1999.

World Bank. 1993. *Ukraine: Country Economic Memorandum.* Report 10029-UA. Washington, D.C.

———. 1995. "Ukraine: Financial Sector Review." Washington, D.C.

ANNEX A: AN AGENDA FOR STRUCTURAL REFORMS

Introduction

Structural reforms are needed throughout Ukraine to accelerate the transition from a soviet economy to a market economy. Some of these reforms will be vital simply to minimize the risk of further poverty-creating financial crises. Almost all of the reforms will be required if Ukraine is to attain the rates of growth that it has targeted in its plan for the year 2010. The reforms needed in Ukraine are grouped below in three thematic areas: changing the role of government, improving social conditions, and structural reforms. All of these reforms should be have been implemented many years ago; all are urgently needed. However, given the situation today, those flagged with a large arrow (➜) are more urgent than others — either to prevent a crisis or to create conditions necessary for the success of other "downstream" reforms. Given the urgency and complexity of the reforms that are needed within the next 18 months to prevent a major economic and social crisis, the list below does not try to cover the longer-term structural measures that will be required to fine-tune the economy for greater efficiency, thus maximizing long-term economic growth.

Critically urgent reforms

Although the most urgent reforms are marked with an arrow in the presentation below, three areas of reform need to be highlighted up front because they are so vitally important in the short run to avoid a serious crisis that could bring economic and social strife to the country. These reforms focus on assuring that the country as a whole and the government in particular lives within its means. This is vital so that Ukraine does not return to the pattern of profligate spending that marked the years after independence. These reforms include:

- Keep budget expenditures in line with revenues at all times, running a small surplus in the short run, for this will make it easier to avoid a debt crisis.

- Avoid printing money to cover budgetary deficits or to finance quasi-budgetary expenditures.

- Allow exchange rate to devalue as necessary to build international reserves and to maintain a stable real exchange rate that makes domestic products more competitive on both foreign and domestic markets.

Although the list of reforms below is long, the number of different ministries, agencies, committees and working groups that can be mobilized to work in parallel on these reforms is formidable in a country with the size and expertise of Ukraine. Therefore multiple reforms can easily proceed in parallel if the will to reform is present. For example, the Ministry of Agriculture can easily move forward with land titling while the Ministry of Health introduces improved energy efficiency in hospitals. The process will be demanding, however. Institutional mechanisms will have to be established to coordinate policy formulation across sectors. Also, technical assistance programs need to be expanded dramatically to help Ukraine develop policy analysts able to evaluate, design and promote implementation of market-oriented economic policies.

Rapid action is technically feasible in Ukraine because, with the support of extensive foreign technical assistance programs, some local policy analysts have been trained and have already started doing policy analysis and formulation in a number of critical areas. Some reforms such as large-scale privatization and expansion of the economic court system will require substantial financial resources. However, if evidence emerges that Ukraine has clearly shifted onto the path of radical economic reforms, the necessary resources could easily be mobilized from private and official external sources. Money is not the problem. What has been lacking is the will to reform.

Structure and actions of Government

➜ *Apparat.* Reform the "Apparat" of the Cabinet of Ministers so that it focuses on policy coordination rather than policy making and delegate to ministers the responsibility for policy making in their sectors (An important precondition is to enact the law on the COM*)*.

➜ *Cabinet structure.* Consolidate the Cabinet so that it becomes a small collegial body focused on strategic policy making.

➜ *Civil service.* Reform the civil service, clearly delimitating political and non-political posts, implementing pay reform, training of senior civil servants, and introducing merit-based promotion principles.

➜ *Deregulation.* Reduce the number of business inspections by half as measured by independent surveys in a random selection of cities; and sharply limit the number of routine State Tax Administration inspections.

Fiscal policy

Budget Process and Policy Issues

➜ *Overall Budget Deficit.* Hold to maximum of 1% or less of GDP at least until adequate credit is available domestically without crowding out productive investments and until more access to international capital on normal conditions is restored. (A primary surplus of at least 2% of GDP is also needed.)

➜ *Inter-governmental fiscal relations.* Implementation of a formula-based transfer system and reduced dependency on tax sharing can improve the incentives for local government tax collection and augment the overall transparency and stability of the fiscal system, and contribute to better management of budgetary resources at all levels of government.

➜ *Budget Process.* Pass and implement a "Law on the Budget System and Budgetary Processes" that creates clear rules of the game, including clear allocation of expenditure responsibilities and revenue generation authority between the sub-national and national levels of government.

- *Budget Coverage.* Bring all revenues and expenditures of the Central Government and its agencies under the consolidated government budget. Extra-budgetary funds such as Road and Innovation should either be abolished or be forced to compete for funds within the consolidated government budget.

- *Treasury operations.* All government revenues and expenses should flow through the Treasury (the term "government" here excludes only state enterprises, which should operate on a commercial basis and, in most cases, be privatized as quickly as possible). The technical capacity of the Treasury needs to be improved so that it can handle the additional work. Fees and fines collected by authorized bodies such as Customs, State Tax Administration and various police agencies should not remain with the bodies collecting them.

- *Treasury deposits.* All government resources should be held by the National Bank, not by commercial banks. Where funds need to be moved to the NBU, however, this should be done in a phased manner to avoid unwarranted banking failures. Any government resources that have to be held in commercial banks as an interim measure should be in interest bearing accounts with interest credited at normal commercial deposit rates. Any payments to commercial banks for handling government revenue collection or disbursement activity should be billed and paid explicitly, not through interest offsets. If commercial bank services are required in the longer term to support treasury operations, periodic tenders should be issued for these services on a competitive basis.

Expenditure Issues

➔ *Budget expenditure levels.* Limit budget expenditure commitment authority of spending agencies to levels consistent with emerging revenues to avoid further accumulation of arrears. Enforce through strong Treasury system.

➔ *Arrears.* Avoid any accumulation of new budgetary expenditure arrears by tightly controlling expenditure commitment authority in line with realistic estimates of revenues. Consider securitizing and factoring outstanding arrears. Avoid writing off tax receivables; this endangers future revenue collections by creating expectations of further write-offs.

➔ *Procurement.* To reduce risk of corruption, use open competitive bidding for procurement for at least 50 percent of the value of government purchases, gradually raising this percentage thereafter.

➔ *Staffing levels and patterns.* Reduce total staffing in line with IMF agreements and streamline the structure of Ministries and the apparat in line with the plans developed for the Public Administration Reform Loan from the World Bank.

- *Subsidies.* Move steadily to at least 80 percent cost recovery during 1999 for all communal public transport services. Put policies in place that will assure full pass-through of cost increases to maintain or further improve cost recovery levels.

- *Privileges.* Eliminate all privileges that allow certain categorical groups to enjoy a variety of government-supplied services at low or no cost. Protect those affected from risk of poverty with a means-tested social safety net system.

- *State Reserve Fund.* Require zero budget deficit in State Reserve Fund Operations effective immediately. Force fund to cover any deficits by sale of assets. Implement full annual review of SRF by outside auditor. All procurement should be done through open, competitive tenders. No barter deals should be allowed.

- *Security.* Reduce expenditures on external and internal security forces.

- *Human services.* The most important areas of government expenditure in terms both of the money involved and the impact of peoples' quality of life are human services— health, education, and the social safety net. Because of the issues related to these programs go far beyond the need to control expenditures, the policy recommendations for these programs are presented separately below.

Revenue issues

➔ *Revenue collection in cash.* A plan should be developed to assure that non-cash payments to the budget are reduced by 30 percent per year over the next three years. More rapid progress would be desirable.

➔ *Tax privileges.* Reduce tax privileges (concessional rates and exemptions) so that all economic activity is subject to essentially the same rates of tax (aside from "sin" taxes on alcohol, tobacco and a limited list of luxury items). To the extent possible, a flat rate of VAT should apply across the board, except for exports which, by international convention, are zero rated. Any budgetary support deemed necessary for poverty alleviation or other reasons should be budgeted explicitly and included in the calculation of the overall budget deficit.

- *Personal income tax.* A flat rate Income tax of about 25 percent with almost no exemptions or deductions, and a liberal minimum income cutoff level before any tax is paid, would increase revenues, reduce corruption, and be reasonably progressive, particularly at the lower income levels.

- *Corporate income tax.* A flat rate equal to the top personal income tax rate with minimum exemptions and deductions would reduce corruption, legal manipulations, and increase tax revenues by encouraging enterprises to rejoin the official sector.

- *Value added tax.* Improve system by operating on international standards in terms of accrual accounting, time allowed for government to rebate VAT credits (overpayments), and auditing procedures for tax rebate claims. Move and keep the VAT on an accrual basis, preferably without the dual accounting system required under current transitional arrangements.

➔ *Bankruptcy and hard budget constraints.* The existence of a credible threat of bankruptcy is one of the most effective ways of assuring the enforcement of contracts. Although Ukraine has a bankruptcy law on the books, it is ineffective. A new draft is available which appears to be consistent with international practice. This should be approved and implemented as quickly as possible to provide the essential foundations for a good business climate in Ukraine.

- *Customs.* Develop a customs code and other international trade laws in line with international standards. Consider contracting out the customs function to a reliable international pre-shipment inspection firm to improve service and reduce corruption.

Monetary and exchange rate policy

- *Monetization.* The current ratio of money to GDP is exceptionally low in Ukraine. This contributes directly to the dominance of barter in the economy, to the exceptionally high cost of capital, and thus to the lack of economic growth. The ratio needs to be increased to more normal levels by establishing a solid balance between monetary and fiscal policy. This should be accomplished largely by tightening fiscal policy, but also by allowing some growth of credit consistent with realistic inflation targets.

External trade policy

- *Customs.* Reduce customs delays, corruption, and losses of revenues to the Government. This could include contracting customs operations to an internationally recognized pre-shipment inspection agency as other countries such as Indonesia have done,

- *Import tariffs.* Gradually reduce import duties to levels consistent with international agreements on tariff reductions under the WTO. Reduce high and variable tariff rates to levels more consistent with average tariffs. Remove most import tariff exemptions, and raise exceptionally low rates closer to the average level.

➔ *Export restraints.* Ukraine badly needs foreign exchange from exports. Virtually all remaining barriers to export such as quotas, duties, advance deposits and forex surrender requirements should be abolished, the only exception being the unfortunate cases where the EU and other countries impose export quotas on Ukrainian industries to protect their own high-cost producers.

- *World Trade Organization.* Complete process of accession to the WTO as quickly as possible, thus allowing Ukraine to participate fully on a stable basis in world trade and the privileges pertaining to WTO membership.

Shadow Economy

➔ *Judicial reform and anti-corruption program.* Implement judicial reform to strengthen courts, ensure effective and efficient enforcement of law, organize a witness protection program, stimulate strong public disapproval of corruption, introduce basic legal and anti-corruption courses at primary education schools, set up more channels of legal information to people, enable wider participation of general public in legislative drafting, etc.

➔ *Tax System Reform.* Decrease the number of taxes and surcharges, reduce tax rates and pay for the cut by eliminating tax privileges, introduce a comprehensive basic tax law (Tax Code) instead of myriad of contradictory laws and regulations, foster voluntary tax compliance, reduce tax evasion and broaden tax base, efficiently and equitably administer taxes, and promote a compliance-based revenue administration equipped with business processes, skills, management systems, and operational tools

- *Reduce regulatory burden*. Reduce incentives to hide in shadow economy by reducing regulatory burden, especially the frequency of inspections. . Restrict the number of days that an enterprise can be visited by inspectors during a given year without an order based on cause from a court of law. Establish rules of engagement for inspections that clearly list the obligations that can be enforced and the rights of enterprises being inspected. Provide adequate right of appeal, including a small-claims window for appeals using simplified procedures.

- *Contract enforcement.* The difficulty of enforcing contracts for delivery and for payment is one of the most frequent complaints of investors in Ukraine today. Major improvements are needed in the nation's economic court system to overcome this problem.

Improving social conditions

Health Care

- *Health-care programs and facilities*. Shift focus of health system from tertiary to primary health care and from curative to preventative care. Retrain doctors so that more of them are general practitioners, not just narrow specialists. Improve access to modern medical equipment for diagnosis and treatment; this will allow more cases to be handled on an outpatient basis and to reduce average hospital stays. This, plus efforts to close under-utilized facilities, to establish non-medical shelters for the homeless, and to increase the energy efficiency of the remaining facilities will help Ukraine reduce the heavy financial burden of maintaining an exceptionally high ratio of hospital beds to population served. Improved equipment and facilities will also help make it possible to reduce the total number of medical staff to levels more consistent with international experience.

- *Health-care financing.* Moving from the current implicit medical insurance program where the state in theory pays almost all costs to an explicit medical insurance program where the people are charged for services rendered and contribute a fraction of the cost through a co-payment scheme would reduce unnecessary use of medical services. It would also allow moving towards a more realistic program of cost recovery, helping reduce the corruption and side-payments that are now common.

Education

- *Education programs and facilities.* Gradually lower the ratio of education workers to students closer to international standards, thus reducing the high burden of staff costs in the sector. To reduce the high energy costs and other maintenance expenses that drive up the costs of education in Ukraine, gradually consolidate schools, limit the number of specialized institutions, invest in energy conservation measures, and remodel to increase the intensity of space utilization.

- *Education financing*. Most countries provide access to essentially free education at the primary and secondary levels, an approach well-justified by the externalities to society of making certain that all citizens have a good basic education. Ukraine goes further and provides essentially free tertiary education. This education is very costly per student. In Ukraine, tertiary education is made even more expensive by the fact that the enrollment ratio at the tertiary level in Ukraine exceeds that in Western European countries. Since the cost of such education can usually be recovered through higher salaries in a market economy, the standard approach internationally is to have students and their families pay a significant part of these costs directly. Introducing basic cost recovery at the tertiary level in Ukraine would help ease the direct burden on the budget. Also, it would bring enrollment ratios more into line with normal international experience and reduce the risk that a large group of university graduates will develop who can not find a job commensurate with their level of education, thus creating a socially volatile group of alienated youths as has happened in countries like Sri Lanka, for example.

Social protection

➜ *Social Insurance Fund (SIF).* Reduce payroll tax rates for SIF, as well as pensions and Chernobyl Fund, thus reducing incentives for employers to hide in the shadows, to avoid creating new jobs, and to deprive workers of their benefits. Shift responsibility for first two weeks of sick leave to enterprises, thus creating incentives for enterprises to watch more closely for abuse of sick leave privileges.

➜ *Social safety net*. Consolidate fragmented social assistance program under the housing support program so that it becomes a comprehensive, means-tested social safety net that is better able to provide adequate protection for the poor because it limits the assistance given to the non-poor under current programs. Review justification for child allowances.

- *Pensions.* Continue work to establish a three-tier pension system where the current pay-as-you-go "solidarity" pension, which provides a minimum defined-benefit pension, is augmented with a second-tier fully-funded mandatory system, and with a third-tier fully-funded voluntary system for those who want to set aside more of current income for future retirement. Carefully review financial implications of all proposals under active consideration to assure that the "transition" problem of moving from a pay-as-you-go system to a fully-funded system is resolved, and that any defined benefits are realistic given anticipated financial and demographic parameters.

- *Chernobyl Fund.* Develop plan to incorporate most Chernobyl activities into normal health and social safety net programs. Special Chernobyl benefits should be granted only on the basis of demonstrated need, not categorical qualifications.

Structural reforms

Agriculture

➜ *Bread of Ukraine.* Privatize 100 percent of all commercial grain storage capacity in Ukraine (current targets based on number of enterprises are not particularly meaningful because targets can be met while retaining a de facto monopoly in terms of total capacity). Intermediate targets in terms of capacity should be set if full privatization would be delayed for more than 12 months. Once facilities are privatized, Government can issue competitive tenders for storage capacity for state reserves if such are still deemed necessary.

➜ *Input supply and output marketing.* Ban all "commodity credit" transactions. Instead extend credit for agricultural inputs on normal commercial terms with repayments to be made in cash. Allow free entry and operation of private sector businesses in supplying inputs and marketing outputs in the agricultural sector, subject only to normal international rules of good business behavior.

➜ *Grain Movement and State Procurement.* Eliminate all forms of government interference at all levels of government with the movement of grain. Place all state procurement on a competitive basis.

➜ *External trade policies in agriculture.* Assure no further reversals, and remove tariff and non-tariff barriers to exports of agricultural products.

- *Land.* Move as quickly as possible to allow effective private ownership and control of agricultural land. If immediate freehold ownership of the kind universal throughout most of the rest of the world is not possible for insurmountable political reasons, at a minimum and on an urgent basis, establish alienable leasehold titles to identified plots with at least 50 year duration for all agricultural land in Ukraine. Establish mechanisms for transferring titles in the case of loan defaults so that the leasehold titles become a credible and acceptable form of collateral for banks.

Manufacturing

➜ *Bankruptcy and hard budget constraints.* The existence of a credible threat of bankruptcy is one of the most effective ways of assuring the enforcement of contracts (see point on bankruptcy above).

➜ *Contract enforcement.* The difficulty of enforcing contracts for delivery and for payment is one of the most frequent complaints of investors in Ukraine today. Major improvements are needed in the nation's economic court system to overcome this problem.

➜ *Deregulation.* As noted above under "Role of government," the scope of government intervention in the daily operations of enterprises should be sharply curtailed in line with the deregulation program developed for the Public Administration Reform Loan.

➜ *Demonopolization.* Certain segments of the Ukrainian enterprise sectors are still dominated by state monopolies that operate at the national level. Where the current scale of operation is not demonstrably necessary for economies of scale, these enterprises should be broken up to encourage efficiency-stimulating competition. Where economies of scale are important, such as in the aerospace industry, ancillary units should be spun off to operate as independent suppliers to multiple buyers, and efficiency of the core monopolies should be encouraged by removing any artificial barriers to international competition.

➜ *Privatization.* To help close the budget and BOP financing gap for 2000, and as a stimulus to creating a more favorable business climate, privatize large enterprises in the industrial sector (including energy and telecoms) sufficient to generate USD 1.0 billion by the end of 2000 through transparent processes consistent with international standards.

- *Privatization.* Complete the privatization of virtually all medium and large enterprises—including the sale of "golden" shares and "blocking" minority positions in all areas including agro-industry. Encourage secondary market for privatization certificates and share holdings to facilitate the emergence of individuals or groups with controlling blocks of shares who can then provide strong corporate governance.

- *Tax legislation.* Move as quickly as possible to a tax code that eliminates the current contradictions among fragmentary bits of legislation and provides a stable, transparent, equitable basis upon which businesses can make the investment and production decisions. If immediate introduction of such legislation is not possible, the Government should announce the intended direction of reform so that investors can plan in terms of the probable future tax environment. The environment should be as consistent as possible with the norms prevalent in Europe to help facilitate direct and portfolio foreign investment.

Energy

- *Electricity.* The financial viability of the electricity sector is a risk because of artificially low tariffs, low collection rates, and even lower cash payments. Without prospects for financial viability, the sector will be unable to obtain the resources needed to invest to increase the efficiency and reliability of the system, thus jeopardizing all areas of the economy and society. Total and cash collection rates should be increased—including through service cuts and bankruptcy procedures as required. A major acceleration of privatization of controlling interests of both generation and distribution companies would provide incentives for imposing the hard budget discipline required to increase collection rates and would provide access to new investment resources and management skills.

➜ *Privatization.* Sell controlling blocks of shares of at least seven oblenergos to strategic investors through competitive tenders with the assistance of internationally reputable privatization advisors.

- *Coal.* The biggest challenge facing the coal industry in Ukraine today is to improve efficiency and safety. This will require closing at least 20 mines a year during the next 10 years. Somewhere between 500,000 and one million workers may be affected. To prevent massive unemployment, highly proactive programs to facilitate labor mobility and to create new jobs in partnership with the private sector will be required, as will adequate social safety nets. New investments in mining should be done with private sector resources on a concession basis, not with government resources.

➜ *Closures.* Transfer at least 20 additional mines to UDKR for closure in the next 6 months and provide no less than UAH 25 million from the state budget every month to cover the costs of statutory benefits for laid-off miners and physical closure of mines.

- *Gas.* Efforts to establish an auction market for transit fee and domestically produced gas have failed—largely because of the fatal flaws in the non-auction market. Consumers are unwilling to pay cash up front for gas on the auction market, regardless of any reasonable price, when they can get it for barter (and sometimes even for free) on the non-auction market. Hard budget constraints and payments discipline need to be introduced in that segment of the gas market by various means, including shutting off those who do not pay. Commercial consumers accounting for the largest overdue unpaid balances should be taken into bankruptcy for reorganization or liquidation. The attractiveness of gas auctions in the future will become a measure of the success of Ukraine's efforts to impose a hard budget discipline in the consumption of gas.

➜ *Transmission Privatization.* Award a long term concession for the operation and management of the entire gas transmission system to an international consortium of strategic investors through a competitive tender.

- *Gas – cost recovery.* Other measures required in the gas sector include the widespread introduction of gas meters and strict limits on the ability of government organizations to commit to purchasing gas. Full cost recovery and full payment in cash are other objectives that should be accomplished as soon as possible. The Government should not accept residual payment responsibility for gas or other energy debts, other than those related to its own consumption. Privatization of all medium and large enterprises, coupled with the effective threat of bankruptcy, would make a major contribution to assuring the success of these efforts. Likewise, to assure a level playing field for all economic activity, the consumption of energy should be subject to the standard VAT rate just like any other commodity or service.

  - *District heating.* As with other parts of the energy sector, urgent measures are needed to improve the financial viability of district heating so that it can pay for its energy supplies and so that it can invest to improve the quality and efficiency of district heating services. Tariffs that allow full cost recovery are urgently needed, as are improved collection rates. Improvements in accounting standards, building code standards for energy efficiency, and the elimination of the privileges that allow concessional or free district heating to certain groups of people are also needed.

Banking system

➔ *Foreign exchange reserves.* Central Bank should defend reserves, not the exchange rate. The rate should be allowed to move in a steady manner to preserve a competitive real rate that leads to a sustainable trade balance..)

➔ *Bank closures.* Initiate the closure of any bank not showing any real prospects for recovery out of the seven large banks which signed Commitment Letters with the NBU.

• *Law on National Bank.* This law should be implemented in a way which assures the Bank can continue to operate without political interference.

• *Law on Banks and Banking Activity.* The law should be approved and implemented to provide clear, modern rules of the game for banking sector development.

  • *Commercial bank independence.* Government interference in lending decisions of commercial banks converts such banks into welfare and political arm of government, destroying their ability to function as a normal financial intermediary. Government should sell the shares of banks that it holds today and abstain from placing any political pressure on banks to lend to specific enterprises—or to the government through t-bill purchases or other instruments.

  • *Kartoteka 2.* Under this old soviet system, the government can take money out of private bank accounts without due process or effective right of appeal. This policy has had a seriously negative impact on the ability of enterprises to retain the working capital that they need to stay in operation and earn the money required to pay their bills. It has also tended to destroy confidence in the banking system, prevents enterprises from setting priorities among creditors, and drives enterprises into the shadow economy. At time of writing it appeared that Kartoteka 2 was being abolished. This is good news—especially if an alternative market-friendly means of enforcing contracts for payment such as bankruptcy and creditor-led workouts is put into place.

  • *Commercial bank supervision and prudential regulation.* Bring supervision of commercial banks up to international standards. Strictly enforce requirements regarding minimum capitalization, capital/asset ratios, and provisioning. Banks unable to meet the requirements should be subject to merger or closure.

ANNEX B: UKRAINE'S GROWTH PROSPECTS: A COMPARATIVE PERSPECTIVE

A nation's ability to provide decent standards of living for its people depend crucially on the long-run rate of economic growth. Over long periods of time even a small difference in rates of growth can translate into a major difference in per capita levels of income—the most adequate measure of an economy's level of development and well-being[1]. However, even over time intervals short by historical standards significant changes in the prosperity of nations and their comparative economic strength. In 1991 Ukraine and Poland started the transition from command economy with very similar level of GNP per capita. Ukraine's GNP at 1,580 dollars per person was only 120 dollars lower that of Poland (Table 1). By 1998 situation has changed dramatically.

In September 1989 the first non-communist government of Poland started to implement an ambitious and comprehensive Economic Transformation Program which harmoniously combined the goals of the short-term macroeconomic stabilization with structural reforms—financial system reform, public enterprise restructuring and privatization, modernization of social safety net. These decisive measures revitalized the economy—since 1992 GDP grew at an average rate of 5% creating jobs and raising prosperity. Poland's GNP per capita by the end of the decade is estimated at over 4,000 dollars.

Table 1. Atlas GNP per Capita in Ukraine and Poland, 1991-1998[2]

	1991	1992	1993	1994	1995	1996	1997	1998
Poland	1,700	1,870	2,250	2,430	2,810	3,230	3,590	3,900
Ukraine	1,580	1,660	1,400	1,310	1,350	1,210	1,040	850

Source: World Development Indicators

While Poland's reform was starting to bear fruit and the life of people has been improving, Ukraine's feeble attempts at restructuring the economy which showed little commitment brought about further decline of Ukrainian economy and living standards. By 1998 the gap in GNP per capita between Poland and Ukraine has widened to over 3,000 dollars and Ukraine is wavering on the brink of being included into the list of the poorest countries of the world[3].

The divergence of Ukraine's and Poland's growth paths in 1990s exemplifies the critical importance of the choice of development strategy and associated economic policies for the longer-term economic growth and improvement in the welfare of people. Despite the differing legacy of the command system in Ukraine and Poland, the countries have so many ethnical, historical, natural, and economic similarities that the claims of radically different cultures, mentality or natural resource endowment often cited to diminish comparisons of Ukraine with Japan or Thailand do not hold water in the case

---

[1] For example, in 1880, Norway was poorer than Argentina. By the late 1990's situation reversed. Due to higher growth rates in Norway compared to Argentina over the past 130 years, Norway's GNP per capita reached 36,000 dollars in 1998 exceeding Argentina's about 4 times.

[2] To minimize effects of exchange rate fluctuations on per capita incomes in the cross-country comparisons, the World Bank calculates dollar GNP per capita using a special Atlas method. According to this method, local currency GNP per capita is converted into dollars at the average exchange rate for the current and two previous years adjusted for the difference in inflation rates in the country and G-5 countries (United States, United Kingdom, France, Germany, Japan).

[3] According to the World Bank definition which is revised annually, in 1998 a country was classified as poorest (IDA-eligible) if Atlas GNP per capita was below the 895 dollars operational cutoff.

of Poland. There are no compelling reasons why Ukraine under a liberal macroeconomic and structural policy mix cannot achieve growth rates similar to those of Poland or other successful transition economies of Eastern Europe.

Today Ukraine is at an economic crossroads again. The question now is not about choosing a set of short-run policy measure. At issue now is the economic strategy that will shape the future of the economy in 5-10 years from now and which must put Ukraine firmly on the path of the long-awaited economic growth and prosperity. This Memorandum has presented three macroeconomic scenarios modeled to reflect the two basic economic strategy options facing Ukrainian government at present—pushing ahead with an ambitious structural reform (Optimistic and Base Case Scenarios) or trying to restore economic growth through inflationary monetary policies, external borrowing, or a return to the central planning (Low Case Scenario)—and the pace of implementing reforms under reform scenario.

The comparison of the results of the three scenarios convincingly demonstrate that the optimal choice for Ukraine is to quickly implement structural reforms that would help to build up its export performance, attract foreign direct investment, and fix the state budget. The alternative to this policy of reforms is unsustainable and fraught with disastrous consequences. Attempts to restore economic growth without fiscal adjustment and implementation of proper structural measures is a road to nowhere.

OPTIMISTIC AND BASE CASE SCENARIOS

The failure of financial stabilization to bring about economic growth between 1995 and the first half of 1998 has clearly shown that the muddling-through course pursued by the successive government of Ukraine in the past five years has been a major cause of its current economic difficulties and forcefully argues in favor of another strategy—the export-oriented growth—strategy that has brought economic progress and higher living standards to many a developing and transition economy. Ukraine has long been dependent on trade across its borders (foreign turnover today is close to 80% of GDP). Improving export competitiveness, opening domestic economy to foreign investments, cutting-edge technology and know-how are Ukraine's pass to a prosperous future.

The *Optimistic and Base Case Scenarios* are based on the assumption that a package of comprehensive second-generation macroeconomic and structural policies set out in the Memorandum is implemented. However, the term over which the measures are taken and the resolution with which the authorities approach them differ under the two scenarios. While Optimistic Scenario assumes that most of the policy measures are implemented over the 2000-2001 period in the optimum sequence and with due care, the Base Case shows the cost of wavering over the implementation of reform or choosing a sub-optimal reform order. These policies would help quickly overcome the aftereffects of the Russian crisis and develop resilience to the external shocks in the future. These reforms would also lay the foundations of the growth in the real sectors of the economy and would enhance the most important determinants of output growth—savings, investments, productivity.

Table 2. Gross and Net Investment in Ukraine, 1990-1998 (% of GDP)

	1992	1993	1994	1995	1996	1997	1998
Gross domestic fixed investment	27.1	24.3	23.5	23.3	20.7	19.8	19.3
Net domestic investment	8.3	4.3	4.5	5.0	2.7	1.3	0.5

Source: State Statistics Committee

Like many other transition economies, Ukraine has large unutilized productive capacity. Labor is abundant in Ukraine as evidenced by low real wages and physical capital is not as scarce as in many developing countries. With efficient use of existing stocks of capital and labor, the Ukrainian economy could generate output growth even with minimum of investments. However, due to high degree of capital stock depreciation (estimated at around 65% in industry), neglect during the depression years as well as technological obsolescence of capital, a good deal of investment, not least in capital repair and technological upgrading, will be needed for the output to reach and exceed the pre-transition level. Despite the high gross investment (19-20% of GDP in 1996-1998), net investment—an increase in the productive capital economy has at its disposal which determines the incremental production capacity of the economy has been steadily decreasing and in 1998 stood at just 0.5% of GDP. A return to economic growth will require gross domestic investments to rise from the current depressed level of about 19% of GDP to about 25% or more, which is more consistent with the levels observed in the fast growing transition economies.

An important step towards increasing net investment and improving growth prospects is lowering the cost of private sector borrowing. The fiscal adjustment and monetary policies described in the Memorandum—including balancing of the budget by 2000-2001; banking system reform which builds confidence among depositors and promotes a smooth flow of savings from households to businesses; a slowly but steadily growing money supply that keeps inflation under control—are designed to bring down the cost of medium-term borrowing from the current highs of 60-70% per annum to a level more acceptable for business borrowers. Under the Optimistic Scenario, cheaper and more readily available investment financing is assumed to be forthcoming within one-two years after the second-generation reform push is initiated. However, the cost of borrowing cannot be brought by fiscal and monetary policies alone. Downward rigidity of interest rates in Ukraine is partly caused by high risk of doing business in Ukraine and by structural weaknesses of the Ukrainian economy. Improving bankruptcy procedures, eliminating vagueness of ownership rights that make collateral ineffective, development of efficient arbitration system capable of dealing with recovery and distribution of collateral among creditors, all of which have been recommended in the Memorandum, are indispensable in order to bring the cost of private sector borrowing down and expand investment.

Equally important, the efficiency of investment needs to be dramatically improved. This will happen only if investment growth comes primarily from increases in private investment as is projected in the Optimistic and Base Case Scenarios. While public capital expenditures will also rise slightly as a percentage of GDP, for example through increased spending on market economy infrastructure, the role of the locomotive of growth firmly belongs to private investments.

National savings, now at just 18% of GDP, are insufficient to finance the economic recovery and growth. Under the Optimistic Scenario the Ukrainian authorities will aim at increasing national savings by creating conditions for shadow savings to come back from the unofficial economy and offshore zones abroad. Wide-ranging deregulation and liberalization, including possibly an amnesty for shadow capital of non-criminal origin, together with tax reform cutting the

Chart 1

———. 1996a. *Poverty in Ukraine.* Report 15602-UA. Washington, D.C.

———. 1996b. *World Development Report 1996: From Plan to Market.* New York: Oxford University Press.

———. 1997. "Ukraine: Public Investment Review." Washington, D.C.

———. 1998a. *Assessing Aid: What Works, What Doesn't, and Why.* A Policy Research Report. New York: Oxford University Press.

———. 1998b. *World Development Indicators 1998.* Washington, D.C.

World Economic Forum. 1997. *Global Competitiveness Report.* Geneva.

number of tax privileges and reducing tax burden on businesses will give a boost to national savings and improve domestic financing of investment. More realistic Base Case Scenario recognizes the Government's hesitance in dealing with tax privileges and tax reform. The Base Case Scenario also assumes that the measures are implemented more slowly reducing economic growth by several percentage points.

The current composition of national savings in Ukraine is unsatisfactory. The single biggest economic player—the government—has big dissavings in the form of a budget deficit, which encroaches on the savings of the private sector and deprives the economy of credit resources -- and growth. Under the Optimistic Scenario the investment-savings gap would be closed through foreign savings of 2-3% of GDP and an improvement in the structure and magnitude of foreign savings is achieved by balancing the fiscal position of the government as early as 2000. The Base Case Scenario allows for a slower implementation of budget reform and more gradual fiscal adjustment. As a result, the consolidated government deficit, while lower than in 1996-1998, is not eliminated completely and continues to put pressure on national savings and to restrain economic growth. However, under both the Optimistic and Base Scenarios the importance of creating an attractive climate for foreign direct investments and restoring Ukraine's access to international capital market is hard to overestimate. To attract foreign savings Ukraine needs to distinguish itself among the many countries that are vying for foreign capital. Establishing its credibility both with foreign and domestic investors by pursuing tight but growth-oriented monetary and fiscal policies, creating a stable and transparent business environment is the first step in this direction.

Under the Optimistic scenario, an estimated 1.7% GDP decline in 1998 will be followed by –1% GDP growth in 1999 as the effects of the Russian crisis persist. In the subsequent years Ukraine is projected to achieve an GDP average growth of up to 8% per year by 2010 with an average of 7.3% from 2002. Compared to Optimistic Scenario, the Base Case Scenario is more realistic concerning Ukraine's economic prospects. Under the Base Case Scenario an average GDP growth in 2000-2010 is projected at about 4%, which still produces a cumulative growth of about 50% over the decade. Per capita incomes in dollar terms may rise even more as the hryvnia appreciates in real terms due to good export performance.

However, the very ambitious growth rate projected under the Optimistic Scenario is not unprecedented. A number of Eastern European transition economies achieved rates of growth as high or even higher, although admittedly not over such extended periods of time. As can be seen in Chart 1, Poland's economic growth path during 1990s was very similar to that projected for Ukraine under the Optimistic Scenario. If Ukrainian authorities learn from its neighbor's mistakes and demonstrate extraordinary commitment to, and persistence in, pursuing reforms, many of which are described in the Memorandum, Ukraine may very well become the next success story among transition economies.

LOW CASE SCENARIO

The Low Case—an alternative scenario which is likely if reforms proposed in the Memorandum are not implemented—shows that the economic growth achieved through money supply expansion and external borrowing is nowhere as rapid and lasting as growth achieved through the resolute implementation of free market reforms. This Low Case scenario also demonstrates that even deviations from a reform path will lead to crisis and the loss of many previous achievements, in particular macroeconomic stability. This scenario demonstrates the negative consequences that a failure to implement policy reforms can have for the economy and people of Ukraine. Despite the unsustainability of this alternative, it reflects in some aspects policies often put forward by certain political circles in Ukraine.

The Low Case Scenario assumes that Ukrainian authorities either change the economic strategy dramatically with a view to replace the regulatory functions of the market with a form of quasi-command system of economic management or commit serious slippages in reform process losing control of the economic policies.

In both cases the first result of the anti-market policies would be the destabilization of macroeconomic situation. Inflation will surge as the government tries to avoid addressing serious structural problems and instead keeps uncompetitive industrial enterprises afloat with directed loans from the Central Bank. Government will also support enterprises with direct and indirect subsidies from the State budget, boosting the budget deficit and causing further monetary emission. Attempts to enlist support of the poorer strata of population through generous subsidies from the state budget will further aggravate the state of public finances.

As the inflation and budget deficit pick up, so will interest rates on bank loans to the private sector (assuming it still exists). Unless banks are nationalized and ordered to comply with government lending priorities, which would imply all but a transition to a command economy, the banks will virtually suspend the loss-making long-term lending to the economy depriving economy of credit resources needed to finance capital investment and production expansion. Public investments orchestrated by the government will only partly compensate for reduced commercial banking credit and the efficiency of such investment in public enterprises would be far lower than the efficiency of investment in private enterprises. Inflation which will soon turn into hyperinflationary spiral will eat up the working capital in most industries as only enterprises with the highest rates of working capital turnover will be able to safeguard their working capital against rapid depreciation. With nominal and real interest rates high (the latter reflecting the commercial banks' uncertainty about the extent of future inflation and exchange rate depreciation) enterprises will not be able to replenish the rapidly depreciating working capital and soon will have to switch to barter operations reducing the demand for money and further accelerating inflation.

With little hope that the banking system will be able to maintain nominal interest rates above the inflation level and lacking the trust in the stability of the banking system in general, households will choose to consume more and invest the lower savings via purchases of foreign exchange and durables thereby reducing the depositor base of the banking system and thus resources available for onlending to enterprises. The foreign exchange and goods markets will come under pressure. As demand for foreign exchange rises and the exchange rate of the national currency hits new lows, the government will introduce a multiple exchange rate regime to hold back the depreciation and imported inflation, to provide low-cost imports to privileged interest groups and to minimize the local currency cost of servicing foreign debt. Exporters will be required to surrender their currency earnings, normally at an unfavorable exchange rate, and a massive capital flight will start. Then the government will have to takes over from the market the responsibility for foreign exchange allocation with all the associated inefficiencies and corruption. However, as foreign exchange supply plummets, the government will face a problem of financing critical imports. International capital markets will be closed for a country pursuing such a policy mix. Given the lack of foreign financing, country's foreign exchange reserves will be depleted even if the country defaults on its external obligations

Chart 2

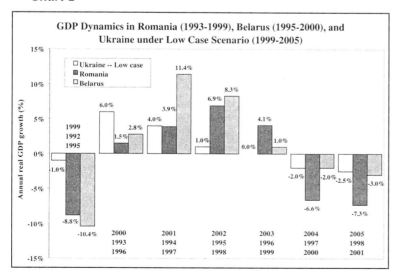

GDP Dynamics in Romania (1993-1999), Belarus (1995-2000), and Ukraine under Low Case Scenario (1999-2005)

and the authorities will be forced to introduce rationing of food, oil, electricity and other imported goods.

As popular dissatisfaction with constantly rising prices increases the authorities will have to respond by introducing price controls for a wide range of consumer products, especially foodstuffs, causing mass shortages. As prices for many industrial products are likely to remain less regulated, agriculture—whose products will be purchased by the government at below-market prices—will fall into decay, unable to buy the required machinery and inputs. As excessive inventories accumulate, both agricultural and industrial production will declines and the country will be under risk of hunger. Population whose welfare has fallen as a result of the policies will replace the government that brought the country to the brink of economic collapse.

The consequences of the reversal in the reform policies described above have been taken to an extreme. However, the stark choice facing Ukraine is obvious—either the country resolutely pursues market reforms to the end or resort to full-scale state planning whose results will be similar to the one described above, however they will take longer to become apparent.

Despite their damaging consequences, many of these policies have been tried or are still being implemented by the countries in Eastern Europe, including Ukraine in early 1990s. The two prime examples of market reforms going awry and an attempt to return to a revised form of command economy in the Eastern Europe are, respectively, Romania whose policy errors in mid-1990 lead to a demise of the fledgling economic recovery and three consecutive years of economic decline, and Belarus whose administrative methods of economic management reached its limits less than three years after their adoption (Chart 2). With such examples close at hand, Ukraine would commit a gross mistake to follow in their footsteps to a few years of miserable growth followed by economic collapse. Out of the two generic policy alternatives facing Ukraine at present, only one—fundamental economic and structural reform projected in the Optimistic/Base Case Scenarios—will put Ukraine on a path of long-term, sustainable outward-oriented growth capable of raising the living standards of the people of Ukraine to the level they deserve.

ANNEX C: THE SHADOW ECONOMY IN UKRAINE. METHODS OF CALCULATING ITS SIZE

This note reviews the methods used by Professor Borodiuk and MP Turchinov in their study of the shadow economy in Ukraine[1] for estimating its size. Discussed below are their methodologies, the probable errors of each in estimating the size of the shadow economy, and possible quick fixes that could improve the estimates.

Methods

Borodiuk and Turchinov (**BT**) analyzed three methods of calculating shadow economy in their article "Methods for calculating the size of shadow economy," (*Economy of Ukraine*, 1997, No 5, pp. 41-53). They empirically tried to measure the applicability of those methods for Ukraine (see box 1).

Box.1 *Problems with the basic methods of estimating the size of the shadow economy in Ukraine*

Electricity-consumption method	Used by Kaufmann and Kaliberda in Ukraine, and by other researcher in other countries, this method has proven its usefulness, providing overall estimates of size as well as indications of trends. However, given a changing situation in electricity energy sector of Ukraine including sharply higher energy prices that should lead to at least some gains in energy efficiency, it is far from foolproof. Also, there may be problems in data collection, processing, and verification of electricity consumption
Monetary method (Monetary and money velocity)	In Ukraine, Russian and some other FSU countries, money in banks can directly feed into informal sector transactions. Unstable legislation, weak financial sector, inefficient regulatory control of commercial banks by the central bank, ineffective management of public money, quasi money, growing unsecured budget arrears in wages and pensions, netting-out operations, non-bank means of payment like barter and arrears, and writing off enterprise debts to the budget make accounts based on monetary and banking system indicators subject to a high degree of error.
Cash in circulation and taxation	Tax legislation is cumbersome and does not foster implementation of compliance-based tax system. Accounted taxes and fines/penalties, as well as property under execution, remain virtual (existing on paper only) in terms of not turning to cash budget revenues fully. Granting tax privileges, accepting tax payments in kind, and writing off tax arrears, make this method questionable.

- *Electricity consumption.* The first method involves computing a real GDP based on GDP of a known date in the past and changes in electricity-consumption since that date. The result, which assumes that electricity consumption will reflect changes in real GDP, is then compared with official data on GDP and with the estimated share of GDP in the shadow economy in a base period (they used 14% in

---

[1] V.M. Borodiuk and O.V. Turchinov. "Shadow Economy Policy," Chpater 7 in *Economic Growth with Equity: Ukrainian Perspectives (part of the Country Economic Memorandum project jointly sponsored by the Ministry of Economy of Ukraine, the World Bank, and the International Center for Policy Studies, 1999.*

1990). On this basis, they estimated the shadow economy at 38.1%, 50.1%, and 56.4% of the official Ukrainian GDP in 1993, 1994, and 1995, respectively.

- **Monetary Method.** The second approach, the so-called monetary method, assumes that the size of shadow economy depends on amount of cash in circulation outside the banks. The size of shadow economy is then estimated by examining changes in key monetary aggregates including (a) cash in circulation vs. money supply, (b) deposits vs. monetary supply, or (c) cash in hands vs. deposits. Using these methods, the shadow economy was estimated at 101%, 32%, and 158% of the official Ukrainian GDP in 1995, respectively.

Figure 1

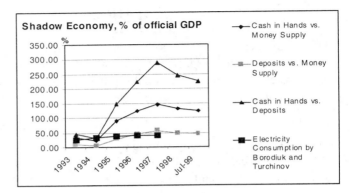

Source: NBU data and Bank staff estimates.

As a modification of the second method (cash in hands vs. deposits), another approach takes into account the velocity of money in informal sector. Higher velocity means higher share of shadow economy. Mathematically, the formula is multiplied by a coefficient ω, which reflects the increase of the velocity in shadow sector towards the velocity in official economy, On this basis, the shadow economy was estimated at 186% of the official Ukrainian GDP in 1995, which shows that ω in 1995 was 1.18.

Table 1

Shadow Economy Size Calculation Methods, 1993-1995

No.	Methods of calculations	Basic Year	Size of Shadow Economy, UAH mn.			Size of Shadow Economy, % of the official GDP		
			Year			Year		
			1993	1994	1995	1993	1994	1995
1	Monetary Method: Cash in Hands vs. Money Supply	1992	549	3 732	53 462	37	31	101
2	Monetary Method: Deposits vs. Money Supply	1992	133	-843	16 939	9	-7	32
3	Monetary Method: Cash in Hands vs. Deposits	1992	742	4 454	83 634	50	37	158
4	Monetary Method: Cash in Hands vs. Deposits, taking into account money velocity	1992			98 455			186
5	Cash in Hands and Taxation	1992	446	6 619	40 912	30	55	77,3
6	Electricity Consumption: Input-output balance	1990	565	6 031	29 854	38,1	50,1	56,4
7	Electricity Consumption: Data of Goscomstat of Ukraine	1990	526	6 163	371 179	35,4	51,2	68,2
8	Electricity Consumption: by the World Bank	1990	599	6 440	31 231	40,4	53,5	59

Source: Based on Borodiuk and Turchinov, op. cit

- **Cash in circulation and taxation.** The third method was suggested by the Institute of Russia to the National Academy of Science of Ukraine. It focuses on measuring influence of cash in hands and size of taxation on the size of shadow economy. The size of taxation reflects tax base, tax rate, and percent of collected taxes towards the planned figures in the budget. The formula puts the size of shadow economy in direct proportion to the amount of cash in hands and in inverse proportion to the size of taxation. On this basis, the shadow economy was estimated at 30%, 55%, and 77.3% of the official Ukrainian GDP in 1995, respectively. This method was used by BT for contributing to the paper "Growth with Equity" (table 1). These methods have also been used to provide estimates of the size of the shadow economy for more recent years (figure 1).

Deviations and errors

BT note a variety of risks that can seriously undermine reliability of calculations and forecasts made by the above methods.

- High risk of making a wrong assumption on shadow economy share in the basic year for calculation. This is clearly a problem for Ukraine, as well as for other countries of FSU, because of deliberately inaccurate data on economy inherited from the Soviet times.

- Weak capacity of existing Ukrainian statistics system to ensure reliability and completeness of information. Data collection is inefficient and there is not enough data to compute without making too many presumptions.

We would like to stress on the importance on dealing with the second risk of inefficient and ineffective statistics system. In addition to the shadowization of markets of products, financial resources, and factors, this weakness makes impossible to calculate basic economic aggregates correctly, monitor the situation and forecast future trends. Thus, it creates a vicious circle when results of government's, households', and companies' activities, being unmeasured[2], to a certain extent contribute to the growth of shadow markets, which, in their turn, introduce more distortions to the functioning of those three players (see Figure 2).

Quick Improvements

First, reform the statistics system. Instead of collecting all possible data,[3] move to a fully equipped, efficient system that coordinates information flows and provides reliable outputs based on internationally accepted conventions such as the System of National Accounts (SNA) and the system of Government Financial Statistics (GFS).[4]

Second, implement continuing work on measuring the shadow economy. The shadow economy continues to grow under current policies and will probably remain a most difficult issue for the government to deal. At modest costs, local researches with experience in the field can do modeling of informal sector data that keeps information up to date and gradually improves the methodology, reducing deviations and errors.

Finally, and by far the most important, implement policies that will encourage otherwise legitimate shadow activity to move into the formal economy. Measuring the shadow economy does not solve the shadow economy problems such as low tax revenues and excessive tax pressure on legal firms. We already know that this is a serious problem. While measurements may help focus attention on the issue, a

---

[2] Existing unmeasured part of GDP blocks accurate monitoring and forecasting of economic development. 'Unmeasured' may often means 'untaxed', e.g. it causes untaxed informal trade / smuggling and corruption at customs offices if custom declarations of individuals are collected by customs offices but remain unprocessed until destroyed upon expiration of limitation period.

[3] Experts of Goscomstat agree they force enterprises to submit many overlapping data, part of which, by the way, is never processed. Goscomstat sees the main problem in changing legislation and normative acts of statistics. However, one may think that this is just a kind of institutional fear to lose the significance by restructuring the agency, removing useless procedures and requirements, and, if needed, cutting off redundant staff.

[4] Statistics System Reform is one of the firs-tier components of ID APL.

much higher priority is to shrink the relative size of shadow activity so that its measurement ceases to be an important issue.

Figure 2

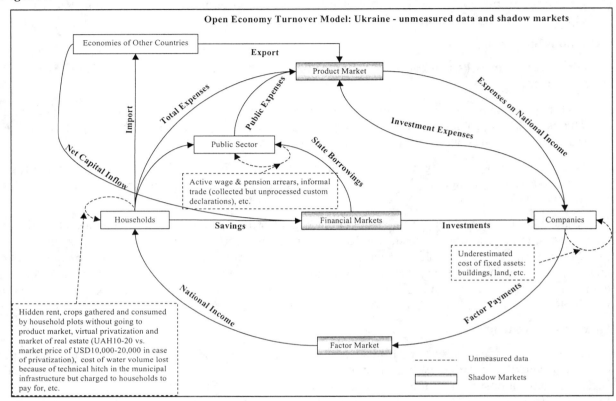

Source: Bank staff

ANNEX D: LIST OF UKRAINIAN CEM PROJECT CONTRIBUTORS

Preparation of this and the other documents generated by the participatory country economic memorandum project involved dozens of Ukrainian professionals from a wide range of backgrounds in a year-long process of discussing, researching, writing, and reviewing some of the key macroeconomic and sectoral issues facing Ukraine today. The members of the eight research groups that participated in this process and the experts who helped advise and review the work of these researchers are listed below.

A great debt of gratitude is owed to these people. Their work contributed greatly to the quality of the discussions and the final products of this participatory process.

AGRARIAN POLICY

Ukrainian research group	Ukrainian experts, who commented on the analytical materials
P.T. Sablouk, *Director, Agrarian Policy Institute, Ukrainian Academy of Agrarian Sciences* **A.A. Fesina,** *Leading Research Fellow, Agrarian Policy Institute, Ukrainian Academy of Agrarian Sciences*	**P.I. Hajdutsky,** Deputy Head, Presidential Administration **O.M. Golovanov,** Chief, Department for Problems of the Economy of Agro-industrial Complex, R&D Institute of the Ministry of Economy **Y.Y. Luzan,** First Deputy Minister of the Economy of Agro-industrial Complex of Ukraine **L.G. Shmorhun,** Head, Chief Department for Agro-industrial Policy, Ministry of Economy **O.M. Shpychak,** Secretary, Academy of Agrarian Sciences **V.V. Yurchyshyn**, Head of Department, Agrarian Policy Institute, Ukrainian Academy of Agrarian Sciences **V.V. Demjanchouk,** Head, Secretariat for Agrarian Reform at the Vice Prime Minister

EDUCATION

Ukrainian research group	Ukrainian experts, who commented on the analytical materials
Y.M. Vitrenko, *Head of the Department for Economy of Education, Culture and Health Care, the Ministry of Health Care of Ukraine*	**A.G. Bohomolov,** Deputy Minister of Education of Ukraine **I.P. Dryhus,** Head of Secretariat, Verkhovna Rada Science and Education Committee **O.I. Kiliyevich,** Assistant Professor, Chair of Economics and Finance, State Administration Academy under the President of Ukraine **K.V. Korsak,** Expert in Education, International Staff Academy **L.H. Kostyliov,** Director, Kyiv School #155 **Y.V. Lukovenko**, Deputy Director for Projects, ICPS **V.M. Matviychouk,** Deputy Minster of Finance of Ukraine

	A.V. Furman, Professor, Chief of Chair for Pilot Systems in Education, and Deputy Editor of *Education and Administration*, Academy for Managerial Educational Personnel

ENERGY POLICY

Ukrainian research group	*Ukrainian experts, who commented on the analytical materials*
A.G. Vrublevsky, *First Deputy Minister of Economy* **V.I. Kiriniachenko,** *Head, Department of Fuel-power Complex of the Ministry of Economy* **V.G. Skarshevsky,** *Expert, Prime Minister Service*	**P.S. Ambrosevich,** Head, Department of Fuel-power Complex, Antimonopoly Committee **Y. Halynovsky,** Chief of Sector, Research and Development Institute of Economics, the Ministry of Economy **O.L. Zolotariova,** Head of the Board, Association of Independent Electric Power Suppliers **V.G. Nosov,** Researcher, "Quarterly Predictions" Project, ICPS

FISCAL POLICY

Ukrainian research group	*Ukrainian experts, who commented on the analytical materials*
M.V. Chechetov, *Deputy Minister of Economy* **V.G. Skarshevsky,** *Expert, Prime Minister Service* **V.Y. Lomynoha,** *Head, Department for Forecasting Revenues and Expenditures of the State Budget of Ukraine, Chief Department of the State Treasury of Ukraine* **V.V. Soldatenko,** *Head of Sector, Chief Department of Economic Analysis of the State Tax Administration of Ukraine*	**V.I. Lysytsky,** Head, Group of Advisers to the NBU Governor **I.A. Shumylo,** Deputy Minister of Economy **A.A. Maksiuta,** Head of Sector, Chief Budget Department of Ministry of Finance of Ukraine **O.V. Mostovenko,** Deputy Head, Chief Department of Tax Enforcement of the State Tax Administration **S.F. Obozny,** Deputy Head, Department of Financial Activity of Business Structures of the Ministry of Economy of Ukraine **H.O. Piatachenko,** Director, R&D Financial Institute of the Ministry of Finance of Ukraine **O.I. Soskin,** Advisor to the President of Ukraine **M.M. Shapovalova,** Deputy Head, Chief Budget Department **O.I. Shytria,** Deputy Head, State Tax Administration **I.D. Yakushyk,** Head, R&D Tax Policy Center of the State Tax Administration

HEALTH CARE

Ukrainian research group	*Ukrainian experts, who commented on the analytical materials*
Y.M.Vitrenko,	**R.V. Bogatyryova,** Minister of Health Care of Ukraine

Head of the Dept. for Economy of Education, Culture and Health Care, the Ministry of Health Care of Ukraine	**T.F. Baranova**, Head of the Main Department of Economy, Minister Ministry of Health Care of Ukraine
	L.S. Gryrovych., Deputy Head Committee on Health Care, Maternity and Childhood Protection, Parliament of Ukraine
A.M.Nagorna,	**I. B.Demchenko,** Advisor to the Minister of Health Care of Ukraine
Deputy Director of the Ukrainian Institute for Public Health	**V.D.Zukhin,** Member of the Association of Administrators of Private Medicine
	B.P. Kryshtopa, Honored Doctor of Ukraine, Ph.D., Head of the Department of Health Care, Kyiv Medical Post-graduate Academy
	O.M. Lukianova, Director of the Institute of Pediatrics, Obstetrics and Gynecology
	O.Ye. Poladko, Deputy Head of the Main Department for Medical and Preventive Treatment, the Ministry of Health Care of Ukraine
	V.M. Rudyi, Head of the Secretariat of the Committee for Health Care, Maternity and Childhood Protection, Parliament of Ukraine
	V.F. Sayenko., Director of the Institute of Clinic and Experimental Surgery
	O. Smyrnova, Deputy Head of Kyiv Oblast State Administration for Education, Culture and Health Care
	Y.Subotin, Head of the Bureau of World Health Protection Organisation on Coordination and Relations with Ukraine
	M.K. Khobzey., Head of the Department for Health Care, Lviv Oblast State Administration

INDUSTRIAL AND FOREIGN TRADE POLICY

Ukrainian research group	*Ukrainian experts, who commented on the analytical materials*
A.G. Vrublevsky, *First Deputy Minister of Economy* **G.O. Tryneyev,** *Head, Chief Department of Economy of Inter-sector Relations, Ministry of Economy*	**Y.M. Bazhal,** Chief of Department, Institute of Forecasting, National Academy of Sciences
	I.S. Byk, Deputy Head, Financial-economic Department, Ministry if Industrial Policy
	O.S. Samodurov, Head, Department of Cooperation with CIS Member States and Baltics, Ministry of Economy
	V.M. Horbachouk, Expert, Ukrainian Union of Industrialists and Entrepreneurs
	S.H. Hrischenko, Deputy Minister of Industrial Policy
	Y.A. Zhalilo, Chief, Department of Policy Studies, National Institute for Policy Studies
	V.H. Sharshevsky, Expert, Prime Minister Service

M.M. Yakubovsky, Deputy Director, R&D Institute of Economics, Ministry of Economy	L.M. Sokolov, Chief of Sector, Institute for Broad Transport Problems T.M. Solianik, Deputy Head, National Agency of Ukraine for Development and European Integration Y.P. Shkarban, Deputy Head, Economic Department, Ministry of Foreign Economic Relations and Trade

SHADOW ECONOMY

Ukrainian research group	*Ukrainian experts, who commented on the analytical materials*
V.M. Borodiuk, *Doctor of Economics, Professor Corresponding Member of the National Academy of Sciences, Adviser, Accounting Chamber of Ukraine* **O.V. Turchinov** *Doctor of Economics, Parliament Member, Head of Subcommittee for State Budget Expenditures, Budget Committee of Verkhovna Rada*	**Y.M. Bazhal,** Doctor of Economics, Head of Department, Institute for Economic Forecasting, National Academy of Sciences **A.V. Bazyliuk,** Doctor of Economics, Head of Department, Research & Development Institute of Economics, Ministry of Economy of Ukraine **Y.B. Bazyliuk,** Candidate of Economics, National Institute for Policy Studies **B.F. Besiedin,** *Doctor of Economics, Professor, Deputy Director, Research & Development Institute of Economics, Ministry of Economy of Ukraine* **G.M. Bilous,** Head of Department, Ministry of Economy of Ukraine **V.I. Golikov,** Doctor of Economics, Professor, Corresponding Member of the National Academy of Sciences, Head of Department, Institute for Economic Forecasting, National Academy of Sciences **B.A. Holovco,** Deputy Head, State Committee for Statistics **B.M. Horbansky,** Head of Department, State Tax Administration of Ukraine **V.M. Horbachouk,** Doctor of Economics, Expert, Ukrainian Union of Industrialists and Entrepreneurs **V.I. Lysytsky,** Chief, Group of Advisers to the NBU Governor **D.V. Liapin,** Executive Director, Association for Promotion of Small and Medium Business Development, *Yednannia* **O.I. Paskhaver,** Honorary Chairman, Association of Consulting Enterprises of Ukraine, *UkrConsulting* **N.V. Prokopovych,** Head of Department, State Committee for Business Development **A.P. Revenco,** Doctor of Economics, Head of Department, Institute for Economic Forecasting, National Academy of Sciences

	O.I. Soskin, Doctor of Economics, Adviser to the President of Ukraine
	V.I. Terekhov, Doctor of Economics, Professor, Senior Specialist, Accounting Chamber of Ukraine
	O.V. Tkachenco, Executive Director, Economic Reform Institute
	M.V. Chechetov, Deputy Minister of Economy of Ukraine
	V.T. Shlemco, Candidate of Economics, National Institute for Policy Studies
	I.A. Shumylo, Deputy Minister of Economy of Ukraine

SOCIAL PROTECTION

Ukrainian research group	*Ukrainian experts, who commented on the analytical materials*
O. S.Yaremenko, *Deputy Minister of Economy*	**N. E.Burkat,** Director, Social Reforms Project, Institute for Market Reforms
	V. P.Bevz, Head of the Social Policies Division of the Cabinet of Ministers of Ukraine
M.O. Soldatenko, *Head of the Main Department of population income policies and employment, the Ministry of Economy*	**I. F.Hnybidenko,** Head of the Main Department of complex analysis and projections for social development and information, Ministry of Labor and Social Policies of Ukraine
	E. M.Hrygorenko, Head of the Department of economic and social policies, Administration of President of Ukraine
N. I. Zinkevych, *Deputy Head of the Main Department of population income policies and employment, the Ministry of Economy*	**V. M.Novikov,** Advisor to President of Ukraine
	V. M.Ruddenko, Deputy Minister of Labor and Social Policies of Ukraine
	Y.I. Sayenko, Deputy Director, Institute of Sociology, NASU

STATISTICAL APPENDIX

STATISTICAL APPENDIX

STATISTICAL APPENDIX PREFACE

This appendix provides statistical series describing Ukraine's economy and its sectors from different perspectives. In the majority of cases, time series data back to 1991, the year Ukraine gained its independence. However, in some cases (e.g., balance of payments statistics and foreign trade statistics) data series start later. Ukrainian statistics, just like the country itself, had to go through a transition. From being a source of data for the state planner who needed a wide variety of physical indicators to control the public production process, the Ukrainian statistical system has turned into a supplier of information on prices and other market conditions for market participants to make educated decision on the efficient allocation of scarce economic resources to most productive uses.

Structure. The appendix contains 72 tables in 10 sections covering population and employment, national accounts, balance of payments and international trade, debt, public finances, monetary sector, agriculture and industry, prices, and pace of economic transition, in particular privatization.

Data sources. The data presented in the appendix have been drawn from various official sources. The basic source of data is the State Statistics Committee (SSC) which publishes *Statistical Yearbook* and monthly *Statistical Bulletin* as well as a number of specialized publications like *Ukraine: National Accounts* and *Foreign Direct Investments in Ukraine.* Other important official publications containing valuable statistical data on various aspects of Ukrainian economic and social development are Presidential Administration's *Ukraine and its Regions*, Ministry of Economy's *Macroeconomic Indicators*, NBU's *Monthly Bulletin* and *Balance of Payments Quarterly.* From among unofficial sources of statistical data which were extensively used during the preparation of the Statistical Annex we would particularly like to note the publications of the Ukrainian-European Policy and Legal Advice Center, especially its monthly *Ukrainian Economic Trends.* A number of tables in the Annex, in particular on external debt, are based on World Bank and IMF staff calculations.

Data coherence and methodological notes. International organizations have done considerable work to improve the quality of Ukrainian statistical data and bring it up to international standards. A number of IMF and World Bank statistical missions worked in Ukraine over the past four years to verify the methodologies of monetary and banking statistics, balance of payments, national accounts, consumer and producer price indices. In all those areas Ukrainian statistics were judged to comply with international methodological guidelines.

However, there are two areas of potential inconsistency in the foreign trade and public finance data presented in the Annex which deserve special mention. In Ukraine, preparation of the balance of payments statistics (BOP) is the responsibility of the National Bank of Ukraine while the foreign trade balance (FTB) is compiled by the SSC. NBU and SSC use different methodologies. The BOP is prepared using the methodology laid out in the 5th (1993) edition of IMF's *Balance of Payments Manual.* The FTB is compiled in accordance with the methodological guidelines of the United Nations' Statistical Commission. The main differences between the two include:

- *Timing of goods' registration:* For FTB purposes, a product is considered exported or imported at the moment it physically crosses the border. Under BOP the time of import/export is taken to be the moment of ownership rights transfer;

- *Sources of information:* FTB data are based on customs statistics and on reports of enterprises. BOP also draws on additional information about international financial transactions collected by the NBU through commercial banks;

- *Price bases used and geographical classification of transactions:* In FTB merchandise exports is accounted for on FOB terms while merchandise imports based on CIF terms. In BOP, both exports and imports are recorded at FOB prices. In

FTB, geographical structure of exports and imports is

- determined by country of destination and country of origin respectively, while in BOP geographical breakdown of foreign trade flows is based on the country-owner of merchandise;

- Periodicity: FTB data is release monthly while BOP data is released quarterly with a 90 day lag.

The second source of data inconsistency lies in difference between consolidated budget data calculated in accordance with IMF's 1986 *Government Financial Statistics* methodology and official Ukrainian numbers. Budget tables 5.1 - 5.4 in the Annex are based on the IMF methodology. According to IMF calculations consolidated budget deficits were much higher in the early years of independence than officially reported by Ukrainian authorities. The higher IMF deficit numbers reflect primarily the inclusion of the quasi-fiscal expenditures—directed bank lending at government's request. Since 1995, the government has sharply reduced directed lending, which reduced the difference between the two public finance data sources.

Three key differences between IMF-GFS methodology and the official Ukrainian numbers remain. First, on the revenue side, privatization proceeds are classified by the IMF as below-the-line financing, not current revenues. Second, on the expenditures side, the amortization of foreign and domestic loans is also reclassified by the IMF as a financing item rather than a current expenditure. Finally, changes in government deposits are subtracted by the IMF in calculating net revenues. In 1998, as a result of the partial switch to the GFS methodology, the Government of Ukraine moved the amortization of foreign and domestic loans below the line, thus eliminating one of the differences.

The IMF is calculating the accrual deficit by adding budget expenditure arrears to cash deficit but not adding tax collection arrears to revenues. This treatment is based on the assumption that tax arrears will not be paid, while expenditure arrears will eventually be paid. This asymmetric treatment is probably justified given that the government has a moral obligation to pay for its consumption sooner or later while, on the other hand, a major share of taxes are owed by enterprises that are effectively bankrupt and unlikely ever to repay their tax arrears.

It needs mentioning that due to high inflation during the first years of independence State Statistics Committee has used moving base year for constant price GDP calculations rather than a single fixed year. As a result, when GDP components were rebased to 1990 in Table 3.4 in order to produce chain indices of GDP growth, additivity of components has been lost.

SECTION 1

Table 1.1 - Population, 1991-1998

(at the beginning of the year)

	1991	1992	1993	1994	1995	1996	1997	1998
Population, mn persons	51.9	52.1	52.2	52.1	51.7	51.3	50.9	50.5
including								
				mn persons				
urban population	35.1	35.3	35.4	35.4	35.1	34.8	34.5	34.3
rural population	16.8	16.8	16.8	16.7	16.6	16.5	16.4	16.2
males	24.1	24.2	24.2	24.2	24.1	23.9	23.7	23.5
females	27.8	27.9	28	27.9	27.6	27.4	27.2	27
				% of total				
urban population	68	68	68	68	68	68	68	68
rural population	32	32	32	32	32	32	32	32
males	46	46	46	46	47	47	47	47
females	54	54	54	54	53	53	53	53
Memo:								
Birth-rate (per thous. persons)	12.1	11.4	10.7	10	9.6	9.1	8.7	8.3
Death-rate (per thous. persons)	12.9	13.4	14.2	14.7	15.4	15.2	14.9	14.3
Children before year death-rate (per thous. born)	13.9	14	14.9	14.5	14.7	14.4	14.0	12.8
Natural increase in population, thous. persons	-36.2	-100.6	-179.3	-242.8	-299.8	-309.5	-311.5	-300.7
including in rural area	-76.7	-86.6	-106.6	-121	-131.7	-139.8	-143.4	-133.9
per thous. persons	-0.8	-2	-3.5	-4.7	-5.8	-6.1	-6.2	-6.0

Source: State Statistics Committee

Table 1.2 - Labor Force

(thousand persons, unless otherwise indicated)

	1993	1994	1995	1996	1997	1998**
Employment*	23,945	23,025	23,726	23,232	22,598	22300
Job leavers (quits - dismissals), total	165.1	227.7	218.4	363.8	426.7	273.3
Including						
women	110.9	145.7	145.8	239.8	273.4	171.6
persons under 28 years old	--	29.9	25.9	46.4	55.2	32.4
As of the end of the period:						
Unemployed:	83.9	82.2	126.9	351.1	637.1	1003.2
Officially registered						
Including	62.7	59.8	92.2	235.8	416.5	620.4
women	35.3	29.6	47.4	118.8	197.2	319.1
persons under 28 years old						
Of which:	40.0	47.7	74.4	214.6	361.6	532.8
Benefit recipients	1.00	6.29	22.54	40.63	40.13	38.51
Average amount of benefit (Hrn.)						
Memorandum items:	131.6	136.6	86.4	35.2	34.8	34.6
Vacancies						
Officially registered unemployed *** (% of labor force)	0.3	0.3	0.5	1.3	2.3	3.7
Of which:						
Benefit recipients (%)	47.6	58.0	58.6	61.1	56.8	53.1

* Data are presented as an annual average.

** Preliminary data

*** Unemployment level is calculated as a ratio of number of official registered unemployed to labor force

Source: Ministry of Economy, State Statistics Committee

Table 1.3 - Average Employment by Sector, 1992-1997

	1992	1993	1994	1995	1996	1997
Total employment (million):	**24.5**	**23.9**	**23.0**	**23.7**	**23.2**	**22.6**
Industry	7.4	7.0	6.3	5.8	5.3	4.9
Agriculture and forestry*	4.9	4.9	4.8	5.3	5.1	5.0
Construction	1.9	1.8	1.6	1.5	1.4	1.2
Transport and communications	1.6	1.6	1.5	1.5	1.4	1.3
Trade**	1.8	1.7	1.6	1.6	1.5	1.5
Municipal services***	0.9	0.8	0.8	0.8	0.8	0.8
Health care****	1.5	1.5	1.5	1.5	1.5	1.4
Education and culture*****	2.8	2.7	2.7	2.6	2.5	2.3
Finance and insurance******	0.1	0.2	0.2	0.2	0.2	0.2
General administration and defense, public non-profit organizations	0.6	0.6	0.7	0.7	0.7	0.8
Other industries	0.5	0.6	0.5	0.5	0.5	0.4
Other spheres of economic activity	0.5	0.5	0.8	1.7	2.3	2.8
Total employment (percentage of total):	100.0	100.0	100.0	100.0	100.0	100.0
Industry	30.2	29.3	27.1	24.3	23.0	21.6
Agriculture and forestry	20.4	20.7	20.9	22.5	21.8	22.0
Construction	7.8	7.4	7.1	6.3	5.9	5.3
Transport and communications	6.6	6.7	6.5	6.3	6.0	5.8
Trade	7.1	7.1	7.1	6.9	6.7	6.7
Municipal services	3.7	3.5	3.6	3.4	3.3	3.6
Health care	6.2	6.4	6.5	6.3	6.4	6.4
Education and culture	11.6	11.4	11.6	11.0	10.7	10.3
Finance and insurance	0.6	0.7	0.8	0.8	0.8	0.8
General administration and defense, public non-profit organizations	2.3	2.6	3.0	3.0	3.2	3.4
Other industries	1.5	2.0	2.1	1.8	2.0	1.9
Other spheres of economic activity	2.1	2.2	3.6	7.4	10.2	12.2
Total employment (percentage change on previous year):	..	-2.3	-3.8	3.0	-2.1	-2.7
Industry	..	-5.2	-10.9	-7.8	-7.4	-8.5
Agriculture and forestry	..	-0.9	-2.5	10.5	-4.8	-2.1
Construction	..	-7.2	-7.4	-9.4	-8.0	-12.6
Transport and communications	..	-1.1	-7.0	-2.8	-3.5	-6.5
Trade	..	-2.3	-4.8	-0.9	-3.9	-1.9
Municipal services	..	-6.5	-2.4	0.0	-6.1	6.1
Health care	..	0.7	-1.6	0.5	-2.2	-2.6
Education and culture	..	-3.6	-2.5	-2.3	-4.6	-6.7
Finance and insurance	..	12.4	9.0	2.8	-0.4	-1.2
General administration and defense, public non-profit organizations	..	10.9	9.4	6.0	4.2	1.1
Other industries	..	39.9	1.8	-3.9	-1.0	-6.9
Other spheres of economic activity	..	-0.4	63.3	108.5	34.0	16.9

* Including working at household plots
** Including catering, procurement and material supply
*** Public utilities and personal services
**** Including physical culture and social security
***** Education, culture, art, science and science service
****** Including insurance
Source: Ministry of Economy, State Statistics Committee, World Bank staff calculations

---

Statistical Appendix

Table 1.4 - Labor Productivity Indexes by Industry

	1985=100							1990=100						
	1990	1992	1993	1994	1995	1996	1997	1991	1992	1993	1994	1995	1996	1997
Manufacturing	121	113	110	87	83	86	92	98	94	91	72	69	71	76
including														
Fuel Industry	100	75	58	51	50	51	58	90	75	58	51	50	51	58
Ferrous Metallurgy	115	90	71	53	51	56	60	91	78	62	46	44	49	52
Chemical & Petrochemical Industry	123	101	87	71	66	66	71	95	82	71	58	54	54	58
Machine Building & Metal-Working	134	149	172	117	101	85	93	108	112	129	88	76	64	70
Pulp & Paper Industry	129	146	151	108	93	84	86	107	113	117	83	72	65	66
Construction Materials Industry	120	113	102	71	56	42	42	99.3	94	85	60	47	35	35
Light Industry	119	131	116	71	54	47	51	102	110	97	59	45	39	43
Food Industry	117	89	80	67	59	58	52	88	76	68	57	51	50	45

Source: State Statistics Committee

Table 2.1 - Gross Domestic Product by Industry and Expenditure Category at Current Prices
(million hryvnias)

	1989	1990	1991	1992	1993	1994	1995	1996	1997	1998*
By Industry										
Agriculture and Forestry	**0.342**	**0.409**	**0.737**	**10.49**	**319.4**	**1,754**	**7,507**	**9,969**	**11,685**	**12,842**
Agriculture	0.340	0.407	0.733	10.47	318.2	1,731	7,337	9,654	11,385	12,432
Forestry	0.002	0.001	0.004	0.02	1.2	23	170	315	300	410
Industry and Construction	**0.720**	**0.712**	**1.633**	**26.25**	**543.2**	**5,110**	**20,626**	**27,196**	**27,819**	**30,619**
Industry	0.585	0.576	1.367	22.45	440.4	4,215	16,873	22,381	22,995	25,525
Construction	0.136	0.136	0.266	3.80	102.8	895	3,753	4,815	4,824	5,094
Other	**0.429**	**0.480**	**0.927**	**16.93**	**512.8**	**4,619**	**21,853**	**36,011**	**42,593**	**47,353**
Transport	0.098	0.097	0.161	3.72	158.1	760	5,478	8,880	8,843	11,037
Road maintenance	0.004	0.007	0.015	0.20	7.5	93	302	409	576	
Communication	0.017	0.018	0.029	0.31	8.6	119	766	1,433	2,334	2,843
Retail trade and catering	0.053	0.072	0.135	2.48	113.2	619	2,888	4,570	7,387	8,271
Material supply	0.009	0.009	0.025	0.48	56.3	165	625	809	791	859
Procurement	0.006	0.007	0.016	0.32	13.2	92	264	342	380	288
Information and computing services	0.001	0.003	0.007	0.06	0.9	8	44	65	103	112
Other sectors of material production	0.010	0.012	0.017	0.34	14.1	41	242	443	778	802
Housing	0.026	0.025	0.042	0.28	27.3	173	1,279	1,578	1,745	4,975
Public utilities and personal services	0.020	0.021	0.045	0.38	13.0	154	721	2,789	2,870	
Health care, social security, etc.	0.033	0.038	0.088	1.45	40.0	355	2,301	3,786	4,072	4,407
Education	0.045	0.052	0.111	1.85	51.3	407	2,764	4,303	4,598	5,107
Culture and art	0.009	0.011	0.019	0.33	9.4	63	385	726	787	888
Science and research	0.033	0.034	0.049	0.70	14.7	217	581	853	1,094	1,111
Finance, credit and insurance	0.008	0.010	0.065	2.25	150.7	889	1,567	2,011	2,252	6,653
General administration and defense	0.054	0.063	0.101	1.75	53.0	453	1,609	2,879	3,747	
Private non-profit organizations	0.002	0.002	0.004	0.04	1.4	17	12	37	135	236
Total gross value added	**1.491**	**1.601**	**3.297**	**53.67**	**1,595.3**	**11,483**	**49,986**	**73,176**	**82,097**	**90,814**
Financial intermediaries, imp. chrg.	-0.002	-0.003	-0.062	-2.12	-121.4	-684	-1,243	-1,087	-1,030	-1,784
Total GDP at factor cost	**1.489**	**1.598**	**3.235**	**51.56**	**1,473.9**	**10,799**	**48,743**	**72,089**	**81,067**	**89,030**
Taxes on production	0.236	0.282	0.306	5.55	215.8	2,165	8,608	11,877	14,373	16,703
Subsidies on production	-0.191	-0.209	-0.547	-6.78	-207.0	-927	-2,835	-2,447	-2,075	-1,864
Total GDP at market prices	**1.534**	**1.671**	**2.994**	**50.33**	**1,482.7**	**12,038**	**54,516**	**81,519**	**93,365**	**103,869**
By Expenditure Category										
Gross Domestic Expenditures	**1.534**	**1.671**	**2.994**	**50.33**	**1,482.7**	**12,038**	**54,516**	**81,519**	**93,365**	**103,869**
Consumption	**1.092**	**1.230**	**2.140**	**31.99**	**949.3**	**8,166**	**41,651**	**65,119**	**76,198**	**85,479**
Private consumption	0.792	0.915	1.558	21.12	653.5	5,331	27,094	43,469	50,617	58,409
Non-profits	0.034	0.039	0.061	2.03	58.8	504	2,961	3,912	3,252	3,426
Government consumption	0.266	0.276	0.521	8.84	237.0	2,331	11,595	17,738	22,329	23,644
Gross domestic investment	**0.443**	**0.459**	**0.789**	**17.34**	**538.1**	**4,253**	**14,547**	**18,481**	**20,023**	**21,539**
Gross fixed investment	0.389	0.385	0.600	13.66	360.2	2,833	12,692	16,891	18,517	20,048
Change in stocks	0.044	0.057	0.148	3.54	174.6	1,395	1,787	1,467	1,346	1,278
Net acquisition of valuables	0.010	0.017	0.041	0.15	3.3	25	68	123	160	213
Resource balance (net export GNFS)	**-0.001**	**-0.018**	**0.065**	**1.00**	**-4.6**	**-381**	**-1,681**	**-2,081**	**-2,856**	**-3,149**
Export of goods and NFS	0.492	0.462	0.782	12.07	383.7	4,260	25,663	37,215	37,898	41,355
Import of goods and NFS	-0.493	-0.480	-0.717	-11.07	-388.3	-4,641	-27,344	-39,296	-40,754	-44,504
Memo items:										
Gross National Income	**1.559**	**1.709**	**3.056**	**50.28**	**1,446.9**	**11,960**	**53,639**	**80,472**	**92,166**	..
Net factor income from abroad	0.025	0.038	0.062	-0.05	-35.8	-78	-877	-1,047	-1,199	..

* Preliminary data

Source: State Statistics Committee

Table 2.2 - Structure of Gross Domestic Product by Industry and Expenditure Category at Current Prices

(percentage distribution)

	1989	1990	1991	1992	1993	1994	1995	1996	1997	1998*
By Industry										
Agriculture and Forestry	**22.3%**	**24.4%**	**24.6%**	**20.9%**	**21.5%**	**14.6%**	**13.8%**	**12.2%**	**12.5%**	**12.4%**
Agriculture	22.2%	24.4%	24.5%	20.8%	21.5%	14.4%	13.5%	11.8%	12.2%	12.0%
Forestry	0.1%	0.1%	0.1%	0.0%	0.1%	0.2%	0.3%	0.4%	0.3%	0.4%
Industry and Construction	**47.0%**	**42.6%**	**54.5%**	**52.2%**	**36.6%**	**42.4%**	**37.8%**	**33.4%**	**29.8%**	**29.5%**
Industry	38.1%	34.5%	45.7%	44.6%	29.7%	35.0%	31.0%	27.5%	24.6%	24.6%
Construction	8.9%	8.1%	8.9%	7.6%	6.9%	7.4%	6.9%	5.9%	5.2%	4.9%
Other	**28.0%**	**28.7%**	**31.0%**	**33.6%**	**34.6%**	**38.4%**	**40.1%**	**44.2%**	**45.6%**	**45.6%**
Transport	6.4%	5.8%	5.4%	7.4%	10.7%	6.3%	10.0%	10.9%	9.5%	10.6%
Road maintenance	0.3%	0.4%	0.5%	0.4%	0.5%	0.8%	0.6%	0.5%	0.6%	
Communication	1.1%	1.1%	1.0%	0.6%	0.6%	1.0%	1.4%	1.8%	2.5%	2.7%
Retail trade and catering	3.4%	4.3%	4.5%	4.9%	7.6%	5.1%	5.3%	5.6%	7.9%	8.0%
Material supply	0.6%	0.6%	0.8%	1.0%	3.8%	1.4%	1.1%	1.0%	0.8%	0.8%
Procurement	0.4%	0.4%	0.5%	0.6%	0.9%	0.8%	0.5%	0.4%	0.4%	0.3%
Information and computing services	0.1%	0.2%	0.2%	0.1%	0.1%	0.1%	0.1%	0.1%	0.1%	0.1%
Other sectors of material production	0.7%	0.7%	0.6%	0.7%	0.9%	0.3%	0.4%	0.5%	0.8%	0.8%
Housing	1.7%	1.5%	1.4%	0.6%	1.8%	1.4%	2.3%	1.9%	1.9%	4.8%
Public utilities and personal services	1.3%	1.3%	1.5%	0.8%	0.9%	1.3%	1.3%	3.4%	3.1%	
Health care, social security, etc.	2.1%	2.3%	2.9%	2.9%	2.7%	2.9%	4.2%	4.6%	4.4%	4.2%
Education	3.0%	3.1%	3.7%	3.7%	3.5%	3.4%	5.1%	5.3%	4.9%	4.9%
Culture and art	0.6%	0.7%	0.6%	0.6%	0.6%	0.5%	0.7%	0.9%	0.8%	0.9%
Science and research	2.1%	2.1%	1.6%	1.4%	1.0%	1.8%	1.1%	1.0%	1.2%	1.1%
Finance, credit and insurance	0.5%	0.6%	2.2%	4.5%	10.2%	7.4%	2.9%	2.5%	2.4%	6.4%
General administration and defense	3.5%	3.8%	3.4%	3.5%	3.6%	3.8%	3.0%	3.5%	4.0%	
Private non-profit organizations	0.1%	0.1%	0.1%	0.1%	0.1%	0.1%	0.1%	0.2%	0.3%	
Total gross value added	**97.2%**	**95.8%**	**110.1%**	**106.7%**	**107.6%**	**95.4%**	**91.7%**	**89.8%**	**87.9%**	**87.4%**
Financial intermediaries, imp. chrg.	-0.1%	-0.2%	-2.1%	-4.2%	-8.2%	-5.7%	-2.3%	-1.3%	-1.1%	-1.7%
Total GDP at factor cost	**97.1%**	**95.6%**	**108.0%**	**102.4%**	**99.4%**	**89.7%**	**89.4%**	**88.4%**	**86.8%**	**85.7%**
Taxes on production	15.4%	16.9%	10.2%	11.0%	14.6%	18.0%	15.8%	14.6%	15.4%	16.1%
Subsidies on production	-12.5%	-12.5%	-18.3%	-13.5%	-14.0%	-7.7%	-5.2%	-3.0%	-2.2%	-1.8%
Total GDP at market prices	**100%**	**100%**	**100%**	**100%**	**100%**	**100%**	**100%**	**100%**	**100.0%**	**100.0%**
By Expenditure Category										
Gross Domestic Expenditures	**100%**	**100%**	**100%**	**100%**	**100%**	**100%**	**100%**	**100%**	**100%**	**100%**
Consumption	**71.2%**	**73.6%**	**71.5%**	**63.6%**	**64.0%**	**67.8%**	**76.4%**	**79.9%**	**81.6%**	**82.3%**
Private consumption	51.6%	54.8%	52.0%	42.0%	44.1%	44.3%	49.7%	53.3%	54.2%	56.2%
Non-profits	2.2%	2.3%	2.0%	4.0%	4.0%	4.2%	5.4%	4.8%	3.5%	3.3%
Government consumption	17.3%	16.5%	17.4%	17.6%	16.0%	19.4%	21.3%	21.8%	23.9%	22.8%
Gross domestic investment	**28.9%**	**27.5%**	**26.4%**	**34.5%**	**36.3%**	**35.3%**	**26.7%**	**22.7%**	**21.4%**	**20.7%**
Gross fixed investment	25.4%	23.0%	20.0%	27.1%	24.3%	23.5%	23.3%	20.7%	19.8%	19.3%
Change in stocks	2.9%	3.4%	4.9%	7.0%	11.8%	11.6%	3.3%	1.8%	1.4%	1.2%
Net acquisition of valuables	0.7%	1.0%	1.4%	0.3%	0.2%	0.2%	0.1%	0.2%	0.2%	0.2%
Resource balance (net export GNFS)	**-0.1%**	**-1.1%**	**2.2%**	**2.0%**	**-0.3%**	**-3.2%**	**-3.1%**	**-2.6%**	**-3.1%**	**-3.0%**
Export of goods and NFS	32.1%	27.6%	26.1%	24.0%	25.9%	35.4%	47.1%	45.7%	40.6%	39.8%
Import of goods and NFS	-32.1%	-28.7%	-23.9%	-22.0%	-26.2%	-38.6%	-50.2%	-48.2%	-43.7%	-42.8%

* Preliminary data

Source: State Statistics Committee

Table 2.3 – Gross Domestic Product by Industry and Expenditure Category at Comparative Prices
(million hryvnias)

	1990	1991	1991	1992	1992	1993	1993	1994	1994	1995	1995	1996	1996	1997	1997	1998*	1998*
	actual prices	1990 prices	actual prices	1991 prices	actual prices	1992 prices	actual prices	1993 prices	actual prices	1994 prices	actual prices	1995 prices	actual prices	1996 prices	actual prices	1997 prices	actual prices
By Industry																	
Agriculture and Forestry	0.409	0.338	0.737	0.663	10.49	11.07	319.4	288.82	1,754	1,676.8	7,507	6,766.0	9,969	9,875	11,685	11,403	12,842
Agriculture	0.407	0.337	0.733	0.660	10.47	11.06	318.2	286.53	1,731	1,654.8	7,337	6,589.0	9,654	9,583	11,385	11,017	12,432
Forestry	0.001	0.001	0.004	0.003	0.02	0.01	1.2	2.29	23	22.0	170	177.0	315	292	300	386	410
Industry and Construction	0.712	0.641	1.633	1.355	26.25	20.40	543.2	354.12	5,110	4,352.4	20,626	18,664.0	27,196	26,046	27,819	27,774	30,619
Industry	0.576	0.514	1.367	1.205	22.45	17.48	440.4	275.19	4,215	3,742.7	16,873	16,194.0	22,381	21,714	22,995	22,824	25,525
Construction	0.136	0.127	0.266	0.150	3.80	2.92	102.8	78.93	895	609.7	3,753	2,470.0	4,815	4,332	4,824	4,950	5,094
Other	0.480	0.509	0.927	1.048	16.93	14.88	512.8	625.0	4,619	4,146.6	21,853	19,690.0	36,011	34,158	42,593	41,477	47,353
Transport	0.097	0.076	0.161	0.151	3.72	2.24	158.1	136.68	760	724.2	5,478	4,779.0	8,880	8,843	8,843	9,179	11,037
Road maintenance	0.007	0.007	0.015	0.015	0.20	0.15	7.5	}	93	}	302	}	409	576	}	}	}
Communication	0.018	0.017	0.029	0.023	0.31	0.23	8.6	8.04	119	62.5	766	508.0	1,433	1,361	2,334	2,297	2,843
Retail trade and catering	0.072	0.070	0.135	0.105	2.48	1.56	113.2	94.96	619	507.7	2,888	2,848.0	4,570	4,609	7,387	7,030	8,271
Material supply	0.009	0.005	0.025	0.015	0.48	0.44	56.3	40.65	165	140.4	625	593.0	809	790	791	772	855
Procurement	0.007	0.005	0.016	0.011	0.32	0.27	13.2	9.99	92	57.5	264	194.0	342	229	380	235	288
Information and computing services	0.003	0.003	0.007	0.006	0.06	0.05	0.9	0.96	8	6.9	44	34.0	65	50	103	92	112
Other sectors of material production	0.012	0.010	0.017	0.014	0.34	0.18	14.1	3.17	41	34.8	242	233.0	443	514	778	661	802
Housing	0.025	0.025	0.042	0.053	0.28	0.28	27.3	26.15	173	167.2	1,279	917.0	1,578	1,360	1,745	4,641	4,975
Public utilities and personal services	0.021	0.020	0.045	0.036	0.38	0.35	13.0	15	154	113.7	721	651.0	2,789	2,596	2,870	}	}
Health care, social security, etc.	0.038	0.048	0.088	0.049	1.45	1.57	40.0	34.69	355	337.6	2,301	2,191.0	3,786	3,600	4,072	4,064	4,407
Education	0.052	0.053	0.111	0.068	1.85	2.00	51.3	43.72	407	393.6	2,764	2,611.0	4,303	4,028	4,598	4,552	5,107
Culture and art	0.011	0.009	0.019	0.013	0.33	0.13	9.4	7.99	63	59.4	385	359.0	853	702	787	758	888
Science and research	0.034	0.029	0.049	0.046	0.70	0.62	14.7	13.19	217	198.5	581	536.0	739	1,094	1,094	1,014	1,111
Finance, credit and insurance	0.010	0.030	0.065	0.167	2.25	2.53	150.7	140.20	889	916.8	1,567	1,503	2,011	2,101	2,252	6,182	6,653
General administration and defense	0.063	0.098	0.101	0.268	1.75	2.23	53.0	47.97	453	..	1,609	1,699	2,879	2,774	3,747	}	}
Private non-profit organizations	0.002	0.003	0.004	0.008	0.04	0.05	1.4	1.29	12	425.7	37	34	135	133	236	}	}
Total gross value added	1.601	1.487	3.297	3.066	53.67	46.35	1,595.3	1,267.9	11,483	10,176	49,986	45,120	73,176	70,079	82,097	80,654	90,814
Financial intermediaries, imp. chrg.	-0.003	-0.030	-0.062	-0.145	-2.12	-2.30	-121.37	-132.3	-684	-698	-1,243	-1,290	-1,087	-1,057	-1,030	-999.0	-1,784
Total GDP at factor cost	1.598	1.457	3.235	2.921	51.56	44.05	1,473.9	1,135.7	10,799	9,478	48,743	43,830	72,089	69,023	81,067	79,655	89,030
Net indirect taxes	0.073	0.069	-0.241	-0.224	-1.23	-0.88	8.83	7.02	1,238.2	1,097	5,773	5,211	9,430	10,060	12,298	12,077	14,835
Total GDP at market prices	1.671	1.526	2.994	2.697	50.33	43.17	1,482.7	1,142.7	12,038	10,575	54,516	49,041	81,519	79,083	93,365	91,732	103,869
By Expenditure Category																	
Gross Domestic Expenditures	1.671	1.526	2.994	2.697	50.33	43.17	1,482.7	1,142.7	12,038	10,575	54,516	49,041	81,519	79,083	93,365	91,732	103,869
Consumption	1.230	1.164	2.140	2.006	31.99	25.99	949.25	857.32	8,165.8	7,869.4	41,651	38,163	65,119	63,941	76,198	..	85,479
Private consumption	0.954	0.878	1.619	1.471	23.15	17.14	712.26	649.14	5,835.1	5,723.8	30,055	27,199	47,381	46,605	53,869	..	58,405
Government consumption	0.276	0.286	0.521	0.535	8.84	8.85	236.99	208.18	2,330.7	2,145.6	11,595	10,964	17,738	17,336	22,329	..	27,074
Gross domestic investment	0.459	0.363	0.789	0.652	17.34	13.07	538.12	392.11	4,253.1	2,279.2	14,547	10,805	18,528	18,481	20,023	..	23,644
Gross fixed investment	0.385	0.305	0.600	0.510	13.66	9.49	360.17	212.37	2,833.1	1,960.6	12,692	9,813	17,240	16,891	18,517	..	21,535
Change in stocks	0.057	0.036	0.148	0.128	3.54	3.51	174.63	177.07	1,394.9	302.1	1,787	898	1,467	1,135	1,346	..	1,896
Net acquisition of valuables	0.017	0.022	0.041	0.014	0.15	0.07	3.32	2.67	25.1	16.5	68	94	123	153	160	..	213
Resource balance (net export GNFS)	-0.018	0.027	0.065	0.033	1.00	3.54	-4.64	-104.28	-381.2	-119.9	-1,681	-1,677	-2,081	-2,294	-2,856	..	-3,149
Export of goods and NFS	0.462	0.382	0.782	0.412	12.07	10.77	383.70	423.54	4,260.0	4,309.0	25,663	29,994	37,215	35,214	37,898	..	41,355
Import of goods and NFS	-0.480	-0.355	-0.717	-0.379	-11.07	-7.23	-388.34	-527.82	-4,641.2	-4,428.9	-27,344	-31,671	-39,296	-37,508	-40,754	..	-44,504
Statistical discrepancy	0.000	-0.028	0	0.006	0	0.57	0	-2.47	0	546.4	0	1,750	0	-1,092	0	..	0

* Preliminary data and World Bank estimates
Source: State Statistics Committee

Table 2.4 - Gross Domestic Product by Industry and Expenditure Category
(index, 1990=100)

	1990	1991	1992	1993	1994	1995	1996	1997	1998*
By Industry									
Agriculture and Forestry	**100**	**83**	**74**	**78**	**71**	**68**	**61**	**61**	**59**
Agriculture	100	83	74	79	71	68	61	60	..
Forestry	100	91	89	37	74	71	73	68	..
Industry and Construction	**100**	**90**	**75**	**58**	**38**	**32**	**29**	**28**	**28**
Industry	100	89	79	61	38	34	33	32	31
Construction	100	93	52	40	31	21	14	12	13
Other	**100**	**106**	**120**	**105**	**128**	**115**	**104**	**98**	**96**
Transport	100	78	73	44	38	36	32	31	..
Road maintenance	100	100	102	75	65	62	54	54	..
Communication	100	95	77	57	53	28	24	23	..
Retail trade and catering	100	97	76	48	40	33	32	33	..
Material supply	100	56	33	30	22	19	18	17	..
Procurement	100	73	50	43	32	20	15	10	..
Information and computing services	100	133	121	104	115	94	73	56	..
Other sectors of material production	100	87	75	40	9	8	7	8	..
Housing	100	103	130	129	124	120	86	74	..
Public utilities and personal services	100	96	78	71	83	61	55	51	..
Health care, social security, etc.	100	127	71	77	67	63	60	57	..
Education	100	101	62	67	58	56	53	49	..
Culture and art	100	79	54	22	18	17	16	16	..
Science and research	100	85	80	71	64	59	54	47	..
Finance, credit and insurance	100	313	798	899	836	863	827	864	..
General administration and defense	100	156	413	527	477	..	..	..	..
Private non-profit organizations	100	115	228	304	275	..	..	..	..
Total gross value added	**100**	**93**	**86**	**75**	**59**	**53**	**47**	**45**	**45**
Financial intermediaries, imp. chrg.	100	937	2.182	2.368	2.581	2.633	2.732	2.656	..
Total GDP at factor cost	**100**	**91**	**82**	**70**	**54**	**48**	**43**	**41**	..
Net indirect taxes	100	94	88	63	50	44	40	43	..
Total GDP at market prices	**100**	**91**	**82**	**71**	**54**	**48**	**43**	**42**	**41**
By Expenditure Category									
Gross Domestic Expenditures	**100**	**91**	**82**	**71**	**54**	**48**	**43**	**42**	**41**
Consumption	**100**	**95**	**89**	**72**	**65**	**63**	**57**	**56**	**..**
Private consumption	100	92	84	62	56	55	50	49	..
Government consumption	100	104	106	107	94	86	81	80	..
Gross domestic investment	**100**	**79**	**65**	**49**	**36**	**19**	**14**	**14**	**..**
Gross fixed investment	100	79	67	47	28	19	15	15	..
Change in stocks	100	63	55	54	55	12	6	5	..
Net acquisition of valuables	100	129	44	21	17	11	15	19	..
Resource balance (net export GNFS)									
Export of goods and NFS	100	83	44	39	43	43	51	48	..
Import of goods and NFS	100	74	39	26	35	35	40	38	..

* Preliminary data and estimates

Source: State Statistics Committee, the World Bank staff calculations

Statistical Appendix

Table 2.5 - Gross Domestic Product by Industry and Expenditure Category at Comparative Prices
(annual growth rates)

	1991	1992	1993	1994	1995	1996	1997	1998*
By Industry								
Agriculture and Forestry	**-17.4%**	**-10.0%**	**5.5%**	**-9.6%**	**-4.4%**	**-9.9%**	**-0.9%**	**-2.4%**
Agriculture	-17.4%	-10.0%	5.6%	-10.0%	-4.4%	-10.2%	-0.7%	-3.2%
Forestry	-9.5%	-2.0%	-58.2%	99.1%	-4.6%	4.0%	-7.3%	28.7%
Industry and Construction	**-10.0%**	**-17.0%**	**-22.3%**	**-34.8%**	**-14.8%**	**-9.5%**	**-4.2%**	**-0.2%**
Industry	-10.8%	-11.8%	-22.1%	-37.5%	-11.2%	-4.0%	-3.0%	-0.7%
Construction	-6.7%	-43.7%	-23.2%	-23.2%	-31.9%	-34.2%	-10.0%	2.6%
Other	**5.9%**	**13.0%**	**-12.1%**	**21.9%**	**-10.2%**	**-9.9%**	**-5.1%**	**-2.6%**
Transport	-22.1%	-6.1%	-39.7%	} -13.6%	} -4.7%	} -12.8%	} -3.5%	} 3.8%
Road maintenance	0.0%	2.1%	-26.6%					
Communication	-5.1%	-19.0%	-26.3%	-6.8%	-47.6%	-33.7%	-5.0%	-1.6%
Retail trade and catering	-2.8%	-22.1%	-37.2%	-16.1%	-18.0%	-1.4%	0.9%	-4.8%
Material supply	-43.6%	-41.2%	-8.5%	-27.7%	-14.8%	-5.1%	-2.3%	-2.4%
Procurement	-27.2%	-30.8%	-15.6%	-24.4%	-37.4%	-26.4%	-33.0%	-38.2%
Information and computing services	32.7%	-8.7%	-13.9%	10.3%	-18.4%	-22.8%	-23.1%	-10.7%
Other sectors of material production	-12.5%	-14.8%	-46.8%	-77.5%	-15.5%	-3.5%	16.0%	-15.0%
Housing	2.6%	26.7%	-0.8%	-4.1%	-3.1%	-28.3%	-13.8%	} 166.0%
Public utilities and personal services	-4.0%	-19.2%	-9.1%	17.7%	-26.3%	-9.7%	-6.9%	
Health care, social security, etc.	26.9%	-44.4%	8.6%	-13.2%	-4.9%	-4.8%	-4.9%	-0.2%
Education	1.4%	-38.5%	8.0%	-14.7%	-3.2%	-5.5%	-6.4%	-1.0%
Culture and art	-20.5%	-32.1%	-60.0%	-15.4%	-5.1%	-6.8%	-3.3%	-3.7%
Science and research	-14.6%	-6.6%	-10.8%	-10.1%	-8.5%	-7.7%	-13.4%	-7.3%
Finance, credit and insurance	212.7%	155.4%	12.5%	-7.0%	3.2%	-4.1%	4.5%	} 174.5%
General administration and defense	55.7%	165.5%	27.6%	-9.6%	..	5.6%	-3.6%	
Private non-profit organizations	14.9%	98.5%	33.4%	-9.8%	3566.3%	-8.7%	-1.5%	
Total gross value added	**-7.1%**	**-7.0%**	**-13.6%**	**-20.5%**	**-11.4%**	**-9.7%**	**-4.2%**	**-1.8%**
Financial intermediaries, imp. chrg.	837.3%	132.8%	8.5%	9.0%	2.0%	3.8%	-2.8%	-3.0%
Total GDP at factor cost	**-8.8%**	**-9.7%**	**-14.6%**	**-22.9%**	**-12.2%**	**-10.1%**	**-4.3%**	**-1.7%**
Net indirect taxes	-5.6%	-6.8%	-28.3%	-20.5%	-11.4%	-9.7%	6.7%	-1.8%
Total GDP at market prices	**-8.7%**	**-9.9%**	**-14.2%**	**-22.9%**	**-12.2%**	**-10.0%**	**-3.0%**	**-1.7%**
By Expenditure Category								
Gross Domestic Expenditures	**-8.7%**	**-9.9%**	**-14.2%**	**-22.9%**	**-12.2%**	**-10.0%**	**-3.0%**	**-1.7%**
Consumption	**-5.4%**	**-6.3%**	**-18.7%**	**-9.7%**	**-3.6%**	**-8.4%**	**-1.8%**	..
Private consumption	-8.0%	-9.1%	-26.0%	-8.9%	-1.9%	-9.5%	-1.6%	..
Government consumption	3.6%	2.7%	0.1%	-12.2%	-7.9%	-5.4%	-2.3%	..
Gross domestic investment	**-20.9%**	**-17.4%**	**-24.6%**	**-27.1%**	**-46.4%**	**-25.7%**	**0.3%**	..
Gross fixed investment	-20.8%	-15.0%	-30.5%	-41.0%	-30.8%	-22.7%	2.1%	..
Change in stocks	-36.8%	-13.5%	-0.7%	1.4%	-78.3%	-49.7%	-22.6%	..
Net acquisition of valuables	29.4%	-65.9%	-52.1%	-19.6%	-34.2%	38.2%	24.4%	..
Resource balance (net export GNFS)	**-250.0%**	**-49.2%**	**253.3%**	**2147.4%**	**-68.5%**	**-0.2%**	**10.2%**	..
Export of goods and NFS	-17.3%	-47.3%	-10.8%	10.4%	1.1%	16.9%	-5.4%	..
Import of goods and NFS	-26.0%	-47.1%	-34.7%	35.9%	0.0%	15.8%	-4.6%	..

* Preliminary data and World Bank estimates
Source: State Statistics Committee

Table 2.6 - Structure of Gross Domestic Product by Industry and Expenditure Category at Comparative Prices

(percentage distribution)

	1991	1992	1993	1994	1995	1996	1997	1998*
By Industry								
Agriculture and Forestry	**22.1%**	**24.6%**	**25.6%**	**25.3%**	**15.9%**	**13.8%**	**12.5%**	**12.4%**
Agriculture	22.1%	24.5%	25.6%	25.1%	15.6%	13.4%	12.1%	12.0%
Forestry	0.1%	0.1%	0.0%	0.2%	0.2%	0.4%	0.4%	0.4%
Industry and Construction	**42.0%**	**50.2%**	**47.3%**	**31.0%**	**41.2%**	**38.1%**	**32.9%**	**30.3%**
Industry	33.7%	44.7%	40.5%	24.1%	35.4%	33.0%	27.5%	24.9%
Construction	8.3%	5.5%	6.8%	6.9%	5.8%	5.0%	5.5%	5.4%
Other	**33.3%**	**38.9%**	**34.5%**	**54.7%**	**39.2%**	**40.2%**	**43.2%**	**45.2%**
Transport	5.0%	5.6%	5.2%	12.0%	6.8%	9.7%	10.8%	10.0%
Road maintenance	0.5%	0.6%	0.3%					
Communication	1.1%	0.9%	0.5%	0.7%	0.6%	1.0%	1.7%	2.5%
Retail trade and catering	4.6%	3.9%	3.6%	8.3%	4.8%	5.8%	5.8%	7.7%
Material supply	0.3%	0.6%	1.0%	3.6%	1.3%	1.2%	1.0%	0.8%
Procurement	0.3%	0.4%	0.6%	0.9%	0.5%	0.4%	0.3%	0.3%
Information and computing services	0.2%	0.2%	0.1%	0.1%	0.1%	0.1%	0.1%	0.1%
Other sectors of material production	0.7%	0.5%	0.4%	0.3%	0.3%	0.5%	0.6%	0.7%
Housing	1.7%	2.0%	0.7%	2.3%	1.6%	1.9%	1.7%	5.1%
Public utilities and personal services	1.3%	1.4%	0.8%	1.3%	1.1%	1.3%	3.3%	
Health care, social security, etc.	3.1%	1.8%	3.6%	3.0%	3.2%	4.5%	4.6%	4.4%
Education	3.5%	2.5%	4.6%	3.8%	3.7%	5.3%	5.1%	5.0%
Culture and art	0.6%	0.5%	0.3%	0.7%	0.6%	0.8%	0.9%	0.8%
Science and research	1.9%	1.7%	1.4%	1.2%	1.9%	1.1%	0.9%	1.1%
Finance, credit and insurance	2.0%	6.2%	5.9%	12.3%	8.7%	3.1%	2.7%	6.7%
General administration and defense	6.4%	9.9%	5.2%	4.2%	..	3.5%	3.5%	
Private non-profit organizations	0.2%	0.3%	0.1%	0.1%	4.0%	0.1%	0.2%	
Total gross value added	**97.5%**	**113.7%**	**107.4%**	**111.0%**	**96.2%**	**92.0%**	**88.6%**	**87.9%**
Financial intermediaries, imp. chrg.	-2.0%	-5.4%	-5.3%	-11.6%	-6.6%	-2.6%	-1.3%	-1.1%
Total GDP at factor cost	**95.5%**	**108.3%**	**102.0%**	**99.4%**	**89.6%**	**89.4%**	**87.3%**	**86.8%**
Net indirect taxes	4.5%	-8.3%	-2.0%	0.6%	10.4%	10.6%	12.7%	13.2%
Total GDP at market prices	**100.0%**	**100.0%**	**100.0%**	**100.0%**	**100.0%**	**100.0%**	**100.0%**	**100.0%**
By Expenditure Category								
Gross Domestic Expenditures	**100.0%**	**100.0%**	**100.0%**	**100.0%**	**100.0%**	**100.0%**	**100.0%**	**100.0%**
Consumption	**76.3%**	**74.4%**	**60.2%**	**75.0%**	**74.5%**	**77.8%**	**80.8%**	**..**
Private consumption	57.5%	54.5%	39.7%	56.8%	54.2%	55.5%	58.9%	..
Government consumption	18.7%	19.8%	20.5%	18.2%	20.3%	22.4%	21.9%	..
Gross domestic investment	**23.8%**	**24.2%**	**30.3%**	**34.3%**	**21.6%**	**22.0%**	**23.5%**	**..**
Gross fixed investment	20.0%	18.9%	22.0%	18.6%	18.5%	20.0%	21.8%	..
Change in stocks	2.4%	4.7%	8.1%	15.5%	2.9%	1.8%	1.5%	..
Net acquisition of valuables	1.4%	0.5%	0.2%	0.2%	0.2%	0.2%	0.2%	..
Resource balance (net export GNFS)	**1.8%**	**1.2%**	**8.2%**	**-9.1%**	**-1.1%**	**-3.4%**	**-2.9%**	**..**
Export of goods and NFS	25.0%	15.3%	24.9%	37.1%	40.7%	61.2%	44.5%	..
Import of goods and NFS	-23.3%	-14.1%	-16.7%	-46.2%	-41.9%	-64.6%	-47.4%	..
Statistical discrepancy	-1.8%	0.2%	1.3%	-0.2%	5.1%	3.6%	-1.4%	..

* Preliminary data and World Bank estimates

Source: State Statistics Committee

Table 2.7 - Gross Capital Investment by Industry
(million current hryvnias)

	1990	1991	1992	1993	1994	1995	1996	1997
By Industry								
Agriculture and Forestry	**0.072**	**0.115**	**2.65**	**67.81**	**280.49**	**1,065.44**	**1,194**	**1,179**
Agriculture, including fishing	0.072	0.1147	2.65	67.75	265.69	1,032.3	1,165	1141
Forestry	0.0001	0.0004	0.004	0.06	14.80	33.11	29	38
Industry and Construction	**0.151**	**0.231**	**6.62**	**151.59**	**988.13**	**4,579.51**	**7,219**	**7,933**
Industry	0.133	0.202	5.74	136.18	934.54	4,408.25	6,971	7727
Construction	0.018	0.029	0.88	15.41	53.59	171.26	248	206
Other	**0.162**	**0.253**	**4.39**	**140.77**	**1,564.44**	**7,046.59**	**8,478**	**9,405**
Transport	0.028	0.036	0.97	24.89	195.97	993.67	1,860	1789
Road maintenance	0.010	0.022	0.34	12.96	157.58	821.58	604	360
Communication	0.004	0.006	0.11	2.61	34.26	191.23	448	891
Retail trade and catering	0.009	0.011	0.19	11.13	38.21	74.00	120	157
Material supply	0.002	-0.0004	0.12	5.22	23.88	43.39	50	101
Procurement	0.002	0.002	0.05	0.86	5.84	31.98	50	45
Information and computing services	0.001	0.001	0.02	0.29	3.15	1.13	7	6
Other sectors of material production	0.003	0.007	0.29	6.38	56.72	151.44	218	304
Housing	0.051	0.083	1.11	31.12	455.67	2,074.35	2,666	3036
Public utilities and personal services	0.011	0.026	0.29	8.58	161.60	568.59	788	848
Health care, social security, etc.	0.010	0.021	0.26	10.53	149.26	689.23	513	527
Education	0.018	0.026	0.37	9.79	132.82	657.75	335	304
Culture and art	0.003	0.006	0.08	2.46	22.54	70.05	118	132
Science and research	0.005	0.004	0.07	1.68	6.28	18.46	9	15
Finance, credit, insurance, pensions	0.002	0.002	0.06	5.22	99.13	186.14	409	439
General commercial activity	..	..	..	..	0.27	0.10	9	424
Real estate transactions	..	..	..	0.10	..	..	..	14
Administration and defense	0.002	0.001	0.08	6.82	20.71	469.75	265	4
Private non-profit organizations	0.001	0.0003	0.001	0.13	0.55	3.75	9	9
Total gross capital investment	**0.385**	**0.600**	**13.65**	**360.17**	**2,833.06**	**12,691.54**	**16,891**	**18,517**
Memo:								
Gross Capital Investment as a share of GDP	-184.6%	-109.7%	-201.4%	-174.0%	-305.7%	-447.7%	-690.3%	19.8%

Source: State Statistics Committee

Table 2.8 - Gross Capital Investment by Industry at Current Prices
(% of total)

By Industry	1990	1991	1992	1993	1994	1995	1996	1997
Agriculture and Forestry	**18.7%**	**19.2%**	**19.4%**	**18.8%**	**9.9%**	**8.4%**	**7.1%**	**6.4%**
Agriculture, including fishing	18.7%	19.1%	19.4%	18.8%	9.4%	8.1%	6.9%	6.2%
Forestry	0.0%	0.1%	0.0%	0.0%	0.5%	0.3%	0.2%	0.2%
Industry and Construction	**39.2%**	**38.6%**	**48.4%**	**42.1%**	**34.9%**	**36.1%**	**42.7%**	**42.8%**
Industry	34.5%	33.7%	42.0%	37.8%	33.0%	34.7%	41.3%	41.7%
Construction	4.7%	4.9%	6.4%	4.3%	1.9%	1.3%	1.5%	1.1%
Other	**42.1%**	**42.2%**	**32.2%**	**39.1%**	**55.2%**	**55.5%**	**50.2%**	**50.8%**
Transport	7.3%	6.0%	7.2%	6.9%	6.9%	7.8%	11.0%	9.7%
Road maintenance	2.7%	3.6%	2.5%	3.6%	5.6%	6.5%	3.6%	1.9%
Communication	1.0%	1.0%	0.8%	0.7%	1.2%	1.5%	2.7%	4.8%
Retail trade and catering	2.4%	1.9%	1.4%	3.1%	1.3%	0.6%	0.7%	0.9%
Material supply	0.5%	-0.1%	0.9%	1.4%	0.9%	0.3%	0.3%	0.5%
Procurement	0.4%	0.4%	0.4%	0.2%	0.2%	0.3%	0.3%	0.2%
Information and computing services	0.2%	0.2%	0.1%	0.1%	0.1%	0.0%	0.0%	0.0%
Other sectors of material production	0.8%	1.2%	2.2%	1.8%	2.0%	1.2%	1.3%	1.6%
Housing	13.3%	13.8%	8.1%	8.6%	16.1%	16.3%	15.8%	16.4%
Public utilities and personal services	2.9%	4.4%	2.1%	2.4%	5.7%	4.5%	4.6%	4.6%
Health care, social security, etc.	2.6%	3.5%	1.9%	2.9%	5.3%	5.4%	3.0%	2.9%
Education	4.8%	4.4%	2.7%	2.7%	4.7%	5.2%	2.0%	1.6%
Culture and art	0.8%	0.9%	0.6%	0.7%	0.8%	0.6%	0.7%	0.7%
Science and research	1.2%	0.6%	0.5%	0.5%	0.2%	0.2%	0.1%	0.1%
Finance, credit, insurance, pensions	0.5%	0.3%	0.4%	1.4%	3.5%	1.5%	2.4%	2.4%
General commercial activity	··	··	··	··	··	··	0.1%	
Real estate transactions	··	··	··	··	··	··		0.1%
Administration and defense	0.5%	0.1%	0.6%	1.9%	0.7%	3.7%	1.6%	2.3%
Private non-profit organizations	0.2%	0.1%	0.0%	0.0%	0.0%	0.0%	0.1%	0.0%
Total gross capital investment	**100.0%**	**100.0%**	**100.0%**	**100.0%**	**100.0%**	**100.0%**	**100.0%**	**100.0%**

Source: State Statistics Committee

Table 2.9 - Households' Monetary Income

(mln UAH)

	Wages in state sector and co-operatives, bonuses and travel fees	Pensions and other transfer incomes	Total monetary income	Wages (% of total income)	Pensions & others (% of total income)	Real income (bn constant 1990 roubles)*
1992	15.2	6.5	23.7	64.4	27.3	70.0
1993	331.0	247.5	628.5	52.7	39.4	45.8
1994	3,118	1,876	5,389	57.9	34.8	30.7
1995	15,178	10,186	26,498	57.3	38.5	28.9
1996	23,257	15,507	40,311	57.7	38.5	26.8
1997	25,210	22,973	50,069	50.9	45.9	30.3
1992 Q1	1.2	0.3	1.6	73.2	18.9	14.1
1995 Q2	3,202	2,235	5,622	57.0	39.8	7.1
1995 Q3	4,538	2,847	7,809	58.1	36.5	8.2
1995 Q4	5,434	3,540	9,385	57.9	37.7	7.7
1996 Q1	5,326	2,911	8,514	62.6	34.2	6.3
1996 Q2	5,651	3,554	9,549	59.2	37.3	6.5
1996 Q3	6,047	4,134	10,629	56.9	38.9	6.9
1996 Q4	6,233	4,908	11,619	53.7	42.2	7.1
1997 Q1	5,504	4,749	10,598	51.9	44.9	6.5
1997 Q2	6,258	5,354	11,978	52.2	44.7	7.3
1997 Q3	6,986	6,763	14,329	48.8	47.2	8.7
1997 Q4	6,462	6,107	13,164	49.1	46.4	7.8
1998 Q1*	6,047	5,596	12,054	50.2	46.4	6.8
1998 Q2*	6,253	6,204	12,921	48.4	48.0	7.2
Oct-95	1,584	822	2,560	61.9	32.1	2.5
Feb-97	1,796	1,497	3,411	52.6	43.9	2.1
Mar-97	2,011	1,787	3,911	51.4	45.7	2.4
Apr-97	2,172	1,774	4,066	53.4	43.6	2.5
May-97	1,972	1,749	3,835	51.4	45.6	2.3
Jun-97	2,114	18,331	4,077	51.8	44.9	2.5
Jul-97	2,272	2,340	4,788	47.4	48.9	2.8
Aug-97	2,502	2,253	4,949	50.6	45.5	3.0
Sep.-97	2,212	2,170	4,592	48.2	47.3	2.8
Oct-97	2,103	1,993	4,307	48.8	46.2	2.6
Nov-97	1,828	1,763	3,764	48.6	46.8	2.2
Dec-97	2,531	2,351	5,093	49.7	46.2	3.0
Jan - 98*	1,628	1,525	3,279	49.6	46.5	1.9
Feb - 98*	1,911	1,828	3,871	49.4	47.2	2.2
Mar - 98*	2,508	2,243	4,904	51.2	45.7	2.8
Apr - 98*	2,131	2,082	4,365	48.8	47.7	2.4
May - 98*	1,907	1,912	3,965	48.1	48.3	2.2
Jun - 98*	2,215	2,210	4,591	48.3	48.2	2.6
Jul - 98*	2,231	2,605	5,009	44.6	52.0	2.8
Aug - 98*	1,991	2,362	4,514	44.1	52.3	2.5
Sep - 98*	1,970	2,359	4,628	42.6	51.0	2.5
Oct - 98*	2,205	2,498	5,025	43.9	49.7	2.6
Nov - 98*	2,088	2,556	4,930	42.4	51.8	2.4
Dec - 98*	2,771	3,079	6,241	44.4	49.3	3.0

* Preliminary data

** excluding wages of physical persons - entrepreneurs, agricultural workers and

receipts from sales of agricultural products

Source: TACIS' Ukrainian Economic Trends based on State Statistics Committee data

Table 3.1- Balance of Payments. 1990-1998 [1]

(mln. USD)

	1991	1992	1993	1994	1995	1996	1997	1998
CURRENT ACCOUNT:	-2,928	-621	-854	-1,163	-1,152	-1,185	-1,335	-1,296
Net trade in Goods & Services	2,509	-606	-905	-1,366	-1,190	-1,122	-1,536	-1,207
Trade balance	1,994	-622	-2,519	-2,575	-2,702	-4,296	-4,205	-2,584
Exports of Goods & Services & Income Receipts	24,671	11,356	15,876	16,697	17,337	20,449	20,513	17,743
Exports of Goods & Services	24,671	11,355	15,850	16,641	17,090	20,346	20,355	17,621
Exports of Goods	23,988	11,308	12,796	13,894	14,244	15,547	15,418	13,699
Exports of Services	683	47	3,054	2,747	2,846	4,799	4,937	3,922
Imports of Goods & Services & Income Payments	-22,162	-11,977	-16,850	-18,407	-18,961	-22,143	-22,693	-19,821
Imports of Goods & Services	-22,162	-11,961	-16,755	-18,007	-18,280	-21,468	-21,891	-18,828
Imports of Goods, f.o.b.	-21,994	-11,930	-15,315	-16,469	-16,946	-19,843	-19,623	-16,283
Imports of Services	-168	-31	-1,440	-1,538	-1,334	-1,625	-2,268	-2,545
Net income receipts	..	-15	-69	-344	-434	-572	-644	-871
Income receipts	..	1	26	56	247	103	158	122
Income payments	..	-16	-95	-400	-681	-675	-802	-993
Net total current transfers	..	0	120	547	472	509	845	782
Total current transfer receipts	..	..	..	583	557	619	942	868
Total current transfer payments	..	..	..	-36	-85	-110	-97	-86
CAPITAL & FINANCIAL ACCOUNT:	..	-2,141	-423	1,281	1,366	1,819	2,503	782
Net official capital grants	..	0	0	97	6	5	0	-3
Net total private investment inflows	..	170	200	151	261	724	2,184	794
Net direct investment inflows	..	170	200	151	257	526	581	747
Inflows	..	..	..	..	267	521	623	743
Outflows	..	..	..	..	-10	5	-42	4
Net portfolio investment inflows	..	..	..	0	4	198	1,603	47
Inflows	..	..	..	..	16	199	1,605	49
Outflows	..	..	..	..	-12	-1	-2	-2
Net long- and medium-term borrowing	..	361	603	21	3,506	1,140	1,025	130
Disbursements	..	415	627	1,586	4,561	1,951	1,950	1,791
Guaranteed loans	..	..	..	..	4,491	1,745	1,635	1,161
Non-guaranteed loans	..	..	..	..	70	206	315	630
Repayments due	..	0	-114	-1,565	-1,055	-811	-925	-1,661
Guaranteed loans	..	..	..	..	-1017	-708	-869	-1224
Non-guaranteed loans	..	..	..	..	-38	-103	-56	-437
Other LT inflows, net	..	-54	90	..	..	..	..	..
Adjustments to scheduled debt service	0	0	0	0	0	0	0	0
Debt service not paid	0	0	0	0	0	0	0	0
of which Arrears Accumulation	0	0	0	0	0	0	0	0
Reduction in arrears/prepayments (-)	0	0	0	0	0	0	0	0
Other capital flows, net	..	-2,672	-1,226	1,012	-2,407	-50	-706	-139
Net short-term capital	..	..	..	1,012	-2,571	-673	13	-14
Capital flows n.e.i.	..	..	..	0	164	623	-719	-125
FINANCING:	..	-96	37	-546	-488	-873	-383	1,324
Reserves, net change (includes IMF & LCFAR)	..	-96	37	-546	-488	-873	-383	1,324
Foreign exchange & deposits	..	..	..	..	-446	-916	-507	1432
SDR	..	..	..	..	17	94	-5	-108
Securities	..	..	..	..	-59	-51	129	0
ERRORS AND OMISSIONS:	94	-29	14	428	274	239	-785	-810
Memo Items:								
Gross reserves (incl. gold)	..	469	166	664	1,069	1,953	2,345	686
International reserves excl. gold	..	469	162	651	1,051	1,941	2,327	654
Gold reserves	..	0	4	14	18	12	18	32

[1] *Balance of Payments complying with IMF standards has been published in Ukraine since 1994. The only pre-1994 BoP data available are IMF staff estimates.*

Source: National Bank of Ukraine, IMF staff estimates

Table 3.2 - Balance of Payments, 1994-1998

(mln. USD)

	1994 Q1	1994 Q2	1994 Q3	1994 Q4	1994 Full year	1995 Q1	1995 Q2	1995 Q3	1995 Q4	1995 Full year	1996 Q1	1996 Q2	1996 Q3	1996 Q4	1996 Full year	1997 Q1	1997 Q2	1997 Q3	1997 Q4	1997 Full year	1998 Q1	1998 Q2	1998 Q3	1998 Q4	1998 Full year
CURRENT ACCOUNT	-678	-512	-114	141	-1163	-325	-240	-188	-399	-1152	-709	105	-53	-528	-1185	-748	-274	-159	-154	-1335	-714	-305	-448	171	-1296
NET TRADE IN GOODS & NON-FACTOR SERVICES	-698	-625	-223	180	-1,366	-381	-274	-230	-305	-1,190	-702	65	-22	-463	-1,122	-741	-354	-249	-192	-1,536	-722	-261	-364	140	-1,207
EXPORTS OF GOODS & NON-FACTOR SERVICES	3,204	4,231	4,610	4,596	16,641	3,425	4,224	4,570	4,871	17,090	4,667	5,486	5,068	5,125	20,346	4,744	5,040	5,205	5,366	20,355	4,421	4,727	4,147	4,326	17,621
IMPORTS OF GOODS & NON-FACTOR SERVICES	-3,902	-4,856	-4,833	-4,416	-18,007	-3,806	-4,498	-4,800	-5,176	-18,280	-5,369	-5,421	-5,090	-5,588	-21,468	-5,485	-5,394	-5,454	-5,558	-21,891	-5,143	-4,988	-4,511	-4,186	-18,828
TRADE BALANCE	-878	-978	-605	-114	-2,575	-753	-644	-612	-693	-2,702	-1,506	-811	-719	-1,260	-4,296	-1,456	-1,024	-885	-840	-4,205	-1,016	-520	-694	-354	-2,584
EXPORTS OF GOODS	2,710	3,508	3,789	3,887	13,894	2,751	3,505	3,859	4,129	14,244	3,544	4,208	3,995	3,890	15,547	3,527	3,888	3,945	4,088	15,418	3,441	3,750	3,174	3,332	13,699
IMPORTS OF GOODS	-3,588	-4,486	-4,394	-4,001	-16,469	-3,504	-4,149	-4,471	-4,822	-16,946	-5,050	-5,019	-4,624	-5,150	-19,843	-4,983	-4,882	-4,830	-4,928	-19,623	-4,459	-4,270	-3,868	-3,686	-16,283
SERVICES BALANCE	180	353	382	294	1,209	372	370	382	388	1,512	804	876	697	797	3,174	715	670	636	648	2,669	294	259	330	494	1,377
EXPORTS OF SERVICES	494	723	821	709	2,747	674	719	711	742	2,846	1,123	1,278	1,163	1,235	4,799	1,217	1,182	1,260	1,278	4,937	978	977	973	994	3,922
Transportation	…	…	…	…	…	519	550	530	553	2,152	966	1,077	979	1,011	4,033	1,007	939	1,019	1,064	4,029	815	774	811	822	3,222
Railroads	…	…	…	…	…	29	26	25	23	103	59	82	71	95	307	88	90	157	94	429	102	79	123	88	392
Maritime	…	…	…	…	…	158	167	122	170	617	148	204	154	125	631	137	127	131	115	510	125	109	98	119	451
Air	…	…	…	…	…	17	29	35	34	115	27	39	45	29	140	26	38	69	58	182	44	59	69	55	218
Other	…	…	…	…	…	315	328	348	326	1,317	732	752	709	762	2,955	756	684	671	797	2,908	544	536	521	560	2,161
Tourism	…	…	…	…	…	45	35	63	48	191	53	58	65	54	230	57	73	82	58	270	68	94	80	76	315
Construction services	…	…	…	…	…	2	8	10	11	31	7	10	12	13	42	9	13	14	14	50	11	12	10	8	41
Financial services	…	…	…	…	…	33	18	7	8	76	4	10	5	7	26	5	6	14	8	33	7	7	5	4	23
Communication services	…	…	…	…	…	54	57	32	33	176	38	23	30	34	125	30	29	29	26	114	30	26	25	26	102
Other services	…	…	…	…	…	21	51	59	89	220	55	100	72	116	343	109	122	102	108	441	55	64	42	58	219
IMPORTS OF SERVICES	-314	-370	-439	-415	-1,538	-302	-349	-329	-354	-1,334	-319	-402	-466	-438	-1,625	-502	-512	-624	-630	-2,268	-684	-718	-643	-500	-2,545
Transportation	…	…	…	…	…	-115	-99	-118	-122	-454	-59	-132	-132	-101	-424	-105	-94	-156	-121	-476	-115	-117	-148	-107	-487
Railroads	…	…	…	…	…	-23	-30	-21	-26	-100	-14	-47	-48	-33	-133	-36	-37	-77	-53	-203	-49	-35	-69	-49	-202
Maritime	…	…	…	…	…	-25	-22	-32	-31	-110	-26	-40	-38	-33	-137	-24	-22	-25	-20	-91	-23	-27	-22	-22	-94
Air	…	…	…	…	…	-13	-12	-15	-12	-52	-15	-34	-35	-34	-118	-35	-25	-42	-34	-136	-26	-34	-40	-26	-126
Other	…	…	…	…	…	-54	-35	-50	-53	-192	-4	-11	-11	-10	-36	-10	-10	-12	-14	-46	-17	-21	-17	-10	-65
Tourism	…	…	…	…	…	-44	-38	-67	-61	-210	-61	-66	-95	-86	-308	-71	-75	-97	-62	-305	-72	-89	-95	-84	-340
Construction services	…	…	…	…	…	-2	-13	-12	-9	-36	-24	-20	-33	-17	-109	-42	-48	-52	-50	-192	-65	-65	-38	-28	-196
Financial services	…	…	…	…	…	-45	-20	-23	-10	-98	-5	-9	-11	-17	-42	-16	-17	-17	-30	-80	-30	-16	-16	-14	-90
Communication services	…	…	…	…	…	-72	-71	-36	-33	-212	-28	-29	-29	-33	-119	-24	-30	-33	-28	-115	-37	-31	-31	-32	-131
Other services	…	…	…	…	…	-24	-108	-73	-119	-324	-142	-146	-166	-169	-623	-244	-248	-269	-339	-1,100	-365	-386	-315	-235	-1,301
NET INCOME	-93	-48	-50	-153	-344	-93	-110	-37	-194	-434	-127	-102	-159	-184	-572	-165	-150	-148	-181	-644	-205	-238	-269	-159	-871
Receipts	9	10	19	18	56	28	44	97	78	247	19	32	30	22	103	30	28	39	61	158	49	26	24	23	122
Payments	-102	-58	-69	-171	-400	-121	-154	-134	-272	-681	-146	-134	-189	-206	-675	-195	-178	-187	-242	-802	-254	-264	-293	-182	-993
NET CURRENT TRANSFERS	113	161	159	114	547	149	144	79	100	472	120	142	128	119	509	158	230	238	219	845	213	194	185	190	782
Receipts	118	166	166	133	583	169	159	107	122	557	162	156	156	145	619	187	251	266	238	942	231	230	201	206	868
Payments	-5	-5	-7	-19	-36	-20	-15	-28	-22	-85	-42	-14	-28	-26	-110	-29	-21	-28	-19	-97	-18	-36	-16	-16	-86

Note: Balance of Payments complying with IMF standards has been compiled in Ukraine since 1994.

Source: National Bank of Ukraine

Table 3.3 - Geographic Structure of Foreign Trade in Goods

(mln . USD)

	Export*					Import*				
	1994	1995	1996	1997	1998	1994	1995	1996	1997	1998
Total	**10272.1**	**13166.8**	**14400.8**	**14231.9**	**12637.4**	**10745.3**	**16052.3**	**17603.4**	**17128.0**	**14675.6**
Former USSR	*5924.9*	*7225.6*	*7668.6*	*5810.2*	*4433.1*	*8003.2*	*10802.1*	*11463.3*	*10277.5*	*8279.0*
Azerbaijan	79.0	41.5	88.3	87.6	89.9	40.7	53.2	30.8	47.0	27.7
Beloruss	542.3	545.9	722.5	825.5	548.0	339.9	526.4	384.5	391.4	352.9
Armenia	5.5	6.3	25.2	10.7	8.4	1.3	6.0	4.0	8.1	4.5
Georgia	8.8	18.0	183.2	49.4	31.5	3.3	4.9	3.8	7.7	7.8
Kazakhstan	119.2	94.4	90.9	93.7	89.7	164.9	323.3	2.43.6	403.7	345.7
Kyrgyzstan	10.0	8.3	8.1	4.3	12.3	16.1	8.9	9.6	8.7	10.6
Moldova	489.3	151.9	237.8	294.4	180.4	171.9	61.1	72.6	73.8	51.1
Russia	4065.4	5697.9	5577.4	3723.0	2905.5	6349.4	8249.1	8816.6	7837.9	7064.3
Tadjikistan	4.3	11.3	19.1	84.5	76.0	7.1	9.1	8.4	2.5	1.4
Turkmenia	222.0	270.2	274.0	176.7	121.1	687.9	680.5	1541.2	972.3	1.3
Uzbekistan	73.3	114.1	178.7	235.9	139.5	55.0	73.4	60.8	126.4	29.7
Estonia	18.7	36.0	53.9	43.4	51.1	27.4	26.6	38.7	72.8	96.4
Latvia	94.0	63.9	77.9	78.9	78.0	70.3	81.8	92.4	82.9	45.7
Lithuania	193.1	127.3	131.6	102.3	101.7	68.0	129.5	156.3	242.4	239.9
Rest of the World	*4347.2*	*5941.2*	*6732.2*	*8421.7*	*8204.3*	*2742.1*	*5250.2*	*6140.1*	*6850.5*	*6396.5*
Austria	170.8	77.3	101.5	107.7	135.2	99.1	132.6	175.5	224.7	193.8
Belgium	46.0	68.7	78.3	83.2	86.0	21.3	111.3	124.8	152.7	138.5
Bulgaria	129.8	179.2	137.4	154.7	205.4	68.8	128.4	126.1	142.9	100.5
Brazil	2.6	20.1	36.7	40.4	57.9	9.2	137.5	111.6	49.0	64.2
Great Britain	77.0	176.0	135.9	87.4	108.0	58.9	142.5	201.5	232.4	204.7
Virginia Isl.	2.2	36.8	92.2	150.6	56.5	2.2	0.7	1.7	11.5	1.5
Greece	...	39.7	96.9	80.4	59.9	...	84.5	59.6	64.8	34.1
Egypt	58.2	106.3	96.8	184.7	186.9	9.9	8.8	12.2	4.7	7.1
Israel	...	59.9	67.2	72.1	134.1	...	39.9	49.8	51.2	49.2
India	54.2	231.4	82.3	225.3	137.6	24.3	74.3	91.0	82.4	79.3
Italy	200.2	424.6	344.6	395.0	550.2	126.8	271.8	341.8	400.4	408.6
Iran	...	34.9	116.5	189.6	118.5	...	4.2	7.0	8.3	5.5
Ireland	63.6	9.3	64.4	29.9	82.3	22.3	33.9	52.5	48.1	37.3
Spain	...	64.1	90.2	117.5	131.3	...	46.5	57.0	85.1	80.3
Canada	33.7	9.2	14.4	13.9	33.3	23.3	29.0	46.6	37.7	28.2
China	506.1	755.4	768.1	1100.9	737.4	33.0	83.7	90.2	125.6	123.1
Liven	...	141.6	155.9	153.1	72.8	...	1.6	1.5	3.3	1.3
Holland	...	113.3	99.7	121.3	117.7	...	149.2	197.8	192.9	161.5
Germany	282.6	338.7	421.9	568.6	638.7	655.0	958.3	1068.7	1308.9	1263.6
South Korea	67.4	79.3	63.2	51.9	75.3	4.7	27.5	48.0	113.1	196.4
Poland	150.0	274.5	362.7	380.3	313.1	123.2	476.7	510.7	549.9	486.2
Rumania	...	167.3	157.3	149.0	160.9	...	151.5	80.3	86.9	47.8
Syria	17.4	83.8	197.6	260.9	204.1	1.7	11.6	3.2	4.5	8.4
Slovakia	125.4	216.4	230.6	279.3	245.2	75.3	152.8	183.1	204.5	170.4
USA	358.7	273.1	376.3	300.4	502.0	220.2	419.3	569.8	650.9	590.3
Thailand	113.2	124.8	329.3	99.6	15.0	0.5	4.9	16.2	3.2	5.4
Taiwan	87.1	80.2	84.2	303.7	193.1	0.5	6.7	8.6	12.2	18.1
Turkey	116.3	453.0	408.7	670.9	696.3	8.9	67.6	109.8	162.0	135.7
Hungary	170.4	298.1	8.9	318.8	263.1	99.9	169.6	238.3	197.3	193.9
Finland	...	22.9	22.1	37.8	26.2	...	88.4	96.3	120.5	114.9
France	36.7	43.7	111.1	96.7	118.9	64.9	195.3	245.1	307.6	300.2
Check Republic	125.7	118.1	143.0	173.9	171.5	127.5	157.1	239.1	219.7	208.8
Switzerland	326.4	50.3	85.3	71.4	75.6	334.3	131.8	101.3	148.8	120.4
Swiss	...	7.9	11.7	3.7	7.4	...	46.9	66.9	136.7	148.9
Japan	26.2	65.6	81.3	92.8	57.5	30.3	106.9	114.9	150.0	113.8
Other countries	999.3	695.7	1058.0	1254.5	1429.4	496.1	596.9	691.6	556.0	554.8

** In 1996-98 data were obtained from the Customs statistics. For 1994 - 95, data are based on
reports of enterprises, and it is not comparable with data in subsequent years.*

Source: State Committee of Statistics

Statistical Appendix

Table 3.4 - Commodity Structure of Foreign Trade
(mln. USD)

		Export				Import			
		1995	1996	1997	1998	1995	1996	1997	1998
	Total	**11566.5**	**14400.8**	**14231.9**	**12637.4**	**11335.5**	**17603.4**	**17128.0**	**14675.6**
I.	*Live animals*	*485.6*	*593.6*	*438.7*	*272.8*	*75.5*	*316.1*	*190.8*	*221.0*
01	Live animals	50.3	41.5	10.2	0.5	1.8	14.9	11.6	9.3
02	Meat and subproducts	194.8	297.6	260.2	159.6	17.2	156.4	83.6	67.7
03	Fish, etc.	64.4	59.7	58.7	44.7	40.2	117.2	79.6	129.5
04	Dairy products, eggs	174.2	191.7	106.4	65.9	12.7	21.9	13.9	13.0
05	Products of animal origin	1.9	3.1	3.2	2.1	3.6	5.7	2.1	1.4
II.	*Products from plants*	*142.7*	*867.6*	*553.6*	*642.9*	*103.2*	*246.9*	*167.1*	*184.7*
06	Flowers, live plants	0.1	0.6	0.8	0.6	1.5	2.2	3.5	3.5
07	Vegetables and roots	23.8	23.0	29.4	22.8	3	11.3	2.5	3.7
08	Fruits and nuts	2.7	7.5	6.9	7.8	13.5	80.1	40.1	38.9
09	Coffee, tea, mate	1.5	2.1	3.3	2.3	11.5	36.4	34.1	43.0
10	Cereals	47.2	375.7	127.8	313.8	20.3	27.3	19.7	19.1
11	Flour products	50.2	217.5	104.0	51.8	1.9	8.9	16.2	11.8
12	Oil seeds, industrial plants	16	236.4	278.4	241.9	45.7	64.3	44.6	57.3
13	Extracts from plants	1.2	4.8	2.9	1.9	5.7	15.8	6.2	7.4
14	Materials of vegetal origin for threading	0	0.0	0.0	0.0	0.1	0.6	0.2	0.0
III.	*Fats and oils of animal and vegetal origin*	*91.7*	*185.6*	*121.8*	*131.9*	*19.4*	*36.9*	*39.8*	*93.6*
IV.	*Food products*	*979.4*	*1402.0*	*686.7*	*331.8*	*273.5*	*848.3*	*500.3*	*551.9*
16	Fish/meat preparations	63.6	85.9	131.9	53.6	6.1	48.8	19.7	34.1
17	Sugar & confectionery	544.8	675.9	314.6	108.6	162.9	309.9	16.3	43.0
18	Cacao products	2.3	10.5	21.2	22.7	25.9	55.8	72.6	83.1
19	Products from flour, cereals	11.3	16.6	14.4	12.4	8.2	47.2	53.7	17.8
20	Vegetable and fruit preparations	36.4	46.9	37.1	30.1	6.9	26.3	25.5	27.3
21	Mixed food products	4.5	15.1	5.7	2.7	12.4	107.6	56.5	40.8
22	Alcoholic beverages and soft drinks	268.5	445.8	112.6	52.4	17.3	90.5	69.7	88.2
23	Wastes (food industry) and animal feed	15.3	66.7	20.9	18.8	2.3	7.2	10.8	11.8
24	Tobacco	32.7	38.6	28.3	30.5	31.5	155.0	175.4	205.9
V.	*Mineral products*	*1220.9*	*1244.6*	*1282.9*	*1163.6*	*6281.1*	*8781.4*	*8152.9*	*6320.8*
25	Salt, cement. etc..	106.2	123.2	140.9	140.5	99.9	162.3	184.4	151.1
26	Iron ore, ash, slags	603.5	495.4	538.9	502.4	193.3	212.4	161.1	229.1
27	Petroleum products	511.2	626.0	603.1	520.7	5987.9	8406.7	7807.4	5940.7
VI.	*Chemicals*	*1125*	*1674.7*	*1504.4*	*1278.8*	*614.3*	*1025.9*	*1241.8*	*995.1*
28	Inorganic chemicals	284.5	597.7	537.9	508.2	88	121.1	87.2	67.6
29	Organic chemicals	305.6	168.8	217.9	159.6	148.6	159.2	144.8	131.8
30	Pharmaceutical products	29.3	72.5	90.4	60.2	110	255.5	423.5	305.9
31	Fertilizers	301.8	572.3	432.7	328.7	2.5	4.5	7.8	4.7
32	Coloring materials, pigments, ink	90.7	87.2	68.9	68.8	70.1	89.6	111.5	105.7
33	Oils, essence, perfumes	2.8	15.4	18.9	20.7	31.4	70.7	109.8	84.1
34	Soap and detergents	39.1	48.0	20.0	8.7	16.3	39.0	44.0	49.7
35	Glues, albumin	36.9	64.0	57.2	68.4	9.1	14.6	19.0	17.9
36	Explosives, matches	3.5	4.5	8.5	2.5	18.2	13.0	12.1	12.7
37	Photographic materials	0.8	5.0	3.5	2.0	6.8	16.0	18.3	11.3
38	Other chemical products	30	39.3	48.5	50.9	113.3	242.7	263.8	203.7
VII.	*Plastic goods*	*322.4*	*402.0*	*369.4*	*316.3*	*412*	*768.5*	*724.9*	*674.8*
39	Plastic goods	69.8	91.5	67.5	74.0	159.6	288.1	366.6	354.5
40	Rubber	252.6	310.5	301.9	242.3	252.4	480.4	358.3	320.3
VIII.	*Skins, hides, etc.*	*67.3*	*121.2*	*141.8*	*97.9*	*35.1*	*51.6*	*51.8*	*52.0*
41	Skins and hides	60.7	107.5	129.9	86.3	23.7	29.9	34.6	35.9
42	Products of skin, travel goods, bags	0.6	2.1	2.3	3.8	2.9	7.3	6.5	6.5
43	Furs	6	11.6	9.6	7.8	8.5	14.4	10.7	9.6
IX.	*Wood and wood products*	*31.1*	*55.2*	*61.1*	*100.2*	*79*	*119.8*	*90.4*	*75.7*
44	Wood and wood products	31	55.2	61.0	100.2	77.6	118.2	88.5	73.5
45	Cork and cork products	0	0.0	0.0	0.0	1.3	1.5	1.8	2.0
46	Straw products	0.1	0.0	0.0	0.0	0.1	0.1	0.1	0.2
X.	*Paper, products from paper*	*79.8*	*138.8*	*147.7*	*137.9*	*206.5*	*392.2*	*409.7*	*397.4*
47	Pulp	1.3	0.4	0.2	0.1	43.1	50.2	38.6	38.7
48	Paper, carton	72.3	100.7	106.0	106.3	154.5	305.3	327.2	307.9
49	Printed materials	6.2	37.7	41.5	31.5	8.9	36.7	43.9	50.8

** In 1996-98 data were obtained from the Customs statistics. For 1995, data are based on
reports of enterprises, and it is not comparable with data in subsequent years.*

Table 3.4 - Commodity Structure of Foreign Trade (continued)
(mln. USD)

		Export				Import			
		1995	1996	1997	1998	1995	1996	1997	1998
XI.	Textiles	314.8	382.8	449.7	501.6	352.3	495.9	491.6	541.7
50	Silk	0.1	0.3	0.1	0.5	1	0.6	0.5	0.5
51	Wood, animal hair	21.4	13.7	14.2	7.9	36.7	45.2	59.2	65.5
52	Cotton	16.3	12.7	8.1	10.0	73.7	96.0	66.5	69.0
53	Other fibers	16.7	8.5	7.7	6.3	6.5	10.5	7.0	6.2
54	Chemical fibers	38.1	30.7	60.9	64.6	56.7	67.5	59.1	70.8
55	Chemical staple-fibers	11.1	5.0	4.5	3.4	54.8	70.0	91.6	105.8
56	Cotton wool	7.8	11.5	18.6	17.4	18.8	31.9	36.9	30.2
57	Carpets, floor coverings	1	0.5	1.9	2.1	2.4	5.0	7.1	7.7
58	Special materials (decorative materials)	0.6	0.4	0.2	0.5	10.4	11.3	12.6	13.6
59	Textile materials (printed)	18.5	24.1	16.5	12.6	26.4	51.0	46.8	54.5
60	Knitted fabrics	0.8	0.6	1.1	0.5	8	9.4	17.5	22.7
61	Clothes of knitted fabrics	13	18.5	19.6	23.6	12.6	15.8	17.0	18.6
62	Clothes (not knitted)	164.5	244.5	286.4	342.1	26.1	27.7	30.9	36.2
63	Other ready-made textile goods	4.9	11.8	9.9	9.8	18.2	54.0	38.9	40.4
XII.	Shoes, hats, umbrellas	53.1	70.2	59.3	61.9	36.1	69.2	50.4	39.4
64	Shoes, boots	51.5	68.9	57.7	60.4	35.4	67.3	48.0	36.0
65	Hats, caps	1.5	1.3	1.6	1.4	0.2	0.5	0.7	1.6
66	Umbrellas, canes	0	0.0	0.0	0.0	0.1	0.8	1.3	1.5
67	Artificial flowers	0.1	0.0	0.0	0.0	0.4	0.6	0.4	0.3
XIII.	Products from stone, cement, asbestos	171.5	172.8	133.7	108.5	92.8	159.6	202.6	161.3
68	Goods from stone, cement, asbestos	49.8	60.6	52.0	36.8	29.8	42.4	59.8	50.8
69	Ceramics	67.3	56.0	45.4	42.5	35.9	61.1	78.3	58.9
70	Glass and glass products	54.4	56.2	36.3	29.2	27.1	56.1	64.5	51.6
XIV.	Natural pearls	72.2	0.0	0.0	0.0	69.7	0.0	0.0	0.0
XV.	Ferrous and other non-precious metals	4189.9	4763.2	5904.2	5335.7	539.3	791.9	665.4	628.8
72	Ferrous materials	3112.6	3417.0	4495.7	4204.4	224.7	279.0	213.9	207.6
73	Goods from ferrous materials	786.3	1008.3	957.9	644.9	99.1	162.1	174.3	141.8
74	Copper and copper products	25.6	69.3	145.8	131.3	51.1	73.1	54.4	54.0
75	Nickel and nickel products	0.4	0.5	0.4	9.0	34.8	39.4	32.7	24.5
76	Aluminum and products of aluminum	159.7	161.9	221.6	282.0	59.7	93.3	91.6	93.8
78	Lead and lead products	2.6	7.3	4.3	2.9	1.3	2.6	2.6	3.5
79	Zinc and zinc products	0	0.0	0.4	0.5	13.9	16.1	13.9	18.5
80	Tin and tin products	0	0.0	0.0	0.0	3	2.6	1.8	0.5
81	Other non-precious metals	72	53.4	38.3	30.7	11.9	10.8	8.8	8.2
82	Instruments from non-precious metals	11.9	16.8	9.8	13.1	20.3	35.2	48.7	48.4
83	Other goods from non-precious metals	18.8	28.7	30.0	16.9	19.5	77.7	22.7	28.0
XVI.	Machinery	1360.1	1406.7	1370.0	1104.7	1689.2	2407.9	2594.9	2284.7
84	Non-electrical machinery, reactors	905.6	936.7	909.4	761.4	1266.8	1781.1	1961.0	1614.3
85	Electrical machinery	454.5	470.0	460.6	343.4	422.4	626.8	633.9	670.4
XVII.	Transport	743.7	635.4	540.4	617.0	286.6	570.4	861.0	887.3
86	Locomotives	204.1	210.8	142.8	134.6	51.2	108.5	109.6	110.6
87	Transport except railway	411.4	234.5	193.0	130.2	221.6	448.5	639.3	752.7
88	Aircraft	25.6	51.5	113.2	153.1	6.4	9.7	109.9	12.9
89	Ships	102.6	138.6	91.4	198.9	7.4	3.7	2.2	11.1
XVIII	Equipment	62.3	61.7	62.1	64.1	104.2	207.3	237.8	242.0
90	Optical, photografical, control, medical equip.	59.5	60.9	59.1	63.6	98.5	200.2	231.3	236.4
91	Watches, clocks	0.2	0.0	1.6	0.1	4.9	5.1	4.7	4.3
92	Musical instruments	2.6	0.8	1.4	0.4	0.8	2.0	1.8	1.3
XIX.	Other goods	52.9	55.0	55.2	44.4	65.6	152.3	157.6	112.8
94	Furniture	41.5	43.9	42.4	31.7	43.1	101.0	121.2	81.0
95	Toys	10	9.2	11.2	11.3	11.7	29.5	12.5	9.8
96	Other	1.4	1.9	1.6	1.4	10.8	21.8	23.9	22.0
XX.	Collectors' items, antiques	0.1	0.0	0.0	0.0	0.1	0.1	0.1	0.2
XXI.	Other	..	167.6	345.7	319.7	..	116.5	122.0	77.3
XXII.	Goods purchased in ports	..	0.1	3.5	5.7	..	44.7	175.1	133.1

* In 1996-98 data were obtained from the Customs statistics. For 1995, data are based on
reports of enterprises, and it is not comparable with data in subsequent years.

Table 3.5 - Commodity Structure of Foreign Trade (mn. USD)

		Export*					Import*				
		1994	1995	1996	1997	1998	1994	1995	1996	1997	1998
	Total	9708.2	11566.5	14400.8	14231.9	12637.4	9989.2	11335.5	17603.4	17128.0	14675.6
I.	Live animals	340.1	485.6	593.6	438.7	272.8	61.1	75.5	316.1	190.8	221.0
II.	Products from plants	81.9	142.7	867.6	553.6	642.9	94.9	103.2	246.9	167.1	184.7
III.	Fats and oils of animal and vegetal origin	55.6	91.7	185.6	121.8	131.9	5.0	19.4	36.9	39.8	93.6
IV.	Food products	560.4	979.4	1402.0	686.7	331.8	164.6	273.5	848.3	500.3	551.9
V.	Mineral products	1015.0	1220.9	1244.6	1282.9	1163.6	5495.8	6281.1	8781.4	8152.9	6320.8
VI.	Chemicals	1024.0	1125	1674.7	1504.4	1278.8	555.4	614.3	1025.9	1241.8	995.1
VII.	Plastic goods	304.4	322.4	402.0	369.4	316.3	384.7	412	768.5	724.9	674.8
VIII.	Skins, hides, etc.	47.0	67.3	121.2	141.8	97.9	52.4	35.1	51.6	51.8	52.0
IX.	Wood and wood products	15.9	31.1	55.2	61.1	100.2	265.4	79	119.8	90.4	75.7
X.	Paper, products from paper	129.6	79.8	138.8	147.7	137.9	84.1	206.5	392.2	409.7	397.4
XI.	Textiles	159.4	314.8	382.8	449.7	501.6	265.4	352.3	495.9	491.6	541.7
XII.	Shoes, hats, umbrellas	25.3	53.1	70.2	59.3	61.9	38.9	36.1	69.2	50.4	39.4
XIII.	Products from stone, cement, asbestos	170.7	171.5	172.8	133.7	108.5	65.5	92.8	159.6	202.6	161.3
XIV.	Natural pearls	5.9	72.2	0.0	0.0	0.0	9.2	69.7	0.0	0.0	0.0
XV.	Ferrous and other non-precious metals	3513.4	4189.9	4763.2	5904.2	5335.7	410.9	539.3	791.9	665.4	628.8
XVI.	Machinery	1372.0	1360.1	1406.7	1370.0	1104.7	1417.9	1689.2	2407.9	2594.9	2284.7
XVII.	Transport	705.5	743.7	635.4	540.4	617.0	410.7	286.6	570.4	861.0	887.3
XVIII	Equipment	52.1	62.3	61.7	62.1	64.1	123.2	104.2	207.3	237.8	242.0
XIX.	Other goods	130.0	52.9	55.0	55.2	44.4	84.1	65.6	152.3	157.6	112.8
XX.	Collection, antique	0.0	0.1	0.0	0.0	0.0	0.0	0.1	0.1	0.1	0.2
XXI.	Other	167.6		167.6	345.7	319.7			116.5	122.0	77.3
XXII.	Goods purchased in ports	0.1		0.1	3.5	5.7			44.7	175.1	133.1

* In 1996-98 data were obtained from the Customs statistics. For 1994 - 95. data are based on
reports of enterprises, and it is not comparable with data in subsequent years.

Source: State Committee of Statistics

Table 3.6 - Commodity Structure of Export, 10 major products (mln. USD)*

1996			1997			1998		
Code	Product	Value	Code	Product	Value	Code	Product	Value
	Total	**14400.8**		**Total**	**14231.9**		**Total**	**12637.4**
72	Ferrous materials	3417.0	72	Ferrous materials	4495.7	72	Ferrous materials	4204.4
73	Goods from ferrous materials	1008.3	73	Goods from ferrous materials	957.9	84	Non-electrical machinery, reactors	761.4
84	Non-electrical machinery, reactors	936.7	84	Non-electrical machinery, reactors	909.4	73	Goods from ferrous materials	644.9
17	Sugar & confectionery	675.9	27	Petroleum products	603.2	27	Petroleum products	520.7
27	Petroleum products	626.0	26	Iron ore, ash, slags	538.9	28	Inorganic chemicals	508.2
28	Inorganic chemicals	597.7	28	Inorganic chemicals	537.9	26	Iron ore, ash, slags	502.4
85	Electrical machinery	573.3	85	Electrical machinery	460.6	85	Electrical machinery	343.4
31	Fertilizers	495.4	31	Fertilizers	432.7	62	Clothes (not knitted)	342.1
26	Iron ore, ash, slags	470.0	17	Sugar & confectionery	314.6	31	Fertilizers	328.7
22	Alcoholic beverages and soft drinks	445.8	40	Rubber	301.9	10	Cereals	313.8

* Data is based on the Custom statistics

Table 3.7 - Commodity Structure of Import, 10 major products (mln. USD)*

1996			1997			1998		
Code	Product	Value	Code	Product	Value	Code	Product	Value
	Total	**17603.4**		**Total**	**17,128.0**		**Total**	**14675.6**
27	Petroleum products	8406.7	27	Petroleum products	7,807.4	27	Petroleum products	5940.7
84	Non-electrical machinery, reactors	1781.1	84	Non-electrical machinery, reactors	1,961.0	84	Non-electrical machinery, reactors	1614.3
85	Electrical machinery	626.8	87	Transport except railway	639.3	87	Transport except railway	752.7
40	Rubber	480.4	85	Electrical machinery	633.9	85	Electrical machinery	670.4
87	Transport except railway	448.5	30	Pharmaceutical products	423.5	39	Plastic goods	354.5
48	Paper, carton	309.9	39	Plastic goods	366.6	40	Rubber	320.3
17	Sugar & confectionery	305.3	40	Rubber	358.3	48	Paper, carton	307.9
39	Plastic goods	288.1	48	Paper, carton	327.2	30	Pharmaceutical products	305.9
72	Ferrous materials	279.1	38	Other chemical products	263.8	90	Optic., photo., control, med. equip.	236.4
30	Pharmaceutical products	255.5	90	Optic., photo., control, med. equip.	231.3	26	Iron ore, ash, slags	229.1

* Data is based on the Custom statistics

Source: State Committee of Statistics

Table 3.8 - Geographic Structure of Foreign Trade in Services
(mln. USD)

	Export				Import			
	1994	1995	1996	1997	1994	1995	1996	1997
Total	**2118.35**	**2621.52**	**4746.40**	**4738.39**	**309.37**	**631.11**	**1204.54**	**1418.34**
Former USSR	*1114.55*	*1642.30*	*3490.83*	*3351.21*	*90.42*	*271.03*	*367.07*	*422.38*
Azerbaijan	2.36	2.06	4.05	5.95	0.47	0.16	0.87	0.65
Beloruss	10.50	21.01	57.82	38.76	6.23	9.39	14.06	19.05
Armenia	0.38	1.57	1.84	1.28	0.15	0.41	0.31	0.17
Georgia	2.91	2.80	1.87	4.56	0.64	1.28	0.96	0.55
Kazakhstan	16.15	20.98	15.93	20.10	3.13	4.39	3.56	7.36
Kyrgyzstan	0.01	0.07	0.45	0.36	0.10	0.02	0.11	0.71
Moldova	5.63	21.78	34.67	31.10	1.88	5.80	12.43	20.31
Russia	1062.31	1540.90	3333.46	3213.64	71.04	236.11	310.13	344.99
Tadjikistan	0.09	0.45	0.72	0.32	0.01	0.01	0.08	0.18
Turkmenia	1.22	1.08	2.28	3.81	0.01	0.00	0.34	0.30
Uzbekistan	5.04	14.17	23.65	13.39	1.23	2.91	1.95	3.25
Estonia	2.20	6.39	3.11	2.76	1.90	1.70	2.69	2.98
Latvia	3.14	4.61	5.27	8.89	1.97	5.66	8.79	12.71
Lithuania	2.61	4.43	5.71	6.29	1.66	3.19	10.79	9.17
Rest of the World	*1003.80*	*979.22*	*1255.81*	*1387.18*	*218.95*	*360.08*	*837.47*	*995.96*
Austria	20.25	38.76	83.60	75.49	3.69	10.77	7.76	7.20
Belgium	3.54	7.70	14.62	39.44	0.88	4.62	6.15	5.11
Bulgaria	33.92	27.67	38.69	36.88	7.65	8.30	9.46	9.68
Great Britain	27.66	40.00	93.26	108.62	12.72	33.46	34.94	82.45
Greece	18.81	34.47	42.56	48.63	11.03	15.63	22.14	11.30
Egypt	11.51	12.70	14.23	16.14	7.19	2.61	3.91	1.07
Israel	18.82	16.42	27.92	28.28	2.60	6.16	6.64	15.45
India	31.39	25.05	16.99	30.23	18.19	4.45	3.08	2.49
Italy	30.00	37.88	42.25	48.96	18.84	41.99	20.75	14.12
Iran	11.61	4.58	26.26	14.62	0.01	0.23	0.74	0.66
Spain	2.91	5.07	7.03	10.83	5.47	4.03	8.66	9.98
China	16.35	4.77	11.99	24.99	0.09	4.42	2.65	2.65
Cyrpus	9.62	12.10	34.45	54.61	5.84	7.30	14.33	11.15
Liven	9.31	9.12	11.14	4.50	1.01	1.15	0.59	0.10
Holland	10.52	21.46	29.82	29.11	5.48	4.12	4.13	16.15
Germany	70.85	79.50	88.10	118.52	23.87	22.18	33.11	77.89
Poland	31.55	18.60	28.73	37.78	9.87	11.52	14.71	17.33
Rumania	41.71	4.37	11.66	12.54	2.42	1.48	2.37	2.01
Slovenia	0.71	4.09	5.68	4.37	1.11	0.20	2.78	2.78
Slovakia	1.31	8.66	8.24	22.99	2.53	5.59	19.38	21.59
USA	32.31	52.19	88.39	142.92	13.21	29.61	253.78	283.26
Turkey	32.37	30.29	52.28	57.21	5.32	22.36	33.77	22.31
Hungary	26.18	24.15	33.13	43.81	4.96	4.23	5.34	7.41
France	10.90	16.79	19.44	28.13	3.28	2.83	15.14	16.67
Check Republic	4.37	5.83	10.70	15.01	4.33	2.77	5.30	9.52
Switzerland	17.42	22.78	51.30	68.54	2.43	7.77	15.33	15.40
UAE	9.60	5.41	13.33	10.78	1.92	15.58	18.99	8.07
Vietnam	11.55	3.81	2.76	3.17	0.21	1.36	0.15	0.03
Other countries	456.76	405.01	347.26	250.08	42.80	83.37	271.39	322.13

Source: State Statistics Committee

Table 3.9 - Foreign Trade in Services
(mln. USD)

	Export				Import			
	1994	1995	1996	1997	1994	1995	1996	1997
Total	**2118.4**	**2621.5**	**4746.6**	**4738.4**	**309.4**	**631.1**	**1024.5**	**1418.3**
Transportation services	1748.4	2110.5	4065.8	3983.6	144.9	106.5	241.7	328.3
including								
marine transport	684.4	616.4	598.7	510.3	118.9	72.9	76.8	65.6
air transport	129.5	115.0	140.1	188.3	6.1	13.6	21.4	57.8
car transport	99.3	104.1	111.3	142.5	5.8	4.4	9.1	11.6
rail transport	38.4	127.9	337.9	361.0	12.5	8.8	132.5	184.9
pipelines	785.1	1112.7	2817.0	2685.8	0.0	6.4	0.2	0.1
other transport	11.7	34.4	60.8	95.7	1.6	0.4	1.7	8.3
Repair of fixed assets	84.6	49.2	47.1	35.7	5.1	60.5	37.6	33.8
Communication services	78.2	176.3	137.6	109.3	83.0	211.4	119.2	121.3
Construction services	15.2	30.1	40.6	50.6	33.6	35.9	48.5	44.2
Assembly & repair services	107.2	78.4	100.7	139.3	12.4	9.4	17.3	36.4
Insurance services	0.6	2.5	1.3	2.5	1.7	10.8	25.0	20.5
Financial services (excluding insurance & pensions)	14.6	22.7	10.8	27.4	7.1	17.1	10.7	76.5
Rresearch & development	4.6	19.0	93.2	60.2	2.8	29.2	14.5	12.2
Legal, accounting & management consulting services, engineering & other technical services	15.5	42.6	67.1	74.2	6.1	22.4	35.7	64.4
Non-material non-financial assets (patents, licenses, know - how, etc.)	1.4	2.1	1.7	5.8	1.7	1.2	3.9	12.8
Hotel & restaurant services	13.6	28.8	38.9	54.2	0.8	1.0	2.8	2.1
Tourism	11.3	3.1	6.1	8.7	3.3	42.0	63.2	22.5
Other business services	5.4	41.2	113.6	152.3	3.5	78.4	578.3	630.0
Other private services	17.8	15.0	22.1	34.6	3.4	5.3	6.1	13.3
Other services (total)	23.2	56.2	135.7	186.9	6.9	83.7	584.4	643.3

Source: State Statistics Committee

Table 3.10 - Barter in Foreign Trade in Goods
(mln. USD)

	Export (FOB)				Import (CIF)			
	1995	1996	1997	1998.0	1995	1996	1997	1998
Total	**4356.7**	**3132.6**	**1477.4**	**941.7**	**3191.1**	**2095.0**	**1615.5**	**1042.5**
Former USSR	*2942.2*	*2354.5*	*1138.5*	*727.5*	*2219.3*	*1516.1*	*1319.7*	*886.1*
Azerbaijan	27.5	37.1	21.5	*12.6*	37.3	23.0	17.2	10.1
Beloruss	272.2	246.3	228.5	147.5	231.7	183.5	166.5	125.2
Armenia	4.0	3.4	1.7	1.3	2.0	1.6	2.1	2.2
Georgia	9.1	8.7	10.8	4.1	3.1	2.3	2.6	1.4
Kazakhstan	32.0	18.0	6.8	2.7	42.0	10.9	9.3	3.5
Kyrgyzstan	2.0	1.5	0.8	0.5	2.4	0.6	0.3	0
Moldova	38.5	36.1	92.6	66.0	28.3	19.7	17.0	8.8
Russia	2366.6	1730.1	614.2	436.8	1754.0	1201.5	597.8	717.1
Tadjikistan	4.4	5.3	20.7	1.4	5.6	2.8	0.4	0.1
Turkmenia	82.2	177.0	89.9	24.2	22.0	7.9	469.8	0.5
Uzbekistan	29.3	30.4	17.4	11.7	16.9	10.4	7.3	3.5
Estonia	12.6	10.8	5.8	2.9	10.2	8.2	6.8	3.6
Latvia	19.0	17.8	12.7	5.9	24.6	15.2	7.5	2.6
Lithuania	42.8	32.4	15.1	9.9	39.2	28.5	15.1	7.5
Rest of the World	*1414.6*	*778.1*	*338.9*	*214.2*	*971.8*	*578.9*	*295.8*	*156.4*
Austria	6.8	11.8	9.6	1.0	18.2	9.6	9.8	2.4
Australia	2.0	0.1	0.0	0.1	16.2	21.0	0.0	0
Belgium	7.2	1.7	1.4	0.7	28.5	8.7	6.0	3.5
Bulgaria	53.3	21.6	12.2	9.5	39.9	20.5	6.5	6.6
Brazil	0.9	...	...	0.3	54.8	17.1	2.0	0
Great Britain	4.8	4.5	1.1	0.5	9.6	6.1	5.8	1.5
Greece	8.6	1.5	1.2	0.8	5.5	0.4	0.5	0.5
Egypt	16.5	9.4	3.4	1.2	3.1	0.6	0.3	0
India	5.7	4.7	2.0	0.0	15.4	14.2	1.6	0.7
Italy	124.9	12.8	4.5	4.0	42.7	11.5	4.3	4.1
Indonesia	11.2	9.4	3.3	1.0	7.1	11.7	12.5	19.8
Iran	6.7	9.8	5.9	3.3	2.3	3.1	0.6	0.1
Spain	18.0	6.5	7.9	1.3	11.1	4.2	2.2	0.6
China	307.4	131.4	19.2	4.7	33.9	12.8	5.4	3.6
Liven	59.5	33.2	4.8	2.9	0.1	0.1	0.0	0
Holland	10.9	7.1	7.0	2.8	18.3	4.8	6.1	0.6
Germany	36.3	15.6	18.3	13.7	91.7	48.8	28.0	13.6
Poland	70.2	56.7	38.2	34.0	185.5	87.9	58.4	47.7
Rumania	63.2	27.6	18.0	11.9	36.8	12.0	6.2	3.3
Slovakia	60.4	72.7	66.9	41.7	45.9	44.2	23.3	11.6
USA	38.2	3.2	3.9	1.0	18.8	17.3	38.0	2.1
Thailand	25.6	28.0	1.2	0.0	0.1	1.0	0.0	0
Taiwan	17.7	0.5	1.8	0.3	0.4	0.0	0.0	0
Turkey	121.0	41.8	8.5	4.6	9.3	6.8	2.5	0.7
Hungary	115.7	84.2	46.0	34.0	44.3	69.6	11.4	5.9
France	3.5	1.3	0.6	1.1	21.5	23.6	9.3	2.2
Check Republic	36.3	40.7	19.4	16.7	33.9	59.7	18.4	6.4
Switzerland	14.0	5.2	3.2	0.5	21.5	6.9	2.6	0.7
Japan	3.5	12.4	0.0	0.0	11.1	5.3	1.5	1.7

* In 1996-98 data were obtained from the Customs statistics. For 1995, data are based on
reports of enterprises, and it is not comparable with data in subsequent years.

Source: State Statistics Committee

Table 3.11 - Ukraine: Foreign Economic Position

(mn USD. unless other stated)

	Merchandise trade and services balance	Current account balance	Current account balance as % of GDP	Net FDI	Portfolio investments	Increment of gross international reserves	Gross international reserves in weeks of imports	Gross foreign debt, end of period	Gross foreign debt as % of GDP	Debt service ratio in % of exports
1994	-1365	-1163	-3.1	151			1.8	7,167	18.9	11.2
1995	-1190	-1152	-3.1	257	16	488	3.2	8,217	22.2	8.0
1996	-1122	-1185	-2.7	526	199	873	4.8	8,840	19.8	6.6
1997	-1536	-1335	-2.7	581	605	383	5.3	9,555	19.2	7.5
1998	-1207	-1296	-3.1	747	49	-1324	2.7	11,483	27.1	
1995 Q1	-381	-325	-5.0	42	2	-64	2.2			
1995 Q2	-274	-240	-3.2	75	12	986	4.6			
1995 Q3	-230	-188	-1.9	65	2	-415	3.2			
1995 Q4	-305	-399	-3.3	75	0	-19	2.7			
1996 Q1	-702	-709	-8.8	129	26	-361	1.6	8,090	21.6	
1996 Q2	65	105	1.1	78	24	216	2.0	8,300	21.1	
1996 Q3	-22	-53	-0.5	122	36	373	2.9	8,350	20.7	
1996 Q4	-463	-528	-3.4	197	113	835	4.6	8,840	20.1	
1997 Q1	-741	-748	-7.3	96	336	87	4.9	8,790	19.2	8.4
1997 Q2	-354	-274	-2.5	109	410	257	5.6	8,890	19.0	6.7
1997 Q3	-249	-159	-1.3	139	391	189	5.9	9,270	19.5	7.1
1997 Q4	-192	-154	-1.0	237	468	-150	5.5	9,555	19.3	7.2
1998 Q1	-722	-714	-6.7	153	651	139	6.3	10,547	20.9	6.2
1998 Q2	-261	-305	-2.6	276	-205	-748	4.5	10,656	21.0	10.4
1998 Q3	-364	-448	-3.7	155	-368	-692	2.6	10,966	22.3	21.5
1998 Q4	140	171	1.9	163	-29	-23	2.7	11,483	26.5	21.5

Source: TACIS Ukrainian Economic Trends based on Derzhkomstat data

Table 3.12 - NBU interventions

		Satisfied demand = Total volume of USD sales	NBU interventions at UICE	NBU interventions at UICE and inter-bank	NBU interventions at inter-bank	Ministry of Finance
1995	Jan	332,083	30,960	30,960		
	Feb	377,543	-10,350	-10,350		
	Mar	489,826	-28,310	-28,310		
	Apl	413,590	-52,100	-52,100		
	May	535,794	4,550	4,550		
	Jun	871,510	-13,290	-13,290		
	Jul	901,035	2,390	2,390		
	Aug	1,010,515	-40,860	-40,860		
	Sep	1,042,022	76,820	76,820		
	Oct	1,135,325	-14,860	-14,860		
	Nov	1,009,800	-19,340	-19,340		
	Dec	1,098,353	-72,790	-72,790		
1996	Jan	1,080,386	64,180	69,252	5,072	
	Feb	1,419,807	-88,920	-95,927	-7,007	
	Mar	1,577,602	-130,660	-48,695	81,965	
	Apl	1,746,398	-103,200	17,974	121,174	
	May	1,508,352	-64,800	-10,420	54,380	
	Jun	1,734,522	-243,980	-138,902	105,078	
	Jul	2,051,792	-85,510	14,989	100,499	
	Aug	2,294,292	7,740	136,633	128,893	
	Sep	1,654,626	87,900	30,304	-57,596	
	Oct	1,992,884	151,990	-78,490	-230,480	
	Nov	1,789,216	120,880	-1,613	-122,493	
	Dec	2,208,701	-14,240	-129,631	-115,391	
1997	Jan	1,915,613	-152,170	-152,170		0
	Feb	2,114,989	-62,560	-62,560		20,900
	Mar	1,953,342	-630	-1,070	-440	116,500
	Apl	2,049,901	-47,970	-47,970		24,900
	May	2,268,602	-94,390	-94,390		10,100
	Jun	2,569,843	-253,330	-194,720	58,610	94,700
	Jul	2,881,809	-181,580	-160,240	21,340	55,900
	Aug	2,542,801	-211,470	-153,800	57,670	-197,205
	Sep	3,713,002	297,180	334,700	37,520	-66,364
	Oct	3,838,999	95,160	52,428	-42,732	-30,000
	Nov	2,941,693	247,370	274,636	27,266	0
	Dec	3,602,178	158,720	158,720		
1998	Jan	2,353,890	249,850	249,850	0	65,360
	Feb	2,844,357	275,510	248,310	-27,200	-167,600
	Mar	2,968,376	99,590	85,709	-13,881	-470,226
	Apl	3,045,924	146,360	140,060	-6,300	22,393
	May	2,797,174	227,650	195,878	-31,772	-120,994
	Jun	3,238,059	169,640	199,170	29,530	68,054
	Jul	3,368,006	196,240	175,940	-20,300	106,057
	Aug	2,641,720	265,610	199,264	-66,346	458,830
	Sep	962,291	26,490	26,490	0	0
	Oct	780,356	-78,660	-78,660	0	19,667

Table 3.13 - Exchange Rates, Nominal and Real

(average for the period)

	Official exchange rate (UAH/USD)	Official exchange rate (UAH/DEM)	Official exchange rate (UAH/ECU)	Non-commercial inter-bank exchange rate	Real exchange rate of cash (index June'92=100)	Real exchange rate index
1992 Q3	0.002			0.003	99.3	20.6
1992 Q4	0.006			0.008	142.9	14.3
1993 Q1	0.014			0.019	121.4	16.9
1993 Q2	0.033			0.031	98.2	20.9
1993 Q3	0.059		0.062	0.084	66.3	30.9
1993 Q4	0.086		0.094	0.267	63.5	32.3
1994 Q1	0.126	0.073	0.142	0.356	41.3	49.6
1994 Q2	0.141	0.090	0.164	0.435	42.1	48.7
1994 Q3	0.214	0.137	0.263	0.467	41.2	49.8
1994 Q4	0.786	0.515	0.971	1.102	46.4	44.2
1995 Q1	1.207	0.814	1.531	1.428	30.6	67.0
1995 Q2	1.347	0.964	1.792	1.514	25.6	80.1
1995 Q3	1.567	1.094	2.054	1.656	23.5	87.2
1995 Q4	1.771	1.245	2.333	1.839	20.5	100.0
1996 Q1	1.866	1.271	2.402	1.911	17.8	115.2
1996 Q2	1.845	1.213	2.316	1.869	16.3	125.8
1996 Q3	1.767	1.167	2.226	1.785	14.9	137.6
1996 Q4	1.839	1.202	2.320	1.840	14.7	139.5
1997 Q1	1.857	1.125	2.194	1.861	14.5	141.4
1997 Q2	1.849	1.079	2.114	1.841	14.3	143.4
1997 Q3	1.858	1.030	2.034	1.851	14.4	142.4
1997 Q4	1.882	1.071	2.113	1.886	14.4	142.4
1998 Q1	1.967	1.082	2.139	1.967	14.7	139.5
1998 Q2	2.049	1.142	2.247	2.045	15.3	134.0
1998 Q3	2.357	1.342	2.642	2.642	17.9	114.5
1998 Q4	3.426	2.066	4.042	4.043	23.8	86.1
Jan-97	1.891	1.186	2.313	1.891	14.8	138.5
Feb-97	1.844	1.104	2.155	1.856	14.4	142.4
Mar-97	1.837	1.083	2.113	1.837	14.3	143.4
Apr-97	1.848	1.082	2.118	1.842	14.3	143.4
May-97	1.843	1.079	2.113	1.839	14.2	144.4
Jun-97	1.858	1.076	2.112	1.841	14.3	143.4
Jul-97	1.857	1.039	2.056	1.836	14.3	143.4
Aug-97	1.856	1.011	2.000	1.847	14.4	142.4
Sep-97	1.861	1.039	2.045	1.869	14.4	142.4
Oct-97	1.871	1.063	2.091	1.877	14.4	142.4
Nov-97	1.879	1.083	2.137	1.886	14.4	142.4
Dec-97	1.895	1.068	2.111	1.895	14.3	143.4
Jan-98	1.909	1.053	2.082	1.911	14.3	143.4
Feb-98	1.957	1.078	2.130	1.958	14.7	139.5
Mar-98	2.034	1.114	2.205	2.031	15.2	134.9
Apr-98	2.040	1.122	2.199	2.038	15.2	134.9
May-98	2.049	1.153	2.272	2.045	15.3	134.0
Jun-98	2.059	1.150	2.269	2.051	15.4	133.1
Jul-98	2.103	1.168	2.306	2.082	15.8	129.7
Aug-98	2.183	1.221	2.405	2.196	16.5	124.2
Sep-98	2.785	1.637	3.216	2.809	21.3	96.2
Oct-98	3.423	2.090	4.090	3.539	24.7	83.0
Nov-98	3.427	2.054	4.019	3.545	23.5	87.2
Dec-98	3.427	2.054	4.020	3.547	23.2	88.4
Jan-99	3.427	3.982	3.559	3.427	23.0	89.1
Feb-99	3.471	3.891		3.471	23.1	88.7

Source: TACIS

Table 3.14 - *Auction Exchange Rate*

(average for the period)

	US Dollar		Deutsche Mark		Russian Rouble	
	Hrn/USD	Volume (mn USD)	Hrn/DM	Volume (mn DM)	Hrn/RUR	Volume (mn RUR)
1993	0.089					
1994	0.522	909.7	0.357	88.8	0.238	326.2
1995	1.503	3007.9	1.037	237.7	0.319	2905.7
1996	1.838	2147.8	1.225	196.9	0.361	1433.7
1997	1.861	2990.4	1.088	132.6	0.321	476.2
1998	2.679	3896.6	1.481	313.3	-	-
1995 Q1	1.213	700.8	0.806	53.3	0.285	603.7
1995 Q2	1.349	888.6	0.990	54.4	0.265	827.4
1995 Q3	1.568	927.3	1.099	76.3	0.344	940.8
1995 Q4	1.774	491.2	1.254	53.8	0.382	533.8
1996 Q1	1.867	495.1	1.277	56.1	0.389	458.2
1996 Q2	1.845	630.1	1.215	44.6	0.365	372.3
1996 Q3	1.767	367.5	1.187	38.7	0.332	344.0
1996 Q4	1.842	474.8	1.215	42.9	0.340	211.2
1997 Q1	1.850	558.6	1.123	37.9	0.327	146.2
1997 Q2	1.848	699.3	1.085	43.7	0.317	123.7
1997 Q3	1.858	799.4	1.032	30.8	0.319	88.3
1997 Q4	1.883	933.1	1.079	20.2	0.319	118.0
1998 Q1	1.973	815.5	1.088	27.3	0.326	104.1
1998 Q2	2.051	622.1	1.153	18.9	0.333	73.9
1998 Q3	2.417	935.1	1.525	75.1	-	-
1998 Q4	3.426	1524.0	2.158	192.1	-	-
Jan-97	1.890	180.3	1.176	14.7	0.335	47.9
Feb-97	1.820	226.5	1.109	9.9	0.325	52.7
Mar-97	1.840	151.8	1.084	13.3	0.321	45.7
Apr-97	1.849	168.0	1.168	20.4	0.321	46.4
May-97	1.836	247.0	1.083	14.6	0.318	34.8
Jun-97	1.857	267.6	1.078	8.8	0.321	42.5
Jul-97	1.857	192.2	1.044	14.3	0.320	23.6
Aug-97	1.856	293.2	1.009	7.2	0.318	29.6
Sep-97	1.862	314.0	1.043	9.3	0.318	35.0
Oct-97	1.872	390.1	1.069	7.2	0.319	35.0
Nov-97	1.882	277.7	1.094	5.9	0.319	39.0
Dec-97	1.895	265.3	1.072	7.2	0.319	44.1
Jan-98	1.917	270.6	1.057	9.8	0.317	41.4
Feb-98	1.966	308.5	1.085	8.9	0.326	28.5
Mar-98	2.034	236.4	1.121	8.5	0.335	34.2
Apr-98	2.041	167.6	1.134	8.3	0.333	29.3
May-98	2.051	227.3	1.164	5.7	0.333	24.2
Jun-98	2.061	227.2	1.162	4.9	0.332	20.4
Jul-98	2.100	273.0	1.175	7.6	3.378	34.7
Aug-98	2.218	252.3	1.353	11.8	3.050	17.700
Sep-98	2.933	409.9	2.048	55.6	-	-
Oct-98	3.423	502.2	2.177	61.2	-	-
Nov-98	3.427	504.8	2.147	68.5	-	-
Dec-98	3.427	517.0	2.151	62.4	-	-

Source: TACIS

Table 3.15 - External Reserves (mn. USD).

	Q4-92	Q1-93	Q2-93	Q3-93	Q4-93	Q1-94	Q2-94	Q3-94	Q4-94	Q1-95	Q2-95	Q3-95	Q4-95
Gross International Reserves *minus* Gold	468.8	119.6	128.9	311.5	161.6	46.9	43.8	61.6	650.7	642.6	1,584.7	1,149.7	1,050.6
Net International Reserves Total Foreign Borrowing			9.3	182.6	-149.9	-114.7	-3.1	17.8	589.1	-8.1	942.1	-435.0	-99.1
(LMT loan *plus* T-bills)	0.0	180.0	200.0	300.0	210.0	160.0	160.0	160.0	400.0	2,409.0	1,156.0	281.0	661.0
Net Portfolio Invest-ment Inflow -- Debt Securities	0.0	0.0	0.0	0.0	0.0	0.0	0.0	0.0	0.0	2.0	12.0	2.0	0.0
Long- and Medium-Term Loans -- Disbursements		180	200	300	210	160.0	160.0	160.0	400.0	2,407.0	1,144.0	279.0	661.0

	Q1-96	Q2-96	Q3-96	Q4-96	Q1-97	Q2-97	Q3-97	Q4-97	Q1-98	Q2-98	Q3-98	Q4-98
Gross International Reserves *minus* Gold	618.2	812.9	1,109.7	1,960.0	2,045.0	2,299.1	2,468.3	2,341.1	2,493.2	1,743.7	938.0	1,240.0
Net International Reserves Total Foreign Borrowing	-432.4	194.7	296.8	850.3	85.0	254.1	169.2	-127.2	152.1	-749.5	-805.7	302.0
(LMT loan *plus* T-bills)	69.0	445.0	677.0	707.0	525.0	586.0	1,040.0	841.0	599.0	189.0	330.0	250.0
Net Portfolio Invest-ment Inflow -- Debt Securities	8.0	11.0	28.0	106.0	305.0	366.0	352.0	334.0	479.0	139.0	-100.0	0.0
Long- and Medium-Term Loans -- Disbursements	61.0	434.0	649.0	601.0	220.0	220.0	688.0	507.0	120.0	50.0	430.0	250.0

Source: IMF Statistics, WB staff calculations

Statistical Appendix

Table 4.1 - External Debt Outstanding, 1992-1998

(mln. USD, end of period)

	1992	1993	1994	1995	1996	1997	8/31/98
Total Debt Outstanding	**3,691**	**4,474**	**5,667**	**8,691**	**9,463**	**9,555**	..
1. Public and publicly guaranteed	396	3,624	4,828	8,217	8,839	9,555	10,243
A. Official creditors							
i) Multilateral	29	157	600	2,215	3,444	4,025	4,043
IMF	0	0	371	1,565	2,263	2,392	2,417
World Bank	0	0	101	503	905	1,215	1,231
EBRD	0	0	5	33	35	66	83
Other (EC)	29	157	123	114	241	352	312
ii) Bilateral	370	3,467	4,228	4,528	4,127	3,760	3,573
FSU	0	2,733	3,445	3,787	3,085	2,600	2,389
Russia	0	2,704	2,704	3,060	2,381	2,001	1,896
Turkmenistan	0	0	713	708	704	599	493
Other	0	29	28	19	0	0	0
Non-FSU							
Japan	0	0	0	0	182	187	144
Germany	196	401	645	670	597	463	463
USA	174	333	123	71	215	448	453
Other	0	0	15	0	48	62	124
iii) Other	0	0	0	274	148	91	189
B. Private creditors	0	0	0	0	0	559	1,213
C. "Gazprom" Bonds	0	0	0	1,200	1,120	1,120	1,225
3. National Bank of Ukraine	2,398.5	279.9	7.3	22.1	36.6	..	..
2. Private non-guaranteed	896.3	570.4	831.8	452.0	587.4	464.0	..
Memo:							
External Public Debt Service, paid out of budget	144.8	344.3	1,420.5	1,112.3	1,276.8	1,531.9	..
External Public Debt/GDP (%)	1.4%	21.7%	20.9%	22.7%	19.9%	19.2%	34.3%

Source: Ministry of Finance

Table 4.2 - Ukraine - External Debt Stocks and Flows
(US$ millions at current prices)

Base-case (most likely) projection

	Actual[a]				Estimate[a]		Projection[a]					
	1994	1995	1996	1997	1998	1999	2000	2001	2002	2003	2004	2005
A. Gross disbursements												
Public & publicly guaranteed	431.0	732.0	954.0	1221.0	255.0	481.0	140.0	103.0	69.0	45.0	25.0	13.0
Official multilateral creditors, of which	113.0	525.0	552.0	452.0	172.0	417.0	110.0	90.0	64.0	43.0	24.0	13.0
IDA	0.0	0.0	0.0	0.0	0.0	0.0	0.0	0.0	0.0	0.0	0.0	0.0
IBRD	102.0	401.0	406.0	306.0	117.0	358.0	78.0	73.0	59.0	40.0	24.0	13.0
Official bilateral creditors	39.0	25.0	202.0	56.0	23.0	27.0	16.0	9.0	4.0	2.0	1.0	0.0
Private creditors, of which	279.0	182.0	200.0	713.0	60.0	37.0	14.0	4.0	1.0	0.0	0.0	0.0
Bonds	0.0	0.0	0.0	0.0	0.0	0.0	0.0	0.0	0.0	0.0	0.0	0.0
Private creditors nonguaranteed	94.0	69.0	120.0	268.0	0.0	0.0	0.0	0.0	0.0	0.0	0.0	0.0
Total LT[b] loan disbursements	525.0	801.0	1074.0	1489.0	255.0	481.0	140.0	103.0	69.0	45.0	25.0	13.0
Net ST[b] credit	306.0	165.0	283.0	803.0	-1488.0	-550.0	-577.0	-647.0	-557.0	-534.0	-510.0	-510.0
Drawings from IMF	357.0	1196.0	778.0	285.0	0.0	0.0	0.0	0.0	0.0	0.0	0.0	0.0
Total disbursements (LT+ST+IMF)	1188.0	2162.0	2135.0	2577.0	-1233.0	-69.0	-437.0	-544.0	-488.0	-489.0	-485.0	-497.0
B. Amortizations												
Public & publicly guaranteed	158.0	595.0	723.0	637.0	1592.0	991.0	648.0	702.0	612.0	557.0	533.0	519.0
Official multilateral creditors, of which	39.0	127.0	1.0	1.0	9.0	19.0	48.0	119.0	214.0	238.0	250.0	250.0
IDA	0.0	0.0	0.0	0.0	0.0	0.0	0.0	0.0	0.0	0.0	0.0	0.0
IBRD	0.0	0.0	0.0	0.0	0.0	2.0	25.0	73.0	155.0	155.0	155.0	155.0
Official bilateral creditors	15.0	38.0	515.0	502.0	746.0	636.0	284.0	288.0	144.0	140.0	131.0	131.0
Private creditors, of which	104.0	430.0	207.0	134.0	837.0	336.0	316.0	295.0	254.0	179.0	152.0	138.0
Bonds	0.0	200.0	80.0	0.0	121.0	121.0	121.0	121.0	121.0	121.0	121.0	121.0
Private creditors nonguaranteed	60.0	40.0	68.0	52.0	150.0	39.0	69.0	47.0	15.0	22.0	2.0	3.0
Total LT loan amortization	218.0	635.0	791.0	689.0	1742.0	1030.0	717.0	749.0	627.0	579.0	535.0	522.0
Repayments to IMF	0.0	0.0	0.0	0.0	104.0	549.0	770.0	512.0	214.0	112.0	112.0	28.0
Total amortization (LT+IMF)	218.0	635.0	791.0	689.0	1846.0	1579.0	1487.0	1261.0	841.0	691.0	647.0	550.0
C. Net disbursements												
Public & publicly guaranteed	273.0	137.0	231.0	584.0	-1337.0	-510.0	-508.0	-599.0	-543.0	-512.0	-508.0	-506.0
Official multilateral creditors, of which	74.0	398.0	551.0	451.0	163.0	398.0	62.0	-29.0	-150.0	-195.0	-226.0	-237.0
IDA	0.0	0.0	0.0	0.0	0.0	0.0	0.0	0.0	0.0	0.0	0.0	0.0
IBRD	102.0	401.0	406.0	306.0	117.0	356.0	53.0	0.0	-96.0	-115.0	-131.0	-142.0
Official bilateral creditors	24.0	-13.0	-313.0	-446.0	-723.0	-609.0	-268.0	-279.0	-140.0	-138.0	-130.0	-131.0
Private creditors, of which	175.0	-248.0	-7.0	579.0	-777.0	-299.0	-302.0	-291.0	-253.0	-179.0	-152.0	-138.0
Bonds	0.0	-200.0	-80.0	0.0	-121.0	-121.0	-121.0	-121.0	-121.0	-121.0	-121.0	-121.0
Private creditors nonguaranteed	34.0	29.0	52.0	216.0	-150.0	-39.0	-69.0	-47.0	-15.0	-22.0	-2.0	-3.0

Table 4.2 - Ukraine - External Debt Stocks and Flows (continued)

(US$ millions at current prices)

Base-case (most likely) projection

	Actual[a]				Estimate[a]			Projection[a]				
	1994	1995	1996	1997	1998	1999	2000	2001	2002	2003	2004	2005
Total LT[b] loan net disbursements	307.0	166.0	283.0	800.0	-1487.0	-549.0	-577.0	-646.0	-558.0	-534.0	-510.0	-509.0
Net ST[b] credit	306.0	165.0	283.0	803.0	-1488.0	-550.0	-577.0	-647.0	-557.0	-534.0	-510.0	-510.0
Net credit from IMF	357.0	1196.0	778.0	285.0	-104.0	-549.0	-770.0	-512.0	-214.0	-112.0	-112.0	-28.0
Total net disbursements (LT+ST+IMF)	970.0	1527.0	1344.0	1888.0	-3079.0	-1648.0	-1924.0	-1805.0	-1329.0	-1180.0	-1132.0	-1047.0
D. Interest and charges												
Public & publicly guaranteed	69.0	440.0	352.0	463.0	459.0	379.0	335.0	300.0	259.0	221.0	183.0	144.0
Official multilateral creditors of which	10.0	13.0	40.0	71.0	118.0	139.0	147.0	151.0	146.0	133.0	117.0	99.0
IDA	0.0	0.0	0.0	0.0	0.0	0.0	0.0	0.0	0.0	0.0	0.0	0.0
IBRD	0.0	8.0	32.0	59.0	80.0	100.0	105.0	107.0	105.0	97.0	89.0	80.0
Official bilateral creditors	3.0	293.0	159.0	214.0	172.0	120.0	88.0	68.0	52.0	42.0	33.0	24.0
Private creditors, of which	56.0	134.0	153.0	178.0	169.0	120.0	100.0	81.0	61.0	46.0	33.0	21.0
Bonds	0.0	87.0	96.0	99.0	93.0	83.0	72.0	62.0	52.0	42.0	31.0	21.0
Private creditors nonguaranteed	5.0	7.0	22.0	64.0	50.0	12.0	20.0	7.0	11.0	2.0	0.0	0.0
Total interest on LT loans	74.0	447.0	374.0	527.0	509.0	391.0	355.0	307.0	270.0	223.0	183.0	144.0
Interest on ST credit	7.0	12.0	18.0	40.0	0.0	0.0	0.0	0.0	0.0	0.0	0.0	0.0
Interest on IMF drawings	0.0	42.0	74.0	102.0	118.0	107.0	74.0	40.0	20.0	11.0	5.0	1.0
Total interest (LT+ST+IMF)	81.0	501.0	466.0	669.0	627.0	498.0	429.0	347.0	290.0	234.0	188.0	145.0
E. External debt (DOD)c												
Public & publicly guaranteed	4771.0	6541.0	6608.0	6978.0	5639.0	5129.0	4621.0	4022.0	3480.0	2968.0	2460.0	1954.0
Official multilateral creditors of which	225.0	619.0	1125.0	1493.0	1656.0	2054.0	2116.0	2087.0	1937.0	1742.0	1516.0	1279.0
IDA	0.0	0.0	0.0	0.0	0.0	0.0	0.0	0.0	0.0	0.0	0.0	0.0
IBRD	102.0	491.0	859.0	1111.0	1228.0	1584.0	1638.0	1638.0	1542.0	1427.0	1296.0	1154.0
Official bilateral creditors	3533.0	3687.0	3360.0	2892.0	2168.0	1559.0	1291.0	1012.0	873.0	735.0	605.0	474.0
Private creditors, of which	1013.0	2235.0	2123.0	2593.0	1815.0	1516.0	1214.0	923.0	670.0	491.0	339.0	201.0
Bonds	0.0	1200.0	1120.0	1120.0	999.0	878.0	757.0	636.0	515.0	394.0	272.0	151.0
Private creditors nonguaranteed	45.0	84.0	184.0	432.0	283.0	244.0	175.0	127.0	113.0	91.0	89.0	86.0
Total LT DOD	4816.0	6625.0	6792.0	7410.0	5922.0	5373.0	4796.0	4149.0	3593.0	3059.0	2549.0	2040.0
ST debt	417.0	223.0	444.0	1089.0	1089.0	1089.0	1089.0	1089.0	1089.0	1089.0	1089.0	1089.0
Use of IMF credit	364.0	1542.0	2262.0	2402.0	2298.0	1749.0	979.0	467.0	252.0	140.0	28.0	0.0

Table 4.2 - Ukraine - External Debt Stocks and Flows (continued)
(US$ millions at current prices)

Base-case (most likely) projection

	Actual[a]				Estimate[a]				Projection[a]			
	1994	1995	1996	1997	1998	1999	2000	2001	2002	2003	2004	2005
Total DOD (LT+ST+IMF), of which:	5597.0	8390.0	9498.0	10901.0	9309.0	8211.0	6864.0	5705.0	4934.0	4288.0	3666.0	3129.
Principal arrears	602.0	88.0	66.0	235.0	235.0	235.0	235.0	235.0	235.0	235.0	235.0	235.
Interest arrears	205.0	35.0	41.0	43.0	43.0	43.0	43.0	43.0	43.0	43.0	43.0	43.
F. Debt and debt burden indicators (based on data in parts A-E)												
Total debt service (US$ millions)	299.0	1136.0	1257.0	1358.0	2473.0	2077.0	1916.0	1608.0	1131.0	925.0	835.0	695.
Interest (LT + ST + IMF)[b]	81.0	501.0	466.0	669.0	627.0	498.0	429.0	347.0	290.0	234.0	188.0	145.
Principal (LT + IMF)	218.0	635.0	791.0	689.0	1846.0	1579.0	1487.0	1261.0	841.0	691.0	647.0	550.
Total DOD[c] and TDS[d]												
DOD / exports (XGS[e]) ratio	32.8	47.5	45.6	51.7	..			..	..	..	..	
DOD / GDP ratio	15.2	22.7	21.3	21.9	..			..	..	..	..	
TDS / exports (XGS) ratio	1.8	6.4	6.0	6.4	..			..	..	..	..	
IBRD exposure indicators:												
IBRD DS[f] / public loan DS	0.0	0.7	2.8	4.9	3.5	5.0	7.1	11.6	23.5	28.0	29.3	34.
Preferred creditor DS / public DS	21.6	16.9	10.0	14.5	15.4	40.2	56.9	52.9	53.8	54.8	58.1	54.
IBRD DS / exports (XGS)	0.0	0.0	0.2	0.3	..			..	..	..	..	
Country share in IBRD portfolio	..	..	..	..	..			..	..	..	..	
G. Debt and debt burden indicators (based on post-DDSR data for countries with projected debt worksouts; based on adjusted data from Annex C7)												
TDS after DDSR (US$ millions)					..			..	..	..	..	
Interest (LT + ST + IMF)[b]					..			..	..	..	..	
Principal (LT + IMF)					..			..	..	..	..	
Memorandum items												
Factor payments / exports (XGS) ratios												
Interest payments / exports	..	..	..	..								
Total factor payments / exports	2.3	3.9	3.2	3.8								

a. Historical data from Debt Reporting System (DRS); other data projected by country operations division staff.
b. "LT" denotes "long-term," "ST" denotes "short-term."
c. "DOD" denotes "debt outstanding and disbursed"
d. "TDS" denotes "total debt service."
e. "XGS" denotes "exports of goods and services," which comprises exports of goods, nonfactor services, factor receipts, and workers' remittances
f. "DS" denotes "debt service."

Table 4.3 - Direct Foreign Investments in Ukraine
(by industry)

	As at the end of period, mln. USD					Share of total, %				
	1994	1995	1996	1997	1998	1994	1995	1996	1997	1998
Total	**366.7**	**750.1**	**1,355.9**	**2,053.9**	**2,781.8**	**100.0**	**100.0**	**100.0**	**100.0**	**100.0**
Domestic trade	36.2	168.2	395.2	337.6	438.7	9.9	22.4	29.1	16.4	15.8
Food processing industry	52.1	108.4	166.6	422.1	584.6	14.2	14.5	12.3	20.6	21.0
Machine building & metal working	85.6	96.3	138.9	168.7	353.1	23.3	12.8	10.2	8.2	12.7
Health care, physical culture & social security	..	..	74.7	114.9	111.8	..	..	5.5	5.6	4.0
Finance, credit, insurance & pension funds	11.4	55.2	70.7	174.1	197.2	3.1	7.4	5.2	8.5	7.1
Construction & construction materials:	20.4	28.0	69.1	148.9	172.3	5.6	3.7	5.1	7.2	6.2
construction materials	5.5	3.0	..	58.3	57.3	1.5	0.4	2.0	2.8	2.1
construction	14.9	25.1	..	90.6	115.0	4.1	3.3	3.1	4.4	4.1
External trade	27.4	33.1	49.9	28.0	21.1	7.5	4.4	3.7	1.4	0.8
Transportation & communication	18.9	31.0	44.5	59.7	148.4	5.2	4.1	3.3	2.9	5.3
General commercial activity	4.3	29.1	42.7	35.1	50.3	1.2	3.9	3.1	1.7	1.8
Chemical & petrochemical industries:	21.1	31.2	41.4	141.2	125.3	5.7	4.2	3.2	6.9	4.5
Ferrous & non-ferrous metallurgy:	17.8	37.8	33.4	40.9	80.7	4.8	5.0	2.5	2.0	2.9
Light industry	23.5	30.1	31.6	32.5	43.6	6.4	4.0	2.3	1.6	1.6
Science	9.2	10.8	21.0	16.9	1.5	2.5	1.4	1.5	0.8	0.1
Wood & paper industry	5.1	12.0	19.8	44.6	51.9	1.4	1.6	1.5	2.2	1.9
Public services	..	..	47.4	35.6	39.5	..	..	5.6	1.7	1.4
Agriculture	5.6	18.5	17.2	45.9	59.5	1.5	2.5	1.3	2.2	2.1
Coal industry	..	6.0	6.5	..	..	..	0.8	0.5	..	..
Fuel industry	..	3.0	5.0	23.7	78.6	..	0.4	0.4	1.2	2.8
Municipal services	..	..	..	18.4	14.5	..	..	..	0.9	0.5
Catering	..	..	..	17.9	..	..	..	..	0.9	..
Pharmaceuticals	..	..	..	16.9	15.6	..	..	..	0.8	0.6
Other industries	7.9	23.3	80.3	130.3	21.3	2.1	3.2	5.9	6.3	0.8

Source: States Committee of Statistic

Table 4.4 - Direct Foreign Investments in Ukraine
(by country)

	As at the beginning of period, mln. USD					Share of total, %				
	1994	1995	1996	1997	1998	1994	1995	1996	1997	1998
Total	**219.4**	**483.5**	**896.9**	**1438.2**	**2063.6**	**100**	**100**	**100**	**100**	**100**
United Kingdom	14.7	33.8	53.9	100.3	151.4	6.7	7.0	6.0	7.0	7.3
Italy	5.5	14.6	19.3	31.4	51.5	2.5	3.0	2.2	2.2	2.5
Canada	4.7	14.8	19.4	23.5	35.6	2.1	3.1	2.2	1.6	1.7
Cyprus	9.5	28.5	51.5	86.1	126.3	4.3	5.9	5.7	6.0	6.1
Liechtenstein	0.2	1.7	19.3	96.6	111.4	0.1	0.4	2.2	6.7	5.4
Germany	38.0	101.3	156.9	166.5	179.2	17.3	21.0	17.5	11.6	8.7
Poland	8.9	13.1	20.5	25.4	37.1	4.1	2.7	2.3	1.8	1.8
Russia	6.4	19.1	50.0	106.2	152.6	2.9	4.0	5.6	7.4	7.4
USA	50.1	96.6	183.3	263.0	385.0	22.9	20.0	20.4	18.3	18.7
Hungary	2.5	13.7	20.0	26.4	35.7	1.1	2.8	2.2	1.8	1.7
Switzerland	9.9	21.3	38.4	49.7	80.5	4.5	4.4	4.3	3.5	3.9
Swiss	1.1	3.6	19.1	22.1	40.8	0.5	0.7	2.1	1.5	2.0
Other countries	67.3	121.4	245.3	441.0	676.4	30.7	25.1	27.3	30.7	32.8

Source: States Committee of Statistic

Table 4.5 - Ukrainian Direct Investments in Other Countries
(by industry)

	As at the end of period, mln. USD					Share of total, %				
	1994	1995	1996	1997	Jun-98	1994	1995	1996	1997	Jun-98
Total	**16.8**	**29.5**	**82.7**	**133.8**	**97.6**	**100**	**100**	**100**	**100**	**100**
Domestic trade	1.7	3.8	3.6	0.9	0.7	10.40	13.00	4.38	0.64	0.71
Machine building & metal working	4.6	6.5	6.1	7.1	6.8	27.49	22.15	7.36	5.29	6.98
Health care, physical culture & social security	..	..	39.8	26.4	6.4	..	..	48.20	19.73	6.51
Finance, credit, insurance & pension funds	..	0.2	0.3	3.8	3.2	..	0.74	0.32	2.81	3.30
Construction & construction materials	..	0.0	12.6	11.8	4.9	..	0.04	15.26	8.84	5.10
External trade	0.8	0.8	0.7	0.3	0.4	4.69	2.69	0.90	0.24	0.39
Transportation & communication	..	1.0	4.0	67.0	61.8	..	3.34	4.88	50.08	63.31
General commercial activity	1.3	1.0	1.0	..	..	7.70	3.39	1.21	..	..
Chemical & petrochemical industries	2.8	10.0	5.3	4.2	3.7	16.77	33.77	6.47	3.11	3.83
Black & ferrous metallurgy	0.6	0.1	4.6	5.5	3.6	3.86	0.35	5.60	4.14	3.71
Science	..	0.0	..	0.3	0.6	..	0.04	..	0.19	0.59
Coal industry	..	..	0.4	0.4	..	..	..	0.45	0.26	..
Fuel industry	3.7	3.7	3.7	3.7	3.9	22.37	12.54	4.46	2.75	3.95
Municipal services	..	..	..	0.5	0.5	..	..	..	0.38	0.47
Geology, exploration, meteorology	0.5	0.1	0.1	0.2	0.1	3.02	0.38	0.11	0.12	0.11
Fishery	..	2.0	..	..	..	..	6.78	..	..	..
Other industries	0.6	0.2	0.3	1.9	1.0	3.71	0.81	0.41	1.39	1.04

Source: States Committee of Statistic

Table 4.6 - Ukrainian Direct Investments to Other Countries
(by country)

	As at the beginning of period, mln. USD					Share of total, %				
	1994	1995	1996	1997	1998	1994	1995	1996	1997	1998
Total	**11.4**	**20.3**	**84.1**	**97.4**	**127.5**	**100**	**100**	**100**	**100**	**100**
Austria	1.7	0.9	1.6	1.4	1.2	15.3	4.7	1.9	1.4	0.9
Georgia	0.0	0.0	6.1	3.8	4.2	0.0	0.0	7.3	3.9	3.3
Cyprus	0.0	..	2.4	2.4	2.4	0.0	..	2.8	2.4	1.9
Poland	0.2	0.4	0.3	0.3	0.3	1.4	1.9	0.3	0.3	0.2
Russia	2.1	4.2	52.1	47.6	38.2	18.5	20.7	61.9	48.8	30.0
USA	1.3	1.6	1.4	5.3	1.5	11.0	7.9	1.7	5.4	1.2
Hungary	1.9	2.1	7.1	1.7	1.4	16.6	10.2	8.5	1.7	1.1
Switzerland	2.2	8.0	8.1	7.9	7.4	19.0	39.7	9.6	8.1	5.8
Other countries	2.1	3.0	5.0	27.2	70.9	18.3	15.0	6.0	27.9	55.6

Source: State Committee of Statistics

Table 4.7 - Foreign Direct Investment to Ukraine, stock and flows

(mln. USD)

	Total					From CIS and Baltic countries				
	1994	1995	1996	1997	1998	1994	1995	1996	1997	1998
Total capital stock of non-residents In Ukraine (at the beginning of the period)	219.4	483.5	896.9	1438.2	2063.6	7.2	21.4	59.9	167.2	221.6
Flows:										
Increase in the capital of non-residents	176.7	281.5	531.4	759.2	922.4	10.5	22.5	113.0	67.7	57.5
including										
cash contributions	37.5	52.9	170.5	300.8	575.0	5.2	3.8	14.6	24.8	42.8
securities contributions	0.1	36.4	..	35.6	1.9		0.6	..	0.0	0.1
contributions of tangible & intangable assets	122.3	171.4	..	392.9	335.0	4.5	18.0	..	38.3	14.3
including										
deposits in tangible assets	..	170.4	330.8	380.0	298.8	..	18.0	80.4	38.3	14.3
deposits in intangible assets	..	1.0	..	12.9	35.2	..	0.0	..	0.0	0.0
revaluation of capital	0.6	5.2	18.8	14.2	1.9	0.6	0.0	17.9	2.1	0.1
other forms of investments	16.2	15.6	11.3	15.7	8.6	0.2	0.1	0.1	2.5	0.2
Decrease in the capital of non-residents	29.2	14.9	55.4	124.9	179.6	0.2	0.8	8.8	15.1	11.6
including										
withdrawals of money, property or other contributions	24.5	9.3	39.1	80.0	143.8	0.1	0.6	8.4	10.9	3.9
other forms of capital withdrawals	4.7	5.6	16.3	44.9	35.8	0.1	0.2	0.4	4.2	7.7
Foreign exchange gains (losses)	..	..	17.1	18.8	24.7	..	..	3.9	0.3	25.1
Total capital stock of non-residents in Ukraine (at the end of the period)	366.9	750.1	1355.8	2053.8	2781.7	17.5	43.1	160.2	219.5	242.4
Net direct investment inflows	*147.5*	*266.6*	*458.9*	*615.5*	*718.1*	*10.3*	*21.7*	*100.3*	*52.3*	*20.8*

Source: State Committee of Statistics of Ukraine

Table 4.8 – *Ukrainian Direct Investment to Other Countries. stock and flows*

(mln. USD)

	Total					To CIS & Baltic countries				
	1994	1995	1996	1997	1998, I half	1994	1995	1996	1997	1998, I half
	1994	1995	1996	1997	1998	1994	1995	1996	1997	1998
Total capital staock of residents abroad (at the beginning of the period)	11.4	20.3	84.1	97.4	127.5	2.2	5.8	59.9	53.0	43.9
Flows:										
Increase in the capital of residents	8.4	10.8	23.2	49.8	4.6	5.1	0.2	12.5	3.8	1.8
including										
cash contributions	3.2	10.2	7.6	4.4	0.8	0.2	0.2	0.3	0.2	0.7
contributions of tangible assets*	3.3	0.6	4.5	41.7	1.6	3.2	0.0	1.2	1.4	0.0
revaluation of capital	0.8	..	11.1	0.7	0.8	0.7	..	11.0	0.7	0.8
other forms of investment activity	1.1	0.0	0.0	3.0	1.1	1.0	0.0	0.0	1.5	0.0
Decrease in the capital of residents	3.0	1.6	13.6	7.6	8.8	1.2	0.5	0.6	1.2	0.1
including										
withdrawals of money, property or other contributions	0.9	1.4	13.2	1.1	0.9	0.1	0.5	0.2	0.6	0.0
other forms of capital withdrawals	2.1	0.2	0.4	6.5	7.9	1.1	0.0	0.4	0.6	0.1
Foreign exchange gains (losses)										
Total capital stock of residents abroad (at the end of the period)	16.8	29.5	82.7	133.8	97.6	6.1	5.5	62.0	50.6	19.7
Net direct investment flows	5.4	9.2	-1.4	36.4	-29.9	3.9	-0.3	2.1	-2.4	-24.2

* in 1994 investments in tangible & intangible assets

Source: State Committee of Statistics

Table 4.9 - Borrowing in the International Capital Market

Data of Issue	Nominal Amount (mln.) In currency of issue	Nominal Amount (mln.) In US$ equivalent	Amount Actually Received (mln.)	Lead Manager	Nominal Interest Rate	Actual Interest Rate	Maturity	Months to Maturity	Repayment Profile	Placement Price (per bond of 100 units)	Notes
11-Aug-97	USD 450	USD 450	USD 396.9	Nomura International	12%	13.45%	11-Aug-98	12	Fiduciary Loan	-	
17-Oct-97	USD 109	USD 109	USD 98.9	Chase Manhattan	-	10.21%	20-Oct-98	12	Fiduciary Loan	-	
23-Dec-1997 (1st tranche)	UAH 375	USD 197	UAH 278.9	Merrill Lynch	44.00%	46.09% (at least 21.125% in USD)	22-Sep-98	9	T-bills	-	a)
23-Dec-1997 (2nd tranche)	UAH 375	USD 197	UAH 257.4	Merrill Lynch	44.00%	45.84% (at least 21.125% in USD)	22-Dec-98	12	T-bills	-	a)
11-Feb-98	DM 750	USD 421	DM 746.3	Merrill Lynch, Kommerzbank	16%	16.20%	26-Feb-01	36	Eurobond	99.50%	
17-Apr-1998 (additional issue)	DM 250	USD 139	DM 255	Merrill Lynch, Kommerzbank	16%	14.99%	26-Feb-01	34	Eurobond	102.00%	
17-Mar-98	ECU 500	USD 540	ECU 488	SBC Warburg	15%	15.94% (17.5% in US$) 55%	17-Mar-00	24	Eurobond	97.60%	
6-Aug-98	UAH 332	USD 155	USD 155	ING Barings	55.00%	(at least 17.5% in US$)	6-Jun-99	10	T-bills	100.00%	b)

Notes:
a) Interest is payable in UAH but annual return is guaranteed to be not less than 21.125% in USD
b) Coupon is payable semiannually and annual return is guaranteed to be not less than 17.5% in USD
Source: Ministry of Finance

Statistical Appendix

SECTION 5

Table 5.1 - Consolidated Budget, 1992-1998
(million hryvnias)

	1992	1993	1994	1995	1996	1997	1998 [5]
Revenue /1	**17**	**635**	**5,040**	**20,618**	**29,943**	**35,476**	**36,960**
Tax Revenue	16	550	4,485	18,956	28,266	33,237	35,304
VAT	5	172	1,300	4,517	6,293	7,602	7,238
Enterprise Tax	3	145	1,426	4,834	5,451	5,689	5,620
Personal Income Tax	2	29	340	1,601	2,639	3,293	3,561
Land Tax	...	...	...	635	802	1,002	1,105
Excises	1	25	169	401	652	1,158	1,249
Royalties on Gas and Oil	...	...	...	385	1,873	932	62
Foreigh Trade Receipts	...	20	87	429	444	704	972
Pension Fund Receipts	5	134	922	4,160	6,988	8,455	8,930
Chernobyl Fund Receipts	1	25	241	1,026	1,488	1,698	1,416
Other Special Funds /2	...	...	...	42	292	1,048	1,968
Other Tax Revenues	...	...	...	926	1,344	1,655	3,182
Other Revenues	1	85	555	1,662	1,677	2,239	1,656
ow/ NBU Profite	...	...	32	0	21	93	375
ow/ State Reserve Fund	...	20	78	189	264	281	39
Total Expenditure /4	**29**	**1,052**	**6,087**	**23,280**	**32,550**	**40,665**	**39,714**
Current Expenditure	27	1,012	5,657	21,897	31,492	40,129	39,015
Social Protection	4	181	700	3,500	4,066	5,504	4,111
Benefits	2	65	200	866	2,640	2,931	3,011
Subsidies	2	116	500	2,634	1,426	2,573	1,100
Social and Cultural Spending	5	134	1,289	6,021	7,718	9,633	8,715
Education	2	65	622	2,932	3,961	4,959	4,483
Health Care	2	57	555	2,536	3,126	3,912	3,569
Other	1	12	112	553	631	762	663
National Economy	12	226	1,750	2,551	3,453	2,830	2,270
ow/ Directed Credits	7	110	284	89	0	1	0
ow/ Agriculture	...	...	...	...	559	48	306
ow/ State Reserve Fund	...	...	...	...	1,485	1,386	115
Administration and Justice	1	30	296	1,417	2,267	2,975	2,915
Defense	1	27	212	1,033	1,377	1,525	1,338
Pension Fund	4	123	892	4,119	7,025	8,394	8,801
Chernobyl Fund	1	19	227	949	1,524	1,717	1,420
Interest Payments	0	3	131	830	1,281	1,689	2,424
ow/ domestic	0	0	59	620	445	930	1,663
ow/ foreign	0	3	72	210	836	759	761
Other Current Expenditures	1	269	160	1,477	2,782	5,863	7,020
Capital Expenditures	2	40	430	1,383	1,058	536	699
Cash Deficit	**-12**	**-417**	**-1,047**	**-2,662**	**-2,607**	**-5,189**	**-2,754**
Memo:							
Accrual Deficit	-12	-417	-1,047	-4,491	-4,946	-4,822	-3,862
Budget Arrears (flow)	0	0	0	641	2,339	-367	1,108
Tax Arrears (end of period stock)	...	...	...	1,205	1,741	2,012	5,985
GDP	50	1,483	12,038	54,516	81,519	93,365	103,869

1/ 1993 - 1996 data was revised by IMF.

2/ Includes the Road Fund, Industrial Development Fund and Innovation Fund

4/ Ukraine moved to GFS classification on Jan. 1, 1998.

5/ Preliminary data

Table 5.2 - Consolidated Budget, 1992-1998
(percentage of GDP)

	1992	1993	1994	1995	1996	1997	1998 [5]
Revenue /1	**34.2**	**42.8**	**41.9**	**37.8**	**36.7**	**38.0**	**35.6**
Tax Revenue	32.0	37.1	37.3	34.8	34.7	35.6	34.0
VAT	9.7	11.6	10.8	8.3	7.7	8.1	7.0
Enterprise Tax	5.6	9.8	11.8	8.9	6.7	6.1	5.4
Personal Income Tax	3.0	2.0	2.8	2.9	3.2	3.5	3.4
Land Tax	...	...	...	1.2	1.0	1.1	1.1
Excises	1.2	1.7	1.4	0.7	0.8	1.2	1.2
Royalties on Gas and Oil	...	...	...	0.7	2.3	1.0	0.1
Foreigh Trade Receipts	...	1.3	0.7	0.8	0.5	0.8	0.9
Pension Fund Receipts	10.1	9.0	7.7	7.6	8.6	9.1	8.6
Chernobyl Fund Receipts	2.4	1.7	2.0	1.9	1.8	1.8	1.4
Other Special Funds /2	...	...	...	0.1	0.4	1.1	1.9
Other Tax Revenues	...	...	...	1.7	1.6	1.8	3.1
Other Revenues	2.2	5.7	4.6	3.0	2.1	2.4	1.6
ow/ NBU Profits	...	...	0.3	0.0	0.0	0.1	0.4
ow/ State Reserve Fund	...	1.3	0.6	0.3	0.3	0.3	0.0
Total Expenditure /4	**58.4**	**70.9**	**50.6**	**42.7**	**39.9**	**43.6**	**38.2**
Current Expenditure	54.2	68.3	47.0	40.2	38.6	43.0	37.6
Social Protection	7.2	12.2	5.8	6.4	5.0	5.9	4.0
Benefits	3.2	4.4	1.7	1.6	3.2	3.1	2.9
Subsidies	4.0	7.8	4.2	4.8	1.7	2.8	1.1
Social and Cultural Spending	9.3	9.0	10.7	11.0	9.5	10.3	8.4
Education	4.6	4.4	5.2	5.4	4.9	5.3	4.3
Health Care	3.6	3.8	4.6	4.7	3.8	4.2	3.4
Other	1.2	0.8	0.9	1.0	0.8	0.8	0.6
National Economy	23.6	15.2	14.5	4.7	4.2	3.0	2.2
ow/ Directed Credits	13.1	7.4	2.4	0.2	0.0	0.0	0.0
ow/ Agriculture	...	...	...	...	0.7	0.1	0.3
ow/ State Reserve Fund	...	...	...	...	1.8	1.5	0.1
Administration and Justice	1.4	2.0	2.5	2.6	2.8	3.2	2.8
Defense	2.2	1.8	1.8	1.9	1.7	1.6	1.3
Pension Fund	7.2	8.3	7.4	7.6	8.6	9.0	8.5
Chernobyl Fund	2.2	1.3	1.9	1.7	1.9	1.8	1.4
Interest Payments	0.0	0.2	1.1	1.5	1.6	1.8	2.3
ow/ domestic	0.0	0.0	0.5	1.1	0.5	1.0	1.6
ow/ foreign	0.0	0.2	0.6	0.4	1.0	0.8	0.7
Other Current Expenditures	1.2	18.1	1.3	2.7	3.4	6.3	6.8
Capital Expenditures	4.2	2.7	3.6	2.5	1.3	0.6	0.7
Cash Deficit	**-24.2**	**-28.1**	**-8.7**	**-4.9**	**-3.2**	**-5.6**	**-2.7**
Memo:							
Accrual Deficit	-24.2	-28.1	-8.7	-8.2	-6.1	-5.2	-3.7
Budget Arrears (flow)	0.0	0.0	0.0	1.2	2.9	-0.4	1.1
Tax Arrears (end of period stock)	...	...	...	2.2	2.1	2.2	5.8
GDP	50	1,483	12,038	54,516	81,519	93,365	103,869

1/ 1991 and 1992 data do not take into account recent IMF revisions.

2/ Includes the Road Fund, Industrial Development Fund and Innovation Fund

4/ Ukraine moved to GFS classification on Jan. 1, 1998.

5/ Preliminary data

Table 5.3 - Consolidated Budget, 1992-1998
(constant 1990 hryvnias)

	1992	1993	1994	1995	1996	1997	1998 /5
Revenue /1	**45.3**	**44.9**	**28.2**	**22.7**	**20.2**	**21.4**	**19.7**
Tax Revenue	42.4	38.9	25.1	20.9	19.0	20.0	18.8
VAT	12.8	12.2	7.3	5.0	4.2	4.6	3.9
Enterprise Tax	7.4	10.3	8.0	5.3	3.7	3.4	3.0
Personal Income Tax	4.0	2.1	1.9	1.8	1.8	2.0	1.9
Land Tax	…	…	…	0.7	0.5	0.6	0.6
Excises	1.6	1.8	0.9	0.4	0.4	0.7	0.7
Royalties on Gas and Oil	…	…	…	0.4	1.3	0.6	0.0
Foreigh Trade Receipts	…	1.4	0.5	0.5	0.3	0.4	0.5
Pension Fund Receipts	13.4	9.5	5.2	4.6	4.7	5.1	4.8
Chernobyl Fund Receipts	3.2	1.8	1.3	1.1	1.0	1.0	0.8
Other Special Funds /2	…	…	…	0.0	0.2	0.6	1.1
Other Tax Revenues	…	…	…	1.0	0.9	1.0	1.7
Other Revenues	2.9	6.0	3.1	1.8	1.1	1.3	0.9
ow/ NBU Profits	…	…	0.2	0.0	0.0	0.1	0.2
ow/ State Reserve Fund	…	1.4	0.4	0.2	0.2	0.2	0.0
Total Expenditure /4	**77.4**	**74.4**	**34.0**	**25.6**	**21.9**	**24.5**	**21.2**
Current Expenditure	71.8	71.6	31.6	24.1	21.2	24.2	20.8
Social Protection	9.5	12.8	3.9	3.9	2.7	3.3	2.2
Benefits	4.2	4.6	1.1	1.0	1.8	1.8	1.6
Subsidies	5.3	8.2	2.8	2.9	1.0	1.5	0.6
Social and Cultural Spending	12.4	9.5	7.2	6.6	5.2	5.8	4.7
Education	6.1	4.6	3.5	3.2	2.7	3.0	2.4
Health Care	4.7	4.0	3.1	2.8	2.1	2.4	1.9
Other	1.6	0.8	0.6	0.6	0.4	0.5	0.4
National Economy	31.3	16.0	9.8	2.8	2.3	1.7	1.2
ow/ Directed Credits	17.4	7.8	1.6	0.1	0.0	0.0	0.0
ow/ Agriculture	…	…	…	…	0.4	0.0	0.2
ow/ State Reserve Fund	…	…	…	…	1.0	0.8	0.1
Administration and Justice	1.8	2.1	1.7	1.6	1.5	1.8	1.6
Defense	2.9	1.9	1.2	1.1	0.9	0.9	0.7
Pension Fund	9.5	8.7	5.0	4.5	4.7	5.1	4.7
Chernobyl Fund	2.9	1.3	1.3	1.0	1.0	1.0	0.8
Interest Payments	0.0	0.2	0.7	0.9	0.9	1.0	1.3
ow/ domestic	0.0	0.0	0.3	0.7	0.3	0.6	0.9
ow/ foreign	0.0	0.2	0.4	0.2	0.6	0.5	0.4
Other Current Expenditures	1.6	19.0	0.9	1.6	1.9	3.5	3.7
Capital Expenditures	5.5	2.8	2.4	1.5	0.7	0.3	0.4
Cash Deficit	**-32.0**	**-29.5**	**-5.8**	**-2.9**	**-1.8**	**-3.1**	**-1.5**
Memo:							
GDP Deflator (1990=1)	38	1,413	17,902	90,820	148,581	166,124	187,296

1/ 1991 and 1992 data do not take into account recent IMF revisions.

2/ Includes the Road Fund, Industrial Development Fund and Innovation Fund

4/ Ukraine moved to GFS classification on Jan. 1, 1998.

5/ Preliminary data

Table 5.4 - Consolidated Budget, 1992-1998
(percentage of revenue & expenditures)

	1992	1993	1994	1995	1996	1997	1998 [5]
Revenue /1	**100.0**	**100.0**	**100.0**	**100.0**	**100.0**	**100.0**	**100.0**
Tax Revenue	93.6	86.6	89.0	91.9	94.4	93.7	95.5
VAT	28.3	27.1	25.8	21.9	21.0	21.4	19.6
Enterprise Tax	16.4	22.8	28.3	23.4	18.2	16.0	15.2
Personal Income Tax	8.8	4.6	6.7	7.8	8.8	9.3	9.6
Land Tax	...	...	...	3.1	2.7	2.8	3.0
Excises	3.5	3.9	3.4	1.9	2.2	3.3	3.4
Royalties on Gas and Oil	...	...	...	1.9	6.3	2.6	0.2
Foreigh Trade Receipts	...	3.1	1.7	2.1	1.5	2.0	2.6
Pension Fund Receipts	29.6	21.1	18.3	20.2	23.3	23.8	24.2
Chernobyl Fund Receipts	7.0	3.9	4.8	5.0	5.0	4.8	3.8
Other Special Funds /2	...	...	...	0.2	1.0	3.0	5.3
Other Tax Revenues	...	...	...	4.5	4.5	4.7	8.6
Other Revenues	6.4	13.4	11.0	8.1	5.6	6.3	4.5
ow/ NBU Profite	...	...	0.6	0.0	0.1	0.3	1.0
ow/ State Reserve Fund	...	3.1	1.5	0.9	0.9	0.8	0.1
Total Expenditure /4	**100.0**	**100.0**	**100.0**	**100.0**	**100.0**	**100.0**	**100.0**
Current Expenditure	92.9	96.2	92.9	94.1	96.7	98.7	98.2
Social Protection	12.2	17.2	11.5	15.0	12.5	13.5	10.4
Benefits	5.4	6.2	3.3	3.7	8.1	7.2	7.6
Subsidies	6.8	11.0	8.2	11.3	4.4	6.3	2.8
Social and Cultural Spending	16.0	12.7	21.2	25.9	23.7	23.7	21.9
Education	7.8	6.2	10.2	12.6	12.2	12.2	11.3
Health Care	6.1	5.4	9.1	10.9	9.6	9.6	9.0
Other	2.0	1.1	1.8	2.4	1.9	1.9	1.7
National Economy	40.5	21.5	28.7	11.0	10.6	7.0	5.7
ow/ Directed Credits	22.4	10.5	4.7	0.4	0.0	0.0	0.0
ow/ Agriculture	...	...	...	...	1.7	0.1	0.8
ow/ State Reserve Fund	...	...	...	...	4.6	3.4	0.3
Administration and Justice	2.4	2.9	4.9	6.1	7.0	7.3	7.3
Defense	3.7	2.6	3.5	4.4	4.2	3.8	3.4
Pension Fund	12.2	11.7	14.7	17.7	21.6	20.6	22.2
Chernobyl Fund	3.7	1.8	3.7	4.1	4.7	4.2	3.6
Interest Payments	0.0	0.3	2.2	3.6	3.9	4.2	6.1
ow/ domestic	0.0	0.0	1.0	2.7	1.4	2.3	4.2
ow/ foreign	0.0	0.3	1.2	0.9	2.6	1.9	1.9
Other Current Expenditures	2.0	25.6	2.6	6.3	8.5	14.4	17.7
Capital Expenditures	7.1	3.8	7.1	5.9	3.3	1.3	1.8

1/ 1993 - 1996 data was revised by IMF.

2/ Includes the Road Fund, Industrial Development F

4/ Ukraine moved to GFS classification on Jan. 1, 1998.

5/ Preliminary data

Table 5.5 - Budget Financing by Type of Debt Instrument 1998 (mn UAH)

	Approved 1998	Performed 1998	Jan-98	Feb-98	Mar-98	Apr-98	May-98	Jun-98	Jul-98	Aug-98	Sep-98	Oct-98	Nov-98	Dec-98
General Financing														
I. (II+III)	3.38	2.16	..	0.63	1.60	1.42	1.60	1.85	2.00	2.11	2.70	2.07	2.01	2.16
II. Domestic financing	1.13	1.34	0.09	0.12	0.06	0.08	0.00	0.35	0.59	1.52	1.31	1.15	1.00	1.34
Medium term bonds	3.37	0.29	0.07	0.30	0.50	0.37	0.26	-0.08	-0.38	0.23	0.06	-0.03	0.09	0.29
Issue	3.37	3.36	0.24	0.65	1.01	1.23	1.37	1.66	1.97	2.86	3.00	3.00	3.14	3.36
Amortization		3.06	0.17	0.35	0.51	0.86	1.10	1.74	2.36	2.62	2.93	3.03	3.05	3.06
Short term bonds and														
T-bills	-2.24	1.05	0.03	-0.18	-0.44	-0.29	-0.26	0.43	0.97	1.29	1.25	1.18	0.91	1.05
Issue	5.06	4.80	0.40	0.74	1.08	1.54	1.93	2.85	3.51	4.40	4.55	4.55	4.60	4.80
Amortization	7.29	3.75	0.37	0.91	1.52	1.83	2.20	2.42	2.54	3.11	3.31	3.37	3.69	3.75
III. External financing	2.25	0.82	-0.09	0.51	1.54	1.34	1.60	1.49	1.41	0.59	1.39	0.92	1.01	0.82
Long term bonds	2.85	-0.17		0.00	0.00	0.00	0.00	0.00	0.00	0.00	0.00	0.00	0.00	-0.17
Issue	2.85													
Amortization		0.17												0.17
Loans not classified by other categories	-0.60	0.99		0.51	1.54	1.34	1.60	1.49	1.41	0.59	1.39	0.92	1.01	0.99
Loans received	3.00	3.24		0.81	1.90	1.90	2.20	2.20	2.20	2.20	3.00	3.00	3.24	3.24
Loans repaid	3.60	2.26		0.31	0.36	0.56	0.59	0.70	0.78	1.61	1.61	2.08	2.23	2.26

Source: State Treasury

Table 5.6 - State and Local Budgets in Ukraine.

	1990 (bln. krb)			1991 (bln. krb)			1992 (bln. krb)		
	consolidated	state	local	consolidated	state	local	consolidated	state	local
Revenues	**45.1**	**22.4** 0.0	**22.7**	**76.8**	**41.4**	**35.4**	**1,227.5**	**643.7**	**583.8**
including									
Enterprise profit tax	10.9	4.8	6.1	22.7	11.4	11.3	279.1	124.7	154.4
VAT	12.7	4.2	8.5	16.2	9.7	6.5	486.7	277.9	208.8
Excise taxes							59.7	28.0	31.7
Households income tax	4.0	1.1	2.9	9.3	0.0	9.3	143.0	0.0	143.0
Chernobyl tax	-	-	-	2.7	2.7	-	124.2	124.2	0.0
Pension fund*	-	-	-	-	-	-			
Other	17.5	12.4	5.1	25.9	17.6	8.3	134.8	88.9	45.9
Expenditures	**43.8**	**22.6**	**21.2**	**97.9**	**67.2**	**30.7**	**1,919.7**	**1,193.5**	**726.2**
including									
National economy	21.6	13.0	8.6	44.8	37.4	7.4	714.0	599.9	114.1
Social protection, culture & science	20.3	10.0	10.3	41.1	19.6	21.5	865.7	281.6	584.1
Defense							108.7	107.9	0.8
Chernobyl				4.5	4.5	-	114.6	114.6	0.0
Pension fund									
Other	1.9	-0.3	2.2	7.5	5.7	1.8	116.7	89.5	27.2
Balance	**1.3**	**-0.2**	**1.5**	**-21.1**	**-25.8**	**4.7**	**-692.2**	**-549.8**	**-142.4**

*Pension fund revenues & expenditures were included in the State Budget only three years, 1994-96

Source: Ministry of Finance

Statistical Appendix

Table 5.6 – State and Local Budgets in Ukraine (continued)

	1993 bln.krb			1994 bln.krb			1995 mln. UAH		
	consolidated	state	local	consolidated	state	local	consolidated	state	local
Revenues	**49,621.8**	**25,865.8**	**23,756.0**	**523,092.6**	**342,806.7**	**180,285.9**	**20,689.9**	**12,047.6**	**8,642.3**
including									
Enterprise profit tax	14,473.5	5,663.8	8,809.7	142,956.4	47,612.1	95,344.3	4,860.6	1,317.7	3,542.9
VAT	17,206.5	8,519.4	8,687.1	129,937.5	86,949.2	42,988.3	4,529.9	1,525.5	3,004.4
Excise taxes	2,513.8	1,144.8	1,369.0	16,817.7	11,559.2	5,258.5	406.2	304.4	101.8
Households income tax	2,883.4	0.0	2,883.4	33,995.0	11,200.9	22,794.1	1,595.3	736.4	858.9
Chernobyl tax	2,500.4	2,500.4	0.0	24,066.8	24,066.8	0.0	1,026.0	1,026.0	0.0
Pension fund*				94,311.6	94,311.6	0.0	4,189.2	4,189.2	0.0
Other	10,044.2	8,037.4	2,006.8	81,007.6	67,106.9	13,900.7	4,082.7	2,948.4	1,134.3
Expenditures	**57,248.8**	**34,686.7**	**22,562.1**	**630,647.0**	**439,585.2**	**191,061.8**	**24,302.8**	**14,756.2**	**9,546.6**
including									
National economy	11,039.8	10,097.2	942.6	209,117.3	181,832.6	27,284.7	2,336.9	1,683.8	653.1
Social protection, culture & science	32,395.6	15,350.7	17,044.9	209,360.4	60,595.9	148,764.5	9,580.8	1,965.7	7,615.1
Defense	2,765.7	2,743.8	21.9	23,355.7	23,142.5	213.2	1,032.5	1,022.1	10.4
Chernobyl	1,939.2	1,919.8	19.4	22,675.3	22,669.9	5.4	948.7	948.7	0.0
Pension fund				89,729.5	89,729.5	0.0	4,119.2	4,119.2	0.0
Other	9,108.5	4,575.2	4,533.3	76,408.8	61,614.8	14,794.0	6,284.7	5,016.7	1,268.0
Balance	**-7,627.0**	**-8,820.9**	**1,193.9**	**-107,554.4**	**-96,778.5**	**-10,775.9**	**-3,612.9**	**-2,708.6**	**-904.3**

* Pension fund revenues & expenditures were included in the State Budget only three years, 1994-96

Source: Ministry of Finance

Table 5.6 – State and Local Budgets in Ukraine (continued)

	1996 mln. UAH			1997 mln. UAH		
	consolidated	state	local	consolidated	state	local
Revenues	**30,218.7**	**19,266.4**	**10,952.3**	**28,112.0**	**15,973.8**	**12,138.2**
including						
Enterprise profit tax	5,496.6	1,449.1	4,047.5	5,792.1	-	5792.1
VAT	6,246.2	2,765.3	3,480.9	8,242.3	8,242.3	-
Excise taxes	646.2	542.1	104.1	1,207.9	739.0	468.9
Households income tax	2,593.1	1,242.8	1,350.3	3,295.7	-	3295.7
Chernobyl tax	1,490.1	1,490.1	0.0	1,697.9	1,697.9	-
Pension fund*	7,197.1	7,197.1	0.0	-	-	-
Other	6,549.4	4,579.9	1,969.5	7,876.1	5,294.6	2,581.5
Expenditures	**34,182.8**	**22,421.9**	**11,760.9**	**34,312.7**	**20,622.6**	**13,690.1**
including						
National economy	3,450.6	2,584.7	865.9	4,423.6	3,714.8	708.8
Social protection, culture & science	12,404.7	2,870.4	9,534.3	15,949.3	4,332.3	11617
Defense	1,226.6	1,226.6	0.0	1,738.9	1,738.9	-
Chernobyl	1,524.4	1,524.4	0.0	1,746.8	1,746.8	-
Pension fund	7,233.6	7,233.6	0.0	-	-	-
Other	8,342.9	6,982.2	1,360.7	10,454.1	9,089.8	1,364.3
Balance	**-3,964.1**	**-3,155.5**	**-808.6**	**-6,200.7**	**-4,648.8**	**-1,551.9**

* Pension fund revenues & expenditues were included in the State Budget only three years, 1994-96

Source: Ministry of Finance

Table 5.7 - Pension Fund Revenues and Expenditures

(mln. UAH)

	1991	1992	1993*	1994	1995	1996	1
Revenues	**0.30**	**5.08**	**133.62**	**998.93**	**4,400.42**	**7,415.73**	**9,467**
Payroll contributions	0.25	4.77	94.52	943.12	4,181.36	7,072.53	8,483
Transferes from Chornobyl Fund	0.00	0.00	2.31	25.22	87.40	190.20	341
Transferes from State Budget	0.05	0.31	36.79	22.29	83.00	102.54	554
Transferes from Local Budget	0.00	0.00	0.00	8.30	48.66	50.46	88
Expenditures	**0.29**	**3.69**	**123.22**	**892.82**	**4,312.00**	**7,569.80**	**9,530**
Financed by insurance contributions	0.25	3.27	113.75	810.83	3,908.57	6,736.56	8,136
Financed by Chornobyl Fund (for pensions and allowances to Chornobyl victims)	0.00	0.10	4.20	28.34	124.88	251.45	316
Financed by State Budget (for pensions, allowances and compensation payments to servicemen)	0.03	0.28	5.28	40.84	210.19	499.17	650
Financed by Local Budget (for allowances for children of age 1.5 - 3)	0.00	0.00	0.00	12.82	67.58	82.22	77
Other expenditures	0.00	0.04	0.00	0.00	0.78	0.40	350
Pension Fund Balance	**0.01**	**1.389**	**10.401**	**106.103**	**88.42**	**-154.07**	**-63.40**
NBU loan	0.04	0.00	0.00	0.00	62.00	125.00	147

* 1993 transfers from the State budget include a UAH 33.65 mln. budget loan

Source: Ministry of Finance

Table 5.8 – Tax and Expenditure Arrears in Ukraine (mn Hrn)

	1996 Q1	1996 Q2	1996 Q3	1996 Q4	1997 Q1	1997 Q2	1997 Q3	1997 Q4	1998 Q1	1998 Q2	1998 Q3
Total Tax Arrears:											
Total	5,201	6,161	7,644	8,383	9,823	11,402	11,369	13,736	16,555	23,583	31,978
Value-Added Tax	3,025	3,231	3,950	4,049	4,968	5,812	5,210	6,884	8,346	14,394	22,369
Excise Tax	1,266	1,469	1,711	1,695	2,398	2,804	2,422	2,481	3,323	5,561	7,749
Enterprise Profit Tax	84	101	123	114	107	152	225	237	608	739	1,167
Entrepreneurship Activity Profit Tax	890	1,012	1,247	1,229	1,008	1,404	1,135	1,258	1,071	2,587	4,140
Personal Income Tax	3	5	7	8	9	10	12	17	21	29	35
									21	62	97
Land payments	263	200	168	422	555	541	435	553	655	917	1,189
Other taxes and payments	520	444	694	582	891	902	980	2,337	2,647	4,500	7,992
Pension Arrears To:	2,176	2,930	3,694	4,334	4,855	5,591	6,159	6,852	8,209	9,188	9,609
Operational Budgetary Arrears of Ukraine											
State	2,187	3,012	3,606	4,021	3,927	4,466	4,636	3,662	3,364	2,560	3,292
Local	3,974	6,541	8,566	9,501	11,845	14,020	13,803	12,713	12,156	13,705	14,218
Consolidated	6,161	9,553	12,172	13,522	15,772	18,486	18,439	16,375	15,218	16,265	17,509
Pension Arrears From:	418	1,323	2,122	3,043	3,744	4,251	4,302	3,744	4,133	4,855	5,615
Total Operational Arrears	6,579	10,876	14,295	16,565	19,516	22,737	22,741	20,119	19,351	21,120	23,125
Sectoral Arrears:											
Wages and Salaries	1,183	2,020	2,721	3,228	3,670	3,540	3,106	2,282	2,348	2,473	2,834
Social Insurance	622	944	1,254	1,436	1,712	1,656	1,443	1,088	1,115	1,147	1,286
Stipends	124	184	219	274	286	258	281	278	282	250	250
Heating	1,576	2,573	2,758	2,577	2,901	3,693	3,595	3,018	2,480	2,569	2,805
Electricity	276	407	414	348	373	450	485	378	210	241	380
Catering	319	400	423	481	475	354	338	250	200	217	275
Medicine	128	171	224	241	258	267	256	209	187	172	178
Chernobyl	380	258	423	516	554	654	801	900	816	840	1,312

Table 6.1 Summary Balance Sheet of the National Bank
(mln UAH, end of period)

	Foreign Assets	Currency in circulation	Reserves of commercial banks	NBU Credit to Government	NBU Credit to Commercial Banks (refinancing)	Currency % change per month	Real cash balances (index 1992=100)
1992	9	5	17	17	2	25	81.0
1993	32	128	182	113	112	31	20.6
1994	683	793	763	1,244	105	16	25.4
1995	1,994	2,623	960	4,295	349	10	29.9
1996	3,769	4,041	849	5,995	474	4	33.0
1997	4,479	6,132	926	7,096	824	4	45.4
1998	6,172	7,158	1,454	13,479	505	1.3	44.2
1992 Q1		1		0		24	65.1
1992 Q2		2		5		36	100.0
1992 Q3		4	2	9		28	123.3
1992 Q4	9	5	17	17	2	12	81.0
1993 Q1	13	9	32	22	11	22	54.3
1993 Q2	17	17	76	41	21	23	38.2
1993 Q3	30	52	158	69	91	45	38.9
1993 Q4	32	128	182	113	112	35	20.6
1994 Q1	18	230	229	313	117	22	26.8
1994 Q2	14	333	378	565	123	13	33.3
1994 Q3	22	520	752	1,043	150	16	45.7
1994 Q4	683	793	763	1,244	105	15	25.4
1995 Q1	848	1,134	878	1,719	69	13	22.8
1995 Q2	2,247	1,782	914	2,049	187	16	30.9
1995 Q3	1,960	2,235	990	3,271	286	8	30.9
1995 Q4	1,994	2,623	960	4,295	349	5	29.9
1996 Q1	1,397	2,800	964	5,384	243	2	26.4
1996 Q2	1,718	3,324	727	5,726	215	6	30.3
1996 Q3	2,384	3,330	962	5,694	345	0	28.1
1996 Q4	3,769	4,041	849	5,995	474	7	33.0
1997 Q1	3,852	4,306	882	5,856	581	2	33.9
1997 Q2	4,343	5,102	1,000	6,101	608	6	39.5
1997 Q3	4,722	6,031	805	6,403	856	6	46.1
1997 Q4	4,479	6,132	926	7,096	824	1	45.4
1998 Q1	7,816	6,365	806	7,755	528	1	46.4
1998 Q2	6,578	6,390	858	9,386	513	0.1	45.9
1998 Q3	6,158	6,310	1,168	13,238	598	-0.4	44.0
1998 Q4	6,172	7,158	1,454	13,479	505	4.3	44.2

Source: National Bank of Ukraine, TACIS

Table 6.2 - Summary Balance Sheet of Commercial Banks
(mln UAH, end of period)

	Commercial banks credits to the economy (in domestic currency)	Share of credits to private enterprises, households and co-operatives (%)	Credits in foreign currency and net international assets	Deposits (time and demand, in domestic currency)	Share of households in deposits (%)	Deposits in foreign currency
1992	24	21.0	5	18	14.4	2
1993	391	23.5	103	254	12.3	100
1994	1,202	42.0	1,333	1,401	16.3	1,021
1995	3,029	36.2	1,749	2,646	20.0	1,577
1996	4,103	36.1	2,475	3,265	30.9	1,718
1997	5,196	49.4	2,125	4,643	36.5	1,672
1998	5,102	82.2	5,122	5,017	36.4	3,257
1992 Q1	3			3		
1992 Q2	7			5		
1992 Q3	13			8	25.0	
1992 Q4	24	21.0	5	18	14.4	2
1993 Q1	58	22.3		37	12.8	14
1993 Q2	101	19.5		62	12.6	27
1993 Q3	303	16.9		208	6.3	47
1993 Q4	391	23.5	103	254	12.3	100
1994 Q1	538	29.9	130	319	19.0	113
1994 Q2	792	37.8	208	600	18.8	146
1994 Q3	1,253	45.0	347	1,084	14.3	253
1994 Q4	1,202	42.0	1,333	1,401	16.3	1,021
1995 Q1	1,357	37.4	1,817	1,547	18.4	1,254
1995 Q2	2,176	34.7	2,371	2,072	16.7	1,442
1995 Q3	2,886	38.2	2,632	2,409	15.7	1,742
1995 Q4	3,029	36.2	1,749	2,646	20.0	1,577
1996 Q1	2,997	38.9	2,823	2,762	22.1	1,524
1996 Q2	3,060	40.1	2,387	2,753	25.0	1,446
1996 Q3	3,332	38.9	2,320	2,890	26.7	1,372
1996 Q4	4,103	36.1	2,475	3,265	30.9	1,718
1997 Q1	4,126	41.7	1,996	3,734	31.9	1,474
1997 Q2	4,487	46.9	2,095	4,177	32.3	1,692
1997 Q3	5,095	51.3	2,040	4,433	33.2	1,758
1997 Q4	5,196	49.4	2,125	4,643	36.5	1,672
1998 Q1	5,001	78.6	2,414	4,608	38.6	1,863
1998 Q2	5,104	81.0	2,777	4,879	42.4	1,987
1998 Q3	4,985	82.0	4,866	4,563	38.9	3,269
1998 Q4	5,102	82.2	5,122	5,017	36.4	3,257

Source: National Bank of Ukraine, TACIS

Table 6.3 - Monetary Aggregates
(mln UAH, end of period)

	Money Base	Money Base growth (over prior period)	M2 (in domestic currency)	M2 (including time deposits in foreign currency)	M2 growth (over prior period)	Total credits to businesses, households and government	Total credits (incl. credits in foreign currency)	Money multiplier	Actual reserve ratio (%)	Monetization ratio
1992	15		23	25		42	46	1.51	56	0.50
1993	282	1,780	386	481	1,824	505	608	1.42	52	0.32
1994	1,606	470	2,163	3,216	569	2,446	3,706	1.44	49	0.27
1995	3,540	120	5,269	6,846	113	7,324	8,383	1.49	17	0.13
1996	4,882	38	7,306	9,024	32	10,098	11,490	1.50	13	0.11
1997	7,058	45	10,775	12,447	38	12,292	14,392	1.53	15	0.13
1998	8,604	22	12,175	15,432	24	18,581	22,333	1.42	18	
1992 Q1	1		3							
1992 Q2	2	100.0	7							
1992 Q3	5	150.0	11							
1992 Q4	15	200.0	23	25		42	46	1.51	56	1.47
1993 Q1	35	133.3	47	59	136.0	80		1.35	70	1.11
1993 Q2	77	120.0	79	111	88.1	142		1.03	96	0.87
1993 Q3	172	123.4	260	306	175.7	372		1.51	57	0.65
1993 Q4	282	64.0	386	481	57.2	505	608	1.42	52	0.58
1994 Q1	450	59.6	574	681	41.6	852	981	1.27	53	0.46
1994 Q2	693	54.0	927	1,082	58.9	1,358	1,565	1.34	49	0.53
1994 Q3	1,229	77.3	1,596	1,863	72.2	2,296	2,642	1.30	58	0.68
1994 Q4	1,606	30.7	2,163	3,216	72.6	2,446	3,706	1.44	49	0.55
1995 Q1	1,910	18.9	2,681	3,935	22.4	3,076	3,564	1.40	21	0.50
1995 Q2	2,679	40.3	3,850	5,309	34.9	4,225	4,873	1.44	20	0.53
1995 Q3	3,165	18.1	4,645	6,387	20.3	6,157	7,114	1.47	17	0.42
1995 Q4	3,540	11.8	5,269	6,846	7.2	7,324	8,383	1.49	17	0.32
1996 Q1	3,769	6.5	5,562	7,086	3.5	8,381	9,581	1.48	18	0.47
1996 Q2	4,074	8.1	6,077	7,522	6.2	8,786	10,066	1.49	14	0.43
1996 Q3	4,302	5.6	6,220	7,592	0.9	9,026	10,324	1.45	15	0.40
1996 Q4	4,882	13.5	7,306	9,024	18.9	10,098	11,490	1.50	13	0.31
1997 Q1	5,199	6.5	8,040	9,514	5.4	9,982	11,394	1.55	17	0.51
1997 Q2	6,122	17.8	9,279	10,971	15.3	10,588	12,230	1.52	17	0.52
1997 Q3	6,877	12.3	10,464	12,222	11.4	11,498	13,396	1.52	13	0.52
1997 Q4	7,058	2.6	10,775	12,447	1.8	12,292	14,392	1.53	15	0.42
1998 Q1	7,096	0.5	10,973	12,836	3.1	12,756	15,098	1.55	12	0.62
1998 Q2	7,269	2.4	11,269	13,256	3.3	14,490	17,020	1.55	12	
1998 Q3	7,534	3.6	10,873	14,142	10.2	18,223	22,420	1.44	15	
1998 Q4	8,604	14.2	12,175	15,432	16.4	18,581	22,333	1.42	18	

Source: National Bank of Ukraine, TACIS

Table 6.4 - Velocity of Circulation

	Currency Velocity (Ukraine)	Money Base Velocity	M2 Velocity (Ukraine)	M2 Velocity (Russia)	Dollarization ratio(%)	M2 + Changes in Payables Velocity
1994	32.2	15.2	11.8	10.2	56	3.6
1995	32.5	20.7	14.8	11.1	38.4	3.5
1996	24.6	19.7	13.1	8.8	34.6	2.9
1997	17.1	14.4	9.6	8	26.5	2.4
1998	14.9	12.8	8.6		39.6	2.8
1994 Q1	33.8	17.1	13.3	9.2	48	3.6
1994 Q2	27.3	12.8	10.6	10.7	41.2	2.9
1994 Q3	22.5	9.9	7.7	9.9	32.7	2.5
1994 Q4	31.9	14.9	11.1	10.4	48.5	3.9
1995 Q1	36.8	20.8	14.6	10	47	4
1995 Q2	30.7	19	13.9	11.1	42.5	3
1995 Q3	28.8	19.3	13.4	11.3	42.7	3.1
1995 Q4	29	20.5	14	10.9	37.7	3.1
1996 Q1	27.2	20.5	13.9	8	35.8	2.9
1996 Q2	24.5	19.7	13.1	8.1	34.6	2.9
1996 Q3	23.8	19.5	12.9	8.7	32.3	2.9
1996 Q4	23.3	18.8	12.6	9.6	34.5	2.9
1997 Q1	18.3	15	10	7.9	28.3	2.3
1997 Q2	17.9	15	9.8	7.4	28.8	2.4
1997 Q3	16.1	13.7	9.2	8	28.4	2.4
1997 Q4	16	14	9.2	7.9	26.5	2.5
1998 Q1	13.6	11.9	7.8	6.2	28.8	2.6
1998 Q2	13.6	12.1	7.9	6.8	28.9	2.7
1998 Q3	14.7	12.7	8.4	7.6	42	3
1998 Q4	17.3	14.1	10.1		39.8	3

Source: TACIS

Table 6.5 - Interest Rates

	NBU refinance rate (official, % per month)	NBU refinance rate (official, % per year)	NBU refinance real rate (official, % per month)	NBU refinance real rate (official, % per year)	Commercial banks interest rates (weighted average, % per month)		Real interest rate (weighted average, % per month)		Commercial banks interest rates (% per year)		Real interest rate (% per year)	
					on credits	on deposits	on credits	on deposits	on credits	on deposits	on credits	on deposits
1993					15.3	13.2	-20.9	-22.2	452.0	342.7	-94.0	-95.1
1994	19	706.4	4.5	69.6	20.8	17.4	6.8	3.9	865.6	585.5	120.2	58.3
1995	10.7	238.7	1.4	18.2	10.5	5.5	1.4	-3.2	231.4	90.1	18.2	-32.3
1996	5.2	83.7	2.3	31.4	6.7	2.8	3.7	-0.03	117.8	39.3	54.6	-0.4
1997	2	26.8	1.2	15.4	4.1	1.5	3.3	0.7	62.0	19.6	47.6	8.7
1998	5.1	81.6	3.5	51.1	4.5	1.9	3	0.3	69.6	25.3	42.6	3.7
1993 Q1					7.1	6.6	-22.4	-22.7	127.8	115.3	-95.2	-95.4
1993 Q2					13.4	11.1	-18.2	-19.7	352.2	253.6	-91.0	-92.8
1993 Q3	20	791.6	-17	-89.3	18.1	17.7	-17.3	-17.5	636.2	606.8	-89.8	-90.1
1993 Q4	20	791.6	-27.9	-98.0	22.8	17.5	-25.8	-28.9	1075.9	592.6	-97.2	-98.3
1994 Q1	20	791.6	6.8	120.2	30.1	23.3	16	10	2251.4	1134.7	493.6	213.8
1994 Q2	20	791.6	14.3	397.2	24.5	22.9	18.5	17	1286.9	1087.5	666.7	558.0
1994 Q3	13.6	361.9	9.2	187.5	13.5	12.4	9.2	8.2	357.0	306.6	187.5	157.5
1994 Q4	24.1	1234.3	-10.4	-73.2	15.2	10.9	-16.6	-19.7	446.3	246.1	-88.7	-92.8
1995 Q1	20	791.6	2.7	37.7	17.3	10.7	0.4	-5.2	578.5	238.7	4.9	-47.3
1995 Q2	9.2	187.5	3.9	58.3	10.2	5.3	4.9	0.2	220.8	85.8	77.5	2.4
1995 Q3	5.6	92.3	-2.2	-23.4	6.5	2.5	-1.2	-4.9	112.9	34.5	-13.5	-45.3
1995 Q4	8.1	154.6	1.4	18.2	8.4	3.6	-1.7	-2.8	163.2	52.9	-18.6	-28.9
1996 Q1	8.6	169.1	1.8	23.9	9	4.1	2.3	-2.3	181.3	62.0	31.4	-24.4
1996 Q2	5.4	88.0	4.4	67.7	7	2.8	5.8	1.7	125.2	39.3	96.7	22.4
1996 Q3	3.3	47.6	0.7	8.7	5.4	2.2	2.7	-0.4	88.0	29.8	37.7	-4.7
1996 Q4	3.3	47.6	2.1	28.3	5.3	2.2	4.1	0.9	85.8	29.8	62.0	11.4
1997 Q1	2.7	37.7	1.6	21.0	5	1.9	3.8	0.7	79.6	25.3	56.4	8.7
1997 Q2	2	26.8	1.4	18.2	4.3	1.6	3.8	1	65.7	21.0	56.4	12.7
1997 Q3	1.4	18.2	1	12.7	3.6	1.3	3.2	0.8	52.9	16.8	45.9	10.0
1997 Q4	2.1	28.3	1	12.7	3.4	1.4	2.3	0.3	49.4	18.2	31.4	3.7
1998 Q1	3.3	47.6	2.8	39.3	3.9	1.6	3.3	1	58.3	21.0	47.6	12.7
1998 Q2	3.8	56.4	3.3	47.6	4	1.7	3.5	1.3	60.1	22.4	51.1	16.8
1998 Q3	6.7	117.8	5.6	92.3	4.8	2	3.8	1	75.5	26.8	56.4	12.7
1998 Q4	6.6	115.3	2.4	32.9	5.4	2.2	1.2	-1.9	88.0	29.8	15.4	-20.6

Source: National Bank of Ukraine, TACIS

Table 6.6 - Commercial Banks' Interest Rates on Credits in Foreign Currency. by term structure
(% annual)

	Hard Currency		Weak Currency		Hard Currency		Weak Currency
	Jurid. person	Phys. person	Juris. person		Jurid. person	Phys. person	Juris. person
January, 1998	**17.3**	**17.9**	**72.2**	**June, 1998**	**15.6**	**21.3**	**52.2**
up to 1 month	...	...	...	up to 1 month	22.4	21.5	29.1
1 - 3 months	...	...	...	1 - 3 months	12.3	23.9	43.9
3 - 6 months	...	...	...	3 - 6 months	13.2	15	48.3
6 - 12 months	...	...	...	6 - 12 months	24	19	44.5
more than 1 year	...	...	...	more than 1 year	12.7	15.3	119.9
February, 1998	**16.2**	**21**	**25.9**	**July, 1998**	**18.6**	**21.8**	**54.4**
up to 1 month	16.8	26.2	20.5	up to 1 month	20.5	22.5	75.3
1 - 3 months	15.2	...	50	1 - 3 months	18	26.6	31.5
3 - 6 months	13.9	...	34.4	3 - 6 months	18.1	30.6	40.3
6 - 12 months	21.4	15.1	22.5	6 - 12 months	23.2	17	39.9
more than 1 year	13.9	18.5	...	more than 1 year	11.2	19	120
March, 1998	**17.3**	**20.1**	**22.7**	**August, 1998**	**20.5**	**21.7**	**42.5**
up to 1 month	17.9	22.9	32.5	up to 1 month	21.8	22	39.2
1 - 3 months	16.3	10	50	1 - 3 months	18.2	26.6	44.6
3 - 6 months	17.3	3.6	20.4	3 - 6 months	25.5	24.7	54
6 - 12 months	22	10.8	28.6	6 - 12 months	24.3	18.8	40
more than 1 year	12.8	17.8	16.2	more than 1 year	10.9	14.9	120
April, 1998	**16.1**	**18.4**	**54.5**	**September, 1998**	**18.9**	**26.9**	**17.7**
up to 1 month	15.4	22.6	52.6	up to 1 month	15.8	24.3	6
1 - 3 months	15	14.9	53.4	1 - 3 months	17.4	21.6	30.5
3 - 6 months	15.4	15.4	31.8	3 - 6 months	19.7	47.1	...
6 - 12 months	22.3	10.6	48.5	6 - 12 months	25.5	19.8	...
more than 1 year	13.4	17.9	120	more than 1 year	13.4	10.7	...
May, 1998	**15.6**	**21.1**	**47.6**	**October, 1998**	**21.9**	**20.3**	**81.1**
up to 1 month	19.5	21.7	43.6	up to 1 month	16.1	2.7	40
1 - 3 months	14	25.1	49.2	1 - 3 months	30.7	30.6	87.5
3 - 6 months	12.2	14.8	45.7	3 - 6 months	27.8	48.4	...
6 - 12 months	22.8	11	40	6 - 12 months	21.9	23.3	...
more than 1 year	12.9	20.1	78	more than 1 year	13.5	24.8	...

Source: National Bank Of Ukraine

Table 6.7 - Commercial banks' credits to economic entities in Ukraine as of November 1, 1998

(by industries; residual indebtness. mn Hrn)

Industries	Total	currency		short - term			credit (maturity) long - term			Percentage in total credit short - term	long - term
		national	foreign	total	national currency	foreign currency	total	national currency	foreign currency		
Total	8891	4761	4130	7406	4158	3248	1485	603	882	83.3	16.7
including											
1. Credits to juridical persons	8442	4342	4101	7167	3948	3219	1276	394	881	84.9	15.1
Manufacturing - total	3572	1574	1998	3093	1468	1625	479	106	374	86.6	13.4
electric power industry	96	93	3	94	92	2	2	1	1	97.9	2.1
fuel industry	288	55	232	282	50	232	6	6	0	97.9	2.1
ferrous metallurgy	630	245	385	573	236	337	57	9	48	91.0	9.0
machine building	937	443	494	883	415	468	54	28	26	94.2	5.8
food industry	539	277	262	396	256	140	143	21	122	73.5	26.5
Agriculture	343	223	121	257	192	64	86	30	56	74.9	25.1
Transportation	241	87	155	162	69	93	79	17	62	67.2	32.8
Communication	75	25	50	36	16	20	39	9	30	48.0	52.0
Constructions	208	149	58	160	110	50	48	39	8	76.9	23.1
Trade & Catering	2500	1432	1068	2191	1312	879	309	119	189	87.6	12.4
Material - technique supply	162	119	43	122	92	31	40	27	12	75.3	24.7
General commercial activity	157	86	71	140	78	62	17	9	8	89.2	10.8
Municipal services	28	20	8	25	18	7	3	2	1	89.3	10.7
Health & Social protection, sport	52	27	25	42	23	19	10	4	6	80.8	19.2
Culture & Arts	46	26	20	39	26	13	7	0	6	84.8	15.2
Science	67	25	42	35	22	13	32	3	29	52.2	47.8
Financing, insurance, pensions	146	75	71	89	71	18	57	4	53	61.0	39.0
2. Credits to physical person	449	479	30	239	210	29	210	209	1	53.2	46.8

Source: National Bank of Ukraine

Table 6.8 - Inter-Enterprise Arrears

(mln UAH)

	Indebtedness of Ukrain. enterprises registered on their balances		Arrears of Ukrainian enterprises registered by banks		Payables (enterprise balances) in real terms (Bn. 1990 rb.)	Ratio of credits (granted by com. banks) to payables (%)
	Receivables	Payables	Overdue payables of enterprises (cartotheque 2)	Arrears with banks (including overdue interests)		
1992	18	19	4		12.6	125.3
1993	994	1,276	86	40	8.7	30.6
1994	4,904	6,834	1,545	440	8.4	17.6
1995	22,250	30,543	10,955	806	14.5	9.9
1996	48,018	73,168		1,003	28.1	5.6
1997	74,086	102,507		716	40.8	5.1
1998	102,976	137,614			40.5	3.7
1994 Q1	1,714	2,267	267	14	11.6	23.7
1994 Q2	2,470	3,351	527	19	14.8	23.6
1994 Q3	3,400	4,196	646	25	15.4	29.9
1994 Q4	4,904	6,834	1,545	440	8.4	17.6
1995 Q1	11,260	14,605	3,570	652	10.6	9.3
1995 Q2	16,097	20,477	6,514	790	12.7	10.6
1995 Q3	19,794	26,943	8,365	827	13.4	10.7
1995 Q4	22,250	30,543	10,955	806	14.5	9.9
1996 Q1	32,512	45,152	14,721	930	18.5	6.6
1996 Q2	37,340	55,583	18,222	1,002	22.2	5.5
1996 Q3	40,625	60,289	21,539	1,081	25.0	5.5
1996 Q4	48,018	73,168	19,634	1,003	28.1	5.6
1997 Q1	59,312	84,968	20,780	1,033	32.8	4.9
1997 Q2	65,251	95,149	22,263	963	37.2	4.7
1997 Q3	70,219	98,428		1,008	39.2	5.2
1997 Q4	74,086	102,507		716	40.8	5.1
Jan-97	53,202	72,156	19,398	1,041	30.6	5.2
Feb-97	49,925	72,784	20,039	1,054	30.4	5.3
Mar-97	59,312	84,968	20,780	1,033	32.8	4.9
Apr-97	60,118	86,805	n.a.	1,034	35.5	4.9
May-97	60,117	86,134	n.a.	1,050	35.7	5.0
Jun-97	65,251	95,149	22,263	963	37.2	4.7
Jul-97	65,536	92,814		990	38.5	5.0
Aug-97	66,644	93,271		1,009	38.1	5.3
Sep-97	70,219	98,428		1,008	39.2	5.2
Oct-97	70,907	99,138		686	40.0	5.2
Nov-97	72,447	99,847		671	40.3	5.1
Dec-97	74,086	102,507		716	40.8	5.1
Jan-98	70,390	93,979			39.3	5.3
Feb-98	72,843	97,826			38.0	5.1
Mar-98	79,748	103,873			39.7	4.8
Apr-98	80,968	104,902			40.9	4.8
May-98	83,566	108,729			41.8	4.7
Jun-98	85,475	114,015			43.5	4.5
Jul-98	85,778	114,786			44.3	4.5
Aug-98	87,120	114,247			43.8	4.4
Sep-98	92,133	121,125			41.3	4.1
Oct-98	100,210	133,221			40.3	3.6
Nov-98	101,619	134,311			41.0	3.6
Dec-98	102,976	137,614			40.5	3.7

Source: Ukrainian Economic trends, TACIS

Statistical Appendix

Table 7.1 - Ukraine: Agricultural production

	Total production (mn USD)	Share of animal production (%)	Share of private sector (%)	Total production (mn Rb 1983)	Share of animal production (%)	Share of private sector (%)	Total production (current mn Hrn)	Deflator of agricultural production ($ 1990)	Deflator of agricultural production (rb. 1983)	Total production (Hrn 1996)
1990	44,133	31.3	16.5	48,954	55.2	26.7	0.6	1	1	48629
1991	35,903	35.5	20.5	42,493	57.2	30.3	1.1	2	2	42210
1992	34,175	32.2	25.7	38,966	52.6	37.3	14.8	30	30	38707
1993	35,427	27.6	27.0	39,559	47.8	39.9	548.9	1,087	1,080	39287
1994	29,339	31.9	30.0	33,046	52.1	42.9	2,968.7	7,100	6,992	32805
1995	28,727	28.9	32.2	32,217	48.3	46.3	19,374.1	47,320	47,317	31634
1996	21,183	35.3	49.2	29,053	49.2	52.3	26,746.4	88,592	72,206	28643
1997	19,335	34.3	45.0	28,295	45.6	57.9	29,182.1	105,896	80,268	28112
1998	17,343	36.2	49.3	22,633	54.0	60.9	32,800.0	132,697	112,791	25360
1993 Q1	2,325	98.0	34.2	4,361	98.7	38.3	8.5	258	152	
1993 Q2	3,624	76.5	35.2	6,123	88.0	39.4	24.2	469	308	
1993 Q3	19,891	12.0	27.0	19,793	23.7	34.0	318.8	1,125	1,254	
1993 Q4	9,588	24.6	22.1	9,282	48.8	53.7	197.3	1,444	1,654	
1994 Q1	2,030	97.9	40.4	3,667	98.6	44.9	267.5	9,246	5,676	
1994 Q2	3,612	74.1	37.1	5,765	87.5	45.6	259.1	5,034	3,498	
1994 Q3	15,829	15.1	29.3	16,214	27.5	41.2	1,726.9	7,654	8,289	
1994 Q4	7,869	29.2	25.8	7,400	55.4	43.5	715.3	6,378	7,523	
1995 Q1	1,848	97.7	44.5	3,381	98.5	49.1	1,103.7	41,914	25,406	
1995 Q2	2,489	95.3	50.3	5,010	95.5	48.7	1,989.0	56,064	30,898	
1995 Q3	18,094	10.2	27.8	17,175	21.0	42.4	8,312.4	32,233	37,667	
1995 Q4	6,296	34.1	34.7	6,651	57.6	49.3	4,969.1	55,377	58,147	
1996 Q1	1,654	97.7	54.8	3,453	99.3	59.6	2,176.6	92,354	49,062	
1996 Q2	2,072	95.3	53.5	4,493	98.1	55.0	3,598.1	121,832	62,329	
1996 Q3	10,749	17.7	55.4	12,493	26.2	45.9	12,969.4	84,655	80,795	
1996 Q4	6,708	27.8	36.5	8,614	38.4	38.8	8,002.3	83,704	72,298	
1997 Q1	1,517	97.9	60.2	2,923	99.8	61.6	2,006.0	92,796	53,417	2324
1997 Q2	1,792	95.2	61.6	3,519	95.7	62.1	3,854.0	150,902	85,246	3229
1997 Q3	9,019	17.7	45.7	14,132	21.6	52.7	13,780.0	107,203	74,370	15235
1997 Q4	7,008	24.8	36.1	7,810	42.6	61.1	9,542.0	95,540	95,092	7324
1998 Q1	1,323	98	66.9	2,556	98.0	66.6	2,110.0	111,901	64,242	2279
1998 Q2	1,715	95.1	65.3	3,365	95.3	65.1	4,990.0	204,200	115,414	3431
1998 Q3	9,126	16.9	40.8	12,246	24.7	57.2	15,986.0	122,911	101,595	15452
1998 Q4	5,180	32.8	54.7	4,465	73.2	64.5	9,714.0	131,582	169,308	4198

Source: TACIS Ukrainian Economic Trends based on Derzhkomstat data

Table 7.2 - Area cultivated for agricultural crops

(by all types of farms, thous. hectares)

	1985	1990	1991	1992	1993	1994	1995	1996	1997	1998
Overall cultivated area	32656	32406	32021	31542	31264	31008	30963	30061	30304	28790
Grain crops	16077	14583	14671	13903	14305	13526	14152	13248	15051	13718
including										
winter wheat	6651	7568	7013	6315	5749	4507	5324	5985	6486	5543
winter rye	652	518	491	499	510	490	609	636	710	736
spring barley	2897	2201	2557	2833	3467	4985	4130	3367	3516	3677
corn	2581	1234	1462	1160	1343	668	1174	703	1678	1030
millet	302	205	188	207	200	212	167	213	230	368
buckwheat	344	350	399	449	448	524	459	472	472	586
rice	34	28	23	24	24	22	22	23	23	22
leguminous crops	1626	1424	1376	1271	1239	1201	1103	865	750	631
Industrial crops	3669	3751	3611	3563	3507	3505	3748	3652	3348	3770
including										
sugar beat	1641	1607	1558	1498	1530	1485	1475	1359	1104	1017
sunflower	1480	1636	1601	1641	1637	1784	2020	2107	2065	2531
flax	211	172	159	156	136	85	98	65	40	31
Potatoes & Vegetables	2208	2073	2184	2369	2165	2096	2165	2135	2185	2066
including										
potatoes	1528	1429	1533	1702	1552	1532	1532	1547	1579	1513
vegetables (excluding seed stock)	499	456	477	500	474	457	503	476	480	459
Fodder cultures	10702	11999	11555	11707	11287	11881	10898	11026	9720	9236
including grasses										
annual	2188	2583	2604	2241	2353	2590	2879	2771	2505	2176
perennial	4156	3986	3921	4132	4077	4101	3906	4079	3842	3752
Area of fallow ground	1656	1427	1425	1411	1355	1522	1570	2279	2084	3022

Source: State Committee of Statistics

Statistical Appendix

Table 7.3 - Harvest area

(by all types of farms, thous. hectare)

	1985	1990	1991	1992	1993	1994	1995	1996	1997	1998
Grain crops	16064	14552	14571	13816	14224	13244	13963	12506	14502	12756
winter wheat	6644	7549	6977	6294	5726	4453	5299	5747	6328	5408
winter rye	649	517	487	498	498	476	604	627	695	700
winter barley	249	526	630	613	770	192	373	263	382	216
spring wheat	15	9	10	13	22	54	108	145	181	233
spring barley	2893	2186	2511	2812	3445	4900	4040	3163	3322	3345
corn (for seeds)	2580	1223	1459	1137	1331	652	1161	671	1637	908
oats	632	486	489	492	510	604	560	482	554	550
millet	298	197	188	192	197	179	158	129	214	266
buckwheat	346	362	414	447	455	494	448	399	448	495
rice	34	28	23	24	23	22	22	23	23	21
leguminous crops	1638	1414	1361	1276	1237	1191	1085	840	691	577
Sugar beat	1636	1605	1549	1485	1519	1467	1448	1260	1005	893
Sunflower (for seeds)	1487	1626	1585	1630	1629	1725	2008	2025	2001	2431
Flax (fibre)	208	169	156	155	127	79	96	55	32	26
Soy	70	88	101	97	70	43	23	16	14	31
Potatoes	1528	1433	1534	1705	1534	1527	1531	1549	1577	1513
Vegetables	499	447	464	482	464	446	489	452	452	446

Source: State Committee of Statictics

Table 7.4 - Yield for agricultural crops

(by all types of farms, metric centner per harvested area hectare)

	1990	1991	1992	1993	1994	1995	1996	1997	1998
Grain*	35.1	26.5	27.9	32.1	26.8	24.3	19.6	24.5	20.8
wheat:									
winter	40.2	30.3	30.9	38.0	30.8	30.1	23.2	28.5	26.9
spring	30.2	21.7	25.8	27.5	25.2	16.9	14.7	19.2	15.7
winter rye	24.3	20.1	23.2	23.7	19.8	20.0	17.4	19.4	16.2
barley:									
winter	37.2	32.0	30.1	32.8	22.7	26.5	15.6	27.7	22.1
spring	33.0	24.0	29.4	32.0	28.7	21.4	16.8	19.1	16.1
corn (for seeds)	38.7	32.6	25.1	28.4	23.6	29.2	27.4	32.6	25.3
oats	26.8	19.3	25.3	29.0	22.9	19.9	15.2	19.2	13.5
millet	17.2	18.0	11.8	14.9	8.8	17.0	8.9	14.6	9.3
buckwheat	11.6	9.0	7.8	11.6	6.9	7.6	7.5	9.0	6.9
rice	42.5	44.3	37.7	28.9	35.5	36.4	35.7	29.0	34.6
leguminous crops	23.1	14.4	23.4	23.4	22.1	14.5	13.4	15.6	13.4
Sugar beat	276	234	194	222	192	205	183	176	174
Sunflower (for seeds)	15.8	14.6	13.0	12.7	9.1	14.2	10.5	11.5	9.3
Flax (fibre)	6.4	6.8	6.8	5.7	6.3	5.0	3.3	2.9	3.6
Soy	11.3	13.4	7.8	8.8	7.2	9.7	9.5	13.6	11.4
Potatoes	117	95	119	137	105	96	119	106	102
Vegetables	149	128	110	130	115	120	112	114	123

* weight after processing

Source: State Committee of Statistics

Statistical Appendix

Table 7.5 - Private farm cultivated area
and basic agricultural crops gross harvest and yield

	1992	1993	1994	1995	1996	1997	1998
Harvested area, thous. hectares							
Grain crops	65.0	243.8	339.3	344.5	283.4	437.5	385.2
Sugar beat	3.5	16.0	20.7	27.9	28.4	19.1	18.9
Sunflower (for seeds)	17.3	44.7	59.0	89.3	88.9	90.0	141.6
Potatoes	1.6	4.6	2.5	2.3	2.7	3.4	2.6
Vegetables	1.7	3.3	2.4	4.3	3.8	5.2	4.6
Gourds	2.2	5.3	1.5	6.6	6.5	7.8	4.7
Gross harvest, thous. tons							
Grain crops	116	572	595	508	329	685	506
Sugar beat	69	390	453	652	565	394	380
Sunflower (for seeds)	19	52	39	86	61	75	91
Potatoes	15	50	20	16	28	25	21
Vegetables	14	31	18	27	24	34	30
Gourds	9	22	5	27	24	18	12
Yield, metric centner per hectare							
Grain crops	17.8	23.5	17.5	14.7	11.6	15.7	13.1
Sugar beat	196	244	219	234	199	206	201
Sunflower (for seeds)	10.8	11.6	6.6	9.7	6.8	8.3	6.1
Potatoes	96	108	80	70	107	73	80
Vegetables	80	92	76	64	63	65	66
Gourds	41	43	33	42	37	23	26

Source: State Committee of Statistics

Table 7.6 - Basis agricultural product output structure, by unit categories

(% of total output)

	State farms					Household plots					Private farms				
	1993	1995	1996	1997	1998	1993	1995	1996	1997	1998	1993	1995	1996	1997	1998
Grain (weight after processing)	93.0	90.4	88.4	88.6	87.9	5.7	8.1	10.3	9.5	10.2	1.3	1.5	1.3	1.9	1.9
Sugar beats	98.3	95.2	93.1	93.4	90.8	0.5	2.6	4.5	4.4	6.7	1.2	2.2	2.4	2.2	2.5
Sunflower seeds	92.6	92.6	92.3	91.6	90.9	4.9	4.4	4.9	5.1	5.1	2.5	3.0	2.8	3.3	4.0
Potatoes	14.5	4.1	4.5	2.8	2.4	85.3	95.8	95.3	97.0	97.5	0.2	0.1	0.2	0.2	0.1
Vegetables	43.0	26.9	18.0	17.3	15.5	56.5	72.7	81.5	82.0	83.9	0.5	0.4	0.5	0.7	0.6
Meat	59.4	48.0	41.6	34.9	..	40.4	51.7	58.1	64.8	..	0.2	0.3	0.3	0.3	..
Milk	63.6	54.4	48.1	39.1	..	36.3	45.3	51.6	60.5	..	0.1	0.3	0.3	0.4	..
Eggs	51.7	44.2	41.8	37.2	..	48.3	55.7	58.1	62.6	..	0.0	0.1	0.1	0.2	..

Source: State Committee of Statistics

Table 7.7 - Gross output of agriculture by form of ownership

(bln UAH)

Year	Collective agricultural enterprises, inter-enterprise service centers, state agricultural enterprises			Personal self-supporting enterprises, including peasants' and leaseholders' farms		
	gross output of agricultural products	including		gross output of agricultural products	including	
		plant-growing products	output of agricultural products		plant-growing products	output of agricultural products
1990	34.3	18.3	16.0	14.3	6.0	8.3
1991	28.4	14.4	13.9	13.8	5.8	8.0
1992	23.4	12.6	10.8	15.3	7.8	7.5
1993	22.8	13.6	9.2	16.5	9.0	7.5
1994	18.1	10.2	7.9	14.7	7.3	7.4
1995	16.4	9.8	6.6	15.2	8.1	7.1
1996	13.0	7.9	5.1	15.6	8.5	7.1
1997	12.4	8.8	3.6	15.7	8.6	7.1

Source: ICPS Analitycal report "Agricultural policy in Ukraine"

Table 7.8 - Profitability of industrial & agricultural production (by sectors)

	1992*	1995	1996
Industry -- total	30.3	16.6	8.9
Including:			
Electric power production	27.5	9.9	12.9
Fuel industry	22.3	20.4	18.3
Ferrous metallurgy	37.1	13	2.3
Chemical and oil-chemical industry	54	19.5	7.4
Machine building and metal works	32.6	24.3	10.4
Timber and pulp-and-paper industry	27.8	18.7	7.7
Construction materials production	22.4	15.4	3.7
Light industry	36.2	17.5	1.6
Food industry	25.3	22.6	12.2
Agriculture**	99.3	10.6	-11.2
Plant-growing	206.5	55.5	29.7
grain crops and leguminous plants	346	85.6	64.6
sunflower	541.6	170.9	53
sugar beet	142.9	31.2	3.8
potato	233.8	34.3	6.4
vegetables	72.8	12.8	-26.5
Stock-breeding	76.1	-16.5	-39.7
meat of all kinds (live weight)	114.3	-19.3	-42.2
beef	131.2	-19.8	-43.1
pork	95.4	-16.7	-42.1
poultry	32	-18.4	-32.8
mutton	119	-31.9	-51.8
eggs	67.8	36.5	-2.4
wool	108	-61.3	-77.8

* Joint ventures exclusive. All kinds of activity.

Presented is ratio of profit to production costs of sold goods.

** Data cover collective agricultural enterprises

Source: ICPS Analitycal report "Agricultural policy in Ukraine"

SECTION 8

Table 8.1 - Branch Composition of Industrial Production*
(current prices, %)

		Electricity	Fuel	Ferrous Metallurgy	Non-Ferrous Metallurgy	Chemicals	Machine Building	Wood & Paper	Construction Materials	Light Industry	Food Industry	Others
1995		12.3	14	23.4	1.6	7.6	15.1	2	3.1	2.7	14.5	3.7
1996		13.8	12.8	23.6	1.5	7.7	13.8	1.9	2.5	2	15.5	4.9
1997		14.1	11.8	25.3	1.5	6.9	14.2	1.7	2.5	1.6	16.2	4.2
1995	I	14.3	15	22.4	1.5	7.6	15.4	2.1	3.5	3.1	13.4	1.5
	II	12.4	14.3	25.9	1.5	7.6	14.2	1.8	3.7	2.2	14.8	1.5
	III	10.9	13.9	23.8	1.9	7.9	15.3	2	4.1	2.5	16.1	1.5
	IV	12.4	12.6	21.3	1.6	7.8	14.8	2	3.3	2.8	19.7	1.6
1996	I	18.5	13.2	22	1.5	7.7	13.8	2.2	2.5	2.2	14.6	1.9
	II	11.4	13	25	1.6	8.5	15	1.9	3.4	2.1	16.3	1.8
	III	10.4	13.1	25	1.6	7.6	14.3	1.9	3.9	1.8	18.3	1.9
	IV	14.4	12	22.6	1.4	6.9	12.7	1.6	3.1	1.9	21.7	1.7
1997	I	18.7	11.5	24.4	1.6	7.5	14	1.8	2.5	1.6	14.5	1.8
	II	12.2	11.7	27.2	1.6	7.6	15.4	1.8	3.4	1.7	15.7	1.7
	III	10.8	12.3	27.6	1.4	7.3	13.6	1.9	3.9	1.7	17.9	1.7
	IV	14.8	11.8	22.5	1.5	6.1	13	1.5	3	1.6	22.9	1.4
1998	I	18.5	13.1	25.1	1.5	6.8	13.2	1.4	2.8	1.4	13.1	3.1
	II	11.8	12.3	26.5	1.5	7.5	14.7	1.4	3.9	1.5	15.5	3.4
1996	Jan	19.5	13.5	22.5	1.4	7.6	13	1.9	2.4	2.1	14.3	1.7
	Feb	19.9	12.8	20.4	1.3	7.7	14.1	2.3	2.4	2.3	14.8	2
	Mar	16.2	13.3	22.9	1.6	7.7	14.2	2.3	2.7	2.3	14.7	1.9
	Apr	13.3	12.7	24.9	1.5	8.9	14.6	1.9	3.1	2.4	14.8	1.9
	May	10.1	13.1	25.2	1.7	8.6	16	1.7	3.4	1.9	16.3	1.9
	Jun	10.6	13.1	24.9	1.7	7.8	14.5	2	3.8	1.9	18	1.7
	Jul	10.4	12.5	25.9	1.7	7.7	13.6	2	4	1.7	18.6	1.9
	Aug	10.6	13.5	25.3	1.5	7.2	14.4	1.9	3.9	1.9	18	2
	Sep	10.3	13.5	23.9	1.6	7.9	15.1	1.9	3.8	1.9	18.4	1.9
	Oct	11.9	11.9	21.8	1.3	6.6	13.2	1.7	3.4	2.1	24.4	1.7
	Nov	14.2	12.1	22.6	1.3	6.8	11.9	1.5	3.1	1.9	23	1.7
	Dec	16.9	11.9	23.4	1.5	7.1	13.1	1.7	2.9	1.9	17.9	1.7
1997	Jan	21	11	23.9	1.6	7.2	13.3	1.5	2.1	1.3	15.1	1.8
	Feb	18.8	11.2	24	1.6	7.5	14.1	1.9	2.5	1.8	14.7	1.9
	Mar	16.6	12.4	25.3	1.6	7.7	14.5	2	2.8	1.7	13.8	1.7
	Apr	14.4	11.7	26.6	1.5	7.9	15.3	1.7	3.2	1.7	14.4	1.7
	May	11.2	11.8	27.6	1.7	7.5	16	1.7	3.4	1.7	15.7	1.8
	Jun	11	11.7	27.5	1.6	7.4	14.8	1.8	3.8	1.6	17.1	1.7
	Jul	10.9	12	27.7	1.4	7.4	13.3	1.9	3.8	1.7	18.2	1.7
	Aug	10.8	12.5	27.6	1.4	7.1	13.8	1.9	4	1.6	17.7	1.7
	Sep	10.6	11.4	26.7	1.8	6.9	15.2	1.8	3.8	1.8	18.6	1.6
	Oct	11.6	10.8	22	1.6	6.3	12.6	1.5	3.2	1.6	27.5	1.6
	Nov	14.7	12	22.6	1.4	5.8	12.3	1.5	3	1.4	23.8	1.4
	Dec	18.3	12.6	22.9	1.4	6.1	14.3	1.7	2.7	1.7	16.7	1.6
1998	Jan	20.2	12.7	24.9	1.5	6.7	12	1.2	2.4	1.3	13.4	3.6
	Feb	19	12.9	24.7	1.5	6.9	13.4	1.5	2.9	1.4	13	2.7
	Apr	13.5	12.4	26.6	1.4	7.5	14.2	1.5	3.6	1.5	14.3	3.3
	May	10.8	12.7	27.6	1.5	7.8	14.1	1.4	3.8	1.4	15.2	3.6
	Jun	11	11.8	25.2	1.5	7.2	15.9	1.4	4.1	1.5	17	3.4

* Excluding small businesses, collective and cooperative enterprises
Source: Derzhkomstat, calculations of the Ministry of Economy

Table 8.2 - Industrial Production*
(1995=100)

	Electricity	Fuel	Ferrous Metallurgy	Non-Ferrous Metallurgy	Chemicals	Machine Building	Wood & Paper	Construction Materials	Light Industry	Food Industry	Total
1995	100	100	100	100	100	100	100	100	100	100	100
1996	90.6	90.6	108.9	110.2	101.6	74.5	79.6	64.7	73.2	93.4	94.3
1997	87.6	96	119.4	112.5	98.1	70.1	75.1	61	68.2	80.8	93
1995 I	123.8	99.7	93.9	97	96.2	111.3	114	100.5	116.7	80.4	100.4
II	90	103.6	111.7	98.4	98.3	93.2	89.5	98.3	86.2	80.5	96
III	78.6	95.6	98.4	102.6	100.8	97.2	99.6	112	91.1	93.4	95
IV	107.6	101.1	96	101.9	104.7	98.2	96.9	89.2	106.1	145.8	108.6
1996 I	120.4	91.5	99.5	100.3	100.8	79.9	92.4	50.3	77	77.5	94.9
II	78.1	88.4	114.3	115.9	112.5	77.5	78.3	71.5	74.9	83.5	92.6
III	69.2	91.7	111.9	112.3	98.9	72.1	77.3	75.7	66.8	79.6	88.6
IV	94.8	91	109.8	112.5	94.2	68.5	70.3	61.3	74	133.2	100.9
1997 I	110.5	93.3	109.4	110.1	95.6	67.6	73.5	40.1	61.2	64.3	89.7
II	75.8	94.9	126.2	109.3	98.4	73.2	72.1	63.1	69.3	66.9	90.1
III	65.7	96.4	124.5	111.2	101.8	68.8	79.6	74.5	72.9	77.3	90.5
IV	98.4	99.1	117	119.5	96.9	70.7	75	66	69.5	114.5	101.4
1998 I	100.9	102.7	114.4	122.1	91.7	68.9	63.4	58.3	64.3	64.3	90.6
II	70.2	96.3	127.9	126.6	110.1	70.9	79.5	68.5	73.5	72.6	91.9
1996 Jan	130.8	94.8	94	108.4	98.4	73.5	80.6	46.5	67.9	74.6	93.7
Feb	113.4	84.2	94.6	84.3	99	80.3	93.2	46.3	77.7	75.4	90.9
Mar	117	95.6	110.1	108.1	105	86	103.4	58	85.5	82.4	100.1
Apr	91.6	89.2	115.9	111.9	115.2	84.2	85.6	68.4	86	85.4	96.8
May	72.7	88.6	118.8	118.2	105.5	74.1	72.9	71.9	70.4	81.1	91.3
Jun	70.1	87.2	108.3	117.6	116.6	74.3	76.5	74.1	68.3	83.9	89.8
Jul	70.5	88.9	114.3	114.5	98.5	69.3	79	81.8	67.6	84	89.7
Aug	67.6	97.4	113.6	111.3	100.4	67.6	77.8	73.9	68.3	77.3	88.6
Sep	69.6	88.7	107.8	111.3	97.9	79.5	75.1	71.5	64.6	77.4	87.5
Oct	81.2	87.3	106	103.4	92.1	72.3	73.9	67.3	80.5	159.6	102.9
Nov	91.1	93.1	107.6	116.9	91.7	63.2	61.1	59.9	69.6	148.1	101.5
Dec	112.1	92.5	115.8	117.1	98.7	70	75.9	56.6	71.7	91.9	98.2
1997 Jan	122.3	83.1	101	109.3	86.7	62.9	59.6	31.2	52.4	65.9	86.7
Feb	104.2	87.1	100.9	104.4	92.4	65	75.4	39	64.2	62.4	85.1
Mar	104.9	109.7	126.4	116.8	107.7	75.1	85.7	50.2	66.8	64.5	97.2
Apr	91.8	96.1	126.1	114.5	104.3	73.5	74.3	56.8	68.5	64.2	92.7
May	69.9	99	128.1	110.2	95.4	75.5	70.9	62.2	67.8	64.8	89.8
Jun	65.7	89.6	124.3	103.2	95.6	70.4	71.1	70.2	71.5	71.7	87.8
Jul	65.9	97.9	126	100.2	105	66.3	80.5	72.2	80.5	76.6	90.7
Aug	63.8	97.2	122.1	106.9	102.6	65.4	77.8	73.4	68	73.6	88.3
Sep	67.7	92.9	125.2	129	100.3	77.3	80.1	75.3	69	82.6	92.7
Oct	84.5	99.1	119.9	129.9	96	72.5	79.2	72.2	70.2	133.4	103.6
Nov	97.3	95.6	113.6	118.6	98.2	67.7	73.7	61.1	63.1	127.1	101.2
Dec	114	98.7	109.4	116.1	102.5	73	77.1	49.3	73.8	85.2	96.2
1998 Jan	113.4	85	106.4	127.1	104.9	59.1	67.8	43.5	56.5	64.1	86.5
Feb	104.2	96.7	104.7	121.2	103.4	64.9	81.9	48.3	63.6	60.9	87.2
Apr	82.9	100.2	127.6	123.8	114.4	70.9	85	65.1	72.1	68.2	93.6
May	65.8	95.6	129.5	128.5	113.1	68.1	76.2	68.5	71.4	71.6	90.9
Jun	61.8	95	124.3	127.6	102.6	73.7	77.3	71.7	76.5	78.2	91

* Excluding small businesses, collective and cooperative enterprises

Source: State Statistics Committee, Ministry of Economy

Table 8.3 - Industrial Production*
(% change on previous period)

	Electricity	Fuel	Ferrous Metallurgy	Non-Ferrous Metallurgy	Chemicals	Machine Building	Wood & Paper	Construction Materials	Light Industry	Food Industry	Total
1995											
1996	-6.9	-6.7	11.9	8	-3.4	-26.1	-18.6	-34.2	-24.6	-7.2	-5.1
1997	-2.6	4.5	7.7	2.7	-0.6	-3.6	-5.1	-7.9	-7.9	-14.6	-1.8
1995 I											
II	-25.9	0.3	21	-6.3	-4.1	-14.3	-22.6	-0.9	-24.9	6.4	-3.5
III	-8.9	-0.5	4.1	4.1	3.3	2	17.5	17.4	11.7	20.5	-0.1
IV	36.8	-2.5	-0.6	-0.6	3.8	0.9	-2.7	-20.3	16.4	51	14.2
1996 I	11.9	-9.4	3.7	-1.6	-4.6	-18.7	-4.7	-43.8	-27.4	-49.9	-12.6
II	-35.1	-3.5	15	15.6	4	-3.2	-15.2	42.4	-2.9	10.9	-2.5
III	-11.5	3.7	-2.1	-3.1	-7.5	-7	-1.3	6	-10.8	-4	-4.3
IV	36.5	-0.8	-2	0.1	-4.8	-5.2	-9.1	-19.1	10.5	76.9	13.8
1997 I	17.5	1.6	-1.5	-2	2.4	0.2	4.6	-34.4	-16.7	-55.7	-11.4
II	-31.4	1.9	15.4	-0.8	3.3	8.2	-2	57.2	13.3	6	0.6
III	-13.2	1.3	-1.4	2.5	4.3	-4.7	10.2	16.8	4.8	15.3	0.5
IV	49.8	1.9	-8.2	8.5	-3.7	2	-3.5	-17.3	-4.8	54.8	10.8
1998 I	12.5	-1.4	-0.4	4.4	7.9	-8.5	2.8	-24.3	-7.6	-50	-9.6
II	-35.6	0.7	3.7	0.1	0.7	7.3	0.4	50.1	14.3	18.3	-1.3
1996 Jan	5.8	-4.1	-6	19.3	-3.6	-25.7	-17.3	-37.2	-23.7	-24.2	-9.5
Feb	-13.3	-11.2	0.6	-22.2	0	9.3	15.6	-0.4	14.5	-0.9	-3
Mar	3.1	13.5	16.4	28.2	6.8	7	11	25.2	10	11.5	10.1
Apr	-21.7	-6.6	5.3	3.6	9.1	-2.1	-17.2	18	0.6	4.6	-3.3
May	-20.6	-0.7	2.5	5.6	-8.2	-12	-14.8	5.1	-18.2	-4.1	-5.7
Jun	-3.6	-1.6	-8.8	-0.5	-10.6	0.3	4.8	3.1	-3	5.3	-1.7
Jul	0.6	1.9	5.6	-2.7	2.4	-6.8	3.3	10.3	-1	0.9	-0.1
Aug	-4.1	9.6	-0.6	-2.8	2	-2.4	-1.5	-9.6	1	-9.8	-1.2
Sep	2.9	-9	-5.2	0	-2.6	17.6	-3.4	-3.3	-5.5	-0.9	-1.2
Oct	16.6	-1.5	-1.7	-7.1	-5.9	-9.1	-1.7	-5.9	24.7	122.7	17.5
Nov	12.2	6.6	1.5	13	-0.4	-12.6	-17.3	-10.9	-13.6	-6.7	-1.3
Dec	23.1	-0.7	7.7	0.2	7.6	10.7	24.2	-5.6	3.1	-40.8	-3.3
1997 Jan	9.1	-10.2	-12.8	-6.7	-12.1	-10.2	-21.5	-44.8	-26.9	-32.1	-11.7
Feb	-14.8	5.1	1.3	-4.5	7.9	3.6	26.6	24.8	22.5	-4.9	-1.8
Mar	0.7	25.9	24.8	11.9	16.6	15.5	13.6	28.8	4	3.2	14.2
Apr	-12.5	-12.4	-0.3	-2	-3.2	-2.1	-13.3	13.2	2.5	-1.4	-4.6
May	-23.9	3	1.6	-3.7	-8.5	2.8	-4.5	9.4	-1	5.1	-3.2
Jun	-6	-9.5	-3	-6.4	0.2	-6.8	0.2	13	5.5	10.6	-2.2
Jul	0.4	9.3	1.4	-2.9	9.8	-5.8	13.3	2.8	12.6	7.4	3.3
Aug	-3.3	-0.7	-3.1	6.7	-2.2	-1.4	-3.4	1.6	-15.5	-7.3	-2.6
Sep	6.2	-4.4	2.5	20.7	-2.3	18.1	3	2.6	1.4	12.2	5
Oct	24.8	6.6	-4.2	0.7	-4.3	-6.1	-1.1	-4.1	1.7	73.2	11.7
Nov	15.1	-3.5	-5.3	-8.7	2.3	-6.7	-6.9	-15.4	-10.1	-4.5	-2.3
Dec	17.2	3.2	-3.7	-2.1	4.4	7.9	4.5	-19.2	17	-37.7	-5
1998 Jan	1.1	-14.5	-1.5	9.9	1.5	-19.4	-12.5	-23.1	-22.8	-23.8	-9.9
Feb	-8	13.2	-0.3	-4.6	-2.1	8.7	20	16.7	12.5	-5	0.8
Mar	4.9	14.8	17.7	7.8	11.9	13	8.6	26.5	9.7	11.8	12.5
Apr	-24.1	-9	-5.7	-5.4	-1.9	-3.5	-3.8	14.1	2.2	2.6	-7.1
May	-20.7	-4.5	1.5	3.8	-1.1	-3.9	-10.4	8	-0.9	7.6	-2.7
Jun	-6.2	1.5	-5.7	-0.7	-9.6	8.1	1.4	8.1	6.4	10.6	-0.2

* Excluding small - size enterprises and ancillary industry

** Including medical industry

Source: State Statistics Committee, Ministry of Economy

Table 8.4 - Industrial Production*
(% change on a year earlier)

	Electricity	Fuel	Ferrous Metallurgy	Non-Ferrous Metallurgy	Chemicals **	Machine Building **	Wood & Paper	Construction Materials	Light Industry	Food Industry	Total
1996	-6.9	-6.7	11.9	8	-3.4	-26.1	-18.6	-34.2	-24.6	-7.2	-5.1
1997	-2.6	4.5	7.7	2.7	-0.6	-3.6	-5.1	-7.9	-7.9	-14.6	-1.8
1996 I	3.5	-4.3	12.8	-4.7	-1.9	-28.3	-15.7	-47.9	-29.1	-3	-3.6
II	-9.4	-7.9	7.2	17.6	6.4	-19	-7.6	-25.1	-8.4	1.1	-2.5
III	-12	-4.1	13.9	9.5	-4.7	-26.1	-22.4	-32.4	-26.8	-19.5	-6.7
IV	-12.2	-10.1	14.5	10.3	-12.6	-30.6	-27.6	-31.3	-30.5	-5.6	-7.2
1997 I	-7.5	0.9	8.6	9.9	-6.1	-13.8	-20.3	-20	-17.3	-16.5	-6
II	-2.3	6.4	9.2	-5.8	-6.8	-3.7	-7.9	-11.6	-5.8	-20.2	-3.1
III	-4.3	3.9	9.9	-0.4	5.1	-0.9	2.8	-2.5	9.4	-4.1	2.1
IV	4.8	6.7	2.9	8.1	6.3	5.3	9.1	-0.4	-5.8	-16.1	-0.6
1998 I	0.4	3.4	4.1	15.2	12	-3.8	25.7	14.9	4.4	-3.3	1.7
II	-5.8	2.4	-6.5	16.2	9.2	-4.7	17.8	9.6	5.2	7.4	-0.4
1996 Jan	3.8	3.2	11.5	-2.8	2.1	-29.8	-26.1	-46.8	-38.7	-7.4	-3.6
Feb	3.7	-12.7	15.8	-12.5	-1	-23.3	-15.7	-49.5	-28	-3.5	-3.4
Mar	3	-3.9	11.2	-0.1	-6	-30.9	-5.2	-47.2	-22	1.8	-3.8
Apr	-5.6	-6.3	11.6	5.6	11.4	-19.7	4.3	-26.7	-1.5	14.7	0.6
May	-12.7	-12.5	8.5	19.9	5.2	-15.2	-13.3	-19.9	-7.6	-3	-4.2
Jun	-10.9	-5.1	0.8	28.9	2.5	-21	-13.4	-28	-15.9	-6.5	-4.3
Jul	-11.6	-13.4	9.5	8.8	-4.4	-27.7	-19.2	-26.7	-13.8	-6.4	-5.7
Aug	-13.7	3	15.4	11.9	-1.4	-28.7	-19.9	-35.5	-16.1	-18.2	-5.5
Sep	-10.8	-1	17.3	8	-8	-21.7	-27.5	-3.5	-43.1	-31.7	-9
Oct	-10.9	-16.6	9.4	-3.4	-18.9	-28.6	-27.6	-36.6	-36.7	-9.4	-9.5
Nov	-15.7	-6.5	18.5	8.1	-13.1	-33.2	-33.2	-31.7	-32.4	-3.8	-6.7
Dec	-9.4	-6.5	15.9	28.9	-5.3	-29.4	-22	-23.6	-19.5	-1.8	-5.1
1997 Jan	-6.5	-12.5	7.5	0.8	-13.8	-14.6	-26.2	-32.2	-22.7	-12.1	-7.5
Feb	-7.6	2.5	6.1	23.6	-7	-16.6	-19	-15.8	-14.1	-15.5	-6.7
Mar	-9.5	13.7	13.6	8	1.8	-11.5	-17.3	-13.3	-18.5	-21.8	-3.3
Apr	0.8	7	7.5	2.1	-9.6	-10.4	-13.2	-16.9	-17.2	-26.2	-4.6
May	-3.3	10.7	6.7	-6.9	-10.1	3.9	-2.7	-13.6	-2.5	-19.3	-1.8
Jun	-5.6	1.8	13.4	-12.5	0.6	-4.1	-7.1	-5.4	5.6	-15.2	-2.6
Jul	-5.8	9.3	8.8	-12.6	8	-3.4	2.1	-11.9	20.1	-9.6	0.8
Aug	-5	-1.1	6.2	-3.9	3.5	-2.3	0.1	-0.6	0.4	-7.2	-0.5
Sep	-2	3.9	15	16	3.8	2.5	6.7	5.4	7.5	5	6.2
Oct	4.8	12.5	11.7	25.5	5.7	3	7.3	7.1	-12.1	-18.4	0.6
Nov	7.7	1.9	4.5	1.4	8.4	8	20.8	1.9	-8.8	-16.4	-0.5
Dec	2.2	5.9	-6.6	-0.8	5.2	5.3	1.7	-12.8	3.4	-11.8	-2.2
1998 Jan	-5.8	1.8	7.7	16.8	21.6	-6.3	35.8	21.6	8.6	-5.5	0.8
Feb	1.8	9.6	6.4	16.6	10.3	-1.6	26.6	13.6	-0.3	-6.1	3
Mar	6	-0.2	-0.1	12.4	5.8	-3.8	18.4	11.6	5.3	1.8	1.5
Apr	-8	3.7	-5.5	8.4	7.2	-5.1	21.3	12.4	4.9	5.9	-1.3
May	-4.1	-3.9	-5.6	16.9	15.9	-11.3	16.5	11	5	7.8	-0.9
Jun	-4.4	7.8	-8.3	24	4.5	2.8	15.4	6.2	5.9	7.9	1.1

* Excluding small - size enterprises and ancillary industry

** Including medical industry

Source: State Statistics Committee, Ministry of Economy

Table 8.5 - Ukraine: Power Sector Financial Recovery Plan

January 25, 1999

Performance Indicators	97Q3 Actual	Dec 1997 Actual	97Q4 Actual	Jan 1998 Actual	Feb 1998 Actual	March 1998 Actual	98Q1 Actual	April 1998 Actual	May 1998 Actual	June 1998 Actual	98Q2 Actual	July 1998 Actual	Aug 1998 Actual	Sept 1998 Actual	98Q3 Actual	Oct 1998 Actual	Nov 1998 Actual	Dec 1998 Actual	98Q4 Target	99Q1 Target	99Q2 Target
1. Oblenergo electricity collection rate to transit accounts, excl Kievenergo [% of amount billed]																					
1.1 Total	93.9	108.2	100.4	43.2	84.0	72.9	66.1	88.4	101.0	122.8	103.0	87.2	99.0	79.6	88.2	41.2	44.2	99.8	104	106	106
1.2 Cash	10.2	12.6	10.6	9.4	11.6	10.3	10.4	12.3	13.2	11.1	12.2	11.3	9.2	10.0	10.2	7.0	6.3	6.1	22	25	30
2. Energoatom collection rate [% of amount billed]																					
2.1 Total	106.5	122.1	89.7	43.9	65.4	79.1	79.1	110.0	91.0	134.0	110.5	99.2	98.3	119.7	107.0	55.1	73.2	134.1	104	106	106
2.2 Cash	9.3	7.5	7.2	5.8	5.7	7.9	7.9	8.4	8.3	6.0	7.7	6.3	3.6	4.5	4.6	4.5	4.3	3.6	22	25	30
3. Four fossil generators collection rate [% of amount billed]																					
3.1 Total	87.9	112.1	88.2	61	138.3	78.2	90.6	116.1	95.1	94.5	101.2	76.8	88.6	95.6	86.8	27.2	27.9	65.1	104	106	106
3.2 Cash	7.9	8.7	8.2	7	5.6	6.3	6.3	7.2	9.6	6.5	7.7	5.7	5.7	5.7	5.7	3.9	3.5	4	22	25	30
4. Retail tariff adherence [actual tariff as % of market tariff]																			100	100	100
5. Fuel Cost, 4 Fossil Generators [1997$/MWh sold]	5																		24	24	22
6. After-tax profit of 4 fossil generators [1997$/quarter. million]			-7				-6				2.5								30	50	50
7a. Oblenergo debt to Energomarket [1997$ million]	1,368	1,347	1,347	1,450	1,484	1,580	1,580	1,604	1,555	1,508	1,508	1,486	1,412	959	959	1,117	1,292	1,290	1,227	1,120	1,006
7b. Oblenergo debt to Energomarket [Hv million]		2,506	2,506	2,872	2,967	3,160	3,160	3,208	3,203	3,112	3,112	3,171	3,177	3,262	3,262	3,828	4,426	4,421			
8. Oblenergo debt to Energomarket [days, annual]		120	120	129	132	141	141	143	139	134	134	132	126	85	85	100	115	115	112	102	92
9a. Energomarket debt to generators [1997$ million]	1,321	1,338	1,338	1,438	1,416	1,498	1,498	1,463	1,444	1,403	1,403	1,394	1,348	872	872	1,061	1,251	1,291	1,227	1,120	1,006
9b. Energomarket debt to generators [Hv million]		2,488	2,488	2,696	2,832	2,996	2,996	2,926	2,974	2,896	2,896	2,975	3,033	2,964	2,964	3,635	4,287	4,425			
Information Indicators																					
10. Wholesale Purchase Price (from Fossil Generators) [US cents/kWh]	3.22	3.15	3.18	3.15	3.00	3.24	3.13	3.21	3.39	3.37	3.32	3.48	3.34	3.30	3.38	3.62	3.41	3.25			
11. Energoatom Sale Price [US cents/kWh]	2.4	2.4	2.4	2.7	2.7	2.7	2.7	2.7	2.7	2.7	2.7	2.7	2.7	2.7	2.7	2.7	2.7	2.54			
12. Hydro Sale Price [US cents/kWh]	0.96	0.96	0.96	0.96	0.96	0.96	0.96	0.96	0.96	0.96	0.96	0.96	0.96	0.92	0.94	0.51	0.28	0.32			
13. Wholesale Price (to Suppliers) [US cents/kWh]	2.93	2.93	2.93	2.89	2.89	2.96	2.90	2.91	2.67	2.66	2.75	2.90	2.79	2.68	2.80	2.84	2.78	2.65			
14. Average retail tariff (NERC planned) [US cents/kWh]	3.76	3.76	3.76	3.82	3.85	4.12	3.91	3.95	4.15	4.38	4.14	4.23	4.26	3.78	4.08	3.84	3.76	3.79			

Note: The payments collection benchmarks for Energoatom are to be finalized following EBRD's Operation Commission review of the proposed Khmelnitsky 2/Rovno 4 nuclear completion project.

Source: the World Bank

Table 9.1 - Consumer Price Index

(December 1991=100)

	1992	1993	1994	1995	1996	1997	1998
January	385	3,638	256,770	1,308,311	3,326,109	4,341,496	4,738,637
February	444	4,686	289,123	1,545,115	3,572,241	4,393,593	4,748,114
March	498	5,722	305,603	1,721,258	3,679,408	4,397,987	4,757,610
April	536	7,072	323,939	1,821,091	3,767,714	4,433,171	4,819,459
May	613	9,024	340,784	1,904,862	3,794,088	4,468,636	4,819,459
June	775	15,494	354,075	1,996,295	3,797,882	4,473,105	4,819,459
July	947	21,319	361,510	2,100,102	3,801,680	4,477,578	4,776,084
August	1,025	25,945	370,909	2,196,707	4,018,376	4,477,578	4,785,636
September	1,134	46,779	397,986	2,508,639	4,098,744	4,531,309	4,967,490
October	1,274	77,701	487,931	2,736,925	4,160,225	4,572,091	5,275,475
November	1,555	112,899	840,704	2,906,615	4,210,147	4,613,240	5,433,739
December	2,101	215,411	1,079,464	3,040,319	4,248,039	4,677,825	5,613,052

percentage change on same month of the previous year

	1992	1993	1994	1995	1996	1997	1998
January	...	844.5	6957.7	409.5	154.2	30.5	9.1
February	...	955.1	6070.0	434.4	131.2	23.0	8.1
March	...	1049.2	5241.3	463.2	113.8	19.5	8.2
April	...	1220.1	4480.7	462.2	106.9	17.7	8.7
May	...	1372.4	3676.6	459.0	99.2	17.8	7.9
June	...	1898.5	2185.3	463.8	90.2	17.8	7.7
July	...	2152.2	1595.7	480.9	81.0	17.8	6.7
August	...	2430.8	1329.6	492.2	82.9	11.4	6.9
September	...	4025.8	750.8	530.3	63.4	10.6	9.6
October	...	5996.9	528.0	460.9	52.0	9.9	15.4
November	...	7161.3	644.7	245.7	44.8	9.6	17.8
December	...	10156.0	401.1	181.7	39.7	10.1	20.0

percentage change on the previous month

	1992	1993	1994	1995	1996	1997	1998
January	285.2	73.2	19.2	21.2	9.4	2.2	1.3
February	15.3	28.8	12.6	18.1	7.4	1.2	0.2
March	12.1	22.1	5.7	11.4	3.0	0.1	0.2
April	7.6	23.6	6.0	5.8	2.4	0.8	1.3
May	14.4	27.6	5.2	4.6	0.7	0.8	0.0
June	26.5	71.7	3.9	4.8	0.1	0.1	0.0
July	22.1	37.6	2.1	5.2	0.1	0.1	-0.9
August	8.3	21.7	2.6	4.6	5.7	0.0	0.2
September	10.6	80.3	7.3	14.2	2.0	1.2	3.8
October	12.4	66.1	22.6	9.1	1.5	0.9	6.2
November	22.0	45.3	72.3	6.2	1.2	0.9	3.0
December	35.1	90.8	28.4	4.6	0.9	1.4	3.3

Source: Presidential Administration

Table 9.2 - Consumer Price Index by Components (%)

Year	Month	Month-on-month change				Cumulative change since December of the previous year			
		composite	food products	non-food products	paid services	composite	food products	non-food products	paid services
1991						290.0	331.0	248.0	265.0
1992						2,000.0	1,692.0	2,013.0	3,489.0
1993						10,156.0	12,078.0	11,101.0	9,106.0
1994						401.0	373.2	373.1	781.4
1995	January	21.2	23.2	18.8	21.0	21.2	23.2	18.8	21.0
	February	18.1	11.9	10.3	70.0	43.1	37.9	31.0	105.7
	March	11.4	10.0	9.7	18.6	59.5	51.6	43.7	144.0
	April	5.8	4.8	4.9	10.2	68.7	58.9	50.8	168.8
	May	4.6	4.6	3.2	7.1	76.5	66.2	55.6	187.9
	June	4.8	1.0	3.4	16.9	84.9	67.9	60.9	236.6
	July	5.2	-0.1	3.6	19.5	94.6	67.7	66.7	302.2
	August	4.6	4.3	6.5	3.4	103.5	74.9	77.5	315.9
	September	14.2	11.3	8.4	24.6	132.4	94.7	92.4	418.2
	October	9.1	12.0	5.8	6.1	153.5	118.1	103.6	449.8
	November	6.2	7.9	4.7	4.1	169.3	135.3	113.2	472.4
	December	4.6	6.3	3.2	2.1	181.7	150.1	120.0	484.4
1996	January	9.4	6.8	3.1	19.3	9.4	6.8	3.1	19.3
	February	7.4	4.4	3.1	15.7	17.5	11.5	6.3	38.0
	March	3.0	2.3	2.4	4.5	21.0	14.1	8.8	44.2
	April	2.4	1.4	1.5	4.4	23.9	15.7	10.5	50.6
	May	0.7	-0.2	1.1	2.4	24.8	15.4	11.7	54.2
	June	0.1	-1.0	1.0	1.4	24.9	14.3	12.8	56.4
	July	0.1	-2.5	0.8	4.7	25.0	11.4	13.7	63.7
	August	5.7	-1.7	0.8	24.0	32.2	9.5	14.6	103.0
	September	2.0	2.4	1.1	2.0	34.8	12.2	15.9	107.1
	October	1.5	2.0	1.1	1.1	36.8	14.4	17.2	109.3
	November	1.2	1.6	0.8	0.8	38.5	16.2	18.1	111.0
	December	0.9	1.0	0.6	0.8	39.7	17.4	18.8	112.7
1997	January	2.2	3.4	0.5	1.5	2.2	3.4	0.5	1.5
	February	1.2	1.8	0.4	0.7	3.4	5.3	0.9	2.2
	March	0.1	-0.4	0.3	0.6	3.5	4.8	1.2	2.8
	April	0.8	1.1	0.2	0.6	4.4	6.0	1.4	3.4
	May	0.8	1.3	0.1	0.4	5.2	7.4	1.5	3.9
	June	0.1	-0.2	0.1	0.6	5.3	7.2	1.6	4.5
	July	0.1	-0.2	0.1	0.7	5.4	6.9	1.7	5.2
	August	0.0	-0.3	0.1	0.3	5.4	6.6	1.8	5.5
	September	1.2	2.1	0.2	0.3	6.7	8.9	2.0	5.8
	October	0.9	1.2	0.3	0.7	7.6	10.2	2.3	6.6
	November	0.9	1.3	0.5	0.3	8.6	11.6	2.8	6.9
	December	1.4	2.2	0.1	0.9	10.1	14.1	2.9	7.9
1998	January	1.3	1.9	0.1	1.0	1.3	1.9	0.1	1.0
	February	0.2	0.3	0.0	0.1	1.5	2.2	0.1	1.1
	March	0.2	0.3	0.0	0.1	1.7	2.5	0.1	1.2
	April	1.3	1.9	0.1	1.1	3.0	4.5	0.2	2.3
	May	0.0	-1.2	0.0	2.1	3.0	3.2	0.2	4.5
	June	0.0	-1.2	0.0	2.1	3.0	2.0	0.2	6.7
	July	-0.9	-2.3	0.1	0.8	2.1	-0.4	0.3	7.5
	August	0.2	-0.1	0.3	0.6	2.3	-0.5	0.6	8.2
	September	3.8	4.0	6.1	1.9	6.2	3.5	6.7	10.2
	October	6.2	6.7	12.0	1.4	12.8	10.4	19.5	11.8
	November	3.0	4.3	2.9	0.9	16.2	15.2	23.0	12.8
	December	3.3	6.0	0.9	0.2	20.0	22.1	24.1	13.0

Source: Presidential Administration

Table 9.3 - Producer Price Index

(December 1993=100)

	1991*	1992*	1993*	1994	1995	1996	1997	1998
January	...	...	...	134.1	1,129.2	2,458.5	2,799.4	2,951.3
February	...	...	...	162.7	1,257.9	2,529.8	2,810.6	2,977.9
March	...	...	...	176.2	1,374.9	2,603.2	2,827.5	2,998.7
April	...	...	...	185.7	1,445.0	2,642.2	2,852.9	3,013.7
May	...	...	...	190.1	1,547.6	2,663.3	2,861.5	3,013.7
June	...	...	...	195.8	1,680.7	2,674.0	2,872.9	3,019.7
July	...	...	...	204.5	1,753.0	2,690.0	2,884.4	3,037.8
August	...	...	...	228.8	1,866.9	2,700.8	2,884.4	3,074.3
September	...	...	...	258.1	2,051.7	2,727.8	2,887.3	3,363.3
October	...	...	...	310.7	2,224.0	2,730.5	2,919.1	3,723.2
November	...	...	...	650.3	2,317.4	2,763.3	2,913.3	3,853.5
December	...	...	...	874.0	2,377.7	2,788.2	2,927.9	3,965.3

percentage change on same month of the previous year

	1991*	1992*	1993*	1994	1995	1996	1997	1998
January	...	...	...	5902.3	742.1	117.7	13.9	5.4
February	...	...	...	5927.4	673.1	101.1	11.1	6.0
March	...	...	...	5749.1	680.3	89.3	8.6	5.9
April	...	...	...	5120.1	678.1	82.8	8.0	5.5
May	...	...	...	3412.1	714.1	72.1	7.4	5.2
June	...	...	...	1802.9	758.4	59.1	7.4	5.1
July	...	...	...	1416.5	757.2	53.4	7.2	5.1
August	...	...	...	1175.9	716.0	44.6	6.8	6.4
September	...	...	...	715.4	694.9	33.0	5.8	16.3
October	...	...	...	631.6	615.8	22.8	6.9	27.3
November	...	...	...	1050.4	256.4	19.2	5.4	32.1
December	...	...	...	774.0	172.0	17.3	5.0	35.1

percentage change on the previous month

	1991	1992	1993	1994	1995	1996	1997	1998
January	61.8	752.3	118.2	34.1	29.2	3.4	0.4	0.8
February	6.3	29.4	20.8	21.3	11.4	2.9	0.4	0.9
March	4.3	14.9	11.6	8.3	9.3	2.9	0.6	0.7
April	7.6	19.3	18.1	5.4	5.1	1.5	0.9	0.5
May	3.8	8.4	52.2	2.4	7.1	0.8	0.3	0.0
June	1.8	17.4	90.1	3.0	8.6	0.4	0.4	0.2
July	4.5	-0.8	31.0	4.4	4.3	0.6	0.4	0.6
August	3.3	9.0	33.0	11.9	6.5	0.4	0.0	1.2
September	3.1	8.6	76.5	12.8	9.9	1.0	0.1	9.4
October	4.5	25.1	34.2	20.4	8.4	0.1	1.1	10.7
November	9.1	17.8	33.1	109.3	4.2	1.2	-0.2	3.5
December	1.6	27.2	76.9	34.4	2.6	0.9	0.5	2.9

percentage change in quarterly average on the previous quarter

	1991	1992	1993	1994	1995	1996	1997	1998
Q1					105.0	9.7	1.9	1.9
Q2	17.0	52.0	142.5	20.9	24.2	5.1	1.8	1.3
Q3	6.4	11.3	227.4	20.9	21.4	1.7	0.8	4.7
Q4	18.6	44.1	215.6	165.5	22.0	2.0	1.2	21.8
Annual average (%)		2491.7	4698.3	1134.5	488.9	52.0	7.7	13.0

* Before 1994, PPI was calculated by Zaurbeck - Carly formula

Source: Presidential Administration

Table 9.4 - Producer Price Index by Components

percentage change on the previous month

	Total			Energy industry			Fuel industry			Ferrous metallurgy			Chemical industry			Petrochemical industry		
	1996	1997	1998	1996	1997	1998	1996	1997	1998	1996	1997	1998	1996	1997	1998	1996	1997	1998
January	3.4	0.4	0.8	3.6	0.4	3.2	-0.2	0.6	2.1	3.6	0.5	0.6	4.6	-0.1	-0.2	0.0	0.6	-0.1
February	2.9	0.4	0.9	4.4	-2.4	0.3	1.7	-1.9	1.6	3.3	-0.2	2.2	5.0	-0.1	1.4	3.1	2.9	-12.6
March	2.9	0.6	0.7	1.1	1.6	0.0	4.0	1.3	0.3	1.8	-0.9	2.0	2.9	-0.3	2.2	1.7	-0.4	0.1
April	1.5	0.9	0.5	2.1	3.1	0.8	0.1	1.0	0.2	0.7	1.1	-0.1	1.2	-2.1	0.8	0.4	0.7	2.4
May	0.8	0.3	0.0	-1.1	0.2	-0.4	0.9	2.1	-0.5	0.8	-0.4	-0.4	1.4	-0.6	0.4	0.7	-0.1	-0.1
June	0.4	0.4	0.2	3.0	-0.3	1.3	-1.0	-0.3	0.0	0.3	-1.2	0.1	0.0	0.2	0.0	4.4	0.2	0.2
July	0.6	0.4	0.6	-0.1	0.8	1.8	0.2	-0.3	0.3	-0.2	-0.1	1.0	1.1	0.3	1.0	5.3	4.5	0.0
August	0.4	0.0	1.2	2.6	-2.2	3.3	-1.1	-0.4	0.9	-0.4	0.7	1.2	0.3	-0.3	1.6	0.0	0.0	0.3
September	1.0	0.1	9.4	1.7	-0.3	20.4	1.2	0.6	11.6	0.1	-0.7	13.9	0.6	-0.1	12.6	-0.1	0.2	0.7
October	0.1	1.2	10.7	-3.3	2.1	19.5	3.1	0.2	8.8	-1.0	0.4	17.0	0.2	0.2	8.5	0.4	0.0	10.0
November	1.2	-0.2	3.5	8.1	-0.9	4.3	-0.9	1.0	3.4	0.3	-0.4	1.3	1.3	-2.0	3.7	-0.1	0.0	-1.7
December	0.9	0.5	2.9	1.9	0.0	0.2	0.0	0.6	2.7	2.0	0.9	4.6	0.4	0.6	4.4	-0.6	0.0	-0.2

percentage changes on the previous month

	Machine building			Wood & paper industry			Construction materials			Light industry			Food industry[1]			CPI		
	1996	1997	1998	1996	1997	1998	1996	1997	1998	1996	1997	1998	1996	1997	1998	1996	1997	1998
January	6.6	0.7	0.3	6.2	0.8	0.1	4.1	0.2	0.0	2.5	0.8	-0.2	0.2	-1.1	-0.3	9.4	2.2	1.3
February	3.5	3.4	0.8	3.3	0.5	0.2	2.5	0.2	0.2	1.6	0.8	0.0	-1.0	1.1	0.2	7.4	1.2	0.2
March	5.3	1.3	0.4	2.9	0.4	-0.3	4.3	0.1	0.4	3.5	0.4	0.3	0.2	0.3	0.1	3.0	0.1	0.2
April	3.0	1.0	0.5	3.5	1.0	0.0	1.6	0.3	-0.1	2.1	-0.9	1.2	1.3	0.2	0.8	2.4	0.8	1.3
May	1.1	0.8	0.6	1.5	-0.1	0.4	3.6	0.4	0.2	0.5	-1.2	1.4	0.1	0.3	0.7	0.7	0.8	0.0
June	-1.0	-0.2	0.2	-0.4	1.0	0.3	0.7	0.1	0.3	0.6	-0.7	0.1	0.3	1.1	0.7	0.1	0.1	0.0
July	1.1	0.6	-0.3	1.3	0.3	-0.1	1.2	-1.1	0.6	1.6	0.1	-0.1	0.7	2.3	0.0	0.1	0.1	-0.9
August	1.4	0.5	1.3	-0.3	0.1	0.8	0.6	1.1	0.3	0.0	0.2	0.3	0.5	0.7	0.6	5.7	0.0	0.2
September	1.2	1.2	3.9	2.0	-0.3	2.2	1.8	-0.3	2.3	1.0	0.8	2.3	1.2	-0.4	3.8	2.0	1.2	3.8
October	1.0	0.5	6.8	2.1	-0.2	6.9	-1.5	0.5	11.9	0.7	0.5	10.1	-0.6	5.9	2.4	1.5	0.9	6.2
November	0.9	0.7	4.5	-0.2	0.0	3.8	1.2	-0.3	4.8	2.3	0.4	7.8	-1.5	-0.7	0.6	1.2	0.9	3.0
December	0.9	0.6	2.7	0.2	0.1	3.1	0.1	0.4	3.2	-0.1	0.5	1.2	-1.5	-0.4	1.5	0.9	1.4	3.3

[1] Excluding fish, meat, oil & dairy industries

Source: Presidential Administration

Table 9.4 – Producer Price Index by Components (continued)

percentage change on December of the previous year

	Total			Energy industry			Fuel industry			Ferrous metallurgy			Chemical industry			Petrochemical industry		
	1996	1997	1998	1996	1997	1998	1996	1997	1998	1996	1997	1998	1996	1997	1998	1996	1997	1998
January	3.4	0.4	0.8	3.6	0.4	3.2	-0.2	0.6	2.1	3.6	0.5	0.6	4.6	-0.1	-0.2	0.0	0.6	-0.1
February	6.4	0.8	1.7	8.2	-2.0	3.5	1.5	-1.3	3.7	7.0	0.3	2.8	9.8	-0.2	1.2	3.1	3.5	-12.7
March	9.5	1.4	2.4	9.3	-0.4	3.5	5.6	0.0	4.0	8.9	-0.6	4.9	13.0	-0.5	3.4	4.9	3.1	-12.6
April	11.1	2.3	2.9	11.6	2.6	4.4	5.7	1.0	4.2	9.7	0.5	4.8	14.4	-2.6	4.2	5.3	3.8	-10.5
May	12.0	2.6	2.9	10.4	2.8	4.0	6.6	3.1	3.7	10.6	0.1	4.4	16.0	-3.2	4.6	6.0	3.7	-10.6
June	12.5	3.0	3.1	13.7	2.5	5.3	5.5	2.7	3.7	10.9	1.3	4.5	16.0	-2.9	4.6	10.7	4.0	-10.4
July	13.1	3.4	3.7	13.6	3.4	7.2	5.8	2.4	4.0	10.7	1.2	5.5	17.2	-2.7	5.6	16.5	8.7	-10.4
August	13.6	3.4	4.9	16.6	1.1	10.7	4.6	2.0	4.9	10.3	1.9	6.8	17.6	-3.0	7.3	16.5	8.6	-10.1
September	14.7	3.5	14.8	18.6	0.8	33.3	5.8	2.6	17.1	10.4	1.2	21.6	18.3	-3.0	20.8	16.4	8.8	-9.5
October	14.8	4.6	27.1	14.6	2.9	59.3	9.1	2.8	27.4	9.3	1.6	42.3	18.5	-2.8	31.1	16.9	8.8	-0.4
Novemser	16.2	4.4	31.5	23.9	2.0	66.1	8.1	3.9	31.7	9.6	1.2	44.1	20.1	-4.8	36.0	16.8	8.7	-2.1
December	17.3	5.0	35.3	26.3	2.0	66.4	8.1	4.5	35.3	11.8	2.0	50.7	20.6	-4.3	42.0	16.1	8.7	-2.3

percentage change on December of the previous year

	Machine building			Wood & paper industry			Construction materials			Light industry			Food industry[1]			CPI		
	1996	1997	1998	1996	1997	1998	1996	1997	1998	1996	1997	1998	1996	1997	1998	1996	1997	1998
January	6.6	0.7	0.3	6.2	0.8	0.1	4.1	0.2	0.0	2.5	0.8	-0.2	0.2	-2.5	-0.3	9.4	2.2	1.3
February	10.3	4.1	1.1	9.7	1.3	0.3	6.7	0.4	0.1	4.1	1.6	-0.1	-0.8	0.0	-0.2	17.5	3.4	1.5
March	16.2	5.5	1.5	12.9	1.7	0.0	11.3	0.5	0.5	7.8	2.0	0.2	-0.6	0.3	-0.1	21.0	3.5	1.7
April	19.7	6.5	2.1	16.8	2.7	0.0	13.1	0.8	0.4	10.0	1.1	1.4	0.7	0.5	0.8	23.9	4.4	3.0
May	21.0	7.4	2.7	18.6	2.6	0.4	17.1	1.2	0.6	10.6	-0.1	2.7	0.8	0.8	1.5	24.8	5.2	3.0
June	19.8	7.1	2.8	18.1	3.8	0.7	18.0	1.3	1.0	11.3	-0.7	2.8	1.1	2.0	2.2	24.9	5.3	3.0
July	21.1	7.7	2.5	19.7	4.2	0.6	19.4	0.2	1.6	13.0	-0.6	2.7	1.8	4.3	2.2	25.0	5.4	2.1
August	22.8	8.2	3.8	19.3	4.1	1.4	20.1	1.3	1.9	13.0	-0.4	3.0	2.3	5.1	2.8	32.2	5.4	2.3
September	24.3	9.6	7.8	21.7	3.8	3.6	22.3	1.0	4.2	14.2	0.4	5.4	1.7	4.6	6.7	34.8	6.7	6.2
October	25.5	10.1	15.1	24.1	3.5	10.7	20.4	1.5	16.6	15.0	0.9	16.0	2.9	10.8	9.3	36.8	7.6	12.8
November	26.6	10.9	20.3	23.9	3.5	14.9	21.9	1.2	22.2	17.6	1.3	25.0	1.4	10.0	10.0	38.5	8.6	16.2
December	27.8	11.5	23.5	24.1	3.6	18.5	22.0	1.5	26.1	17.5	1.8	26.5	-0.1	9.6	11.7	39.7	10.1	20.0

[1] Excluding fish, meat, oil & dairy industries

Source: Presidential Administration

Table 10.1 – Privatization in Ukraine, 1992 -1997

		Number of objects privatized			Small-scale privatization			Large- and medium-scale privatization			Other		
		Total	State property	Municipal property	Total	State property	Municipal Property	Total	State property	Municipal Property	Total	State property	Municipal Property
1992-94		11,852	4,332	7,520	9,061	2,041	7,081	2,720	2,290	414	71	11	34
1995		16,227	4,114	12,113	13,040	1,770	11,461	3,139	2,334	779	48	21	36
1996		19,487	4,526	14,961	16,197	2,387	14,175	2,995	2,014	1,049	295	204	124
	1st Quater	6,144	1,211	4,933	5,188	605	4,583	934	599	335	22	7	15
	2nd Quater	6,610	1,443	5,167	5,749	893	4,856	832	541	291	29	9	20
	3rd Quater	3,972	987	2,985	3,286	550	2,736	642	422	220	44	15	29
	4th Quater	2,761	885	1,876	1,974	339	2,000	587	452	203	200	173	60
1997		8,574	1,899	6,675	7,000	783	6,320	1,170	868	303	404	268	158
	1st Quater	2,322	591	1,731	1,879	306	1,573	356	237	119	87	48	39
	2nd Quater	2,194	452	1,742	1,805	181	1,624	280	212	68	109	59	50
	3rd Quater	2,173	429	1,744	1,793	157	1,636	263	187	76	117	85	32
	4th Quater	1,885	427	1,458	1,523	139	1,487	271	232	40	91	76	37
Total for 1992-97		56,140	14,871	41,269	45,298	6,981	39,037	10,024	7,506	2,545	818	504	352

Source: Presidential Administration

Table 10.2 – Number of privatized units in Ukraine in 1992 – 1997, by industries

	1992 - 1995	1996	1997	1992 - 1997	1992 - 1995	1996	1997	1992 - 1997
	in units				in percentage			
Total	28079	19487	8574	56140	100	100	100	100
Manufacturing	4142	1679	532	6353	14.8	8.6	6.2	11.3
Agriculture	930	1343	496	2769	3.3	6.9	5.8	4.9
Transportation & Communication	589	422	239	1250	2.1	2.2	2.8	2.2
Construction	1878	871	293	3042	6.7	4.5	3.4	5.4
Trade & Catering	12622	9137	3693	25452	45.0	46.9	43.1	45.3
Material - Technique Supply & Sales	588	361	111	1060	2.1	1.9	1.3	1.9
Purchasing/Reserves	39	69	53	161	0.1	0.4	0.6	0.3
Municipal Services	425	1048	667	2140	1.5	5.4	7.8	3.8
Services	6214	3512	1058	10784	22.1	18.0	12.3	19.2
Science & Science Services	163	100	53	316	0.6	0.5	0.6	0.6
Other Industries	489	945	1379	2813	1.7	4.8	16.1	5.0

* The data exclude the objects with which the purchase agreements were terminated as of January 1. 1999 according to the Center Office of the SPF, its regional branches and representations in the districts and cities

Source: State Committee of Statistics of Ukraine

Table 10.3 - State housing stock privatization
by regions, in 1994 - 1997

	Number of privatized apartments & one-family houses		Including free privatization & privatization with compensation		Total area of privatized stock thous. sq. m
	thous. units	% of total state housing stock*	thous. units	% of total privatized stock	
1994	909.5	13.0	847.0	93	44931.
1995	548.5	7.8	499.1	91	27149.
1996	566.4	8.1	512.0	90	28800.
1997	519.6	7.4	467.7	90	26737.
for 1997:					
Crimea	20.3	6.3	18.3	90	1015.
Vinnytsya	9.1	7.3	8.7	95	462.
Volyn	4.9	5.6	4.4	91	240.
Dnipropetrovsk	62.0	8.3	54.5	88	3271.
Donetsk	52.3	5	45.7	87	2600.
Zhytomyr	8.1	5.9	7.6	94	434.
Zakarpattya	4.2	6.6	3.8	90	226.
Zaporizhzhya	18.1	5.6	16.1	89	936.
Ivano-Frankivsk	8.3	7.3	7.6	92	427.
Kiev region	20.0	10.1	18.8	94	1038.
Kirovohrad	10.3	8.7	9.6	93	516.
Luhansk	21.5	4.1	19.1	89	1095.
Lviv	39.1	11.5	36.2	93	2055.
Mykolaiv	13.0	7.6	12.0	93	642.
Odessa	27.8	8.7	23.7	85	1603.
Poltava	22.6	11.2	20.8	92	1149.
Rivne	6.3	6.3	5.8	93	309.
Sumy	11.2	6.9	10.5	94	515.
Ternopil	10.7	16.3	10.1	94	535.
Kharkiv	34.8	6.6	30.2	87	1744.
Kherson	8.7	6	7.6	87	449.
Khmelnytski	15.5	13.9	15.0	97	794.
Cherkasy	15.3	11.2	14.2	92	789.
Chernivtsi	6.5	9.1	6.0	92	327.
Chernihiv	6.1	5.4	5.7	94	33
Kiev city	57.9	8.7	51.3	89	2975.
Sevastopol	5.1	6.5	4.6	91	249.

* Referred to a total apartment stock of state housing stock as of January 1, 1993

Source: State Committee of Statistics